NEXT CITIES

Mona El Khafif and
Seth McDowell

NEXT
CITIES

Next New York

Contents

Foreword
Mine vs. Ours: Next New York

New York is a truly emblematic American city. It represents and houses the collective multitude—a diverse population of migrants out of which this country was built, while embodying the idea of the modern city as a territory of infinite expansion, industriousness, and opportunity. It is difficult to understand New York's contemporary configuration without a slight detour into its evolution, one that aligns its emergence with the very forces of colonization that captured and settled a continent, instantiated through its highly gridded infrastructure. Whether at the scale of the territorial landscape, city block, or building, the grid, in its agricultural, urban, and architectural formulations, was repeated ad infinitum despite enormous differences in the topographies, climates, and cultures it encountered, or the programs and materials that filled it. From the territorial grid of Thomas Jefferson's Land Ordinance Act of 1784, that subdivided 4/5ths of the continent below the 49th parallel to claim, democratize, and render productive the immense and unseen landscape of this country, to the nineteenth-century Commissioners' Plan of New York that gridded the entirety of Manhattan Island to industrialize and commercialize this modern city, the grid was simultaneously a symbol and vehicle of democracy and a device of control, organization, efficiency, and wealth. Unlike the incremental medieval accretions out of which European cities evolved, or the centered and bound idealized figures that the architects of the Renaissance imagined, the modern grid became the perfect instrument of colonization in the New World order—an a priori numerical net and implicit organizational device that would come to define the underlying logic of spatial distribution and the playing field of the American city for years to come.

By the end of the nineteenth century, first in Chicago and then in New York, the combination of new industrial materials and technologies—steel, concrete, and glass, on the one hand, and the elevator, on the other—enabled the planimetric city grid to be extruded vertically, leading to the emergence of the contemporary skyscraper. This building type would come to dominate New York's skyline and become the architectonic model that both signified and facilitated the densification of the modern city.

The skyscraper was simultaneously a product of industrial mechanization while also being emblematic of the commercialization and capitalization of space since its height could be determined by as many times as it was possible to repeatedly sell the original ground floor area, thus radically amplifying the monetary value of land in the city and distinguishing it from that in the surrounding suburbs.

Notwithstanding the American city's evolution over the last century, the use of the grid as a mechanism to instrumentalize territory to produce capital, still defines the ways in which development has dominated the making of New York's urban fabric, delimiting in advance, as is clear from Ed Mitchell's text *Bigness Is Now Big Business*, the resultant form of the city's architecture. Real estate development, at its simplest, is dependent upon the quantification of land and space (and their reduction to variables in arithmetical operations), regardless of the people, activities, and materials that fill them, standing in stark contrast to more nuanced architectural and urban models and the qualities of life that these might stimulate and support. The changing relationship between the quantification and qualification of space that determines the complexity of its value as this intersects with the idea of what is "mine" versus "ours" in the private/public debate, and the role that governmental agencies, political forces, and individual freedoms play in the making of the city, are key drivers that have determined the shape and evolution of New York City over time.

The public-private dialectic within the context of New York City, made ever so poignant in the proximity of contrasting texts by Seth McDowell and Ed Mitchell, frames *Sharing*—the first of three segments of this book, by revealing the contradictory pressures that determine the intermingling of shared and privatized realms within the city. New York emblematizes the idea of the city as a social condenser, facilitating chance encounters and the entanglement of difference within the public realm. *Sharing* thus exposes the importance of population density, demographic diversity, and cohabitation to the life of this city while underscoring that the urban is constituted by that which is truly shared—the public spaces of the streets, subways, parks, and cafés—rather than the privatized spaces of New York's closet-sized condos and apartments. McDowell makes clear that the cost and valuation of living in the city is therefore not in relation to what one owns or rents, but rather to the plethora of proximate amenities and access to opportunities that the city facilitates, and the capacity of these spaces and services to be publicly shared. The generosity of New York City is therefore in the heterogeneous social, cultural, and spatial complexity of what it offers, yet it is precisely this complexity that is being eroded by the privatization of public space through the capitalized multi-programmed amenities of vertical gated communities (and the highly branded, identity-inducing monocultures these produce), and the emergence of a highly dispersed sharing economy that has cannibalized private space, disintegrated localized communities, and increased gentrification by transforming housing into hotel-like living spaces for temporary tourists. These conditions, stimulated by the ever-increasing opportunities for wealth that drive speculative development in the city, compounded by the financial burdens associated with living in the city, have led to the diminution of investment in, and attention to qualitative public urban spaces as true places for collective interaction as the pressures to monetize every square inch of ground increases.

While the projects presented in *Sharing*, those sited on four blocks directly to the south of Hudson Yards in Manhattan, exemplify overarching strategies that foreground the hybridized, distributed, connected, and/or embedded over the autonomous, closed, and monumental, through numerous formal, spatial, and programmatic tactics that counter those that generated the field of isolated oversized towers that characterize their northern neighbors, *Connecting* focuses on the Broadway Junction in Brooklyn, and attempts to come to terms with the conduits, layers, and knots of a sprawling infrastructural transit hub, its leftover spaces, and underutilized urban surrounds. In contrast to the gridded organizational logic that governs Manhattan and its carpet of extruded skyscrapers, the vector-based logics of modern transit systems—the train lines, highways, and subways—operate as continuous linear conduits transporting goods and people that venerate speed, unimpeded flow, and connectivity over placemaking. Traditionally envisioned through a monofunctional mechanistic model, these highly stratified systems focus primarily on the security and smooth operations of the larger networks themselves with little concern for the neighborhoods on the ground that they disrupt as they hover above, tunnel below, or carve directly through.

Thinking of Broadway Junction, a site that currently operates primarily as an exchange point between transit lines and major thoroughfares at the intersection of six East New York neighborhoods, as an actual place and focal point for these neighborhoods was the first conceptual step in reimagining and transforming the site. Operational approaches outlined by Matthew Jull range from experimenting with the intermixing of new programs injected into the transit hub (a performing arts school, a museum, a library, a swimming pool) to rethinking the architectural project as an unbound, open extended system, rather than an object, to expand its sphere of influence while locally stitching disparate fragments of the surrounding fabric together. The approaches discussed each draw upon, yet complexify existing infrastructural logics by breeding them with architectural and/or urban strategies, so that mobility infrastructure is overlaid with social infrastructure. Linear architectures now overloaded with hybrid programs operate simultaneously as connectors and places. These concurrently navigate many speeds and modes of occupation, while the multiplication of the ground plane, the layering of space, and the permeability of boundaries activate and extend public spaces that enrich the urbanity of the site. By questioning the prevailing paradigm of efficiency and instrumentality that has governed the making of inherited large-scale engineered infrastructures, these architectural urban projects acknowledge that such mobility-driven systems within the city can no longer be thought of as siloed and independent, but rather must be reconceived as wholly intertwined with the spaces that they connect while acknowledging their manifold embedded scales of influence and impact. Kathy Velikov and Geoffrey Thün highlight the logistical challenges demanded by this approach, requiring active stakeholder engagement and more complex interdisciplinary teams that include architects, landscape architects, and designers to synthesize the many interacting conditions surrounding these multi-scaled urban systems. Further, they suggest that an ecological and biological rather than a mechanical paradigm—a soft, complex, relational, and evolutionary model rather than a hard, striated, autonomous, and static one—might be more appropriate to this radical reconception of urban infrastructural systems as part of a larger urban metabolism that addresses current and future challenges not only around mobility and transportation, but also energy, water, food, waste, climate, and environmental issues, among others.

The challenges intrinsic to the debate on what is mine versus ours confronted in the first *Shared Territories* design studio of the New York series, is revisited in the final section of the book—*Partnering*—where New York City public school sites operate as a case-study to reimagine new typological strategies and forms of spatial negotiation for the rebuilding of the city. In the *PublicSURplus* studio, the model of public-private partnerships (PPPs) is employed to capitalize on the land-rich, resource-poor, underzoned, and often dilapidated public school sites while addressing New York City's land and affordable housing crises by accommodating increased residential density on these sites integrated with new programs, amenities, and shared open spaces that simultaneously support the schools' learning environments and the urban neighborhoods in which they are situated. Mona El Khafif underscores the urgent need for profitability to be negotiated with social and environmental sustainability, while making an argument for the invention of new revolutionary, morphogenetic architectural and urban typologies. The school is thus asked to shed its monofunctional program in favor of three new hybridized types that dominate the design projects generated: *compositional aggregations* that fuse two or more generic types, *contextual objects* that recontextualize the objectified architectural monolith, and *distributed fields* that employ the dispersed logics of urbanity to rethink architecture as an open and accessible system.

This notion of emergent educational typologies based on new synthetic genetic mixtures is expanded by Sharon Haar in her essay *Liquid Knowledge* where she not only probes the horizontal grounding of the school as an historical type within the context of the vertical city, but also interrogates the nineteenth century industrial idea of the school as "prototype," and the mass production of education and its public distribution through cookie-cutter facilities, now called into question within the context of contemporary notions of mass customization. The public-private opposition thus gets reconceived again within Haar's text in very different registers as she cross-pollinates John Dewey's idea of the individual mind, a necessity for the creative evolution of public institutions, with Koolhaas's concept of urban individuation (referencing the potential for "three-dimensional anarchy" proposed by Koolhaas above the two-dimensional planimetric grid—a counter to the developer operation of simple extrusion), making a larger argument for reimagining the school in both speculative and urban terms. Drawing a parallel between Dewey's notion of knowledge as liquid and the physical encounter of the student and city, the idea of opening and dispersing the school into a larger context finds its inversion in thinking the city itself as a new public platform and resource for education.

Cities are our largest collective cultural artifacts, and their strategic re-conception is crucial for our future. It is thus hard to imagine how we can remake great cities if our model of city-making values individual wealth over collective resources, or the stockpiling of surplus capital in buildings rather than embodying our collective values in the physical and material environment that surrounds us. Urbanity and its correlate in public space, once seen to be symbolic of the democratizing impulse, is therefore that which is threatened by excessive privatization, not only because of the underlying economics of ownership, but also because the freewheeling machinations of global capital are most often disinterested in the specificity of built artifacts that generate it. These artifacts are the products of our work as architects, urban designers, and planners whose struggle to remake the city is defined as much by the economics and extended terms of the public-private debate as by the characteristics, frameworks, precedents, and procedures that determine the objects of our fields. Mitchell, drawing from Colin Rowe and Fred Koetter's *Collage City* and Manfredo Tafuri's *Architecture and Utopia*, returns us to the parallel between the public-private debate and the opposition between architecture and city—that the former, with its clear boundaries and propensity to contain and objectify space, is a threat to the publicness of the city, just as the latter is precisely what is necessary to redefine the ways in which an urban architecture might be reformulated. These are the very challenges addressed by the design studios and thinking behind *Next New York* where *sharing*, *connecting*, and *partnering* are advanced to bring about new conceptions of city-making through architecture. These draw from yet go far beyond Koolhaas's programmatic exquisite corpse and Koetter's and Rowe's bricolage of bounded public voids and locally stitched architectural fragments, toward the realm of what is both mine and ours—a much-needed urban architecture for collective cohabitation.

Ila Berman, *Next Cities* series editor
Elwood R. Quesada Professor
University of Virginia School of Architecture

Acknowledgments

Next New York is the final outcome of four years of speculative urban research and architectural production. The successful completion of a book project like this involves an extensive network of participants and requires incredible orchestration and collaboration.

We would like to first thank the Next Cities Institute and the Dean's office of the University of Virginia School of Architecture for the financial support to edit the material for this publication. The ongoing guidance by former Dean Ila Berman and Creative Director of Communications Sneha Patel was essential in elevating the book to its present stage. Our thanks are also forwarded to Neil Donnelly and Siiri Tännler for their development of the Next Cities Series graphic design and all the productive discussions that helped to synthesize this volume's content.

In addition, we are tremendously grateful to all of our colleagues who contributed to this book. *Next New York* is framed by an essay contributed by Ila Berman, who generously funded the publication through the Next Cities Institute. Each of the three chapters was enriched by the theoretical voices of Edward Mitchell, Geoffrey Thün, Kathy Velikov, and Sharon Haar, as well as by project-based essays dedicated to the different actions of sharing, connecting, and partnering provided by Thomas Woltz of Nelson Byrd Woltz Landscape Architects, SHoP Architects, and Carrie Moore from SOM. Special thanks to Felipe Correa and Barry Bergdoll for contributing an exhaustive discussion on New York's past, present, and future actions. Tommaso Sacconi's photographs of New York during the COVID-19 pandemic stand out in this publication, and we tremendously appreciate his collaboration and contribution.

The material presented in the following pages would not have been possible without the insightful and critical guidance of faculty and the energetic participation of many student research assistants. In particular, we would like to thank our faculty colleagues Manuel Bailo, Matthew Jull, Katie Kasabalis, Esther Lorenz, Bill Sherman, and Alex Yuen for their efforts in co-teaching the studios and guiding the students' projects.

Last, but not least, a great debt is owed to everyone who was part of the team that under our direction enabled the existence of this book. The following pages represent countless hours of thought and redrawing that extended far beyond the initial studios. We sincerely appreciate the contributions of all the MArch students whose work was selected and of all research assistants who helped with this publication: Andres Soria Galvarro Duran, Harshita Batra, Barrett Weaver, and Luis Medina. In particular, our gratitude goes to Ted Bazil for his skillful editing work and overall help with the production management of this publication. Special thanks go to Paula Woolley, who copy-edited the material with tremendous skill and care.

Mona El Khafif and Seth McDowell
Editors and Studio Coordinators

GRATIS

PARK
AVENUE
SOUTH
MALLS
3M91

NEW YORK
GZP 4915
EMPIRE STATE

NYC
T

El Especialito
EL SEMANARIO DE LA FAMILIA HISPANA

Introduction: The City Is a Verb

In 2025, New York City will enter its fifth century as a hub of commerce, culture, and urban life. Over this 500-year span, a range of innovative, responsive, and pragmatic civic actions have helped to generate, define, and maintain the city's global significance. Early on, most of these actions were pragmatic responses to population density and the accompanying challenges for health and wellbeing. Yet, New York's investment in the public sector resulted in one of the most extensive municipal water systems in the world, one of the oldest and most used public transit systems in the world, and a public park system that maintains 30,000 acres of land, approximately 14 percent of the city, for ecology and recreation. Faced with new scales of building encouraged by the Industrial Revolution, New York was also the first American city to take regulatory action and implemented the Zoning Resolution of 1916 in an effort to maintain the quality of life for people on the street. More recently, under the administration of Mayor Michael Bloomberg, New York took action to rezone large swaths of industrial and manufacturing sites to adapt the city to the changing global economy and promote new, high-profile building projects within the city.

Approaching its next growth cycle, New York is again in the midst of important paradigm shifts that require a reinterpretation of the city's grid as a framework for public and private investment, its infrastructural systems, and architectural models to allow for an open city to balance gentrification. Now, in the twenty-first century, the city has begun to promote a new set of actions responding to urgent concerns over climate change, inequality, affordability, and sustainable density. These actions and their architectural and urban implications are the focus of *Next New York*.

Linked through the city's unique original framework of the Commissioner's Plan from 1811 on one hand, and an understanding of New York as an infrastructural city as outlined in the 1969 Regional Plan on the other, these topics represent emerging actions to address the city's three most critical urban challenges: (1) how to remain an open city, while simultaneously densifying, (2) how to utilize infrastructure as a catalytic driver to establish multifunctional urban centers, and (3) how to productively adjust the legal framework of the urban block to accommodate new models for public-private partnerships. Progress on these fronts was strongly encouraged by the administration of Mayor Bill de Blasio, which published the 2015 roadmap for New York's future entitled "One New York: The Plan for a Strong and Just City." The document outlines a vision for New York centered around the principles of growth, equity, sustainability, and resiliency. Motivated by these principles, New York has in recent years witnessed the initiation of several large-scale projects including the BIG U, a $335 million investment protecting Lower Manhattan from floodwater, storms, and other impacts of climate change; and Sunnyside Yard, where master planning has begun to define a process for incremental development in one of the busiest rail yards in the United States. Other actions set in motion through de Blasio's Housing Plan, released in 2014, and Housing New York 2.0 feature the city's ambition to provide 300,000 new affordable homes by 2026, addressing the problem of social justice.

Next New York captures the city's current momentum with critical writing from scholars and practitioners working on pressing issues, and presents a range of design solutions developed through a series of graduate studios at the University of Virginia's School of Architecture. The book examines New York City's future through three important urban actions: sharing, connecting, and partnering. The publication starts with an essay by Ila Berman, who frames and positions the book through a synthesized overview.

Sharing examines new models of collective, common space in the city at a moment when public space is often designed and maintained by private entities. In this chapter, Edward Mitchell discusses how large-scale private development within the city has produced "black holes" in the urban fabric and Nelson Byrd Woltz Landscape Architects share their work on the public spaces of Hudson Yards. These two perspectives frame the context for a collection of student projects that propose affordable live/work development adjacent to Hudson Yards. *Connecting* examines how infrastructural hubs are being programmed or reprogrammed to enable social, cultural, and economic connections in addition to transit connections. Here, Kathy Velikov and Geoffrey Thün discuss New York's infrastructural icons and highlight how they offer paradigms for hybridity, and SHoP Architects share their work on reconfiguring the city's industrial waterfront for public access and programs. These contributions support a series of student projects which look at transforming Brooklyn's neglected transportation hub, Broadway Junction, into a multifunctional civic hub. Finally, *Partnering* examines new models for public-private partnerships as a productive action for densifying NYC Public School sites. In this chapter, Sharon Haar reflects on the relationship between schools and cities while Carrie Moore of Skidmore, Owings and Merrill discusses their work fusing public schools and private developers.

During the book's editing process in early 2020, COVID-19 spread across the globe and turned New York into one of the first hot spots, which deeply affected the city's culture and daily life. This kind of impact could not be ignored by our contributors, and as editors, we dedicated additional space to the dramatic and unique actions New York took during the summer and fall of 2020. Under *Documenting*, New York-based photographer Tommaso Sacconi walked through the city during the first lockdown in late March 2020. As a resident of the city, he had the urge to observe and capture this unique moment in history as a means of conserving what inhabitants of this restless and vibrant place were experiencing. Hospitals set up medical tents in Central Park for patients *quarantining* outside, while stores in SoHo prepared for vandalism by *closing* up their windows and facades. New York during these weeks seemed desolate and near-abandoned—as if a scene from a dystopian future. Used gloves and face masks lay discarded on the ground; shelves in grocery stores were empty; and for weeks the streets were deserted except for emergency vehicles and service workers *delivering* food via bicycles. At the end of May, Sacconi subsequently documented New York residents *protesting* as part of the Black Lives Matter movement, and—despite the continuing pandemic—the city took action to become an open-air theater for urban interactions, documented under *re-opening*.

The publication closes with the editors' conversation with Felipe Correa, professor of architecture at UVA, and Barry Bergdoll, former chief curator of architecture and design at MoMA New York. *Discussing* New York's recent past, current trends, and future trajectories, the conversation interrogates the extent to which New York's achievements are impacted by the agendas of political leaders. Correa and Bergdoll's roles within the cultural institutions that have shaped the city enable them to offer unique perspectives on New York's past, present, and future.

The design work presented here is selected from more than three years of student investigations produced as part of UVA's Master of Architecture second-year core studio. In this studio, architecture is discussed in its capacity to address urban challenges and to impact its context. Emphasizing a range of cultural, urban, and technical questions that support the development of advanced design skills, the studio consists of a series of interrelated assignments. These include urban analysis and the iterative process of typological massing strategies, and the detailed design of an architectural project challenging students to work across multiple scales—from the city to the detailed development of architectural elements.

Although physically separated from NYC by 345 miles, the students and faculty gain an intimacy with the city through an extensive network of alumni and colleagues living or working there. During these years of study, the research and design work has been supported by collaborations with Thomas Woltz of Nelson Byrd Woltz; Gregg Pasquarelli and SHoP Architects; Carrie Moore of SOM; Koren Manning, former senior planner at NYC Department of City Planning; Neil Thelen of Thelen Design Group; and Adam Yarinksi of ARO, among others. This relationship with the city has enabled the work to be informed critically while also allowing for the production of a provocative and relevant vision for *Next New York*.

Plasticity is also a key element that defines the interiority of the city. The interiors of buildings, dedicated to living and working, are typically seen as speculative spaces: designed not for the nuanced, custom rituals of one or two individuals, but instead as adaptable spaces for changing occupants and activities.
—Seth McDowell

"Bigness" is twenty-five years old, and was already a retrospective thought piece. The Next New York, in its present reality, is evidence of how Koolhaas's idealized conception of Bigness and Somol's idea of the projective possibilities of Shape were disseminated and compromised in the construction of simply big buildings.
—Edward Mitchell

What better example of the Anthropocene than devising an ecology on a suspended platform, an urban terrarium? It is both novel and ancient. Arguably, more than in any other project, the landscape holds all of the elements without which Hudson Yards would not work: structures, flows, functions, tunnels, access, security, and a satisfying urban experience are all dependent on the success of what we unsatisfyingly still call landscape.
—Nelson Byrd Woltz Landscape Architects

Sharing

Sharing Amenities: Why Buy the Cow When You Can Get the Milk for Free?

Seth McDowell

> Spawned by a confluence of the economic crisis, environmental concerns, and the maturation of the social web, an entirely new generation of businesses is popping up. They enable the sharing of cars, clothes, couches, apartments, tools, meals, and even skills. The basic characteristic of these you-name-it sharing marketplaces is that they extract value out of the stuff we already have. Many of these sites depend on millennials disenchanted by the housing bubble and the banking crisis, or uninterested in traditional icons of success such as house or auto ownership.
> —Danielle Sacks, "The Sharing Economy"[1]

Sharing is one of the first lessons parents teach children. In the United States, this early emphasis on collective consumption is all too ironic given the complicated absence of sharing in our national history. The Spanish and English colonizers were not interested in sharing land and resources with the natives they encountered, nor were slave owners interested in sharing a democracy with enslaved Africans. In the post-Civil War American South, racial separation was enforced by Jim Crow laws to prevent the sharing of public facilities with people of color. Even after President Lyndon Johnson signed the Civil Rights Act of 1964, the sharing of rights and physical space by people of different races and socioeconomic statuses continued to encounter systematic obstruction throughout the twentieth century. Across the country, federal, state, and local governments supported divisive urban renewal projects, engaged in housing loan discrimination and redlining, and incentivized "white flight" from urban centers by subsidizing "white only" developments at their peripheries.[2] Today, as Black Lives Matter protests continue across the country, it is clear that, in a country defined by its cultural and racial diversity, the struggle to share rights and physical space remains a difficult and ongoing challenge.

This is also the land of Fordism, where mass production motivated the rise of automobile ownership, single-family home ownership, and a sprawling built environment that minimizes shared space, activities, and objects. The sizable and mostly inhabitable landmass of the United States enables the population to spread out and minimize confrontation with others. In this vastness, sharing often is viewed as a novelty rather than a necessity. In rural Texas, one has to seek out shared space with the same effort that a New Yorker has to search for solitude. It is astonishing that from this national context, boasting stories of self-reliance, manifest destiny, segregation, and—above all—ownership, a city like New York could materialize.

With its spatial and material sharing, New York City is an anomaly within the American landscape. New York's population density, demographic heterogeneity, and economic pressures encourage it to escape the American delusion that success is defined by how much you own and how little you have to share. It is one of the few American cities where shared spaces, in both public and private realms, are generally more generous and stimulating than individual spaces. To live in New York is to be in the street, in the park, in the café, in the subway, at a show—not in a 500-square-foot apartment watching Netflix. Anyone living in New York City during the COVID-19 pandemic in 2020 can testify that New York is a miserable environment when you take away the shared spaces. By discouraging excessive scale and comfort within the domestic space, the city has a built-in mechanism to ensure that common spaces are activated and valued. However, this reliance on communal space is facing new challenges as we move into the third decade of the twenty-first century, not only due to the acute stress of a global pandemic, but more systemically, thanks to two trends that deploy the act of sharing as a marketing tool: the proliferation of autonomous, luxury condo towers and the emergence of a sharing economy.

The Sharing Market

In New York City, these two trajectories exploit the concept of sharing as a financial mechanism, albeit from opposing ends of the spectrum. From the top-down, significant new development caters to the super-wealthy, marketing shared spaces as investment perks—bonus amenities to justify the enormous price tags. This condo-package approach to distributing shared space—as seen in the glossy real estate brochures for the luxury towers in Hudson Yards, Billionaires' Row, Tribeca, and the Financial District—defines shared space and services as an exclusivity to be procured. Indoor pools, rooftop lounges, gyms, and garages are now standard amenities for these towers of luxury. In reading the portfolio of amenities that Extell's *One57* offers, where you can find $90 million condos for sale, it is clear that these spaces are dedicated to decadence rather than democracy:

> Experience the extraordinary every day. Exclusive amenities are paired with the privileges of living above Park Hyatt New York ... The tranquil indoor swimming pool, with a custom-designed Jacuzzi and spa portico, is set within a triple-height space. The experience is enhanced by an underwater soundtrack curated by Carnegie Hall. ... Spa Nalai features the finest services for optimal wellness and relaxation including a unique sand quartz treatment bed and gracious couples spa. ... The private fitness center with personal training and yoga studios is centered around a dramatic three-story pool pavilion 300 feet above Midtown Manhattan. ... The exclusive Resident's Lounge, designed by Thomas Juul-Hansen, offers a curated library, an upholstered billiards table and a 24-foot aquarium. ... Overlooking Carnegie Hall, the exclusive lounge features a Steinway piano, state-of-the-art acoustics and lush tiered seating reserved for *One57* residents.[3]

These large and iconic residential buildings, adorned with lavish, interior playgrounds for the wealthy, are merely the urban equivalents of gated communities with clubhouses and amenities shared only by those of a similar socioeconomic status. They pit architecture against the city by creating interior environments which claim to emulate, if not replace urbanity. This idealized, monocultural urbanity warrants the same criticisms of spatial and social isolation that the sprawling American suburbs have encountered over the last fifty years. As suburbia is now trending toward racial and economic diversity in the United States, is the city now moving toward homogeneity?[4] This high-end *condominiumization*—a term Barry Bergdoll mentions in conversation with Felipe Correa at the end of this book—suggests such is the case, as it devalues the role of urban space in New York and the ability of traditional public spaces like the street, the plaza, the park, the courtyard, and so on to collect diverse populations. While a few autonomous luxury towers are not detrimental to a city's collective environment, the proliferation and concentration of these gated vertical neighborhoods becomes problematic—as seen in Hudson Yards.

To its credit, New York City has attempted to discourage this exclusionary act of building with various programs, both voluntary and mandatory, that offer "lucrative tax abatements, permission to construct larger buildings and bond financing" for private developers that mix market-rate housing with below market-rate housing.[5] Referred to as 80/20 projects, these developments typically set aside 20 percent of the housing units for low- or moderate-income New Yorkers. While this inclusionary zoning has been a long-term development strategy for the city and was championed most successfully by Mayor Michael Bloomberg's administration, one of Mayor Bill de Blasio's signature campaign proposals in 2013 was Mandatory Inclusionary Housing (MIH), which signaled elevated mandates for affordability in the city. Enacted in 2016, MIH applies when an area is rezoned to permit more housing, or when a City Planning Commission special permit allows housing to be built. In theory the mandate is encouraging, but as Eric Kober, adjunct fellow at the Manhattan Institute, describes in his 2020 report, it has yet to be a game changer:

> MIH was explained to the public as a way to increase the total amount of permanently affordable housing. The cost of this housing, whose rentals are, by definition, below the market rate, was supposed to be met by capturing some of the added economic value that rezoning creates for private developers and directing it toward the city's housing goals. In practice, this has rarely occurred. Only 2,065 MIH affordable dwelling units have been approved, in a city of 8.4 million residents. Most of them receive heavy public subsidies.[6]

As Kober points out in the report, "MIH reflects a fundamental failure to recognize that inclusionary zoning is always voluntary."[7] The program's strict restrictions and conditions have limited its effectiveness in bringing affordable housing to strong markets in the city. There is well-funded and well-organized opposition to rezoning in affluent neighborhoods. Developers are reluctant to apply for rezoning when extremely large increases in densities are needed to see a return on their investment if 25 to 30 percent of the units are dedicated to affordability and generate little profit.

Even when these policy initiatives have worked to encourage more diverse neighborhoods within the building's envelope, developers quickly maneuvered to segregate buildings so that below-market-rate renters never mix with the high-end condo owners. Consequently, the chicer shared amenities typically reside on the high-end side of the building, emphasizing the capitalist motto "You get what you pay for." If certain amenities need to be provided to all inhabitants, the financial models seem to predict that it is better to double up—one gym for the poor and a nicer gym for the wealthy—rather than to encourage sharing across socioeconomic boundaries.

This condition of spatial segregation is nothing new for the city; access to exclusive amenities has always been guarded. In a capitalist city, access to capital is a real organizer that separates the "haves" from the "have nots." The criticism that stems from this amenity tower approach is that it eliminates even the slightest possibility of interaction between socioeconomic classes, as residents do not need to leave their building to access everyday amenities. We have to be very cautious with the large mixed-use building program so championed by Rem Koolhaas because as urban amenities transition to the interior, within closer proximity to domestic spaces, they become less available to lower income populations. While it is easy to blame developers for these guarded strategies, they are just building to the market. These amenity towers are not necessarily the cause of this socioeconomic segregation, but rather an effect of cultural tendencies rooted in a reluctance to share with those different from us.

On the other end of the spectrum, the city is struggling to regulate sharing from the bottom up. The technology-based sharing economy and the likes of Airbnb, Uber, and WeWork have put a major kink in some of the city's established, centralized institutions, resulting in an ongoing political and legal war between tech companies and existing industries. The value of owning a Yellow Cab medallion, for instance, has plummeted as Uber pickups surged past NYC taxi fares for the first time in 2017, and the gap has only increased over the last three years. As a result, street congestion has become more difficult to control because Uber puts about 61,000 cars into the city daily while yellow taxis are capped at 13,587.[8] The inundation of Airbnb in the city has also created havoc, leading housing advocates to argue that short-term rentals contribute to rising rents and gentrification. This has led to the NYC Short-Term Rental Law, which prevents entire apartments from being rented out for fewer than 30 days, thereby ensuring that a New York City Airbnb truly is a dwelling space shared with strangers.

As a bottom-up movement, the shared economy has, not surprisingly, encountered regulatory hurdles, but more pertinent for architecture is the effect these distributed processes have on the organization of space. The shared economy works to erode the threshold between individual and collective space as people's most private spaces become open for collective use. Ownership, whether of a taxi medallion or a two-bedroom condo in Chelsea, encourages the predictability of use. As individual spaces become more transient and public, they also become more vulnerable to market forces and the erasure of individual expression. If you are renting a spare bedroom to the public on Airbnb, you do not want to advertise your obscure cultural obsessions, but rather conceal your unique personal aesthetics in favor of the aesthetic of the latest IKEA catalog. The same goes for many of the co-working hubs proliferating in the city. It is not a coincidence that they all look like the same trendy coffee shop or a quintessential tech startup. Shared space, whether it is interior or exterior, requires space to be cleaned of obscurities and presented to the public as a familiar cliché.

The irony is that both of these sharing trajectories in the city have worked to create a huge number of vacancies and ultimately contribute to the de-densification of New York. These are not vacancies in the traditional sense, where spaces sit unrented or unowned. That kind of vacancy would affect the city's rent stabilization laws and completely drive affordability out of the city. Instead, these are vacancies that go unrecognized on paper because someone pays for them, but no one occupies them. Multi-million-dollar condos are bought by foreign billionaires for investment portfolios, but are rarely occupied by inhabitants. Meanwhile, finding affordable long-term leases in New York has become even more difficult, as the profitability of Airbnb encourages individuals with reliable credit or co-signers to collect multiple apartment units for trafficking a never-ending cycle of short-term renters—inserting a transient occupancy into what was once more stable, affordable neighborhoods. Thus, while the towers with their amenities are threatening the vibrancy of the city's public space, the Airbnbs with their transparency apps are threatening the privacy of the interior.

The economic uncertainty which characterized the beginning of the twenty-first century, specifically the sub-prime mortgage crisis of 2008 in the United States and Western Europe and now the economic consequences of the COVID-19 pandemic, have greatly influenced this branding of sharing. After decades of decadence, the U.S. middle class is being hollowed out, and the gap between the poor and the extremely wealthy is widening. This gap is reflected in these two sharing trajectories in New York. The lingering fiscal constraints of the recession have motivated the 1 percent to further isolate, while it has motivated the other 99 percent to decentralize. Technology and digital platforms for communicating, publishing, and tracking have enabled this transformative redistribution of material and immaterial goods.

The Problem of Sharing

In the Spring of 2017 we initiated the first iteration of UVA's New York Studio. Predicating this inaugural Master of Architecture studio on the concept of spatial sharing admittedly ran the risk of generating a lot of hippy-dippy, feel-good, and idealistic proposals. It was therefore crucial from the outset to promote the idea of sharing as a spatial operation so as to avoid deviating too far into utopian social experiments in collective living. This balance was achieved by focusing on the comparatively high density of New York City relative to that in the rest of the United States, which suggests that proximity is a key ingredient in creating valuable and activated collective space. Proximity is salient not only between shared and individual spaces, but also between different individual spaces. In New York, for instance, common areas offer a spatial release from the repetitive stacking of living and working cells.

Another key ingredient we can extract from the successes of New York's spatial sharing strategies is flexibility. Excessively fixed or explicit spaces reduce tolerance and ambiguity, leading to underutilization, undervaluation, and—most problematically—contestation. In order to avoid such fates, spatially or programmatically explicit spaces require a diverse and abundant catalog of spatial types within a single location. Spatial diversity is most easily achieved in large urban projects—a tactic we see employed successfully in many examples from Manhattan: Central Park, all of the avenues, Riverside Park, Washington Square Park, Grand Central Terminal, and the High Line, to name a few. Each of these places offers a multitude of activities for a multitude of user types.

Plasticity is also a key element that defines the interiority of the city. The interiors of buildings, dedicated to living and working, are typically seen as speculative spaces: designed not for the nuanced, custom rituals of one or two individuals, but instead as adaptable spaces for changing occupants and activities. Here, the 5-inch walls separating strangers are shared surfaces, and one person's ceiling is another person's floor. Obeying real estate markets above all else, such interiors therefore constitute an architecture of generalization devoid of spatial autonomy or discreteness. The interior of the city also has the responsibility of being shared among multiple generations of tenants, creating a temporal dimension to this notion of flexibility.

Reacting to these readings of shared space in New York, the site and program of the Shared Territories Studio introduced challenges of adjacency, proximity, and flexibility. Students engaged with a building program based around a shared economy and the demand to situate novel, temporal immediacies between living and working. The brief established a proportional relationship for the project so that 30 percent of enclosed space was dedicated to housing and 45 percent was dedicated to workspaces, leaving 25 percent dedicated to spaces for sharing and services. Drawing inspiration from Rem Koolhaas's technological perversions of Coney Island and spatial juxtapositions of the Downtown Athletic Club in *Delirious New York*, the building was called the Manhattan Innovation Incubator.[9] This spatial program encouraged students to develop narratives for how the transient logics of the shared economy might be deployed to enable creative industries and a working class to reside in Manhattan, New York's most expensive, central borough.

The studio brief was written in a moment when makerspaces and co-working offices were coupled with hipster trends like fixed-gear bikes, farmers markets, microbreweries, and coffee shops to signify the arrival of gentrification. Often these innovation hubs housed all of these fashionable entities under one roof, as with *Neuehouse*, a co-working collective at Madison Square Park where "members can also enjoy a variety of luxurious perks like cultural programming, happy hour, artisan roasted coffee, food and beverage counters, art exhibitions, Linus bikes ... even access [to] a screening room."[10] No doubt, the studio provocation was aimed at this metropolitan yuppyism in hopes of uncovering deeper cultural value for shared programming.

Instead of positioning this incubator in a neighborhood struggling with gentrification in 2017 like Williamsburg, Flatbush, Red Hook, or Bushwick, where it would have been a comfortable cliché, we chose a site adjacent to Manhattan's newest, biggest playground for the wealthy elite: Hudson Yards. The project site—four underdeveloped blocks just south of Hudson Yards' star-studded southwest corner where the High Line lassoes Diller Scofidio + Renfro's retractable Shed and Thomas Heatherwick's reflective Vessel—situated students next to a concentration of developer-driven, shared-amenity towers. From an urbanistic point of view, Hudson Yards is a "black hole" in the city (borrowing Edward Mitchell's term from "Bigness Is Now Big Business: Black Holes for the Cosmos-politan," in this volume). In his essay, Mitchell evaluates how the large urban building creates challenges for linking architecture to the city; similarly, the development at Hudson Yards is a radical shift in scale from the surrounding context, creating an explicit break with the urban fabric. The collective spaces—or rather the territory conceded to the public so that the towers can be taller—are dedicated to the admiring of shiny objects and therefore foster a theme-park-like atmosphere of corporate consumerism.

Shared space at Hudson Yards is not a problem of quantity, as the development strategy provides plenty of ground for a public identity. It is more a problem of disconnection. While Nelson Byrd Woltz worked their magic to knit the isolated towers together with the landscape, there is still an undeniable disconnect between the architecture and the public space that renders us all tourists gawking at the latest global trends. In choosing the four blocks adjacent to this situation, we asked students to take a position on this approach to urbanism. How can this site offer a different form of shared space and bridge the global scale of construction found at Hudson Yards with the industrial scale of construction found further south in Chelsea?

How to Design Shared Space?

As a core studio in the Master of Architecture curriculum, the work is situated within a set of pedagogical objectives that are more foundational than the overarching narrative of sharing. These objectives have worked to inform the underlying approach to all of the studios featured in this book. Within the larger curriculum, this studio focused on developing an urban position for architecture, an agenda which entails confronting fundamental issues of scale, programmatic hybridity, contextuality, regulatory constraints, urban block typologies, and interior/exterior relationships. Students also had to confront the issue of part and whole: is architecture an object within the city, or is it a module dedicated to establishing a larger fabric?

As a foundational studio, the studio began with students engaging in quick conceptual exercises before progressing through urban analysis exercises, iterative site massing exercises, and design development assignments aimed at helping to articulate circulation strategies, materiality, structure, environmental systems, building enclosures, programming, and services (figures 1–3). Drawing upon the technical expertise of Neil Thelen of Thelen Design Group, a New York-based design and fabrication consultant involved with several projects at Hudson Yards, the studio stressed a critical understanding of the relationship between city and architecture through multiple scales. While the expectation was for students to resolve their one-block projects with technical and conceptual proficiency at the intersection of structure and envelope, they also had to establish an urban plan for all four Manhattan blocks outlined as the site. This required students to design connections and relationships beyond an allotted building parcel and conceive of architecture as a unit situated within a shared urban fabric. They also had to understand construction details not as something irrelevant to the urban form, but rather as procedures directly linked to the collective nature of the city. Thelen highlighted this point in a lecture by explaining that the design of high-rise curtain walls in Manhattan is enormously constrained by the window-washing union and the standardization of maintenance in the city. In New York,

Figure 1: Timeline of shared infrastructures in NYC.

whether working with the urban grid or the curtain wall grid, designers must find methods for manipulating the regulations that are at the service of a larger collective.

Beyond these core studio issues, students also addressed the question of how to design and distribute shared space throughout the city. Through analysis and iterative design studies structured by studio assignments, students had to develop theses about the organization of shared territories. This process was aided logistically by pairing students up to develop an inventory of strategies for the parcelization of four Manhattan blocks. They had to address questions such as how are the blocks divided, how is individual building ownership established within this

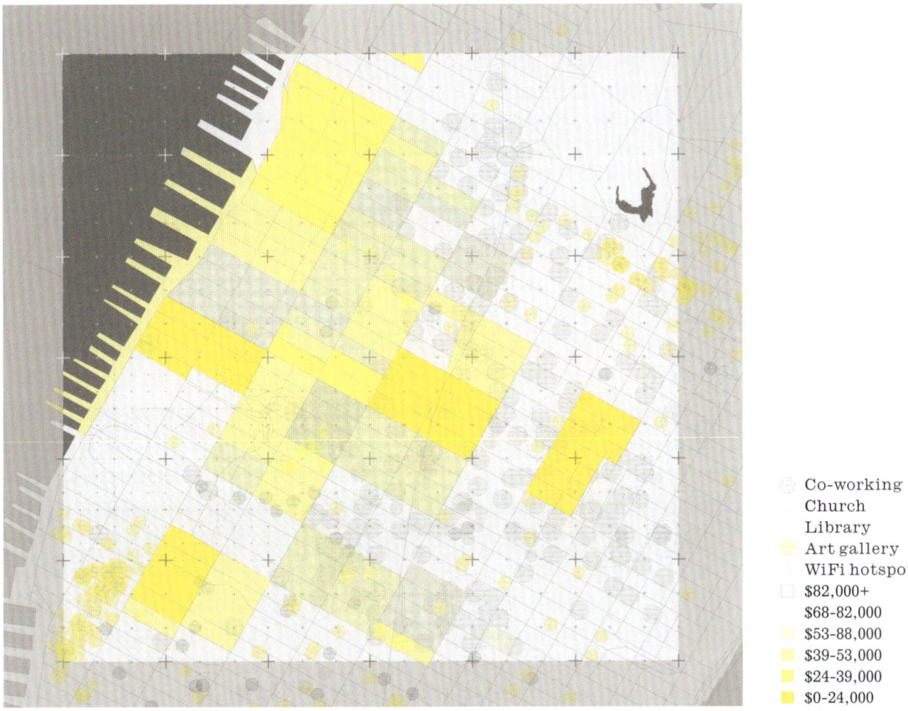

Figure 2: Demographics and shared infrastructure.

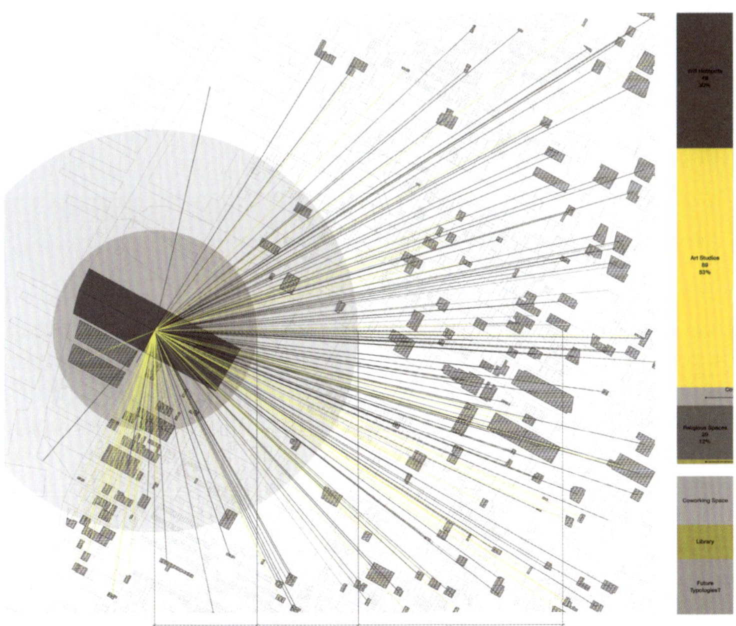

Figure 3: Synthesis and future applications.

territory, and how is sharing created between these individual parcels? Students were tasked to develop a shared syntax for urban development with their teammates and then, within these shared parameters, focus on a specific parcel. To promote flexibility, students could either work individually on a single parcel of their urban plan or continue collaborating with a teammate and tackle a single block as the building project.

The work was guided by an analysis of common city block typologies like the tower and base, the perimeter block, the bar and plaza, and the courtyard. Students were encouraged to disrupt these pure typologies with varying degrees of open space, shared space, or to test forms of hybridization. Working with both physical and digital models, teams developed strategies that conformed to a Floor to Area Ratio (FAR) of eight and provided 10 percent to 40 percent open, public, shared space (figure 4).

Figure 4: Mid-semester typology model review.

As instructors, we avoided a clear definition of what constituted the "site," which unintentionally motivated varied interpretations of territorial thresholds. Students asked: "Should I design all four blocks?... Should I focus on one block?... Should I consider my site as a smaller parcel in the block?" While these questions came with great anxiety about authorship, workload management, and technical resolution, they also hit at larger existential questions about sharing in the city. The answer was always yes. Students had to take a position on territory and how much of it should fall under the jurisdiction of a single designer. Their decisions informed the strategies that later materialized.

Sharing Strategies

Three common spatial strategies for organizing shared experience emerged from the work of the studio: shared space as a linear connector, shared space as a voided room, and shared space as an infrastructure or a distributed field. These strategies are not mutually exclusive, as many projects include all of these strategies to some degree, both internally and externally. Some projects, for instance, interpret shared space as common areas linking diverse programs on the building's interior, while others position shared space as an exterior, public environment structuring the interface between city and building.

Projects that deploy a linear strategy of sharing have an obvious affinity for the city street and its ability to collect a diverse set of activities and people. In these projects, linear movement dissects the building massing and works to knit together various programs. This approach enables projects to link to contextual lines of shared movement, given that the site is sandwiched between the High Line to the east and the West Side Highway, Hudson River Greenway, and Hudson River to the west. "Rifts" by Emily Fiedler, Aisha Sawatsky, and Abe Wilson creates a public alley or rift to organize the two northern blocks of the site, facilitating a shared terrain that connects the Hudson to the High Line. The success of the High Line as a linear space was also a catalyst for Mert Kansu's "Vertical Avenue," which attaches to the elevated park and extends its program upward into the core of his proposal. This linear organizational strategy for shared space gains particular momentum when it connects with existing linear systems in the city which allow it to bridge diverse internal and external environments.

Establishing a kinship to the urban court as a collective device, the second strategy of the void brings to mind the voyeurism of Alfred Hitchcock's *Rear Window* (1954). When positioned toward the interior of the block, these urban rooms offer a protected environment of collectivity for the building's users. This condition is illustrated in Wenpu Chai's "Box and Tower," where shared courts are created by eroding three low-rise "boxes" at the locations where they intersect four vertical towers. As Chai's project shows, these internal voids serve dual functions, as they also allow natural light to be distributed to programmed space from the middle of the block. Relatedly, the subtractive void operation employed by Austin Edwards and Megan Friedman in their project, "The Reciprocal Block," yields a series of sectional modules that allow not only for shared perimeter territories exposed to the city, but also for vertical spaces dramatically carved out of the interior which connect multiple floors to the ground and sky.

The third spatial strategy generated from this studio involves removing rigid public-private thresholds and denoting all or most territory as communal. In this approach, common space is infrastructural and distributed. It is not figural as in the previous approaches; rather, it generates field conditions that promise spatial flexibility and possibility for collaboration, invoking the modernist free-plan philosophy. These projects follow the archetype of a market, where inhabitants are able to swarm freely around structural nodes through a decentralized circulation pattern. Yiwen Xing and Mengdi Rao's axonometric drawings of "Open Space as Structural Element," for instance, captures this quality of open, free space influenced by temporal objects within it. Here, space is designed as the agglomeration of a modular system defined by furniture. Such a strategy mocks current co-working trends, where an open loft is typically filled with chic furnishings. In doing so, it finds itself in alliance with seductive projects like Junya Ishigami's 2008 KAIT Workshop for the Kanagawa Institute of Technology in Japan, where transparency is uninterrupted and space is configured through a field of skinny columns and sleek furnishings.

Regardless of the spatial strategy deployed, it is also interesting to see how varyingly shared space is represented in the projects presented here. In some, the shared space receives graphic hierarchy, as textures, people, and furniture abound—suggesting an animated, urban life not unlike the city street—while the individual dwelling or working spaces are left as blank, austere cells. Yiwen Xing and Mengdi Rao's drawings for "Open Space as Structural Element" exemplify this approach, as does Tyler Mauri's building section for "Emerging Structures of Social + Shared Industry," where visual emphasis is predictably placed on collaborative operations, and not on the space for individual repose. On the other end of the spectrum, however, are projects like Mert Kansu's "Vertical Avenue," where the shared territory, expressed as a vertical avenue cutting from the High Line to the rooftop, is rendered in the section as mostly void of life, while surrounding programmed spaces drive the building's narrative visually, with people shown playing, climbing, performing, sitting, and working within a densely articulated interior. This approach suggests that the shared space is ephemeral and valuable as a visual and auditory connector rather than as a space of physical occupancy. In these two representational approaches, we can see theses for the plasticity of shared space come to fruition.

Sharing, All Grown Up

A child's first lesson in sharing is often met with resistance. They will reluctantly push the desired toy into the arms of the other child, then stare them down as they fumble around with it. No real enjoyment comes from this initial, mandated sharing exercise. While one sulks with possessiveness, the other's play is constrained by inhibition. In looking at these projects of shared territories, one cannot help but think of this awkward interaction. The hope is that this involuntary exercise instills a lifetime of more natural generosity. These projects are trying to transform New York's first directives for sharing into more comfortable and less scripted spaces.

The challenge, then, for the projects of Shared Territories is how to transform novel and uncomfortable spatial relationships motivated by technological progress and wealth redistribution into something familiar. The projects need to be radical, but not so radical as to risk sliding into hippie utopias. They need to channel Raymond Loewy, the wildly successful industrial designer who lived by the philosophy of MAYA: Most Advanced Yet Acceptable. On the surface, the projects shown here convey a newness that resonates with many fashionable architectural tendencies, but what makes them convincing as alternatives to the Hudson Yards model is that they are organized around traditional urban typologies for shared space. Although sometimes working in a covert manner, the street, the court, the park, the square, and the market constitute most of these projects' spatial concepts. The proposals look fresh, they have cool new machines in them, and they have instituted new logistics for access, but deep down in their organizational DNA we can find comfort in the spatial typologies we have known for centuries.

Prioritizing universal, uninhibited access to common, collective spaces enables many of these projects to escape the criticisms of the shared-amenity tower or the co-working hub. In most of these projects, two-thirds of the enclosed area can be read as a public or almost public facility. While the logistics of security may inhibit this perceived openness, and the financial model for profitability is unclear, the ambition for unconstrained sharing is achieved by organizing space relative to duration and flexibility of use. The lobby, New York's gatekeeper between public and private space, is pushed inward in these projects, installing a delay in the public-private threshold.

Projects like "Flex Space" by Lemara Miftakhova even suggest that this delayed moment of arrival can fluctuate with the programmatic flexibility.

Another convincing way some projects counter current trajectories in the city is through clear programmatic separation. Here, program is segregated, not people. Clear separation between commercial, industrial, office, and housing is an old idea but is still useful here, as access can be based on functional demand rather than purchased privileges. When shared programs get distributed throughout the building's section, a predisposition of many contemporary mixed-use buildings, the realities of sharing become strained. The farther you move collective space from the sidewalk, the less public it becomes. So, clear sectional separation enables common space to engage the distributed technologies of a shared economy and become accessible to all, while leaving housing to be dedicated to privacy.

The focus on shared space in this design studio aimed to erode the solidity and monumentality of the presumptive large urban building. In the projects presented in this book, there are very few solutions that promote a pure, archaic, iconic, monumental building massing. Rather, the proposals are jagged, subtracted, compounded, hollowed, staggered, modulated, and dissected. These operations collectively help disguise the bulk of the large urban block project—which in Manhattan measures approximately 264 by 900 feet—and break down the scale to a perceivable human module. This approach stands in strong contrast to the Hudson Yards towers to the north, where the view from a yacht on the Hudson or a helicopter above New Jersey is given priority. At a time when most of our cultural sharing occurs virtually via Twitter, we find in these Shared Territories projects a renewed appreciation for the physical and tangible experience of sharing urban space.

1
Danielle Sacks, "The Sharing Economy," *Fast Company*, April 18, 2011, https://www.fastcompany.com/1747551/sharing-economy.

2
Richard Rothstein, *The Color of Law: A Forgotten History of How Our Government Segregated America*. (New York: Liveright Publishing Corporation, 2017).

3
"NYC Luxury Condos: One57 Condominium," One57, n.d., accessed September 1, 2020, https://one57.com/one57.

4
Of the 488 U.S. counties the Brookings Institution's Metropolitan Policy Program classifies as suburban in larger metropolitan areas, the White share of the population fell in 468 of them from 2000 to 2019, according to calculations by demographer William Frey.

Frey, William H. "American Cities Saw Uneven Growth Last Decade, New Census Data Show." *Brookings*, 26 May 2020, www.brookings.edu/research/new-census-data-show-an-uneven-decade-of-growth-for-us-cities/.

5
Julie Satow, "Living in the Mix," *New York Times*, August 29, 2014, https://www.nytimes.com/2014/08/31/realestate/affordable-housing-in-new-yorks-luxury-buildings.html.

6
Eric Kober, "De Blasio's Mandatory Inclusionary Housing Program: What Is Wrong, and How It Can Be Made Right," *Manhattan Institute report*, January 16, 2020, https://www.manhattan-institute.org/deblasios-mandatory-inclusionary-housing-program.

7
Ibid.

8
Winnie Hu, "Uber, Surging Outside Manhattan, Tops Taxis in New York City," *New York Times*, October 12, 2017, https://www.nytimes.com/2017/10/12/nyregion/uber-taxis-new-york-city.html?rref=collection%2Fsection collection%2Fnyregion.

9
Rem Koolhaas, *Delirious New York: A Retroactive Manifesto for Manhattan* (1978; repr., New York: Monacelli Press, 2014).

10
Stacey Nguyen, "The 7 Best New York City Coworking Spaces of 2020," *The Balance: Small Business*, updated November 20, 2019, https://www.thebalancesmb.com/best-coworking-spaces-in-nyc-4172523.

Bigness Is Now Big Business: Black Holes for the Cosmo-Politan

Edward Mitchell

In the novel *Martin Dressler*, a cigar maker's son rises to the pinnacle of hotel builders in late-nineteenth-century Manhattan. His crowning achievement is the Grand Cosmo, a structure of unfathomable proportions, built by the architect Harwinton who runs an advertising campaign for potential residents: "THE GRAND COSMO: A NEW CONCEPT IN LIVING." The central idea for the campaign is contradictory:

> For if on the one hand he made the claim that the Grand Cosmo, insofar as it contained everything the urban resident could possibly desire, was nothing less than the city itself, so that to dwell within its walls was to be, at every moment, at the center of the city, yet on the other hand he emphasized that the Grand Cosmo was set apart from the city, he presented it as an exotic place that provided sensations available to the mere city-dweller unfortunate enough not to enter its enchanted walls, he did everything in his power to turn the Grand Cosmo into an attraction, an eighth wonder of the world, a place you simply had to see. These two contradictory images of the Grand Cosmo, which at first threatened to lead the campaign into confusion, were brilliantly reconciled by Harwinton in a third image that began to emerge more strongly: the Grand Cosmo as a place that rendered the city unnecessary.[1]

The big building rises again in Manhattan, but the problem is not, as it was in previous generations, one of the "difficult whole," the complex weave of the urban fabric, but that of the hole itself. The big building tears the city fabric. Just as Carl Andre defined sculpture not as cuts in materials, but as cuts in space formed by materials or "A thing is a hole in a thing it is not," we might say that architecture is a black hole. The big building is neither a node in the smooth space of the network nor a continuum of what Bauhaus theorist Sigfried Giedion called Space Time. Modernism also represented itself as a project discontinuous with history. Later claims for autonomy would rend architecture from its spatial and political context.

Architecture is often out of time, if not out of place. Utopias like the fictitious Grand Cosmo are, by definition, timeless and placeless.

The modernist quest for universal space led to a problematic relationship with the object. Two approaches to the city defined this conflict, differentiating object makers from urbanists. The grid and the large building challenged ideological propositions, the traditional forms of the city, and disciplinary rules of composition. Colin Rowe, a notable urbanist but a stalwart defender of architecture, wrote that in the 1960s and 1970s architects were avoiding the object. Quoting José Ortega y Gasset's definition of a cannon as a hole wrapped tightly by steel wire, Rowe and Fred Koetter described architecture's fundamental formal problem as the determination of bounded versus unbounded space.[2] They advocated for an architecture that opposed modernism's utopian tendencies, exemplified by the ubiquity of the grid and a quasi-scientific determinism, in favor of an eclectic and democratic form of the city, characterized by bounded spaces and architectural fragments.

In *Architecture and Utopia*, Manfredo Tafuri took a more overt political position, and linked architecture and power. He laid out three historic modes of architectural production—a cultivated sensualism in which the architectural object would provide specific effects within the more mundane urban fabric; direct claims that architecture represents power; and the Jeffersonian grid, which, he thought, contained the possibilities of a potentially vital and democratic political form. But with the development of the skyscraper, as a result of the concentration of economic power, the grid became anti-urban, and sensual effects became private affairs relegated to the building's interior. The skyscraper, fueled by capital, became an autonomous realm, attached to the urban network but ideologically separate and distinct from the traditional city. Tafuri used Louis Sullivan's drawing of a city to illustrate the problem. Sullivan showed a cityscape made up of self-similar urban blocks topped by stylized skyscrapers. Tafuri saw this as an explicitly American example of "utopian realism" overlapping with "realistic utopianism," a sign of the decline of social utopianism and the rise of the late capitalist "politics of things." The result for architecture was a retreat into the utopia of form as a way of "embracing disorder through order."[3]

Rem Koolhaas's attitude toward the grid and the skyscraper contrasted with the view of his contemporaries. He reveled in the schism between bounded and unbounded spaces and enthusiastically embraced disorder. Drawing similar conclusions to Tafuri in 1978's *Delirious New York*, Koolhaas showed how the Manhattan grid erased ideologies. But *Delirious New York*, a retroactive manifesto, was not yet burdened with prognostication. Rather, it was a piece of detective work about a nearly forgotten past, manifest in the ecstatic dreams of the New York developer of the early half of the twentieth century. Koolhaas embraced the amusement park and the skyscraper; Rowe and Koetter felt that both represented the architecture of kitsch: "the correct analogy [to Disneyland] is that of the New York skyscraper: on the 65th floor is the Rainbow Room where the consumption of Transcendentalist cocktails is the order of the day and then, way, way beneath (out of sight but not out of mind) is the pragmatic sub-basement which facilitates both the upstairs afflatus and public euphoria."[4]

In 1978, collage was the dominant technique. For Tafuri, collage is one result of the delusional utopia of form presaged in the work of Piranesi. For Koetter and Rowe, collage or bricolage offered an operative language that married the modern and traditional city. Koolhaas's version of collage trumped both the pessimism of Tafuri and the guarded republicanism of Rowe and Koetter. The surrealistic juxtaposition of programs he discovered in Manhattanism made ideology obsolete and defied Rowe and Koetter's layered compositional complexity of an architecture of a "difficult whole" that privileged the plan as the generator of ideas. However, whether one subscribed to Tafuri's tragic end game of syntactic play, downed Transcendentalist cocktails with Rowe and Koetter to mollify the casual ecstasy of civic indifference, or ate oysters in boxing gloves with Koolhaas, it all seemed only a matter of taste. Koolhaas, Koetter and Rowe, and Tafuri came to the general consensus that architectural form could not be assigned direct ideological intentions. For Tafuri, the conclusion was tragic; Rowe and Koetter sought solace in the disciplinary project of architecture. *Delirious New York* diagnosed new possibilities of the urban building that were anti-compositional. New forms of program might be engendered by collision and juxtaposition. Koolhaas, despite the cynicism of his writing, held out the possibility of informal and chance encounters as means to new institutional assemblages and a post-critical project.

"Bigness, or the Problem of Large," which informed the UVA brief, followed Koolhaas's earlier observation about the decompositional and institutional potential first identified in the Downtown Athletic Club. Published in a time of financial duress in the OMA offices, "Bigness" diagnosed that large bounded spaces could produce a vast, unbounded interior architecture. The city, according to Koolhaas, was obsolete, but new institutional configurations might arise out of this new spatial paradigm. The projects in *S, M, L, XL*, where the "Bigness" essay appeared, shared affinities with the Grand Cosmo—the city was no longer necessary.

In the essay, Koolhaas made the requisite five points for this new architecture and, in a twist, replaced Le Corbusier's structural propositions gleaned from the Maison Domino: Bigness could not be controlled by any single architectural gesture—there was no new style of the age; the elevator rendered the rules of classic composition inoperable and destroyed the implicit continuity of the modernist ramp; the distance between core and envelope doomed the "honesty" of the interior, which jeopardized the coherent relationship of inside and outside; size entered into an amoral domain beyond good and bad, which eliminated any utopian claims; and, finally, Bigness was no longer part of an urban tissue—or, to quote the author, "fuck context."[5]

Robert Somol riffed on Koolhaas's work in "12 Reasons for Getting in Shape" (2004) in *Content*, and identified an emerging architecture of shape. Somol's short manifesto recognized a subtle shift in OMA's work exemplified by the Whitney Museum and the Seattle Public Library, and brought those projects into a dialogue with buildings like Jan Neutelings's Bruges Concert Hall. The qualifications and potential for an architecture of shape were that it was illicit, easy, expendable, empty, graphic, adaptable, fit, intensive, arbitrary, buoyant, projective, and cool. Somol reclaimed the architectural project excluded by Robert Venturi's argument for complexity and contradiction, the megastructural Duck, and rejected Venturi's project of explicit iconicity and formal rigor. As opposed to the old critical project of form, Somol, paraphrasing Marshall McLuhan, contended that shape could stimulate a productive, seductive, "cool," or low-resolution architecture. This is what I call, in another essay, "Blurred Edges," suggestive and open to interpretation. Architecture, in order to form new institutional possibilities, had to be accessible, vague, and suggestive of new audiences for unprecedented experiences produced "like a visitation from an alternative world."[6]

For the shape architects, the big building is emphatically a thing, but one, like the Grand Cosmo, that perhaps too easily allowed architects to overcome their guilty conscience about making objects at the expense of the politics of the big project. At the same time that Somol wrote his essay, other architects were conspicuously anti-object. Using mapping, distributed systems, and proposals for new infrastructure and landscape urbanism, they used terms like "smoothness" and "network." These advocates for the calculus of the field over the effects of the object attempted to link the urban building to its political and economic influences. Koolhaas's work, to his credit, was broad in scope, and had affiliations with both camps. OMA and AMO in some respects were two minor institutional approaches that could switch between the modalities of object and field.

The buildings of the Next New York—the plethora of apartment towers that have changed nearly every streetscape in the five boroughs—are undoubtedly positioned within the Greater New York network of transportation nodes, and they are emphatically objects, but their presence also has the destructive energy of a black hole. We find ourselves on the edge of yet another event horizon. Koolhaas's Bigness thesis was built around a series of projects where the restrictions of the floorplate allowed the volume of the building to swell beyond conventional types. Libraries, museums, media centers, and convention halls differ by virtue of the codes that inform office buildings and housing, and produce interior effects which differ from the logic of the apartment block. The projects of the early 2000s that are the closest antecedents to the Next New York mega-buildings were shape buildings rather than Big buildings. MVRDV's residential complex in Mirador, Peter Eisenman's 1994 Reinhardt Tower, and OMA's CCTV tower defined the Building with a Hole. Frank Gehry's Fred and Ginger building and the 2002 schemes for the World Trade Center site by Greg Lynn, Foreign Office Architects, UN Studio, Reiser + Umemoto Architects, Kevin Kennon Architects, and Imaginary Forces gave rise to the Kissing Towers.

This brief outline of sources directly and indirectly informs problems set forth in the UVA studio focused on Shared Territories for the Next New York. At the time of the studio, ideas that were percolating in advanced forms of practice and academic speculation had begun to filter into the marketplace. When "Bigness" was written, the World Trade Center still stood, ground had not yet been broken for CCTV tower, the New York City Council had not approved the rezoning of Hudson Yards, Hurricane Katrina had not hit New Orleans, and the G8 summit on climate change had not been convened. Architecture has its own slow period of gestation, often rehearsed in academic think tanks or in speculative propositions. Then it takes several years for those ideas to hit publications and eventually get built. Making a building remains, despite the rapid change in delivery, a slow mode of cultural production. The seeds of architectural thought that take a full generation to bloom into physical structure are quickly dismissed as last year's model. "Bigness" is twenty-five years old, and was already a retrospective thought piece. The Next New York, in its present reality, is evidence of how Koolhaas's idealized conception of Bigness and Somol's idea of the projective possibilities of Shape were disseminated and compromised in the construction of simply big buildings.

Already there was an assumption, a difficult problem that lingers in architecture, that the spatial management of buildings might be connected to discrete political ideologies and programs. The spatial juxtaposition evident in the Downtown Athletic Club and the future-forward playground of Coney Island are the spiritual DNA of the UVA program. The amusement park's incubator building for "preemies—the creation of a private race"[7] is the unacknowledged, programmatic inspiration for UVA's "Manhattan Innovation Incubator." But even those two antecedents have been problematic, as they too are evidence of a generic form that sponsors programmatic juxtaposition.

Program could also be thought of in less obvious ways. Koolhaas, quoting Vico in *Delirious New York*, proposed that "modifications of the mind" reveal principles. It has also been suggested that, while content remains similar, the medium of delivery differs from generation to generation. The city would therefore coincide with desires manifest through new media genres. The mail-order catalogue informed the Jeffersonian grid and helped produce late-nineteenth-century eclecticism. Television was the media of representation for the post-war suburbs and created a false nostalgia for the ideas of neighborhood and the nuclear family. Koolhaas and others claimed a cinematic influence, and produced an architecture of jump cuts and superposition, deconstructing conventional narratives that ordered the traditional program brief. The UVA studio reflects an interest in the urbanism of smart phones, video games, and apps. These might be the generative media and the implicit program of contemporary spatial practice. In other words, social media and cell phone emoji are influencing the big Next New York but not in ways that can be assigned directly to standard architectural representation or program.

Ultimately, as Koolhaas writes, "Bigness instigates the regime of complexity that mobilizes the full intelligence of architecture and its related fields."[8] These questions of form and program frame this brief survey of recently built work in New York City. Reality is complex, revealing the intricate web of disciplinary influences and corporate kickbacks. While political rhetoric speaks one language, backroom deals that are financing the Next New York tell a different story. "Shared territories" are implicated in the financing of the big project, and the adventurous proposals by the students in Next New York have been reduced in the reality of the New York real estate landscape to programs for "the millennial-focused, hipster-amenitized luxury rental developments."[9] Programs pitched as sophisticated urban living are turning into "adult dorm room" lifestyles. Sophisticated algorithms weigh the loss of rentable square footage for an in-house fitness center or conference facility against the increased rental rates. "Bigness," which seemed to promise a liberated chaos, differs from the big business of big buildings.

"Bigger is better—even when it comes to New York City's residential buildings," reported the *New York Post*. In the 2010s, fifty to sixty thousand people moved to metropolitan New York City each year, which has stimulated the construction of a large number of mega-apartment blocks.[10] Changes in demographics began shortly after the economic crash of 2008. Wall Street was deemed "too big to fail" and the rise of tech industries in the financial and media markets produced a young, digitally savvy populace, a new form of "creative class" that eclipsed the romantic notion of the artistic avant-garde who were formerly the denizens of downtown.

Recalling that Koolhaas took a flight of fantasy over Raymond Hood's drawings of "Manhattan 1950," the more recent real estate growth was a plan long in coming. The rebirth of the financial district and the colonization of the Queens, Brooklyn, and New Jersey waterfronts were in the planning agendas of the beginning of the millennium, but they were slowed by the burst of the tech bubble in 2001 and by the 2008 crash. One of the first big projects of the new era was New York by Gehry (2010), developed by Forest City Ratner. At the time of its construction in 2010 it was the tallest residential tower in the Western Hemisphere, boasting 904 units perched on a 100,000-square-foot elementary school base, part of a public-private development strategy to build new infrastructure, which included the extensive waterfront parks of the outer boroughs.

One of the largest areas of new development, Hudson Yards, was part of the visioning plan for the 2012 Olympic bid. It has proven to be as uninspired as the initial plans. Hudson Yards was financed by EB-5, the 1990 federal visa program that allows foreign investors to obtain a green card in exchange for a $500,000 investment. American developers took full advantage of the program to obtain cheap financing for ground-up construction. Visa backlogs, fraud, and misuse plagued the program, but it still has supporters. Related Companies' 35 Hudson Yards, designed by former SOM partner David Childs with interiors by David Rockwell, touts the lifestyle slogan "Live Where It All Comes Together." Certainly with that power lineup, something did. Like other projects, the tower comes with a list of amenities that includes a fitness center, a lounge and bar, a billiards lounge, a golf simulator, a private dining room for sixteen, a library, a screening room, a children's playroom, a board room, Grand Terrace, and Grand Dining Room. This city within a city has come to be the standard fare for Manhattan high-rollers. According to the *Wall Street Journal*, developers, including the Kushner family, "are now looking to U.S. Sen. Lindsey Graham, Chuck Schumer and other powerful elected officials to help ease newly-passed rules" meant to crackdown on abuse of the EB-5 visa program.[11]

While Gehry and Childs have developer history, new firms also emerged on the real estate playing field. SHoP Architects represents a generation facile with digital tools and business savvy. Marrying financial know-how with academic bona fides, they have worked on several large residential projects. The American Copper building, done with JDS Development and Largo and completed in 2017, is one of several big apartment buildings in their portfolio (figure 1). Sheldon Solow, the original developer for the site, tried to construct a seven-tower, $4 billion complex with SOM. That plan would have included a park and a public school.[12] Plans for a twin-tower structure were inherited by JDS and Largo, this time with SHoP. The building's 761 rental units at 626 First Avenue are distinguished by a pair of leaning towers connected by a three-story skybridge that houses a 75-foot pool, a hot tub, a bar and lounge, and terraces. Attempting to seem hip if not hop, former SHoP partner Vishaan Chakrabarti, now the Dean of UC Berkeley, in an obvious nod to Gehry's Fred and Ginger building in Prague, likened the design to Beyoncé and Jay Z dancing.[13] While the architectural merits of the publicly accessible spaces and skin of the building are accomplished, its siting, at the eastern edge of Manhattan near the Queens Midtown Tunnel, is less part of the street grid than it is a node in a network of infrastructure that connects outlying parcels. The relative isolation of the site, which may be only temporary, makes the complex feel less part of the fabric of the city than a Bridge and Tunnel colonial outpost.

The twin-tower typology is also planned for BIG's XI "dancing towers" with developer HFZ Capital Group. The 34-story western tower, named N° I, and the 25-story eastern tower, named N° X, clock in at 895,000 square feet with 247 condominiums, a 137-room Six Senses hotel, 90,000 square feet of retail space, art space, a spa and club, a pool, a lounge and gallery in the glass bridge, a wine-tasting room, a social lounge with billiards tables, a teen room, and a children's playroom. Not the first of BIG's attempts at the two-tower tango, XI is even stiffer than their twisting towers in Coconut Grove, Florida. XI, too, lies at the edge of the city center.

The building with a hole, first seen in Mirador, is popular in the shape lexicon. SHoP's 325 Kent building in Williamsburg, like 35 Hudson Yards, is "Where It All Comes Together." Part of the Domino Sugar Development by Two Trees Management, the 16-story building contains 522 apartments. The amenity package includes a health club, bike storage, residents' lounge, a billiard table, a chef's kitchen for catering, a 2,000-square-foot courtyard on the fourth floor, and a 7,000-square-foot rooftop terrace, both designed by Leeser Architecture and built by Blondie's Treehouse. Again, BIG has made their 2016 entry in this shape category at 625 57 West near the West Side Highway. "Visionary Valiant Unconventional," according to the

Figure 1: American Copper Building, SHoP Architects.

building's website, the 830,995-square-foot, 709-unit tetrahedron-shaped volume is a courtyard type lopped off at an angle to form a pyramid silhouette that marries a conventional plan type with the imageability of the emoji. "We knew that the Far West Side was ripe for a series of large residential buildings that could cultivate community," says Jonathan Drescher, senior vice president at Durst.[14] Visionary valiancy is demonstrated in the building's branding to "Rethink Green Living" by providing an oasis for residents consisting of outdoor terraces, a 22,000-square-foot central space that we are told "shares the exact proportions as Olmsted's Central Park "[15] with 47 species of native plant material. BBQ grills and an eight-screen theater on the ground floor complete the program. Not too far removed in concept from O. M. Ungers's 1975 Roosevelt Island competition entry, 57 West is Manhattan in miniature.

TEN Arquitectos added to the Shape menagerie in 2012 with the Mercedes House, a serpentine 30-story, 864-unit building. But like others they have also made recent additions in downtown Brooklyn with Two Trees Developers. The towering 35-story 379-unit apartment slab at 300 Ashland Place is just down the street from SHoP's Barclay Center and across from the Brooklyn Academy of Music. Located on the site of their unrealized project for the Brooklyn Visual and Performing Arts Library, the program compensates the public with 50,000 square feet of city-owned cultural space, including dance studios, theaters, and a smaller public library.

Not to be outdone in New York's hottest borough, EB-5 partnered with Hudson Development and paid $52 million to redevelop the Public Library's Brooklyn Heights branch library site, aiming to transform the historical building into a 36-story, 139-condo tower with two retail spaces and a new state-of-the-art library and community center. This will add to Hudson Development's local portfolio, which includes plans for two additional residential towers to provide more affordable housing for the community. The David Kramer-led development firm plans to raise up to $110 million for the project through the immigration program.[16]

To an extent, these Shape buildings follow Somol's agenda. Their easily identifiable silhouettes have given them an easy marketability. And while the Somol essay continues to provoke, after seeing several of the early academic instantiations of the agenda at the University of Illinois Chicago in the early 2000s, I asked whether the ubiquitous presence of a chandelier, flock wallpaper, and a bar was the limit of the speculative possibilities of the program. The same question holds true of the buildings of the Next New York. If quirky shapes and colorful panel systems fail to form community identity, and their siting on former edge territories is a challenge, the amenity program of these projects both compensates for their location and adds to their marketability. But in the end, the programs barely distinguish one apartment building from the next. The twin 58-story, 1,359-unit Silver Towers built in 2008 near Times Square have less of the dynamic massing tango of other twin-tower schemes, but the project's website features a building blog of social highlights like an "'80s party" and offers a video of the young tenants staging this ancient passage of history. The online video has all the squirmy embarrassment that made *The Office* a successful sitcom. It shows no evidence of the edgy post-punk downtown vibe of the Lower East Side some of us remember, nor does it re-enact the police crackdown that is credited with turning the tide for the bland development we are seeing today.

Shape and scale would seem to be symptoms or requirements of buildings that want to distinguish themselves from their surroundings. But shape alone is not a distinguishing characteristic of an earlier trend in the market. Cesar Pelli's 4-74 48th Avenue in Long Island City, built in 1997, was a harbinger of things to come. That prototype turned its back to the then low-rise, mixed-use district by attaching a parking garage on the upland side and adding a daycare center in the lobby. Tenants could drop off their children, head to the garage, and speed away without engaging their neighbors. This hermetic idea of the program fits more recent development on the Greenpoint-Williamsburg waterfront. 2 N. Sixth Place in Williamsburg by Douglaston Development is a tower with 550 units. For an added cost, level 9 membership includes access to an indoor/outdoor pool; a whirlpool and steam room; a 24-hour technogym; a yoga studio with stretching equipment; virtual, on-demand fitness classes; a club lounge with game tables and a demonstration kitchen; a party room; a wrap-around terrace with fireplace, grills, and communal lounge/dining areas; a kid's playroom styled as a forest with stage and chalkboard tables; a business center with video conferencing and work stations and free wi-fi in the common spaces. Tall residential towers form a phalanx guarding the public-private spaces of the waterfront park.

What do Next New York residents set inside these self-contained worlds have in common except the need for community? Sky, developed by the Moinian Group and designed by the Rockwell Group, was, at the time of completion, the largest single-tower residence in the U.S. at 1,175 units. The amenity package includes a basketball court designed by Carmelo Anthony. The Hub, "Live High,"[17] in Boerum Hill consisting of 750 units by Steiner Equities, Dattner Architects, and Goldstein Hill & West Architects advertises itself on a website that resembles a Where's Waldo picture book. The images of mixed-race urban hipsters spinning yo-yos, singing in the shower, playing arcade games, wolfing burgers, getting tattoos, and smoking a pipe while bicycling through Downtown Brooklyn are visions of curated, perpetual urban adolescence. Amenities include a 75-foot lap pool, lushly landscaped sundeck and lawn, grilling cabanas, a fully equipped gym and yoga studio, bike storage, indoor and outdoor movie screens, programmed events in the club lounge, a dog run, children's playroom, party room, and a library. "The younger generation is more mobile, more comfortable renting and not aspiring to homeownership the same way past generations [have]," says Doug Steiner.[18]

These post-modern phalansteries that first colonized Manhattan have spread to the nearby neighborhoods of urbanely hip Brooklyn and are now landing on more distant shores. Ironstate Development, "We Go Big,"[19] headed by brothers Michael and David Barry, is packaging a lifestyle brand Urby and has projects in Jersey City, Staten Island, Harrison, New Jersey, and Stamford, Connecticut (figure 2). Already successful with the Standard East Village, W Hoboken hotel, and the Pod Brooklyn Hotel in Williamsburg, the brothers have conjured a brand that combines images of new urban living and the farms that once populated these far reaches of Manhattanism. Designed by Dutch architects Concrete, Urby has captured a middle-brow audience for all that is sustainably vogue. Each project has an iconic, heavy-timber house form (the new primitive hut?) that brings the large apartment blocks down to human scale. Urby Staten Island, with 900 units, has its own resident farmer who tends to the courtyard crops. Urby has the manicured earthy vibe of a Whole Foods market. Jersey City Urby, a 69-story skyscraper located at 200 Greene Street across the Hudson River from

Lower Manhattan, resembles OMA's generic city schemes. Rising 713 feet, it is the tallest residential building and second-tallest building in New Jersey. The amenities include a "creative lab," and a residency program for scientists and artists. The cute entries for the Urby blog read:

Figure 2: Urby Jersey City, Concrete Architects.

> Moving into Urby has changed my life in so many ways I couldn't have imagined. My chakras are so aligned, I don't even have to work anymore. I just think, 'I'd like a Cuban sandwich right now.' And my bank account becomes full.
>
> Being a discerning Pomsky, URBY appealed to me as the kind of place where I'd be welcome to be myself, get petted by adoring fans, and unwind after a long day of being cute. It's perfect.
>
> Somewhere in the midst of lounging in my apartment, kicking it in the café with Jarred and Esther from the fifth floor, and just wandering around the property, it dawned on me: *I never have to leave here. So I haven't since I moved in.*

But living in these Bridge and Tunnel utopias comes with urban problems. The NYPD conducted a raid at the Urby Staten Island apartment complex, where officers discovered cocaine, a scale, and a Mossberg hand-pump shotgun. The perpetrator faces two counts of criminal possession of a weapon, in addition to charges of criminal possession of a controlled substance, criminal possession of a firearm, and criminal use of drug paraphernalia, according to a written statement from the office of the NYPD Deputy Commissioner of Public Information. Newscasters report that the arrest followed a fatal stabbing at the complex in 2018. "It's getting better, but there is [sic] still a lot of shady people that live there," said a tenant.[20]

But if the blog is a forecast, and constant grooming and the capacity to never need to work in the Urby paradise is still possible, the appeal of these outer-borough Edens have not yet been worthy of serious personal investment. Why buy the golden cow if the milk is available for rent? David Barry recognizes that "there's less stigma [to not buying a place], and more effort in the design and amenities."[21] For developers, the renters' market is a safer investment that provides steady income and no long-term financial commitment for residents.

Nowhere is this by-the-hour lifestyle opportunity better captured than with WeLive, who, to date, have been able to realize only one New York residential project. Capitalizing on the hype of the WeWork platform, the Wall Street residence, like many of these other projects, feels part corporate office and part hotel. To compensate for the problem of a continuous change in residents, floors are organized into "neighborhoods," with open staircases and unified decorative schemes. The rental strategy for both long- and short-term stays is aimed at the "modern-day nomad who is just stopping by or dipping your toes in the city before taking the big leap."[22]

Loneliness haunts the new itinerant tech worker.[23] Co-founder Miguel McKelvey thought WeLive might provide the physical context for community building, replacing those institutions that once formed that backbone of New York neighborhoods. If we are to believe the hype, old institutions of family, parish, and school are being replaced by the ubiquitous and generic "We," a nomadic tribe organized by apps and virtual populations of "like"-minded consumers. In this new world order one is guaranteed to find self-curated peers. Soon you'll be able to "feel like you're staying within your community, within the network, wherever you are," according to McKelvey. However, Benjy Hansen-Bundy writes, "WeLive gives me this sinking feeling that what I'm giving up in security and commitment, I'm not necessarily getting back in freedom."[24]

In 2018 WeWork brought in BIG as an equity partner and chief architect. Together they developed WeGrow and several other projects with the ambition to begin with buildings and then WeGrow to cities. WeGrow, the company's for-profit education venture, was a space that featured felt clouds and wooden blobs to enhance the "intuitive" creativity of children. The choice of architects was inevitable. But the venture went under in one year, and during the course of writing this piece, Bjarke Ingels of BIG announced that he was ending his relationship with the company. WeWork's and BIG's ambitions of world conquest slowed considerably after a rough public startup, and rumors abound that WeWork, despite its huge real estate holdings, may soon go bankrupt.

The volatile rental markets coupled with the particulars of the investment strategies for these buildings has left a vacancy problem. Easy money can cloud sound, long-term urban investment. One report shows that a quarter of the new condos built since 2013 in New York City have not found buyers.[25] Steinway Tower, by SHoP, at 111 West 57th Street hit a financial crisis and stopped construction for a time in 2017. Even before 2020, 80 percent of its units were unsold. Similarly, the market glut of high-end real estate caused 100 East 53rd Street to report 72 percent of its units available, and in 2019 53 West 53rd Street had two-thirds of its units for sale. The bigger they are, the harder they can fall.

Mega-buildings made up of hundreds of apartments impact urban planning, increasing demands on the public infrastructure. Residential towers for the small households that are the domain of younger, more affluent New Yorkers are shifting the historic structure of existing neighborhoods as school districts that are now the sites of real estate speculation may see downward swings in elementary school populations. There's also the chance that these huge rentals will decrease overall density in their immediate vicinity. More importantly, New York is qualitatively changed by the instruments of large-scale public-private partnerships. It remains to be seen whether these black holes in the old fabric can live up to their branding and put the cosmos in "cosmopolitanism" or fulfill Koolhaas's aphorism that the "cosmetic is cosmic."

The UVA brief elides the Bigness and Shape agendas, and solicited formal questions: If single gestures, composition, inside/outside continuity, ethics, and context are obsolete, what then do we teach in the studio? What are the methods of control? And what authority establishes criteria for judgment about the success or failure of the work? While these questions are prompts for formal speculation, the brief's program, now three years old, is indebted, no doubt, to the same optimistic projections of the post-critical project envisioned by Koolhaas and Somol. However, companies like Uber, Airbnb, and We Work, the "post-ownership" industries mentioned in the brief, have been less the pioneers of a new condition of "shared territories" than they seem to have fallen into a model of flexibility that, in practice, slips into the generic rather than spatial specificity. Koolhaas, too, shifted in his position that Bigness was a condition that might produce the former surreal chaos of the metropolis, and turned to a steely examination of the Generic City.

In reality, the Next New York has also been reduced by the economic margins of real estate speculation to the generic scenarios of backyard barbeques and horseshoes on elevated terraces, mall-like interiors, and cruise-ship-themed-social-events. When '80s parties take place in Midtown, New York City, once the site of risk and invention, is reduced to predictable and marketable formulas. With the scale of investment in these properties, it is no small wonder that Bigness has yielded the spatial complexity speculated on in the studio but has instead turned into big business.

The new urban network marked by these buildings does fulfill the visionary urbanism of the midcentury as the point towers indicate elevated land values linked to the greater Tri-State development map. Koolhaas once remarked that urban theory developed as the city began to disappear. New York as it once was is also fading. Becoming a New Yorker was once a rite of passage earned on its mean streets. The older city was what Luc Sante and others called an ecosystem for street people, those for whom traditional places and institutions were not designed. Your New Yorker badge is now earned by heavy financial buys-ins. The intricate movements of Jane Jacobs's street ballet will end when a doorman sits guarding the social playgrounds of the new urban interiors, and the towers themselves are left to mutely mimic the old urban street dance. Does anyone still live in New York?

1
Steven Millhauser, *Martin Dressler: The Tale of an American Dreamer* (New York: Vintage Books, 1996), 264–265.

2
Colin Rowe and Fred Koetter, *Collage City* (1978; repr., Cambridge, MA: MIT Press, 1983), 50.

3
Manfredo Tafuri, *Architecture and Utopia: Design and Capitalist Development*, trans. Barbara Luigia La Penta (Cambridge, MA: MIT Press, 1976), 46–49.

4
Rowe and Fred Koetter, 45.

5
Rem Koolhaas, "Bigness, or the Problem of Large," in *S, M, L, XL* (New York: Monacelli Press, 1995), 502.

6
Robert Somol, "12 Reasons to Get Back in Shape," in *Content* (Cologne: Taschen, 2004), 87.

7
Rem Koolhaas, *Delirious New York: A Retroactive Manifesto for Manhattan* (1978; repr., New York: Monacelli Press, 2014), 50.

8
Koolhaas, "Bigness," 497.

9
Penelope Green, "In the '90s, We Had 'Friends.' Now They Call It Co-Living," *New York Times*, August 23, 2017, https://www.nytimes.com/2017/08/23/style/what-is-co-living.html.

10
Zachary Kussin, "Giant, 1,000-Apartment Buildings Are Taking over NYC," *New York Post*, July 13, 2016, https://nypost.com/2016/07/13/giant-1000-apartment-buildings-are-taking-over-nyc/.

11
Cited in Keith Larsen, "New EB-5 Rules Targeting Abuse May Be Eased," *The RealDeal: New York Real Estate News*, January 14, 2020, https://therealdeal.com/2020/01/14/new-eb-5-rules-targeting-abuse-may-be-eased/?utm_source=internal&utm_medium=after_article&utm_campaign=related_article.

12
Charles V. Bagli, "Prime Lot, Empty for Years (Yes, This Is Manhattan)," *New York Times*, August 19, 2013, https://www.nytimes.com/2013/08/20/nyregion/prime-lot-empty-for-years-yes-this-is-manhattan.html?_r=0.

13
Julie Satow, "High-Rises to Replace an East Side Eyesore," *New York Times*, https://www.nytimes.com/2013/08/04/realestate/high-rises-to-replace-an-east-side-eyesore.html?pagewanted=all&_r=0

14
Kussin, "Giant, 1,000-Apartment Buildings."

15
https://big.dk/#projects-w57

16
Larsen, "New EB-5 Rules."

17
https://hubbk.com/

18
Kussin, "Giant, 1,000-Apartment Buildings."

19
https://www.ironstate.net/

20
Kyle Lawson, https://www.silive.com/crime/2019/11/nypd-raid-at-trendy-urby-apartment-complex-yields-cocaine-shotgun.html

21
Kussin, "Giant, 1,000-Apartment Buildings."

22
https://www.welive.com/

23
Benjy Hansen-Bundy, "A Week Inside WeLive, the Utopian Apartment Complex That Wants to Disrupt City Living," *GQ*, February 27, 2018, https://www.gq.com/story/inside-welive. The article appeared in *GQ*, March 2018, with the title "Can the WeLive Experiment Actually Change the Way We Live?"

24
Hansen-Bundy, "A Week Inside."

25
Stefanos Chen, "One in Four of New York's New Luxury Apartments Is Unsold," *New York Times*, September 13, 2019, https://www.nytimes.com/2019/09/13/realestate/new-development-new-york.html.

Infrastructured LandScapes: Civic Frameworks and Engineered Natures

Thomas Woltz

Parks, plazas, and squares are the vital spaces that indicate and reflect the social wellbeing of a city and its citizens. They provide a common platform and, at their best, facilitate democratic conversation among all citizens regardless of demographics. These landscapes, within often dense urban contexts and infrastructure, bring us to some idea of nature—shade, soil, plants, insects, and animals—contributing to our health and the health of the environment around us. In considering the seven-year arc of designing and overseeing the construction of the Hudson Yards Plaza, we reflect on our design team's motivation and vision for this new infrastructure-based landscape, from initial design ideas and ethos, informed by research of the site and the region, to the realities of value engineering and market-driven decisions.

Historically considered a part of Hell's Kitchen, Hudson Yards is named after the previously open-air rail yards along the river and the portion between Eleventh and Tenth Avenues called the Eastern Rail Yards. Today, the 6-acre public plaza functions as the urban fabric that seamlessly stitches together newly minted structures, including the culture-programmed Shed, the monumental installation called Vessel, the High Line, the new number 7

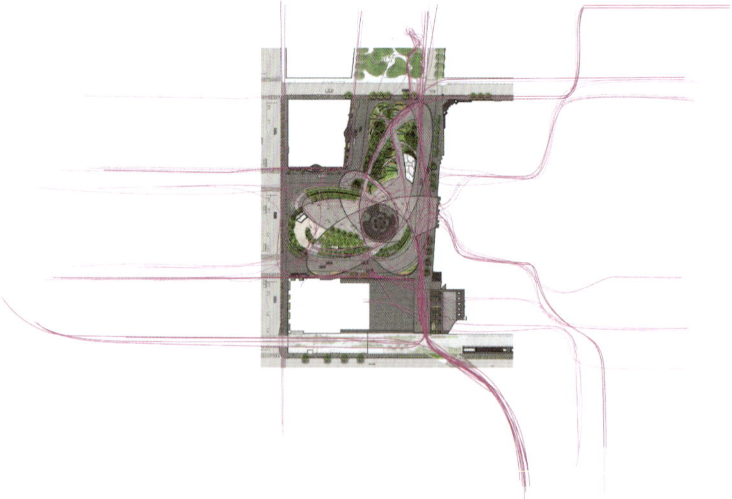

Figure 1: A circulation diagram illustrates how the Plaza was designed to draw visitors in and serve as a physical intermediary between public spaces.

subway station, and surrounding parks and streets on the west side of Manhattan.

The following text explores our design process in creating an infrastructure-landscape hybrid that expresses an openness through formal contextualization and orchestrated physical connections, material and metaphorical, to the ecological and cultural history of the site. Private-public partnerships and ontological evidence of their role in creating and maintaining public spaces with ever-shrinking government budgets will also be briefly considered. The essay concludes with a brief overview of public spaces designed and built on the west side of Manhattan in the past decades—temporally contextualizing the Hudson Yards landscape with other works of landscape architecture.

Research as Inspiration and Origin of Design

The Nelson Byrd Woltz (NBW) team's motivation in designing any public space, including Hudson Yards, lies in the belief that parks, like all public urban zones, are the last democratic territories in the city, where the exchange of thoughts, feelings, and ideas and the possibility for chance encounters flourish—Debord's designed and implied dérive.[1] Our team's design process is informed by a deeply humanistic approach toward achieving urban landscapes that provide connections across physical experiences and temporal states to reveal ecological and cultural stories and traces, mediate the scale of the body with that of the built environment, and support and improve the health of people and the environment.

To achieve these ends, we engage in a research-based design process that digs deeply into cultural archives, in a sense a "paleontology of the present,"[2] looking for clues that reveal the evolution of space in time to arrive at the current condition. In the case of Hudson Yards, two key sources contributed to our research: the first, the ecologically minded Mannahatta Project,[3] by Eric Sanderson and Markley Boyer, which aspires to document to "minute verisimilitude," down to the varieties of moss, the ecology of the island of Manhattan before European contact. The second, culturally focused, is Jill Jonnes's *Conquering Gotham*, which records the monumental efforts to create New York City's infrastructure, and which reflects the country's acceleration of industrialism and material extraction and manipulation.[4] Throughout the design process, the team acknowledged this ongoing dance between the physical and ecological reality and the projected evolution through innovative engineering, and how it created the Hudson Yards site and its surrounds. Throughout, there were gestures towards the poetics of citations and suggestions that, if not obvious, perhaps with time and attention would reveal themselves. As Robert Pogue Harrison has elegantly articulated, gardens "invite us to take the time to learn how to see them; they offer an education in ways of seeing."[5]

Figure 2: The technological achievements of the landscape are a continuation of the site's legacy of innovation—here showing the Greathead Shield used to excavate the tunnel between New Jersey and Hudson Yards.

Designing a Civic Space on Infrastructure

During the hyper-capitalism of the 2010s, Manhattan's desirability as a personal or corporate address attracted global investment, making land less accessible and creating a direct increase in the need for both infrastructure to support a larger populace and park space to ensure elements of community and connections to nature. The economics of urban investment and return leaned heavily toward the prioritization of structures over infrastructural systems and park space. With intense densification of the city, the need for improvements in the public realm has become paramount, and investment in meeting this need has followed.[6] Thus, financially and physically, the public landscape of Hudson Yards was created at the intersection of structural and infrastructural projects within this intensely object-focused era of city building.

Hudson Yards Plaza was designed to offer a satisfying experience for all who visit, without concern for the complexities of coordinating and constructing its structure. A Hudson Valley ecology was plucked from up-river, stylized along the High Line and formalized at Hudson Yards.[7]

What better example of the Anthropocene than devising an ecology on a suspended platform, an urban terrarium? It is both novel and ancient. Arguably, more than in any other project, the landscape holds all of the elements without which Hudson Yards would not work: structures, flows, functions, tunnels, access, security, and a satisfying urban experience are all dependent on the success of what we unsatisfyingly still call landscape.

While the complexities of building architecture on structural columns straddling train lines is impressive and formidable, the complexities of landscape are much more subtle and interconnected. Soils, stormwater, irrigation, temperature considerations above and below, solar aspect, and wind modeling are a few of the considerations in designing at the interface with urban infrastructure. This has meant an intense and instructional process with many collaborators, from structural and civil engineers, to experts on irrigation, soil, and horticulture, to architects.

However, will hyphae, that filamentous structure of a fungus, oomycete, or actinobacterium, form here — dependent on electricity and human calculation for survival? The NBW design team, working with soil consultants and horticulturalists, ensured the potential of this soil communication web between trees, but is it enough? With the consultants, we have created a synthetic hybrid of concrete walls, lightweight cellular concrete fill, EPS fill (expanded polystyrene foam), XPS fill (extruded polystyrene foam for increased insulation performance), sand-based structural soil, and planter soil to negotiate between infrastructure and what we call in the profession a "performing landscape."

On the surface of the 6 acres, the public experience of Hudson Yards East was deliberately conceived to provide myriad agoras while moving people on foot, on wheelchairs, in cars, and other devices seamlessly and with delight. Hardscape and ellipse patterns of granite paving blocks give structure to the experience of the landscape. These formal elements will likely persist the longest at Hudson Yards, manifesting a design intended for future generations of urban dwellers to consider. These mineral elements of Hudson Yards are calibrated within a system of structures, flows, and grades, all carefully and artfully imagined, and reiterated by the structured approach to planting and horticulture. Our team found it useful to create three distinct idealized landscapes—the mineral Plaza, the lush Gardens, and the minimalist Bosque—that follow and reinforce the elliptical lines. Where the Plaza is all about movement, the soft canopy of the Bosque and the Garden were created to slow the movement of pedestrians and provide seating, formal or otherwise, with sheltering plants and focusing views to create sanctuaries of repose.

The designed ecology, the humic foundation of this particular site, manifests a version of nature in an otherwise heavily engineered landscape. For, the process of designing and implementing it was substantial, as exemplified by the black gum trees, which were grown in

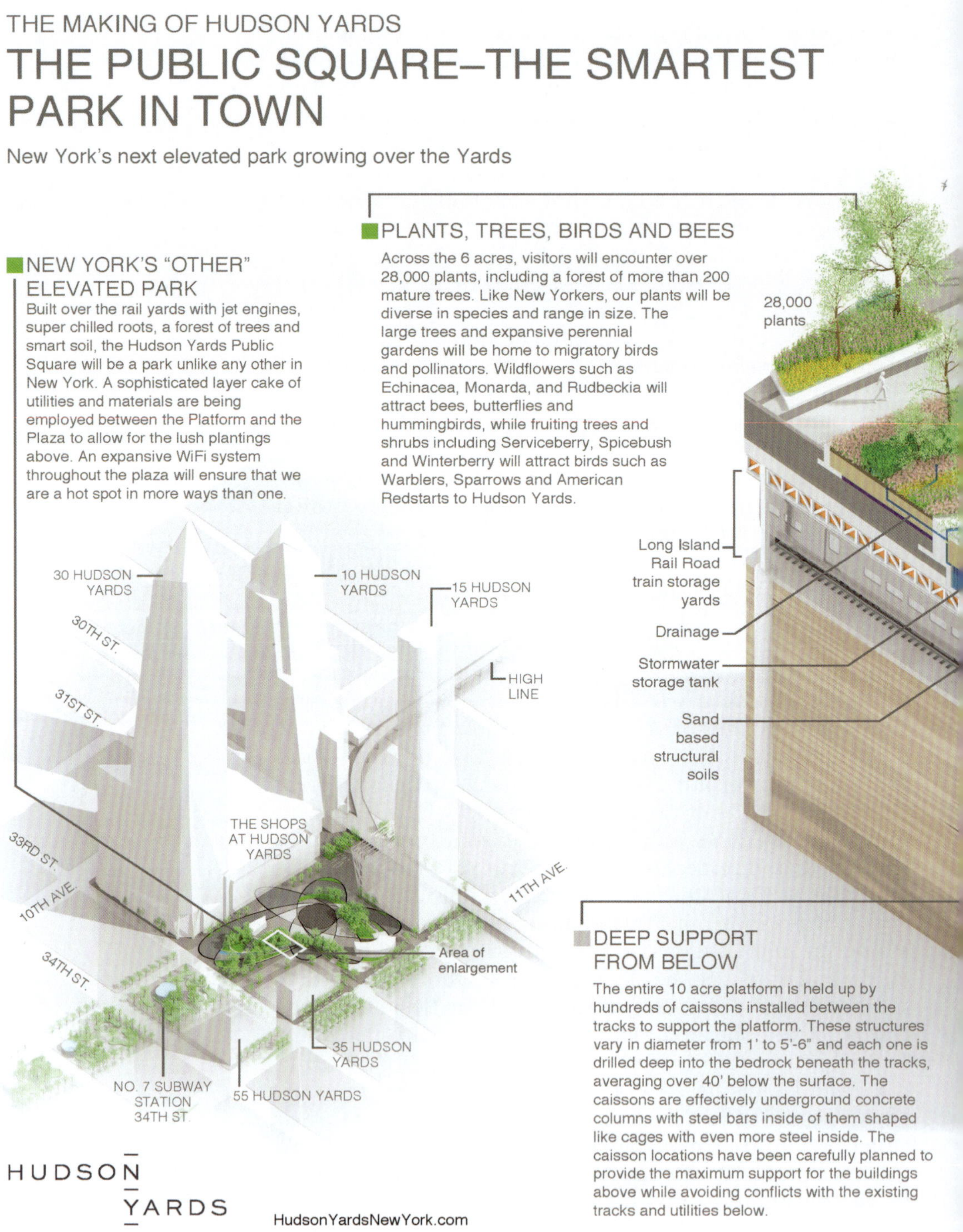

Figure 3: The platform contains an embedded cooling system and engineered soil, sand, and gravel to protect plants from the heat generated by the active rail yards below.

THE SMARTEST SOIL IN TOWN

With a soil depth of 18 inches for plants and only 4 feet for large trees, admittedly we are shallow, but self-aware and over-compensating for it. The soils have been specially designed to provide effective drainage and nutrients for the plants and ensure our roots can run wide, if not deep. Where trees are planted in paving, a specially engineered "soil sandwich" of sand, gravel and concrete slab will protect the roots while allowing them to expand. The sophisticated layering of this system includes provisions for aeration, irrigation, drainage, root development and ongoing control of nutrients, including specially designed soil chemistry and soil biology.

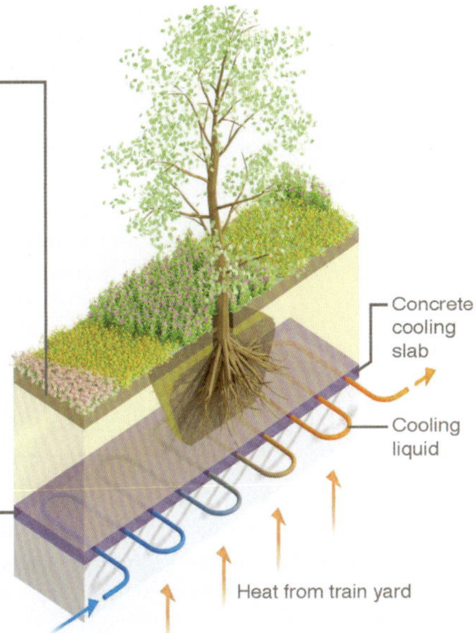

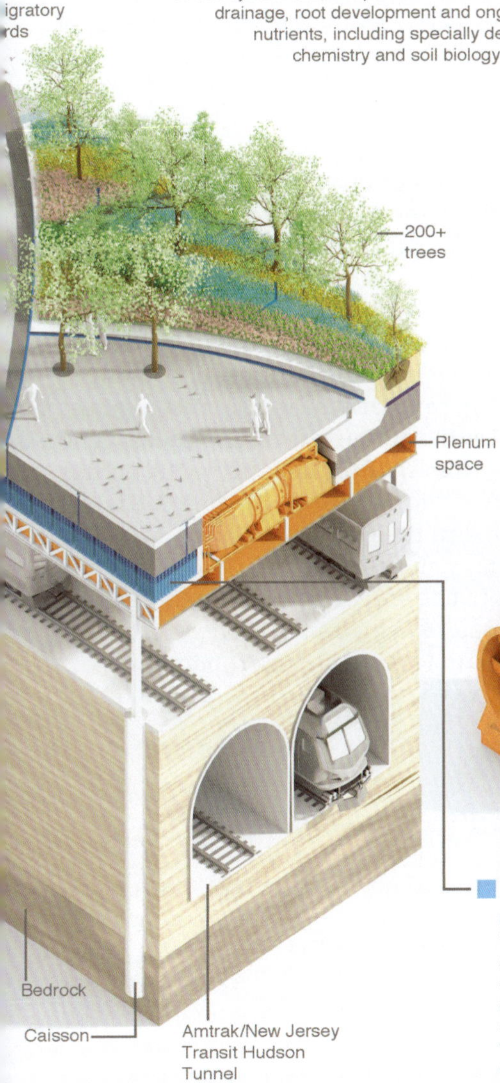

OUR ROOTS ARE COOL, OUR PLANTS ARE PAMPERED

The heat from the train yard below can reach up to 150 degrees, too hot for our city trees. Therefore, AC is in order to keep the roots of our trees and plants healthy. A sophisticated network of tubing is being embedded within the concrete slab to circulate cooling liquids that maintain optimal conditions for our plant's roots. This cooling system will protect the roots, from the train heat below and summer heat above, and ensure that the plants and trees at Hudson Yards will be the most pampered in New York City.

WE HAVE BIG FANS, LITERALLY!

A ventilation system powered by fans, usually found in jet engines, will remove the heat generated from the train equipment below by covering the rail yards. Consisting of 15 large fans, this ventilation system supplies fresh air at 45 MPH to the track level.

RAIN, RAIN, (DON'T) GO AWAY!

Every drop of rainwater that falls on Hudson Yards will be collected into a 60,000 gallon tank and used for irrigating our plants and trees. This collection saves space in the NYC sewer system and helps keep the Hudson River clean. We also save 6.5 megawatt hours of energy and offset 5 tons of greenhouse gas (GHG) every year by collecting our own water. That GHG savings, combined with the savings from diverting the water from NYC treatment plants, is equivalent to the carbon output over 4 acres of forest!

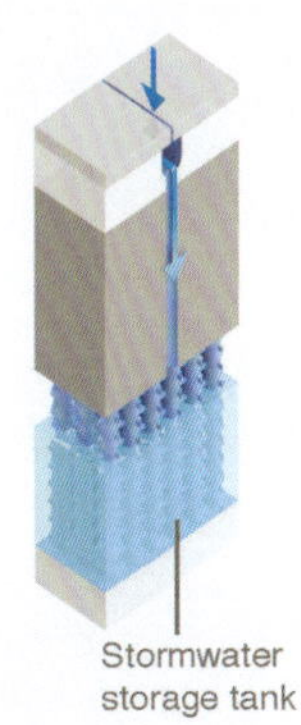

a nursery in Georgia, brought to New Jersey to acclimate over a two-year period with several root prunings, a crown pruning, and injections of phosphorous acid and fungicide to prevent cankers, before being delivered and installed in the darkness of night by large cranes to avoid interference with the public and other construction.

The platform slab and finish grade topography vary continuously in elevation at both levels, creating an ever-changing buildup condition. NBW and the design team led by project architect KPF studied and modeled the platform and surface elevations so there would be adequate depths for paving, planting, and pedestrian and traffic connections. NBW noted areas of conflict that resulted in modifications to the structural system and structural steel to accommodate the landscape design.

Originally, there were several vertical vent shafts and fans. In order to limit their intrusion into the landscape, the design team oriented the fans horizontally and located them in the platform build-up and incorporated the vent shafts in buildings in the landscape. This required an innovative and complex engineering solution. The design team developed an unprecedented mechanical soil-cooling system to combat buildup temperatures harmful to plant life, caused by idling trains underneath the plaza. The concrete plenum, varying in thickness from 18 inches to 7 feet throughout to accommodate both conditions above and beneath, are embedded with cooling tubes at the bottom of all primary planting beds. The system is activated when sensors in the soil profile indicate that the temperature has exceeded 75 degrees F 6 inches above the lower platform slab. We anticipate this will be necessary only in summer heat wave conditions. A monitoring system reports temperature and moisture.

On Open Spaces and the City

Flows and variety are crucial to the survival of any system, and urban systems are no exception. Open spaces, to be active, well-functioning, and truly public, must respond to their environment, simultaneously providing a change in scale of aperture and gathering energy from their surroundings.

Well-designed open spaces in the city carefully consider the flows of people, views, contact with nature, and relationships to the scale of the built environment. Our

Figure 4: The Plaza provides a common ground for the surrounding architecture and a gathering place for the community.

Figure 5: The gardens surrounding the plaza immerse visitors in native plant species of the Hudson Valley, selected in response to the carefully studied lighting and environmental conditions.

Figure 6: In the shadow of a minimalist bosque, a long arcing bench gradually reclines to a chaise form.

design engages the infrastructure-landscape hybrid project and provides openness through formal contextualization and connections, material and metaphorical, to the ecological and cultural history of the site. Unlike an approach that prioritizes the individual structure above its context, which then leads to a breakdown in the integrity of experience and function in the urban grid,[8] our approach prioritized physical, ecological, and cultural connections.

As has been pointed out, New York City has for decades allowed for the creation of nodes of open space that primarily serve developers and corporations. Much of Manhattan is still dominated by spaces of denial and privilege.[9]

However, it is also, as Rebecca Solnit points out in *Nonstop Metropolis*, ripe for excavating buried layers. Or for adding another cultural or ecological overlay of understanding that can be teased out just long enough to consider its impact on the whole. The beauty of this project and landscape architecture in general is that it provides the chance to manifest these complexities in the landscape, to engage and reveal history, to give a voice even if it is subtle and perhaps not always audible in the chaos of the city. We strive toward achieving a poetic beauty, a metaphorical openness to creating spaces and moments

Figure 7: A radiating series of elliptical forms guide circulation and reinforce the formal arrangement.

Figure 8: The surrounding gardens mitigate the imposing skyscrapers to provide respite at the human scale.

for exploration, in this case "to conjure [...] the ghosts of the wolves and elk that once lived in Manhattan."[10]

The Hopes and Realities of Public-Private Partnerships in Creating Civic Spaces

> You could celebrate New York as a capital of democratic public life, except that it is also the capital of the opposite.[11]

Public-private partnerships are complex composites, uniquely formed around particular infrastructure or other construction projects, and they occur in large part in the urban public realm. On a rudimentary level, these partnerships operate on the assumption that there is both public and private investment, generally in the form of assets and finances, respectively, and both public and private return, by way of quality designed and maintained urban spaces or civically accessed amenities, and then a growth in value of real estate or tax benefits. Legal frameworks for public-private partnerships also vary, and they can incorporate quasi-public entities such as water authorities or organizations that oversee tax increment zones.

New York City's POPS program was started in 1961 to encourage private developers to provide publicly accessible spaces, specifically plazas and arcades, on private property in exchange for bonus floor area in certain high-density

Figure 9: In response to existing conditions and program, both the platform and finish-grade topography continuously vary in elevation, creating an ever-changing perspective.

districts. The intent was to "bring light, air, and more usable open space to our city streets, at a time when many bulky buildings and skyscrapers were being constructed."[12] Between the program's inauguration and 2007, over 550 of these spaces were created in the city's five boroughs with mixed success,[13] leading to incremental changes to POPS requirements and a formalization of the program that focused on the quality of successful spaces, calling for them to be "Open and Inviting, Accessible, Safe and Secure, Comfortable and Engaging."[14]

However, these projects are originated by these partnerships with little to no input from designers. Adjusting the legal framework is not in a landscape architect's purview. As landscape architect Margaret Jankowsky put it, "Clients have already figured out what kind of project it will be, the physical boundary, the budget, and the overall goals."[15] This approach limits the quality of the project, not only in its inception but throughout its life as a designed public space.

Furthermore, most public-private partnerships in the last decades in New York City have used design processes structured on a top-down paradigm: decisions happen at the very top, with little or no input from the public users of the space. Even so, the City of New York has produced myriad examples of quality public spaces based on this model. If you focus only on the Hudson River side of the island, you can find some of the most recognized architecture and landscape architecture firms at work: from Battery Park City and Teardrop Park, to the Salt Shed, the High Line, the Shed at Hudson Yards, and the soon-to-be-inaugurated Little Island. These designed jewels adorning the west side of the city point to the dynamics of public space-making and will endure, as long as they are found relevant, as a statement to the socioeconomic conditions that created them.

According to James Lima of James Lima Planning + Development (JLP+D), there are three primary tools that the public entity in the partnership has for leveraging power, and these occur at very specific times in the life of a project. The primary tools are:

> When contributing the land, providing deed restrictions and covenants in favor of the public.
>
> When providing the top loss risk of investment dollars for a project, generally the initial investment, subsidies, and/or discretionary funds requested by the government from the private sector can again benefit the public.
>
> Land use through zoning and environmental reviews are perhaps the best known and the greatest power a government has in maintaining a balance that favors the public.

JLP+D's work in partnership with the Urban Land Institute and others for the development of the edges of the Gowanus Canal in Brooklyn points to a manageable precedent for leveraging the power of reviews in ensuring a multivalent, equitable design, in this case by focusing on the heat-island effect and its direct correlation to the amount of canopy or presence of trees.[16]

Many successful public parks have created staggering financial benefits for developers and adjacent land values, while failing to capture any percentage of that profit for their own maintenance through built-in subsidies or increments. It is a significant failure to not use available tools for the improvement of the social realm by claiming a portion of the value these landscapes create for their own maintenance. For example, despite the huge success that the High Line has become as a public space, it missed the opportunity to build in subsidies for the maintenance of this most celebrated public space. Even with billions of dollars being invested in the development on its edges designed by accomplished design firms (and certainly with

Figure 10: Stratified walls with a range of texture and vertical alignment reference underlying geology and are set at a datum to reveal topography as visitors traverse the landscape.

no small measure of profit), the High Line has not been able to leverage funds toward its coffers; or even better, to transfer that energy toward other parks in the city or even elsewhere in the country. And when considering such a shared maintenance coming from Hudson Yards, there is even less of a chance of incorporation within an open-space shared economy—the agreement structure between city and developer stipulates no such possibility, less so, any incentive or obligation. Every open space contributes to a city's or community's wellbeing, be it ecological, salutogenic, financial, or otherwise, much as the mycorrhizae and hyphae benefit forests and individual trees benefit from the networked community.[17]

As the public plaza at Hudson Yards is celebrating a year since major completion, we have the benefit of assessing its near-term successes and failures. If some of the horticultural elements of the design have been lost to impulses for immediate satisfaction, we can see that the structure of the plaza, the flows of people, and the way spaces are being used work; and even if security personnel control activities in this hybrid space, the colors of urban life continue to find their way in.

1
For more on Guy Debord, see "Psychogeography," *Wikipedia*, accessed June 18, 2020, https://en.wikipedia.org/wiki/Psychogeography.

2
Robert Macfarlane, *Underland: A Deep Time Journey* (New York and London: W.W. Norton and Company, 2019), 75–77.

3
Eric Sanderson and Markley Boyer, *Mannahatta: A Natural History of New York City* (Harry N. Abrams; Illustrated Edition, May 28, 2013).

4
Jill Jonnes, *Conquering Gotham: Building Penn Station and Its Tunnels* (New York and London: Viking Penguin, 2007).

5
Robert Pogue Harrison, "Robert Pogue Harrison Discusses His Book *Gardens*," interview with Brian Sholis, *Artforum*, July 2008, https://www.artforum.com/interviews/robert-pogue-harrison-discusses-his-book-gardens-20793.

6
From the website of the quasi-public Hudson Yards Infrastructure Corporation, accessed June 18, 2020, https://www1.nyc.gov/site/hyic/index.page.

7
Damian Holmes, "The Hudson Yards Public Square and Gardens Were Envisioned as a Contemporary Plaza," *World Landscape Architecture*, January 15, 2020, https://worldlandscapearchitect.com/the-hudson-yards-public-square-and-gardens-envisioned-as-a-contemporary-plaza/#.XknVb2hKguU.

8
Coined by Barcelonan architect and urbanist Manuel de Sola Morales, "Environmental art as urban acupuncture is an artistic way of injecting a healthy dose of natural elements and human scale into the mechanized urban grid." see "Urban Acupuncture," *Wikipedia*, accessed June 18, 2020, https://en.wikipedia.org/wiki/Urban_acupuncture, and expanded by others, including Nicholas de Monchaux in his *Local Code: 3659 Proposals about Data, Design, and the Nature of Cities* (New York: Princeton Architectural Press, 2016).

9
Michael Kimmelman refers to "the so-called POPS (Privately Owned Public Spaces) of the 1960s and subsequent decades, which, partly through City Hall's failure to provide oversight, produced many windswept plazas and heavily policed, frequently shuttered office building lobbies — unwelcoming sites that prioritized the privacy developers actually wanted all along." Michael Kimmelman, "Hudson Yards Promised a Park. They Didn't Mention the Giant Wall," *New York Times*, January 10, 2020, https://www.nytimes.com/2020/01/10/arts/design/hudson-yards-expansion.html.

10
Jedediah Britton-Purdy, "The Concession to Climate Change I Will Not Make," *The Atlantic*, January 6, 2020, https://www.theatlantic.com/science/archive/2020/01/becoming-parent-age-climate-crisis/604372/.

11
Rebecca Solnit and Joshua Jelly-Schapiro, *Nonstop Metropolis: A New York City Atlas* (Oakland: University of California Press, 2016), 117, introduction to the chapter "Public/Private."

12
"New York City's Privately Owned Public Spaces: History," New York City Planning, accessed June 18, 2020, https://www1.nyc.gov/site/planning/plans/pops/pops-history.page. For more on POPS, see Jerold Kayden with New York City Department of City Planning and The Municipal Art Society of New York, *Privately Owned Public Space: The New York City Experience* (New York: Wiley, 2000).

13
"New York City's Privately Owned Public Spaces—History."

14
"Chapter 7: Zoning Resolution," New York City Planning, last amended October 17, 2007, https://zr.planning.nyc.gov/article-iii/chapter-7.

15
Julia Gamolina, "Landscape's Influence: Margaret Jankowsky on Urban Life...," *Madame Architect*, August 21, 2019, https://www.madamearchitect.org/interviews/2019/8/16/margaret-jankowsky.

16
James Lima et al., "Gowanus, Brooklyn: A Vision for a Greener, Healthier, Cooler Gowanus: Strategies to Mitigate Urban Heat Island Effect," *Urban Land Institute*, New York, January 2018, https://ulidigitalmarketing.blob.core.windows.net/ulidcnc/2019/06/ULI-TAP-Gowanus-Report_v11_web_Final.pdf.

17
Robert Macfarlane, "The Understorey," in *Underland*, 85–117.

Box and Tower

Student
Wenpu Chai

Instructor
Mona El Khafif

With private space at such a premium in New York, public spaces often serve as secondary living rooms: a phenomena particularly important and challenging to address during the cold winter months. Box and Tower's site strategy—providing needed, multi-seasonal public space—is based around a full-block podium of offices, residences, and commercial spaces punctuated by a series of interior voids and vertical extrusions containing community programming, pedestrian circulation, and green spaces. These shared, interstitial spaces—clad in frit-patterned glass and operating as passive heating and cooling measures—are not only comfortably occupiable year-round, but also help activate the surrounding private and semi-public programming, and contribute to a broader rejuvenation of the surrounding city fabric and Hudson riverfront.

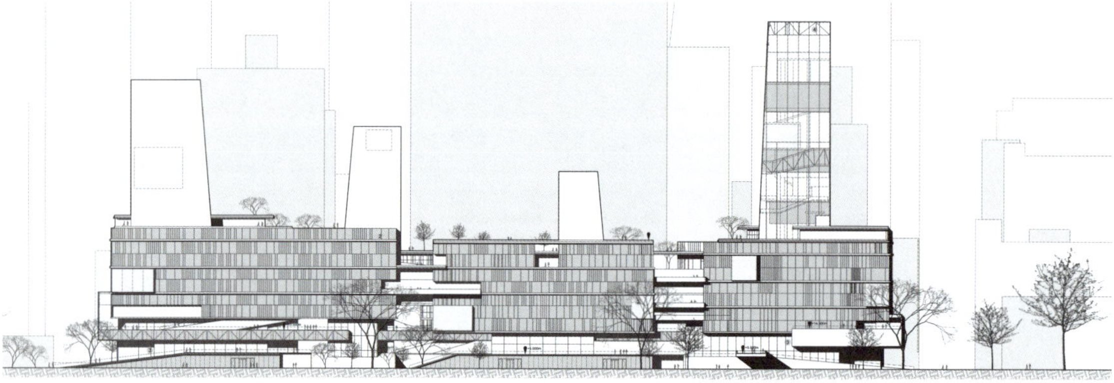

Street elevation

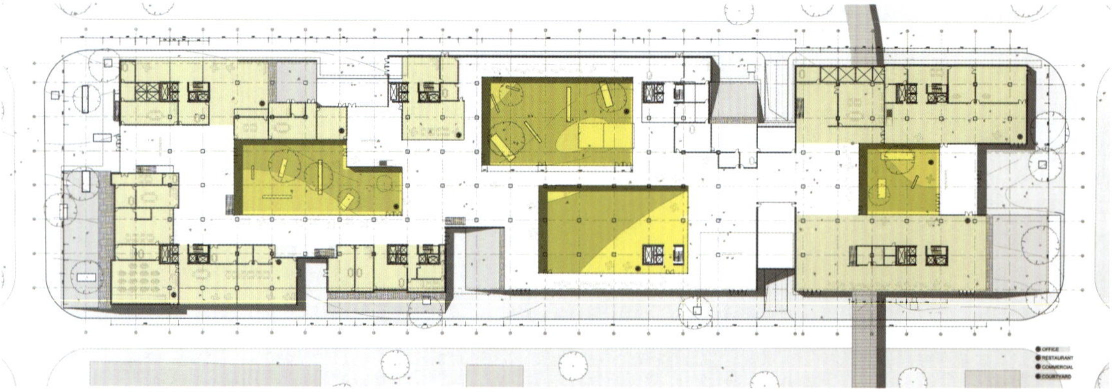

Typical floorplan showing interior void spaces

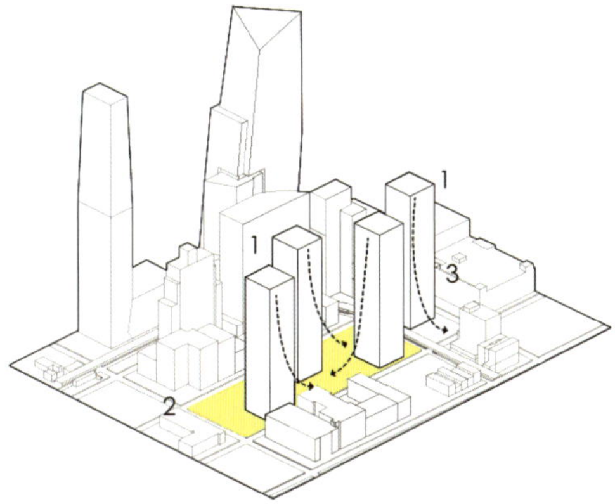

Step 1: Vertical circulation

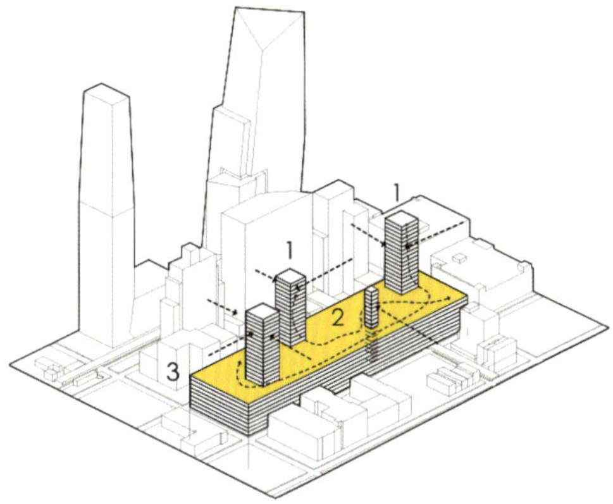

Step 2: Podium box and towers

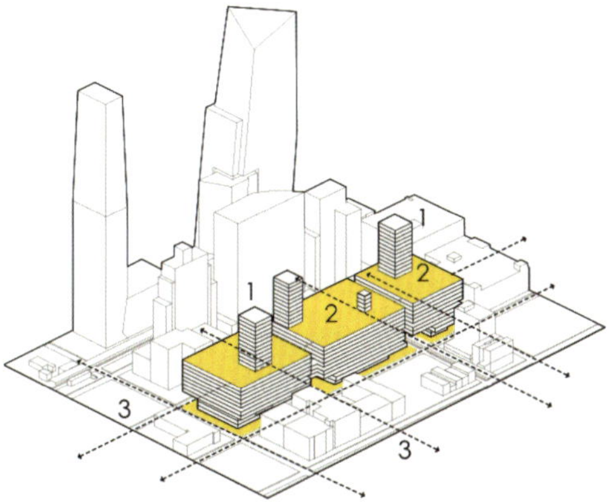

Step 3: Mid-block subdivisions

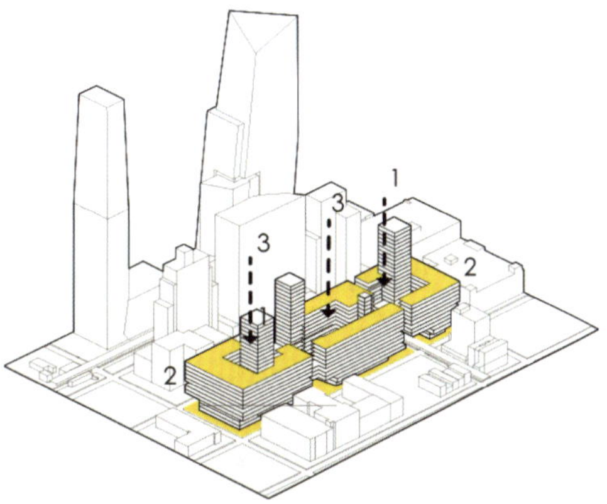

Step 4: Interior courtyard voids

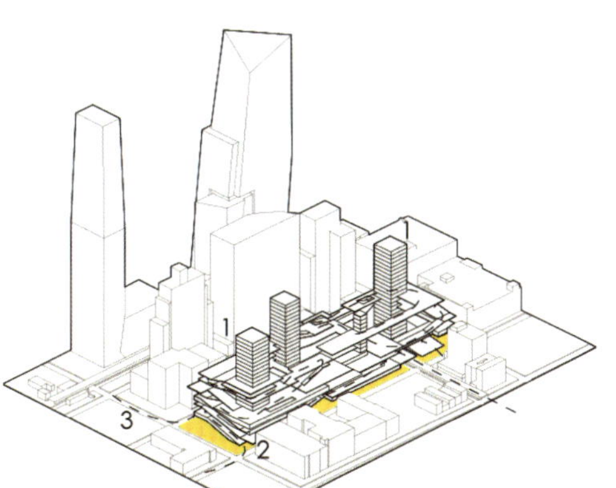

Step 5: Interior circulation network

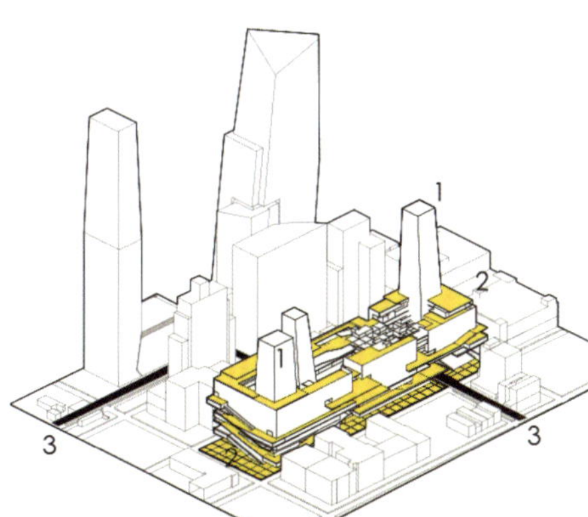

Step 6: Green space network

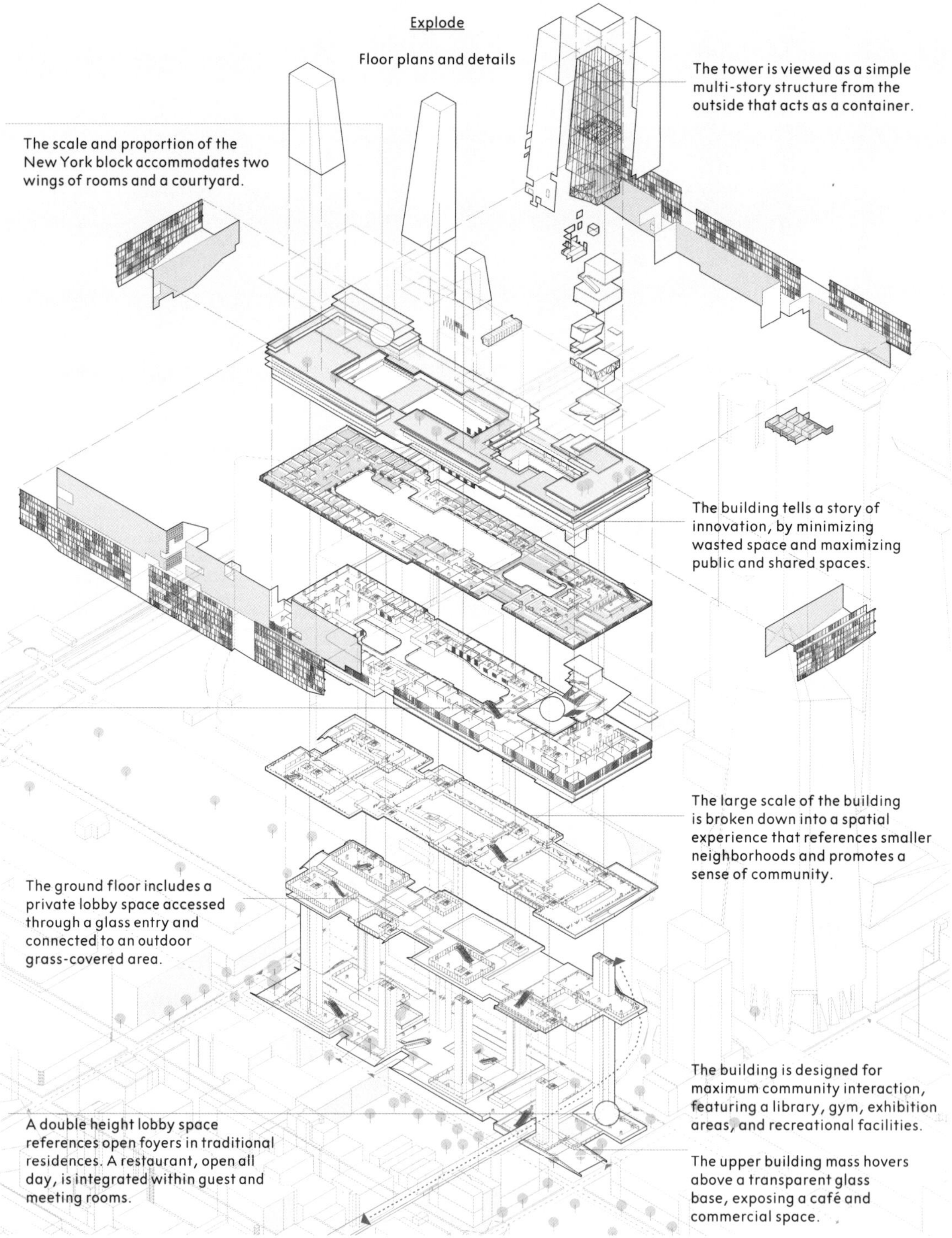

Delayered isometric drawing illustrating the distribution of program across the site

Section perspective through podium, void, and tower

"Box and Tower"
Wenpu Chai

Symbiotic Matrix

Student Team
Andrew Morrell
Joshua Cruz
Kelly Suppes

Instructor
Mona El Khafif

Symbiosis conceptualizes the city as a vast, pixelized grid where the distribution and density of internal programming exists in a state of permanent temporal change. The massing and site strategy is accordingly defined by primary and secondary grid systems—both subdivisions of the city-wide "Greatest Grid"—intended to constrain private development to modular and parametrically aggregatable spatial units responsive to future changes in city population, demographics, economics, and industry. Following pre-configured, grid-based aggregation patterns, these spatial units will accumulate metabolically over time into tower-like formations: maximizing the site's public and green spaces, and protecting them in perpetuity from the encroaching pressures of private market development.

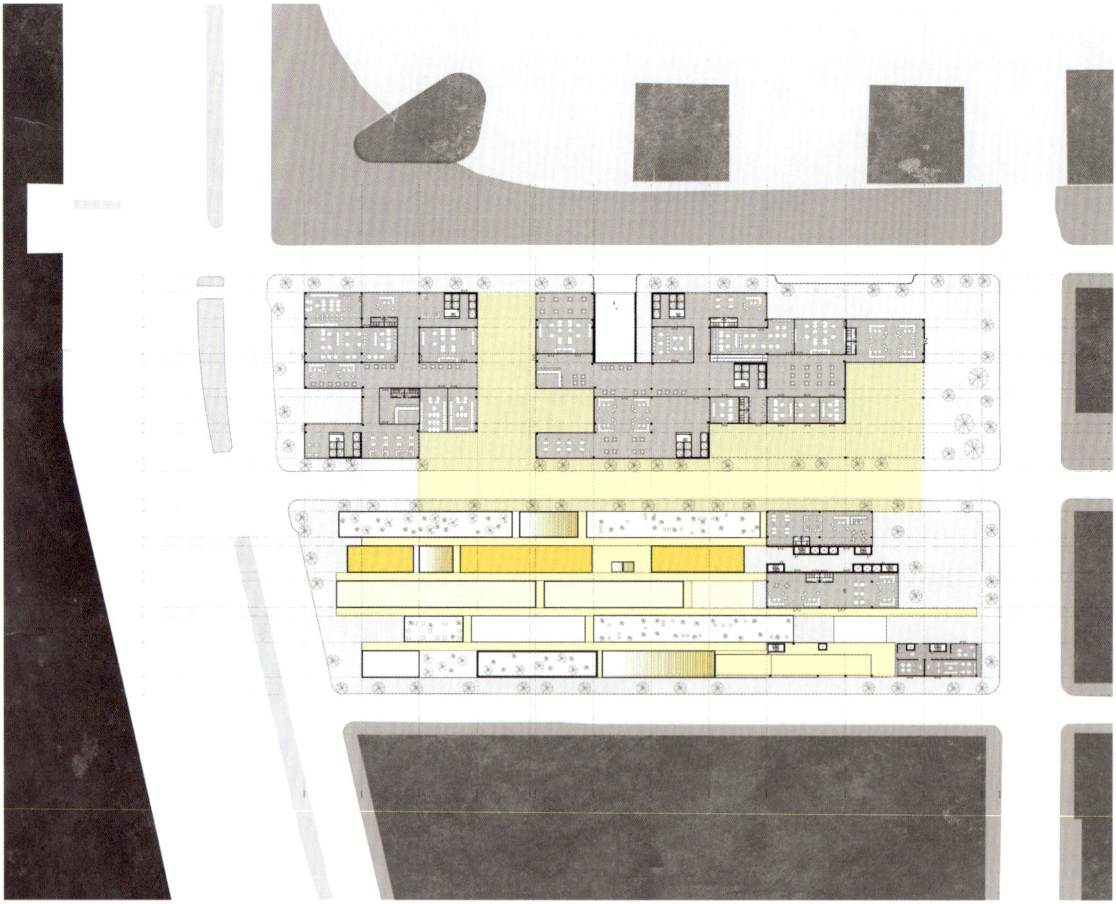

Site plan at ground floor

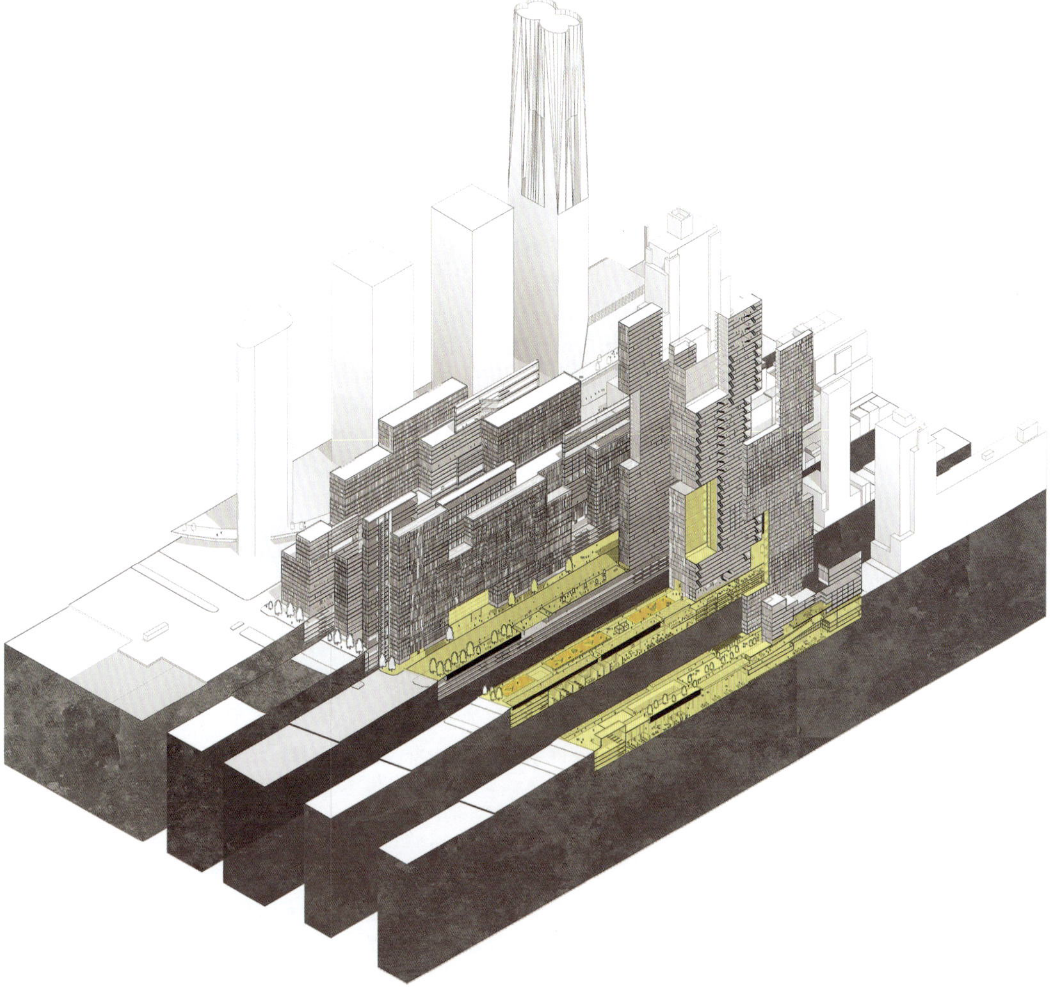

Isometric view of site aggregation

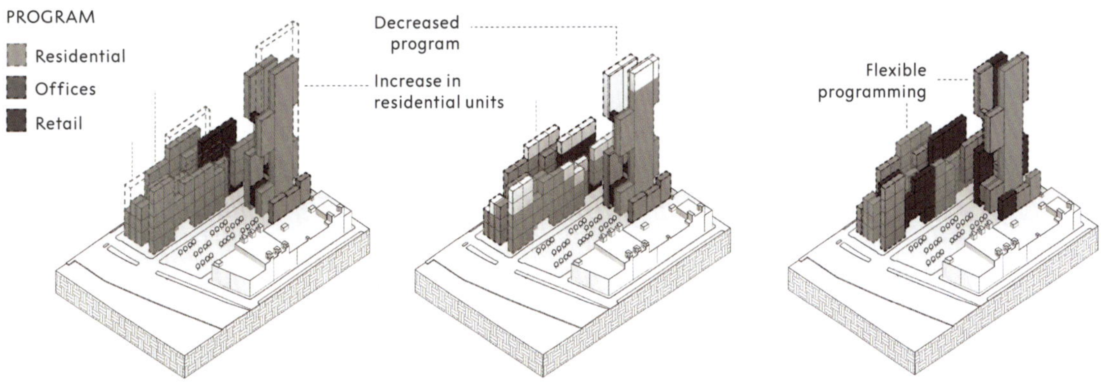

Year 2100 maximum density

Year 2200 low density event

Year 2500 independent city

Student
Lemara Miftakhova

Instructor
Bill Sherman

Flex Space

Flex Space establishes a malleable, intra-block framework for facilitating shared occupancy and maximizing the use of public space. The proposed block, containing interior offices and residences, outdoor public spaces, and an interior network of shared interstitial flex spaces, is formally split into four volumes to allow sunlight and air flow to reach the deep interior voids. These internal public spaces are, in turn, connected to the broader urban context through a greenbelt system running alongside and atop the main structure. The dominant formal image of the project is generated by a fluid, mesh-like volume which contains the contiguous network of interstitial flex spaces. This structure is supported and formally articulated by a combination of trusses, a structural diagrid, and tensile suspended floor plates.

Private program

Shared program

Public program

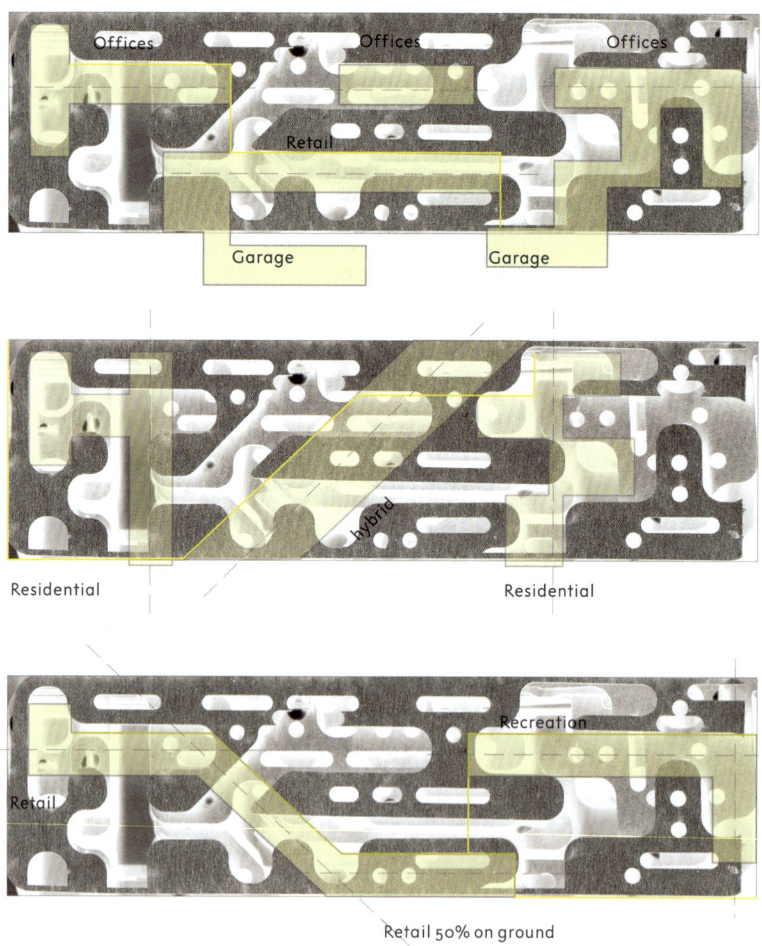

Diagrammatic floor plans illustrating the balance of private and public flex programming

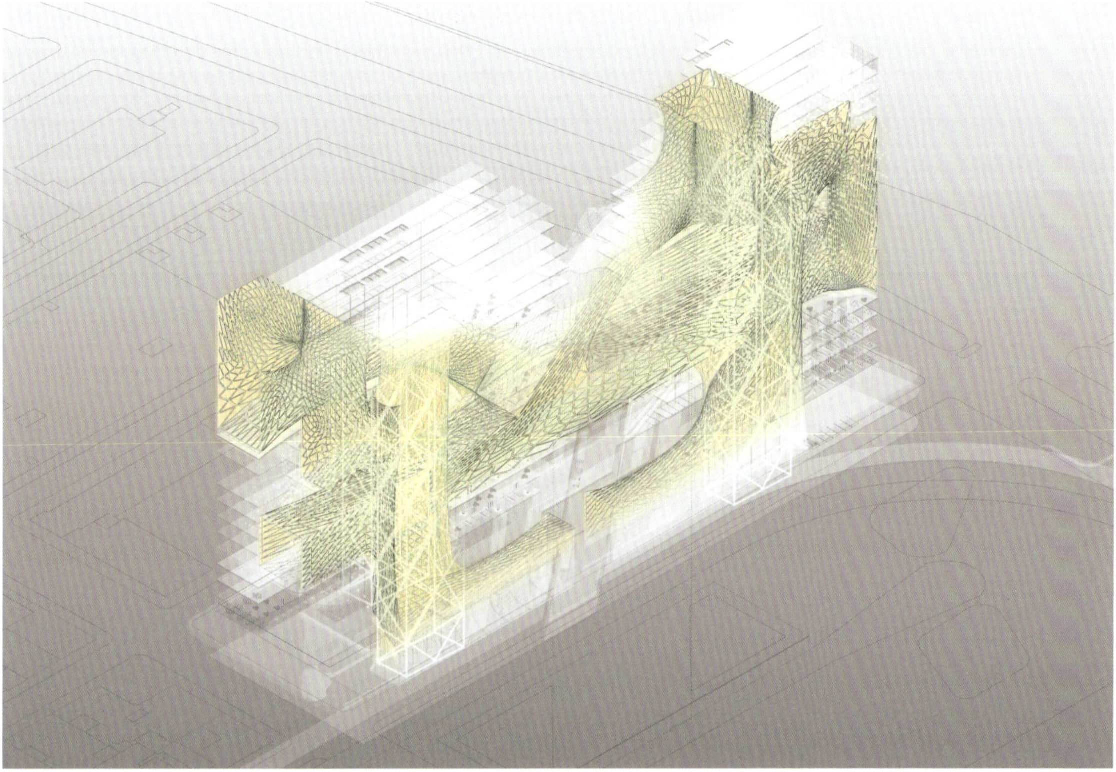

Isometric view illustrating interstitial flex space network (yellow)

Cross-section through vertical voids and interstitial flex space network (yellow)

Isometric sections through shared flex spaces (yellow)

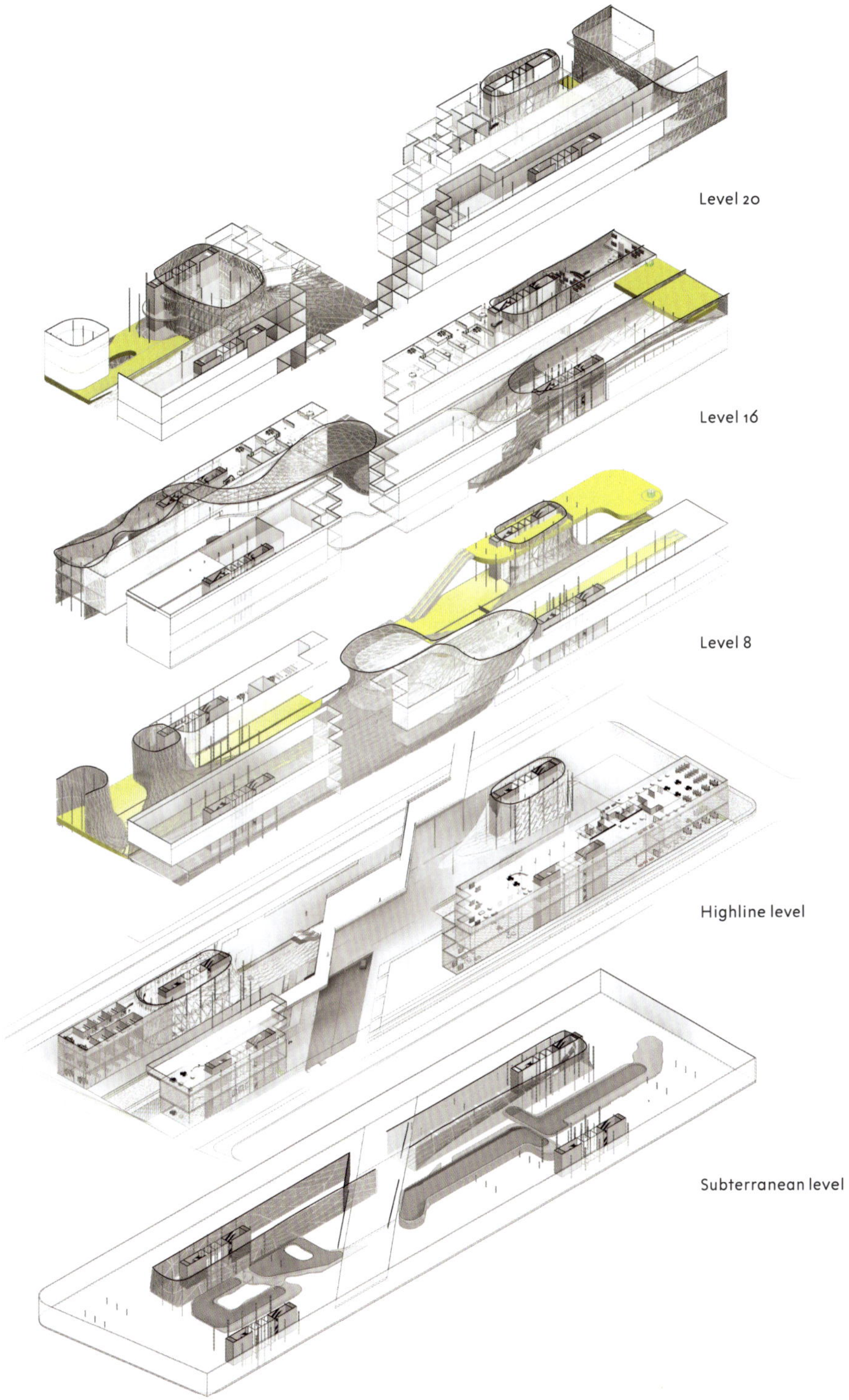

Delayered isometric drawing illustrating vertical distribution of program and green spaces

The Wellness Ratio

Student
Elizabeth Kulesza

Instructor
Manuel Bailo

In *Delirious New York*, Rem Koolhaas conceptualizes the high-rise as a typology defined by the pursuits of maximized density and interior autonomy: the "Culture of Congestion" and "Great Lobotomy," respectively. The Wellness Ratio, however, deconstructs this formal and programmatic construction. Here, interior living and working spaces exist not in self-contained vertical strata, but amid a variegated fabric of urban connectivity, organized around the rhythmic introduction of open, centralized public spaces. No longer dependant on the privatizing "Great Lobotomy," the urban "Culture of Congestion" can instead be both supported and activated by moments of communal respite.

Urban skyline elevation diagram

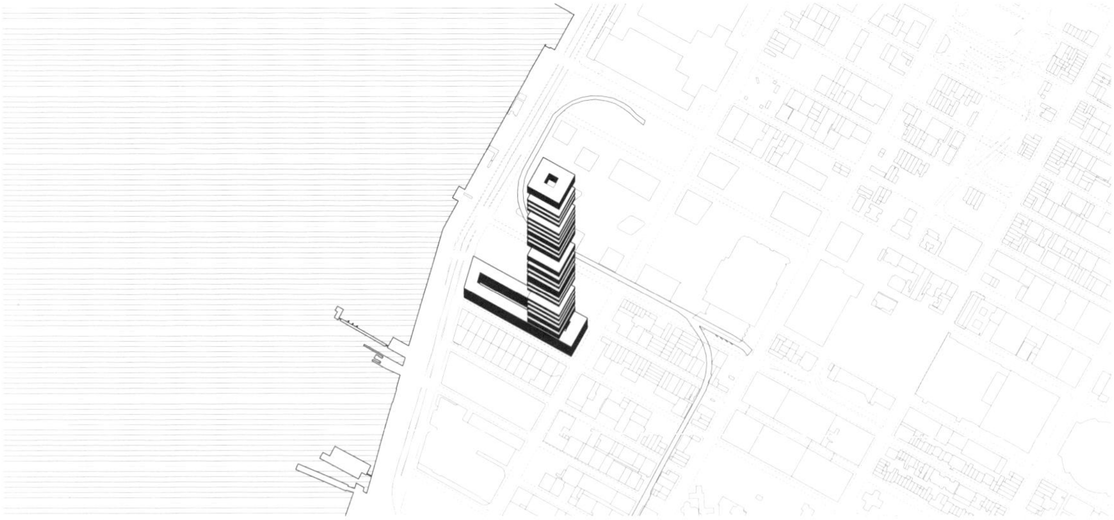

Isometric urban context drawing

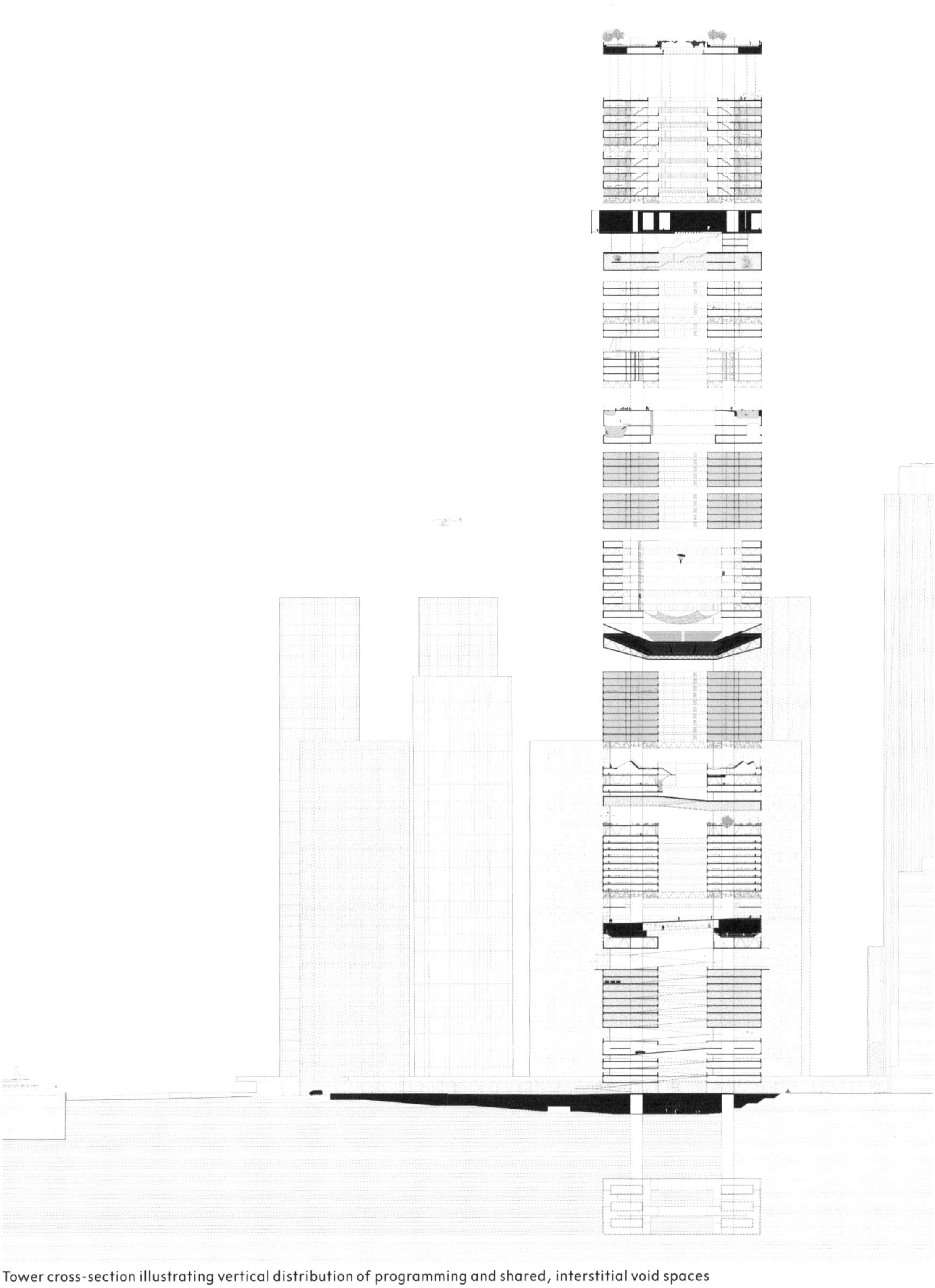

Tower cross-section illustrating vertical distribution of programming and shared, interstitial void spaces

The Reciprocal Fabric

Student Team
Austin Edwards
Megan Friedman

Instructor
Mona El Khafif

Vibrant city blocks, far from being self-contained miniature cities, are dense, porous, and multi-faceted entities operating within larger metabolic systems. In New York, large mono-functional block typologies, such as high rises and warehouses, are often lacking urban vibrancy, programmatic overlap, and public accessibility. The Reciprocal Block, however, adopts a hybrid approach to address these challenges: spatially through a parcel slicing strategy, where interior and exterior voids are removed from a series of gridded section typologies, and programmatically, through a granular interweaving of programming including residences, makerspaces, and gathering areas.

Manufacturing

Residential

Makerspace

Perspective view at street level showing carved-away public spaces

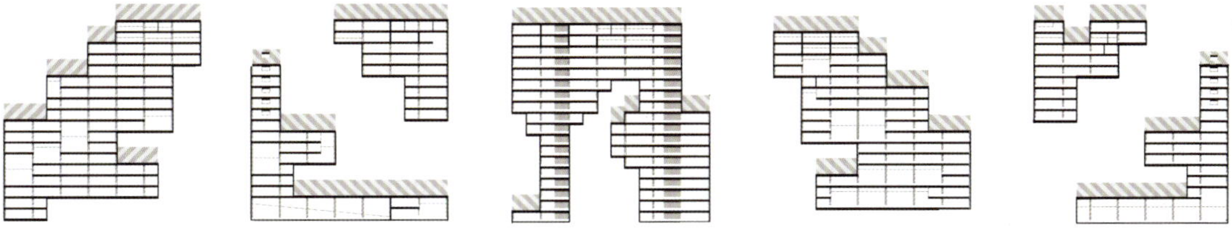

Sectional "slice" typologies

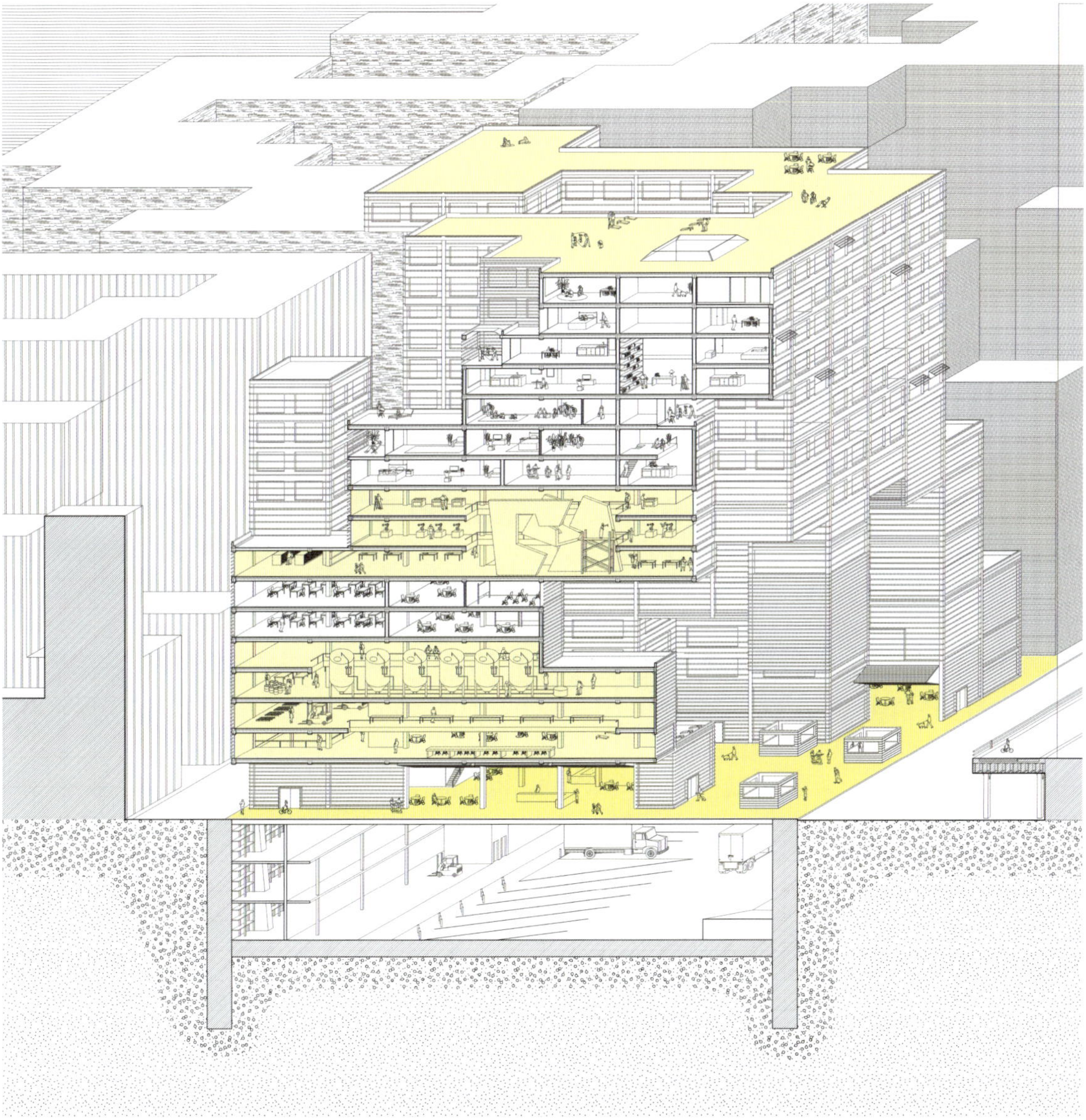

Isometric section of "slice" typology showing interior voids, open spaces, and shared programming (yellow)

1:500 site model, "The Reciprocal Block"

1:200 sectional model, "The Reciprocal Block"

Open Space as Structural Element

Student Team
Yiwen Xing
Mengdi Rao

Instructor
Manuel Bailo

While Manhattan is known for both the extreme verticality of its skyline and the extreme horizontality of open spaces like Central Park, most blocks in the city are also defined by a human scale diversity of form, program, and open space. This proposal catalogs the tableau of such extant spatial typologies, and re-contextualizes them as a granulated field condition within the otherwise high-contrast context of Hudson Yards. A radiating gradient is established between the predominantly private spaces at the site's center and the predominantly public and shared spaces along the periphery.

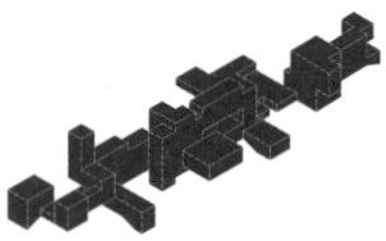

Open spaces

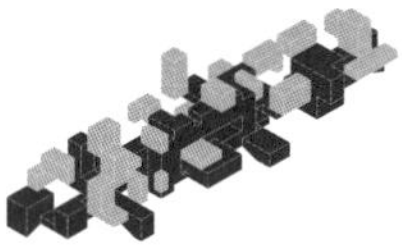

Shared spaces

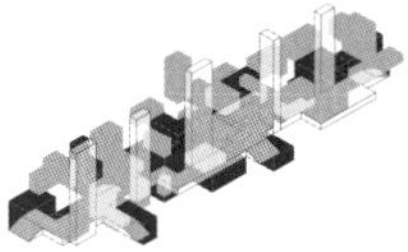

Circulation and service

Commercial spaces

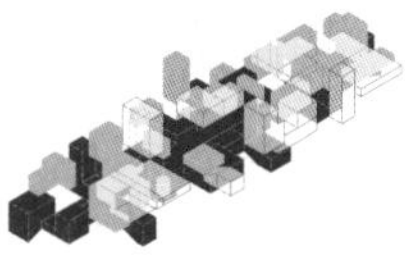

Public programming

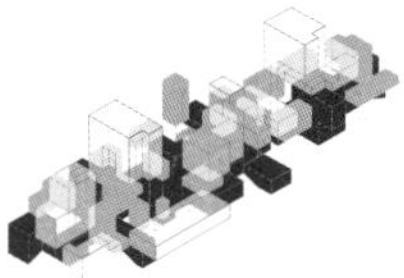

Creative industry

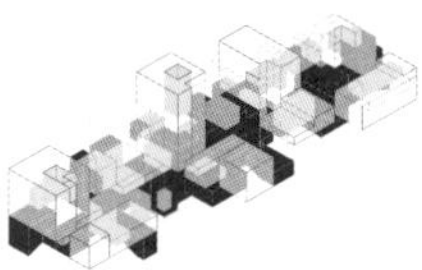

Office spaces

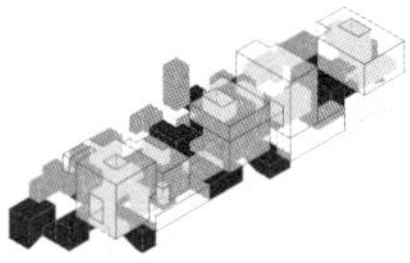

Housing

Site-scale massing aggregation strategy

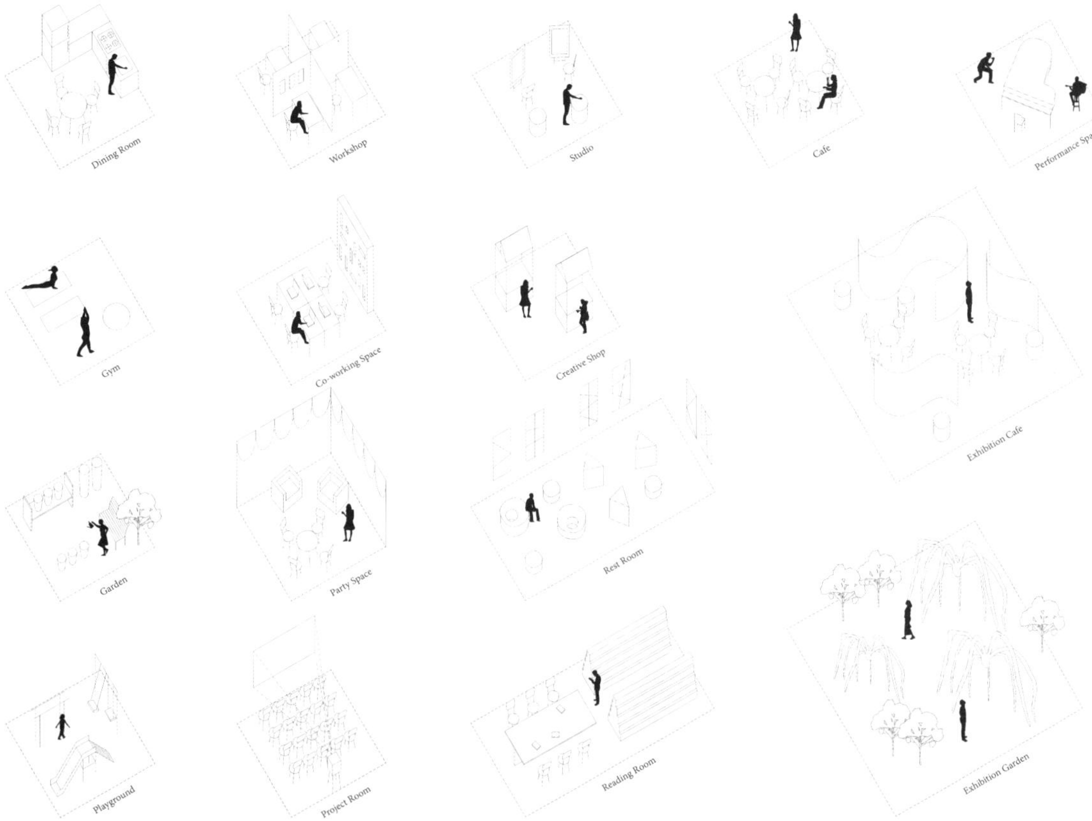

Programmatic module typologies

Programmatic gradient map

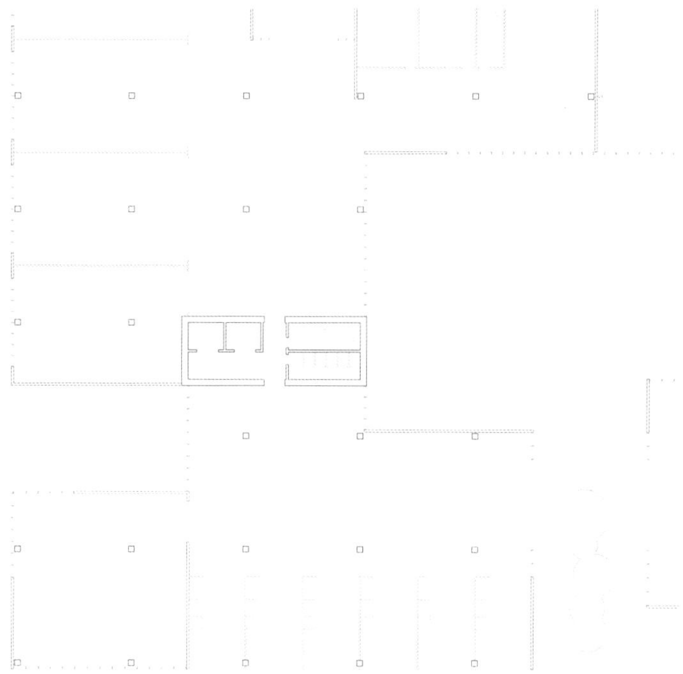

Partial upper level plan

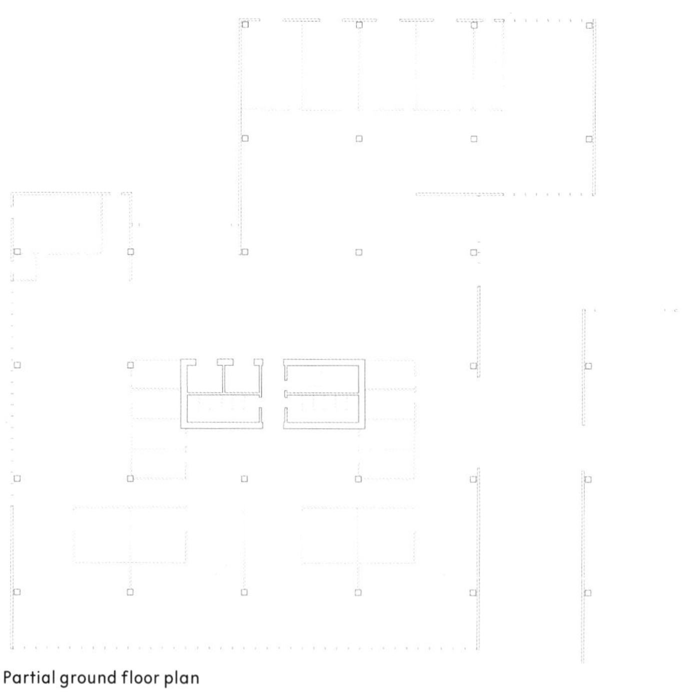

Partial ground floor plan

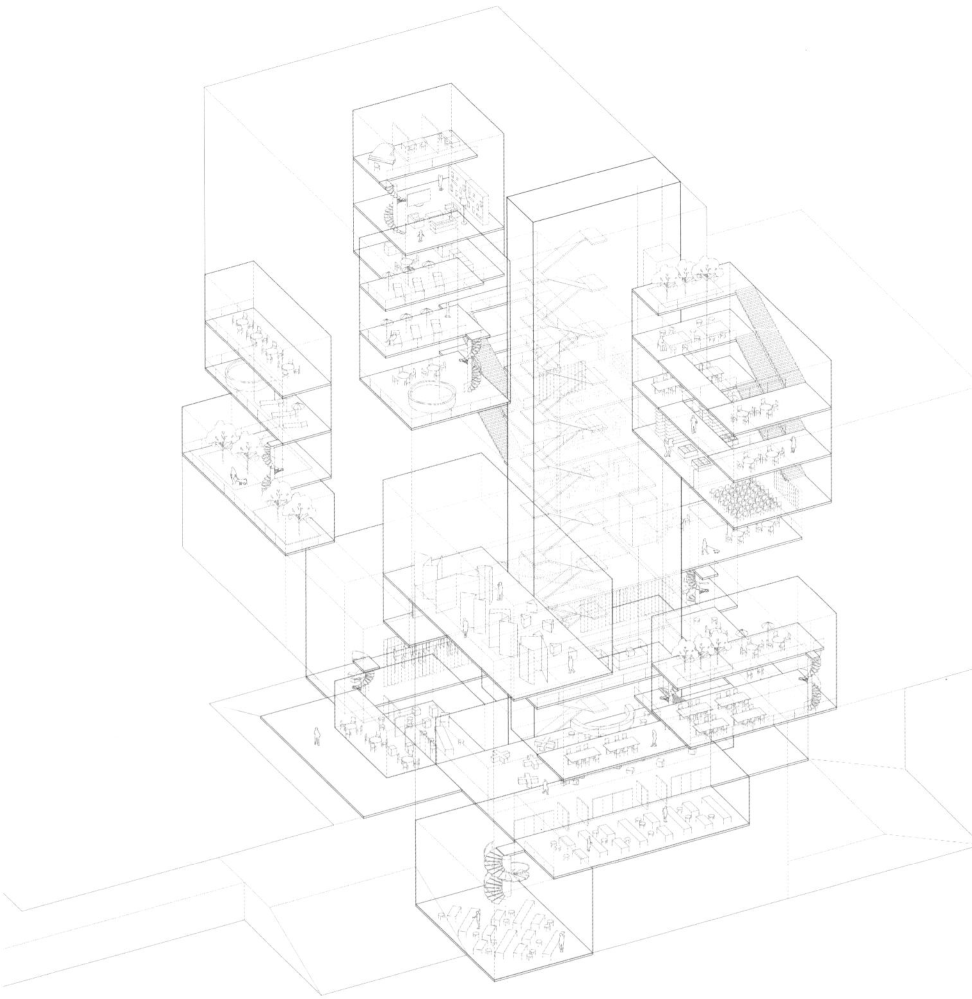

Exploded isometric of envelope and programmatic modules

Vertical Avenue

Student
Mert Kansu

Instructor
Seth McDowell

While the Industrial Revolution led to the segregation of living and working spaces, the contemporary knowledge and maker economy has yielded new opportunities for programmatic hybridization and spatial fluidity. New York's dominant spatial strategy has historically been the vertical stack. However, this floor-by-floor approach unnecessarily silos human activity and inhibits cross-party collaboration. Vertical Avenue addresses these challenges by establishing a new internal vertical axis as a streetscape extension of the adjacent High Line park. The resulting interior void, serving as a spatial catalyst for public activation, engagement, and collaboration, is flanked by an array of private and semi-public spaces whose formal gestures and edge conditions are adapted from a catalogue of spatial operations collected along the High Line: stepping, bordering, framing, and carving.

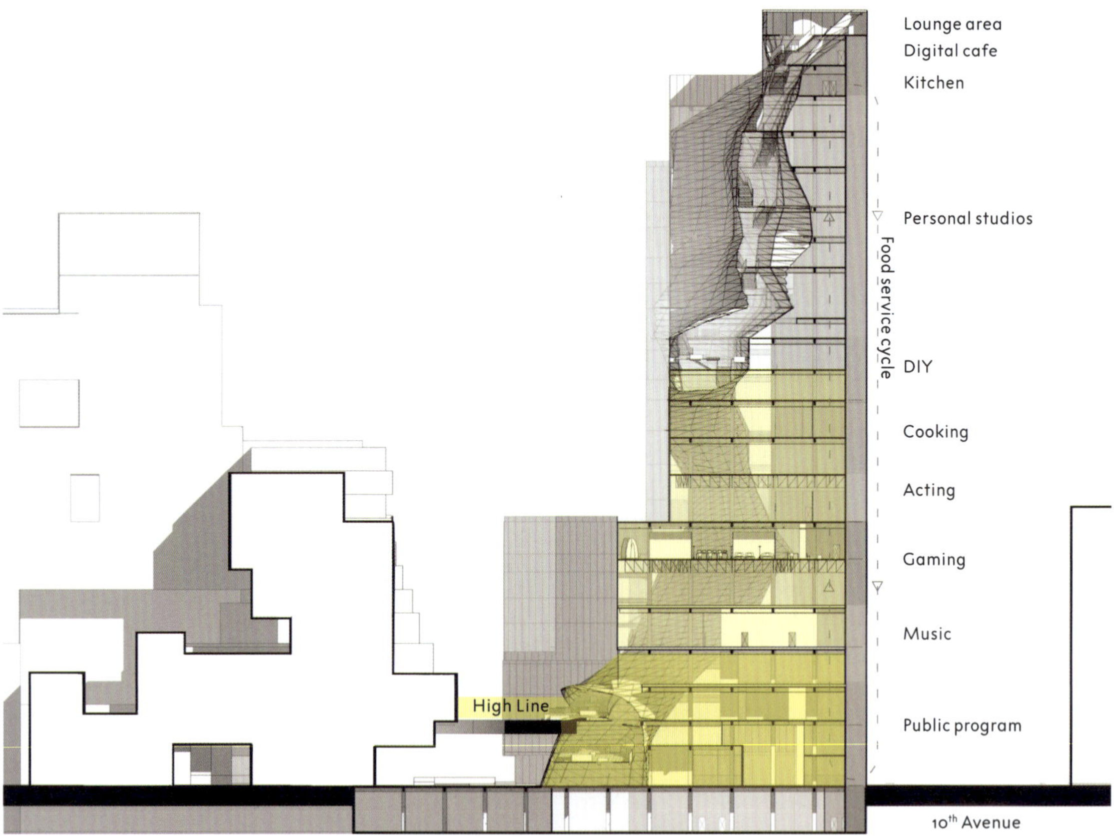

Diagrammatic section showing vertical distribution of public and private programming

Perspective view toward project tower from High Line park

Perspective view of entrance to "Vertical Avenue" from High Line park

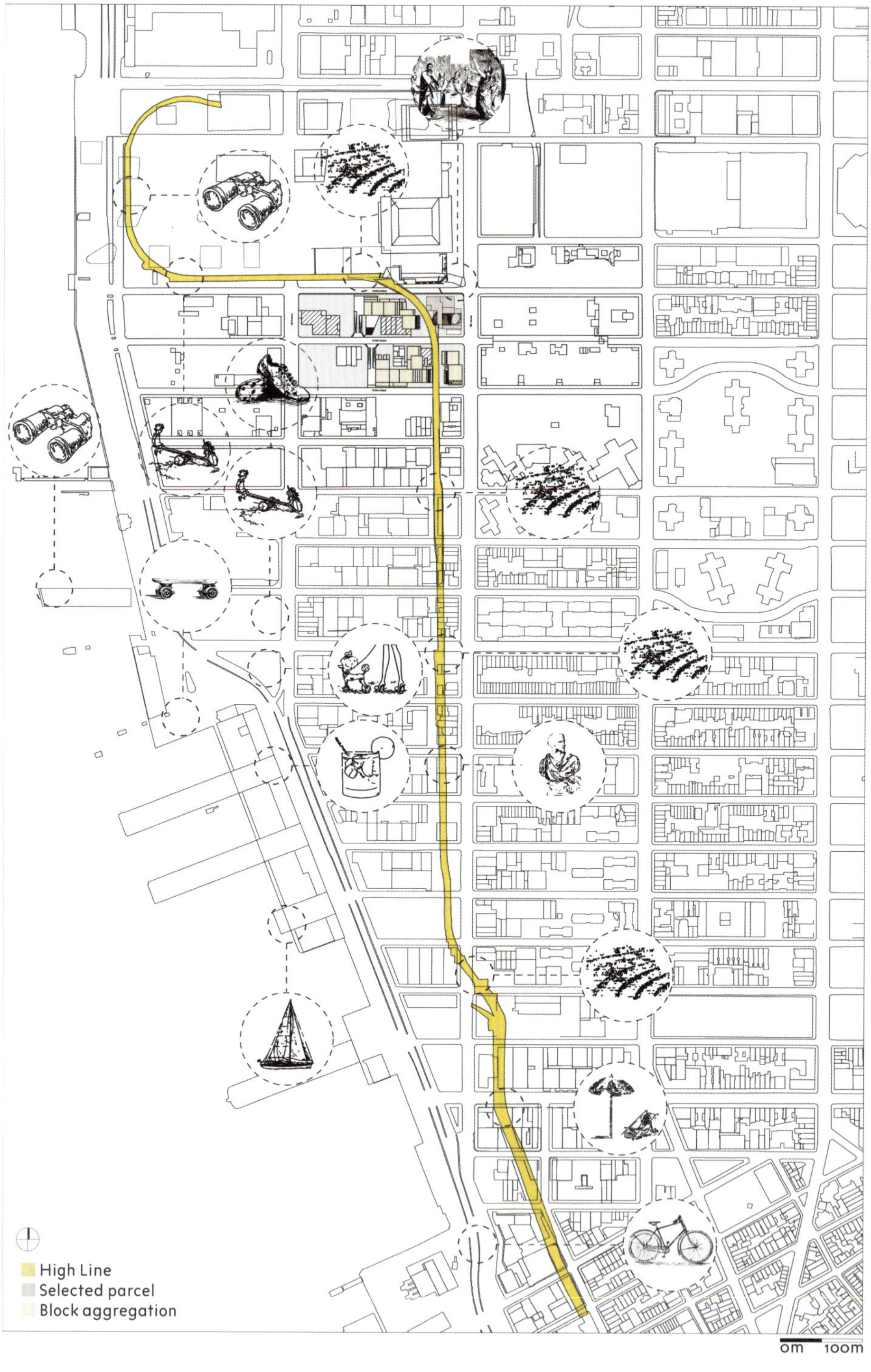

Urban context map of site in relation to High Line park

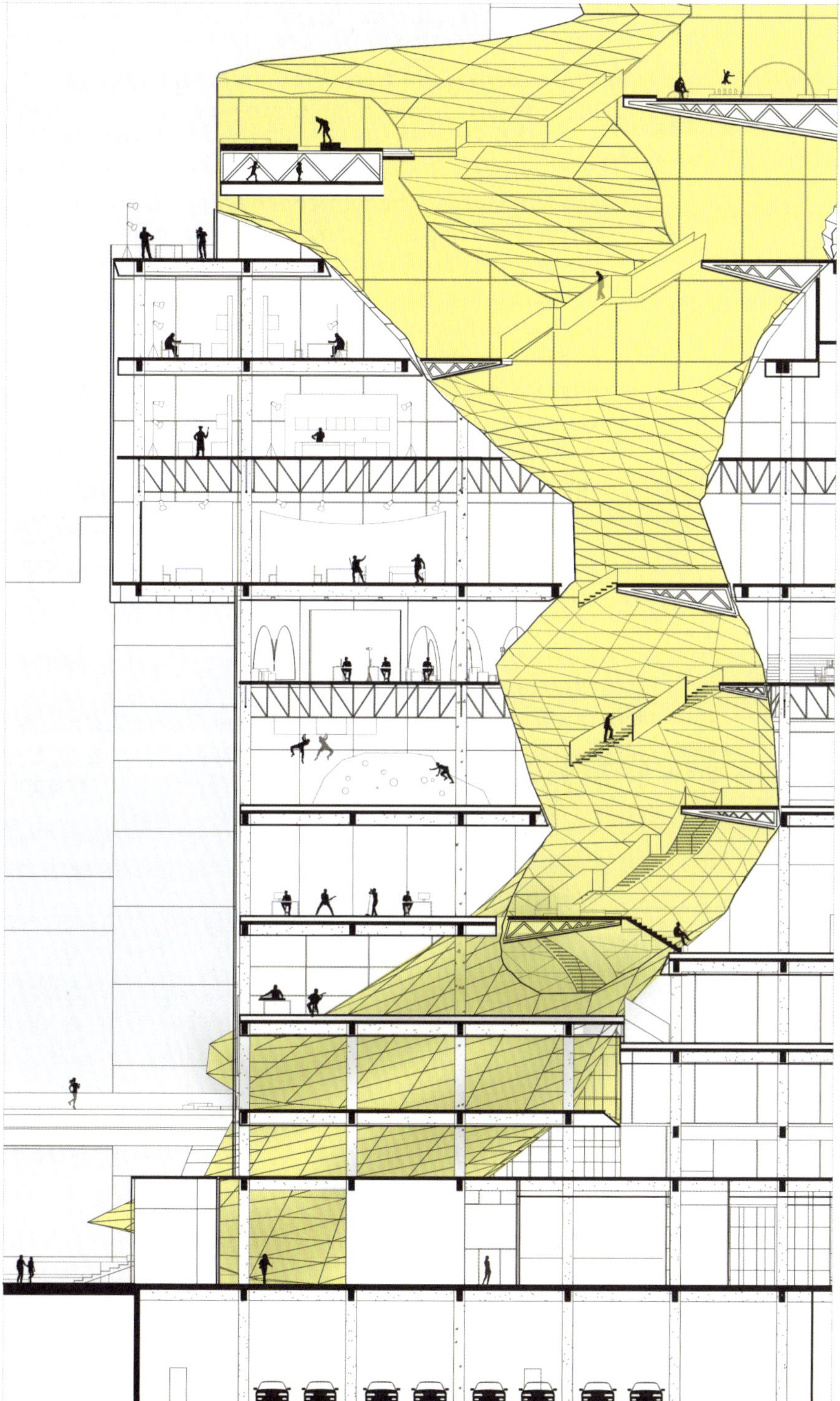

Detailed building section through tower and "Vertical Avenue"

Student
Tyler Mauri

Instructor
Bill Sherman

Emerging Structures of Social + Shared Industry

Until recently, Hudson Yards' main function was to facilitate the logistics of unloading, processing, and distributing goods across Manhattan Island. However, rapid de-industrialization of the waterfront and growth in the global knowledge economy turned the former pedestrian dead-zone into an attractive living environment, albeit sans industry. This architectural proposal aims to close the emerging gap between thinkers and creators by establishing closed and positive feedback loops that support cooperative living, local artisanship, and sustainable manufacturing practices. This programmatic balance is articulated through a spatial strategy of layered vertical spaces and overlapping production floors, which collectively operate as an open and flexible territory of mutual collaboration.

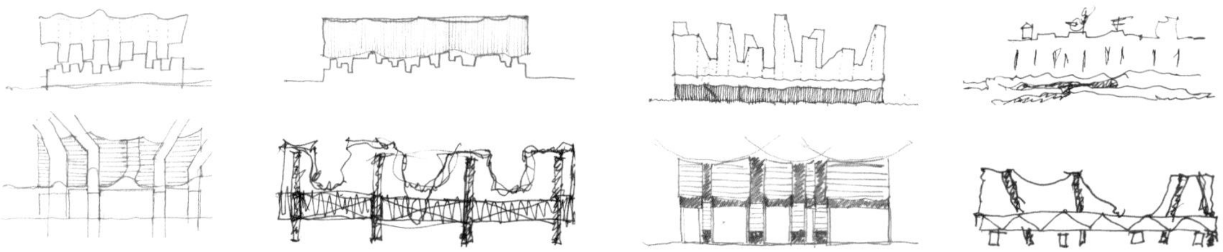

Massing concept sketches

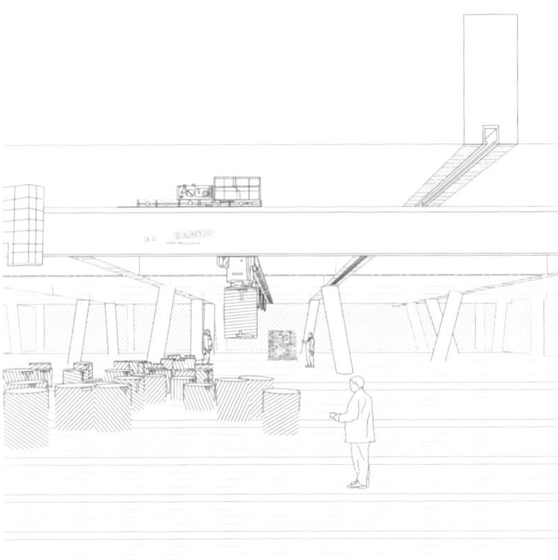

Interior perspective at production floor

Street perspective from river promenade

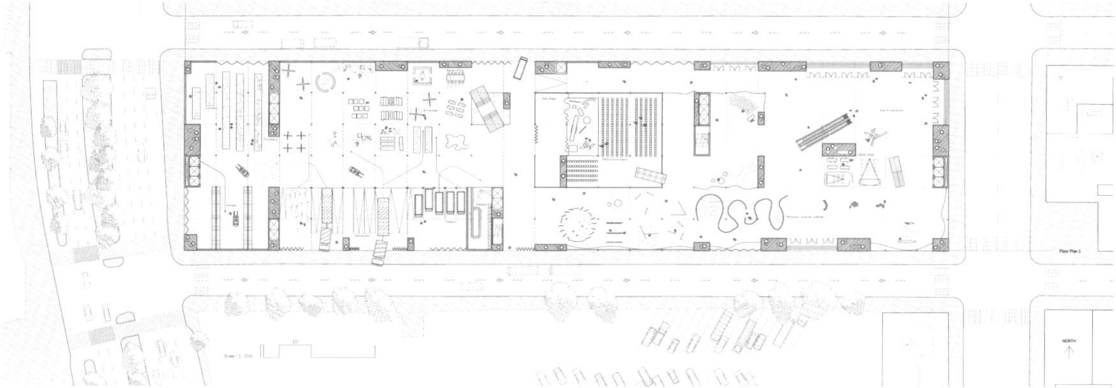

Ground level site floorplan

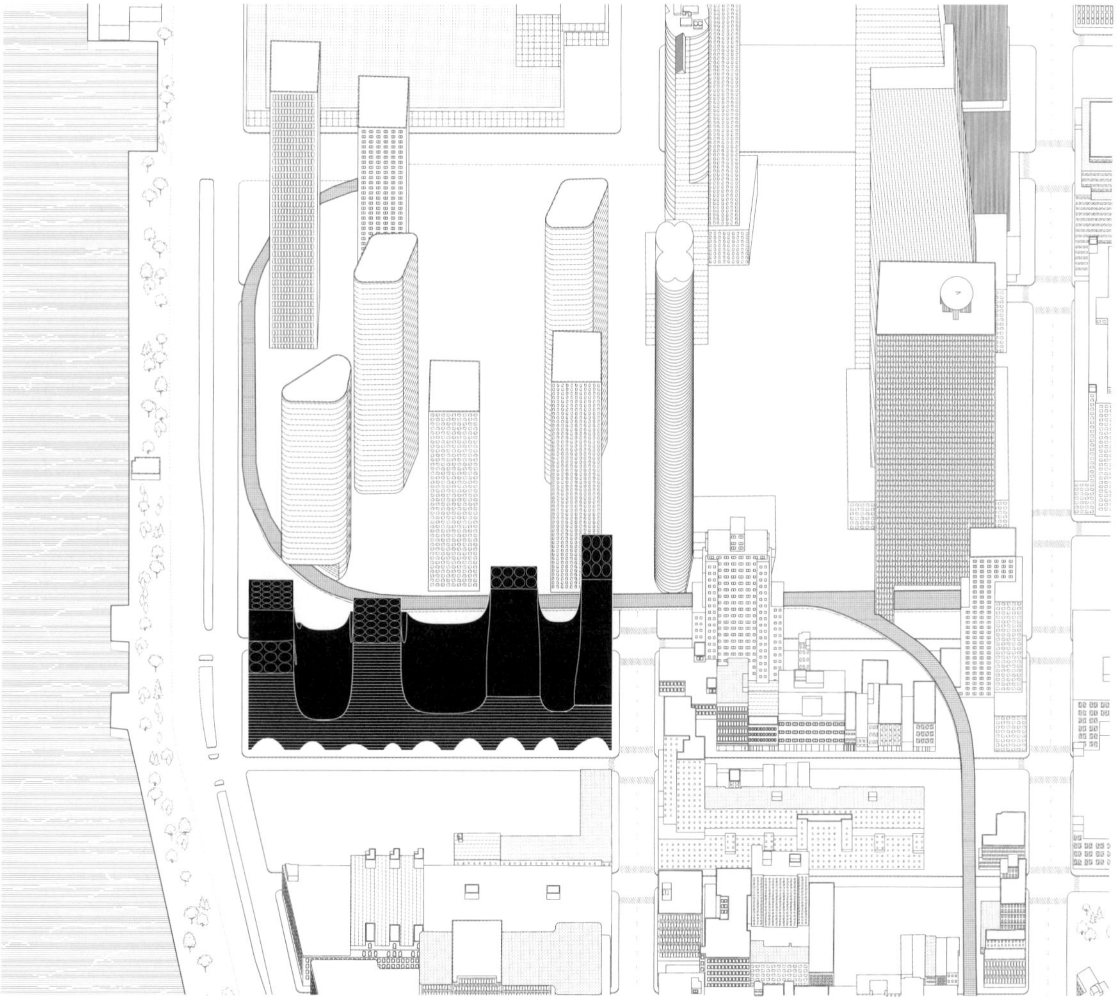

Urban context, elevation oblique

Site longitudinal section through manufacturing production floors

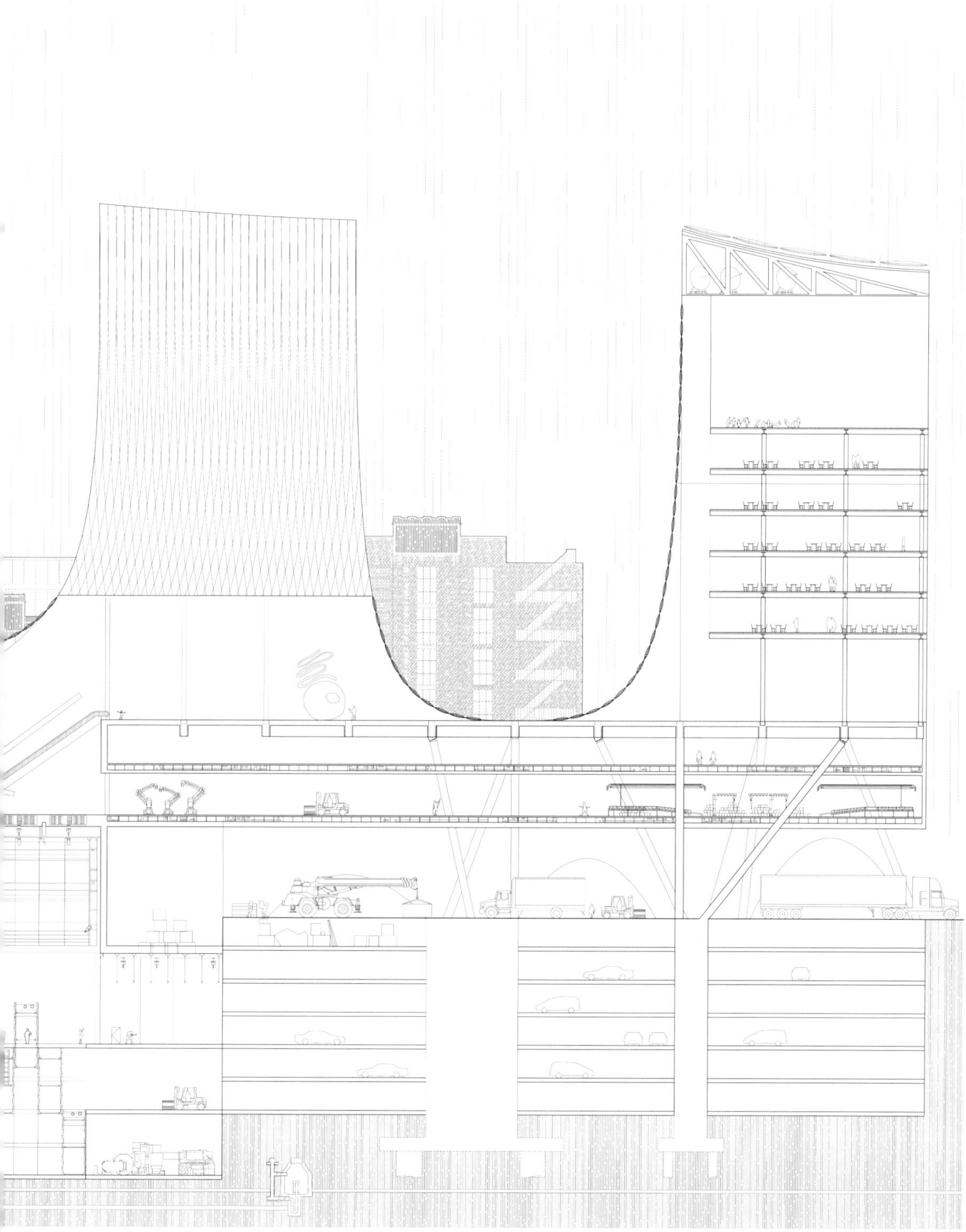

11.5th Avenue, NYC

Student
Yi Yang

Instructor
Bill Sherman

11.5th Avenue, NYC seeks to draw the dynamic and diverse urban streetscape into the interior of the project. Three programmatic elements—open offices and outdoor decks, an industrial innovation area, and a network of pedestrian ramps—are distributed across the two blocks between 10th and 12th Avenues. These elements not only house the main programs and circulation spaces, but also contribute toward an architectural language of poetic contrasts: theatricality and tranquility; monumentality and ephemerality. The ramp system, for instance—a combination of interstitial spaces surrounding the innovation hub—doubles as a shared theatrical stage, while tranquility and monumentality not only mark the project's main entrance along 10th Avenue, but also establish zones of quiet serenity for gallery and library programs.

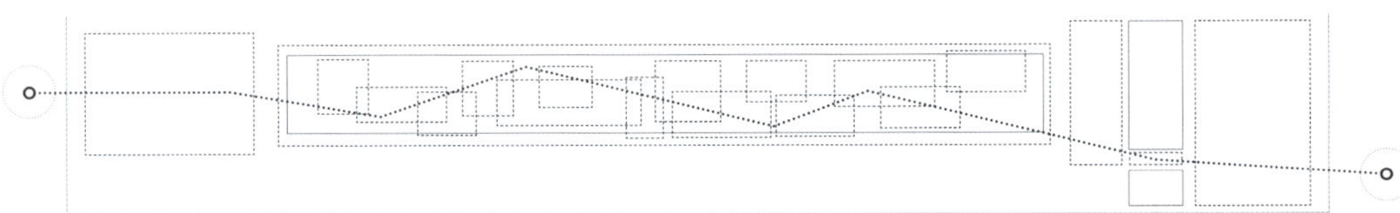

Program distribution diagram (plan)

Program distribution diagram (section)

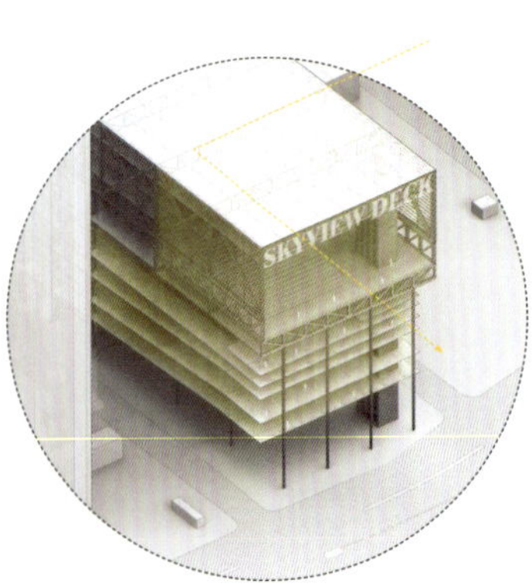

Open offices and sky-view deck

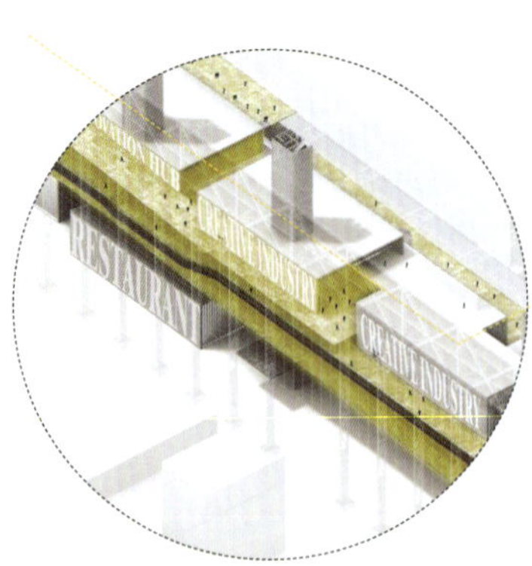

Circulation system / theatrical stage

Monumental entrance and gallery

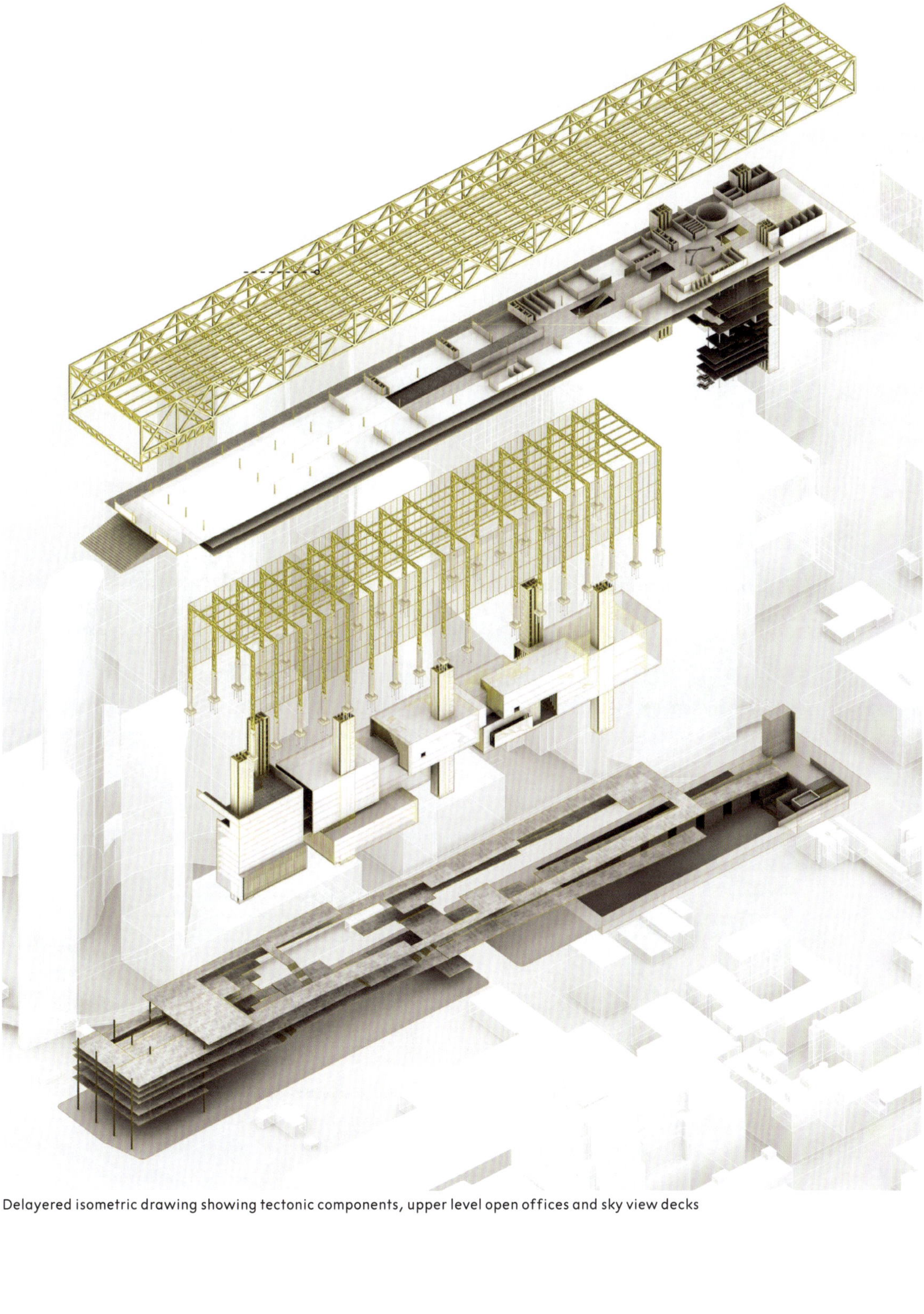

Delayered isometric drawing showing tectonic components, upper level open offices and sky view decks

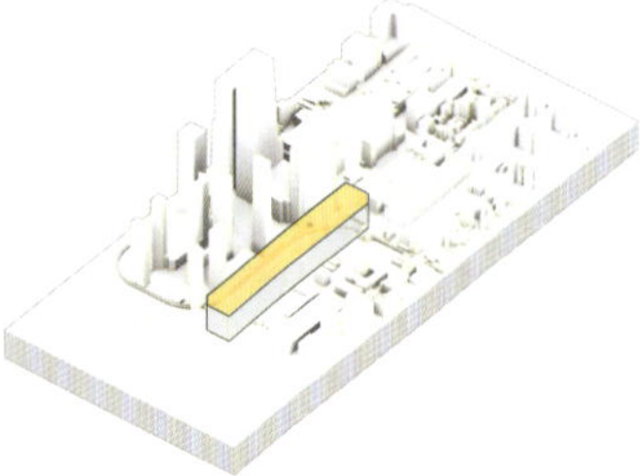
Office space

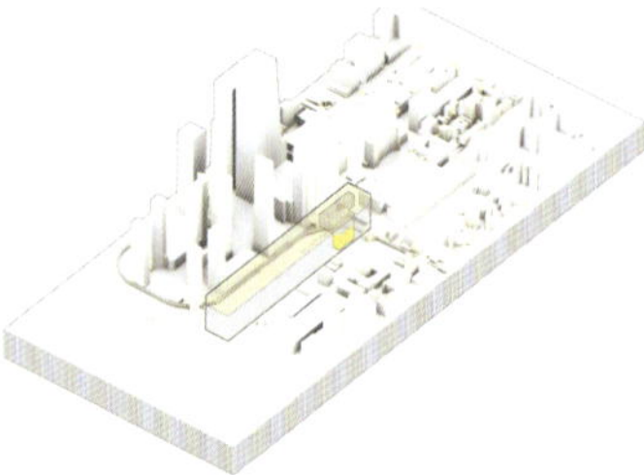
Public library / gallery

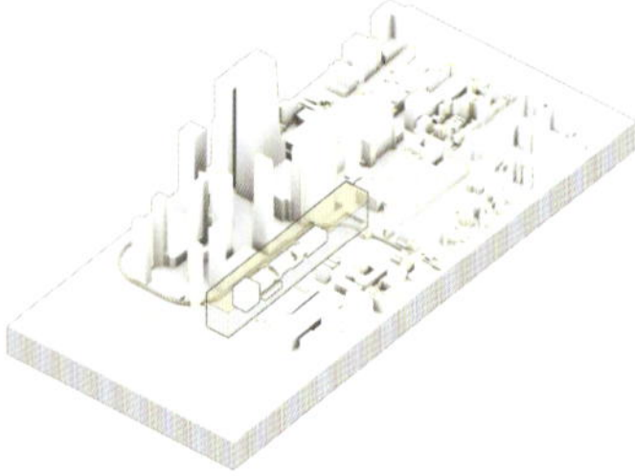
Innovation hub / industrial area

Interior perspective under floating mass

Exterior perspective at streetcorner

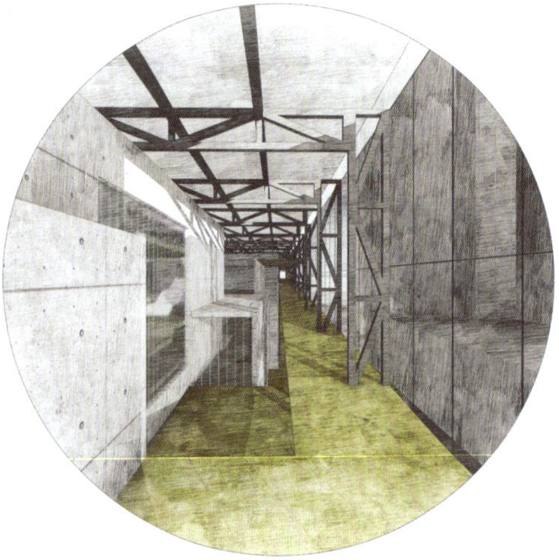
Interior perspective within floating mass

Exterior perspective of facade and interior circulation system

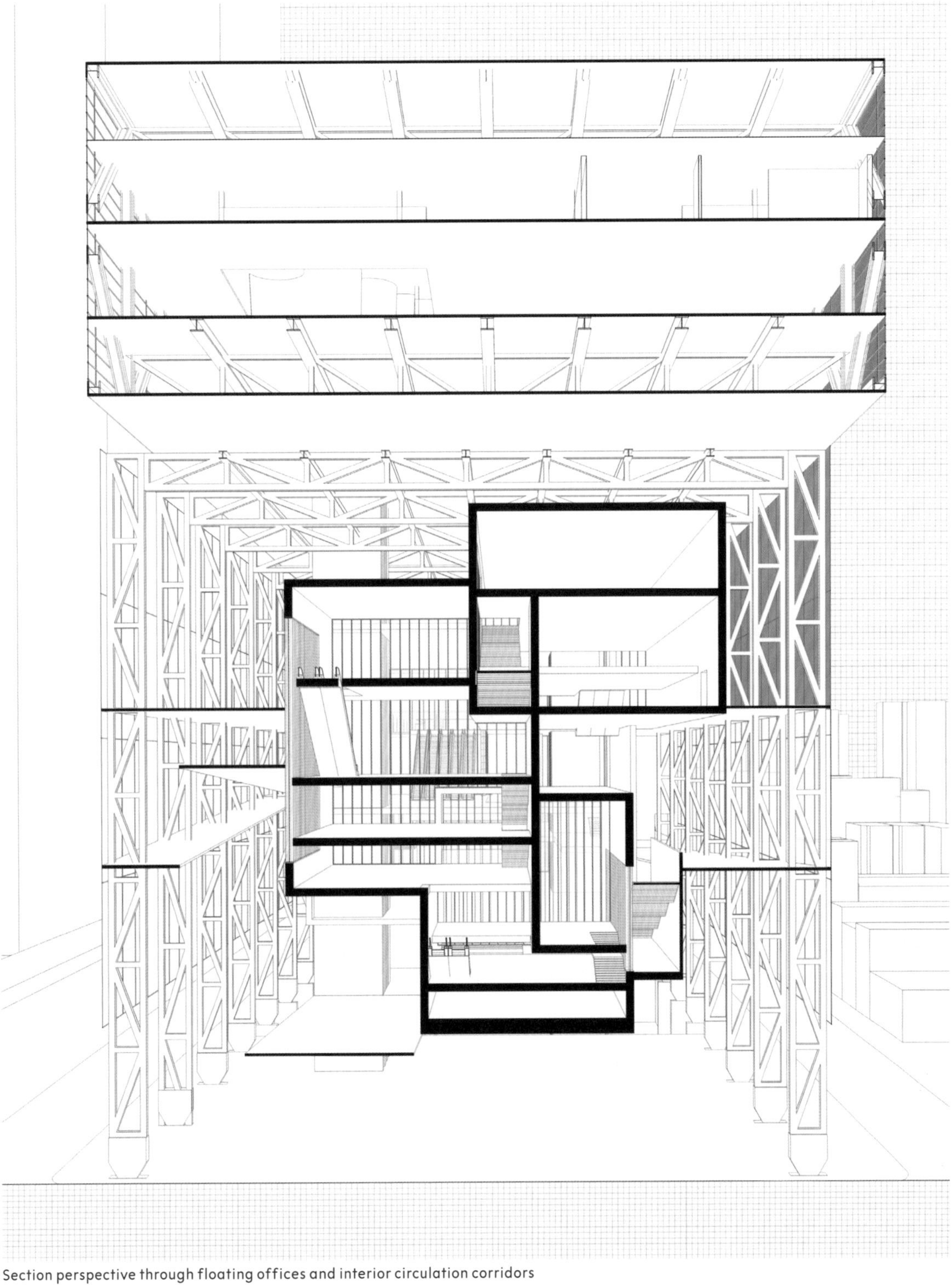

Section perspective through floating offices and interior circulation corridors

Rifts

Student Team
Emily Fiedler
Aisha Sawatsky
Abe Wilson

Instructor
Seth McDowell

To address a growing dissociation between New York's natural ground plane and its greater urban fabric, as illustrated by recent projects such as the High Line, Rifts proposes a new artificial ground plane sensitively calibrated to the needs of both human-scaled public space and the natural environment, thereby engaging the streetscape rather than hovering in isolation above. The formal gesture of the massing, which houses a range of spaces including classrooms and workspaces devoted to environmental sustainability and earth sciences, recalls the natural geology of Manhattan, whose angular cleaves run contrary to the modern city grid. The resulting interstitial rifts serve as the architectural basis for a new network of shared public and private spaces.

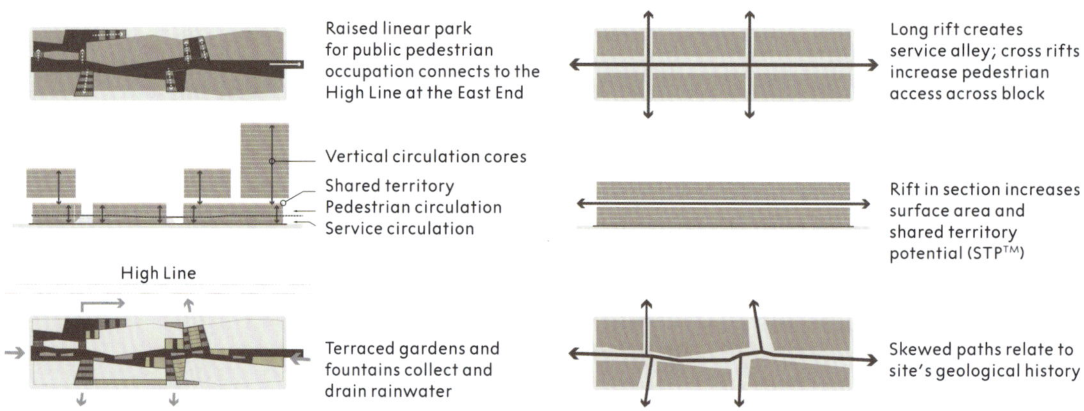

Concept diagrams illustrating block massing and "rifts"

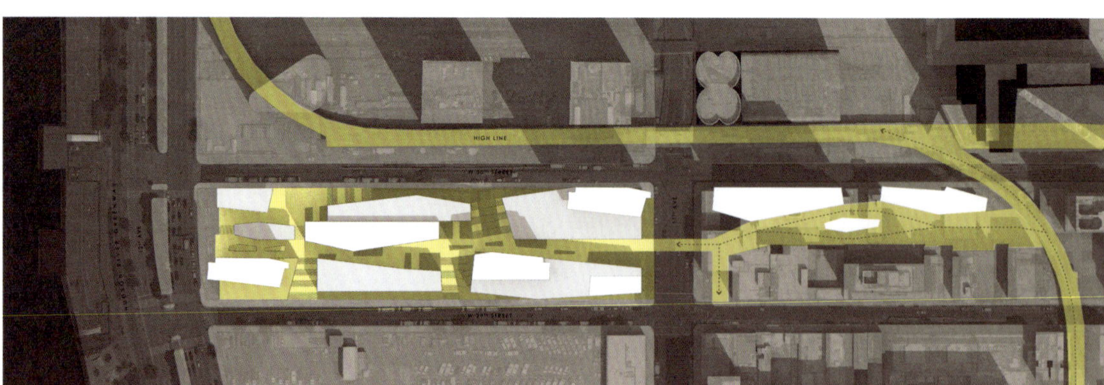

Site plan

Transverse section drawing through towers and interstitial "rift" space

Upper level floor

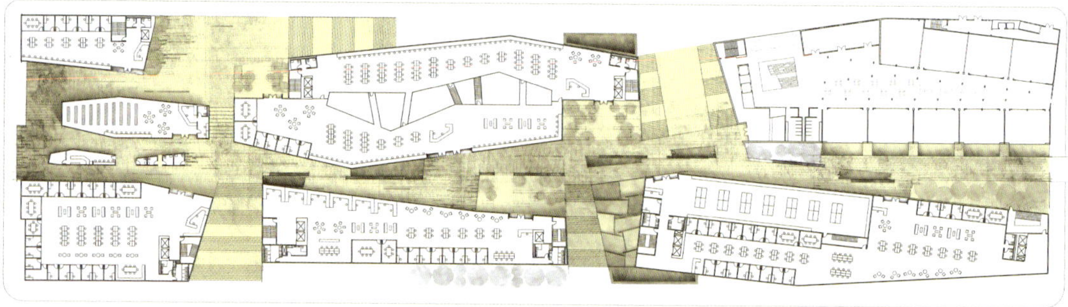

"New" ground level floorplan

Street elevation

Perspective view showing interstitial "rift" space between building masses

Perspective view at street level looking toward site and new, raised ground

Maker Park

Student
Sicheng Zhou

Instructor
Seth McDowell

Maker Park re-imagines Hudson Yards as symbol of New York's global ideas: an architecture and landscape complex conceptually anchored around sharing, learning, and creating. Maker Park encompasses a diverse range of programs: public plazas, playgrounds, fabrication workshops, digital farms, restaurants, commercial spaces, and residences. The physical massing maintains a continuity with the adjacent streetscape, and a focus on the preservation of human-scaled space, however it also generates a rich and varied series of overlapping interior voids which make for ideal shared territories. Some, such as the main, centralized void, contain the primary vertical circulation for the project, while others function as balconies, visual openings to below, and mezzanines.

Perspective view showing spatial overlapping of programmatic blocks

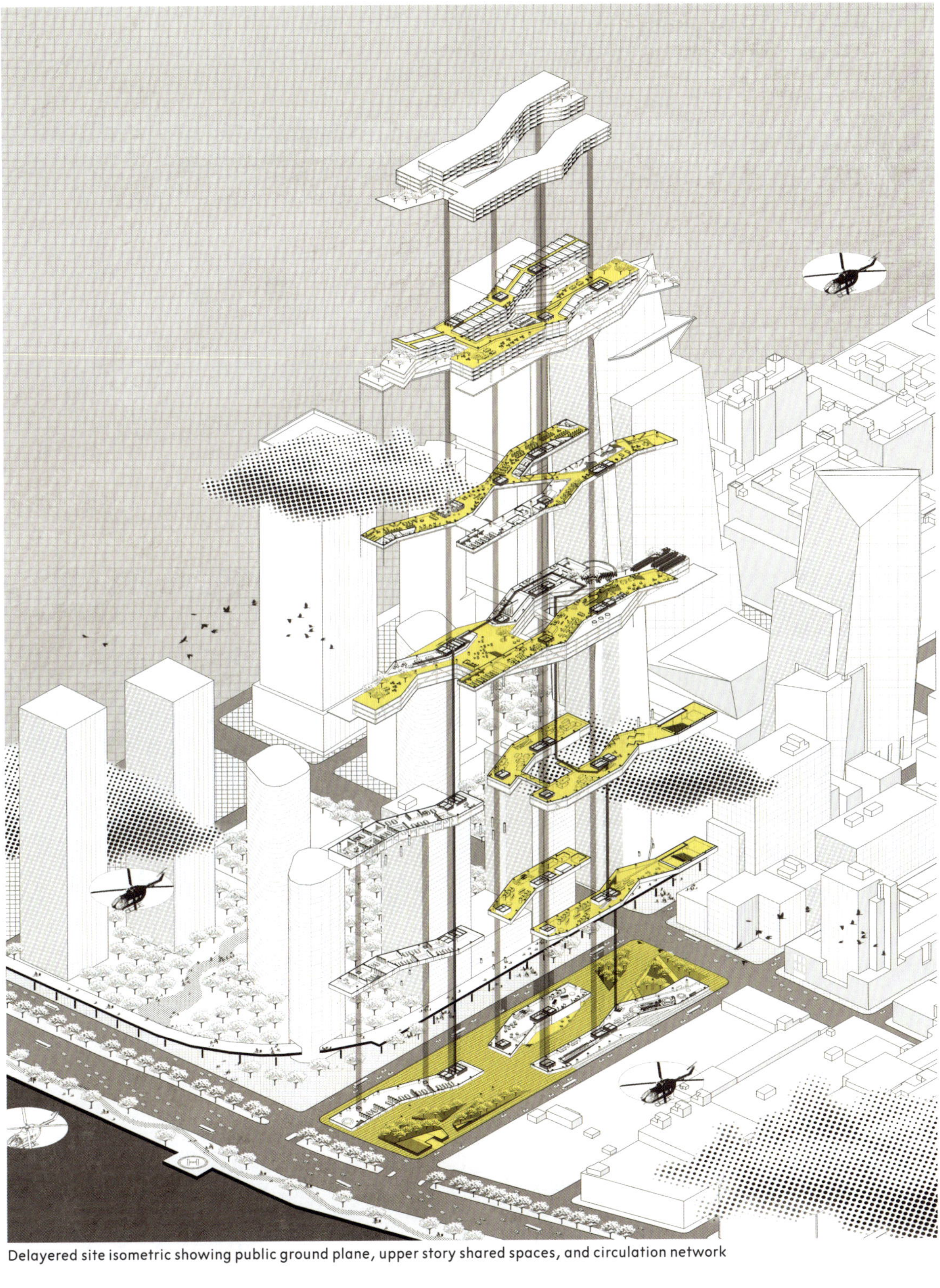

Delayered site isometric showing public ground plane, upper story shared spaces, and circulation network

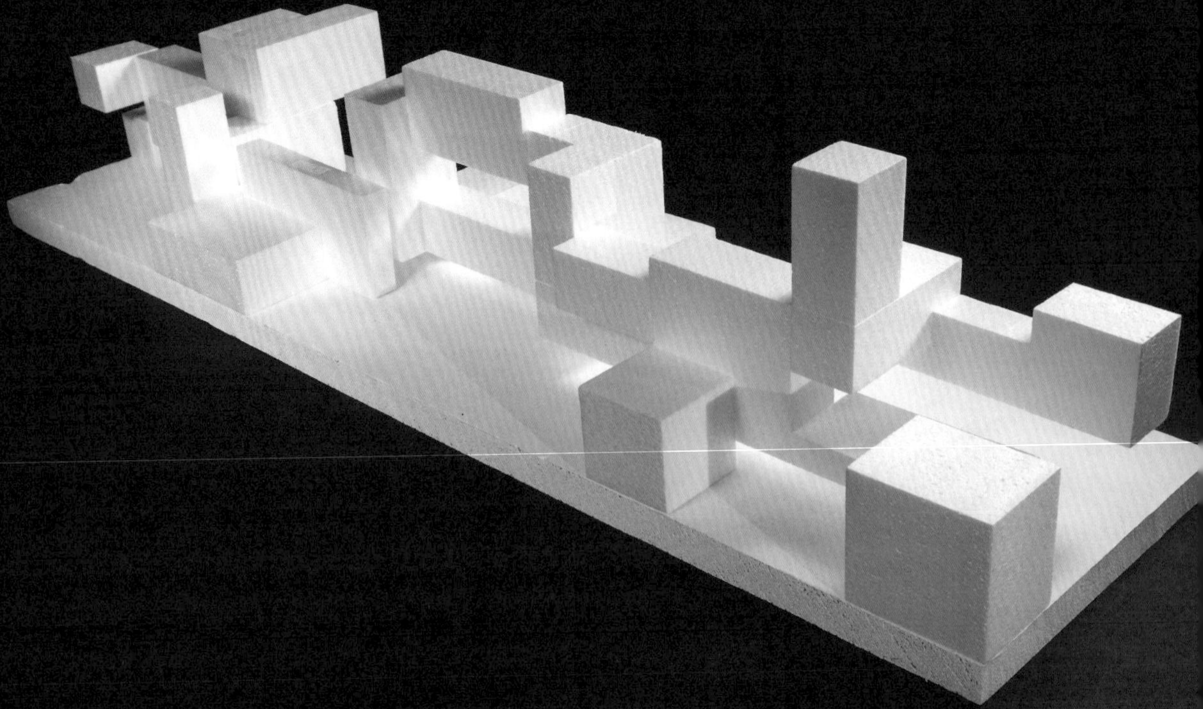

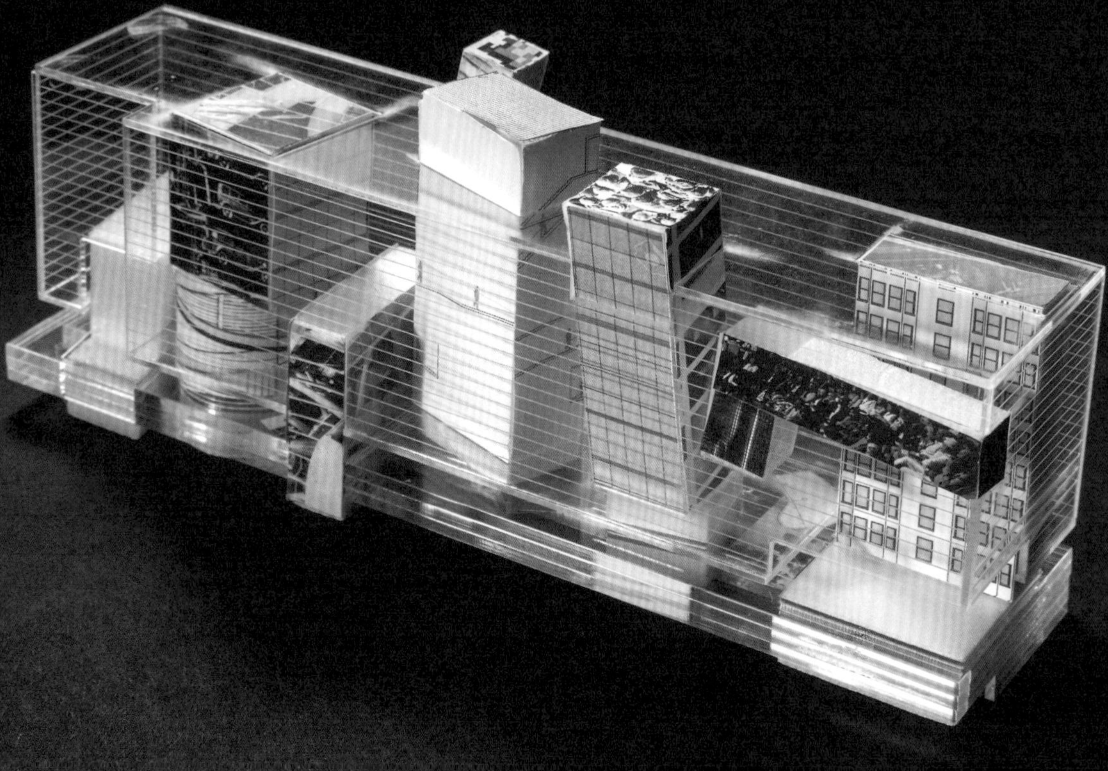

Freeing itself from the limiting confines of the building envelope, architecture as an urban project looks beyond the site boundary and expands its domain of influence to the systems and component of cities, from public spaces to infrastructural elements and networks. Such design operations are often most effective when they release and redirect potentials that have built up over successful iterations of development.
—Matthew Jull

Looking forward to future mobility infrastructures and interchange nodes in an already mature and densified city like New York, new structures will most often need to be conceived as adaptations, modifications, and grafts to what has previously been constructed. Designers and planners will also need to ask themselves important questions beyond the instrumentality of these works, such as for whom these infrastructures will be built, what kind of collective and social space will they produce, whose finances will build them, and what will be the politics of their architectural expression and materialization?
—Kathy Velikov and Geoffrey Thün

Sites along the water's edge, atop railyards, and underneath highway overpasses—where the rigor of the city grid is broken by centuries-long patterns of functional use—must also succeed in realizing something more subtle and rare, and far more likely to be overlooked: the return of a sense of infrastructural utility to the site, and the leveraging their native assets and location to serve in silent support of city life.
—SHoP Architects

Connecting

Catalyzing Urban Transfiguration: The Broadway Junction Laboratory

Matthew Jull

Cities are inherently unstable assemblages of nonlinear and complex agglomerations of both planned and unplanned physical structures.[1] Within this milieu, architecture seeks to transcend the imperatives of commerce and functional demands. In a city like New York, buried under a mountain of architectural ambition, the larger edifice of the city is foregrounded as a decades-long expression of planning decisions punctuated by infrastructure-scale urban elements. What is the role of architecture within this urban context? How and where should architecture begin, end, or operate within the seemingly endless array of spatial and material expression?

Architecture is most potent when it aspires to operate at the scale of the city. Freeing itself from the limiting confines of the building envelope, architecture as an urban project looks beyond the site boundary and expands its domain of influence to the systems and components of cities, from public spaces to infrastructural elements and networks. Such design operations are often most effective when they release and redirect potentials that have built up over successful iterations of development. By forming, relinking, and short-circuiting physical or spatial connections, or by inserting programmatic catalysts, it is possible to reorder the functional, economic, and social capacities of cities. Combined with the curation of mobility, cities can be transfigured into new forms of spatial and programmatic potential.[2] It is at these moments that architecture is at its most significant, expanding beyond the bounds of an exercise in the autonomous, isolated expression of commerce-driven development to become a spatial system of influence that catalyzes the reordering of the city through both explicit and implicit means.

It is somewhat ironic that many of the best-known examples of this type of transfiguration are projects from the canon of the "architectural icon"—most notably the Pompidou Center in Paris (1977) and the Guggenheim Bilbao, Spain (1997).[3] Described by Richard Rogers as "not a building but a town where you find everything—lunch, great art, a library, great music," the Pompidou Center was conceived as a transformational element for the city at a particularly tense moment in its cultural evolution; fundamentally, it was urban in its negotiation of public space and introduction of multivalent functionality and public accessibility. Similarly, the Guggenheim Bilbao was introduced into a failing industrial city. Situated along the edge of a neglected waterfront, the result—merging a major cultural institution brand with an architecture of spectacular formal and material expression—became the foundation for defining a new urban force. The "Bilbao effect" is now universally understood as the reworking of economic, cultural, and social prospects catalyzed by an architectural project. In a similar vein, albeit subtler and more powerful in the absence of a physical edifice, is the recent High Line project in New York (2009). The repurposing of an abandoned elevated railway line into new public space has radically altered the urban and architectural landscape of Lower Manhattan. The project flickers between being an object and an infrastructural catalyst; possessing less of a clear formal identity, the High Line radically reworks the relationship between the pedestrian, the city, and its abutting buildings. It is perhaps best described in the following: "Presenting a scripted urban imaginary, the High Line suspends visitors in a state of collapsed time and space organized into cinematic images—one that invites them to reflect on the collective experience of the metropolis."[4]

Building on these ambitions, we seek to explore the multivalent potentials of architecture in the new cultural, social, and environmental landscape of the twenty-first century. What are the future operational modes of architecture as an urban catalyst that seek out a systems-based approach, prioritizing cultural and social optimization while not being simply another object in a city? To answer this question, we posit that the most fertile moments for such experimentation are found at the intersections, edges, and boundaries of cities, where maximum dislocation and discontinuity are latent with potential.

East New York

Extending the work developed in a series of urban-scale, hybrid architectural studios taught by the author (with Manuel Bailo) at UVA focusing on Atlantic City, NJ, starting in 2013, the Broadway Junction Studio in East New York was developed with co-instructors Mona El Khafif and

Seth McDowell to explore the potentials of architecture as an urban project within an alchemy of program, public space, and infrastructure. As a site latent with potential, Broadway Junction was described in 2017 by the *New York Times* as a "sprawling ... transit hub [that] ... serves as the unofficial welcome center in a fast-growing part of New York City. ... The dingy warren of passageways and platforms linking the A, C, J, Z, M and L are so packed that rush hour turns into a crawl. Outside, bus stops and a Long Island Rail Road station are plopped down in a depressing terrain of trash-strewn streets, chain-link fences rimmed with barbed wire and panhandlers camped out on sidewalks."[5]

Broadway Junction is comparable to other major hubs that serve as or are planned to become regional destinations, such as Atlantic Terminal or Jamaica Center. By public transit, it can be reached from locations across a broad swath of Brooklyn, Queens, Manhattan, and Long Island. Travel between Broadway Junction and Downtown Brooklyn or Lower Manhattan takes about twenty minutes; Midtown can be reached within forty-five minutes. While the convergence of transportation elements provides easy access to destinations across the city and region, the resultant infrastructure is layered across several different levels above and below ground, impacting the physical landscape. Despite also being one of the fastest-growing areas in New York, the area in the immediate vicinity of Broadway Junction is underutilized and poorly developed. Characterized by low-rise buildings, elevated transportation infrastructure, fragmented land uses encompassing residential, commercial, and industrial programs, and many vacant and underutilized sites, the site has little activity at street level, and accordingly, the station is used primarily as a transfer point between different transit services and not as a destination. Yet, Broadway Junction's location is not wholly peripheral to the city; it also sits at the crossroads of six East New York neighborhoods, is bounded by major thoroughfares: Atlantic Avenue to the south, Pennsylvania Avenue to the east, Bushwick Avenue to the north, and Eastern Parkway to the west, and is featured prominently within the larger New York City Department of City Planning (NYCDCP) East New York Neighborhood and Sustainable Communities Plans.

A comprehensive NYCDCP study found that "both residents and visitors have a very poor perception of the area, mostly due to the physical condition around the Broadway

Junction subway station."[6] At community meetings, residents often described the area as unsafe, deserted, and neglected. It was also pointed out that the area lacked a diverse mix of services and retail, particularly basic neighborhood services like supermarkets, pharmacies, and financial services, as well as sit-down restaurants, cafés, bars, and entertainment, cultural, and recreational facilities. The problems identified by area residents were caused in part by physical barriers and development constraints imposed by the transportation infrastructure. Land in the area is underutilized, with few businesses or other services located around the transit stations, in turn leading to reduced public activity at the street level. With few destinations in the area around the station, the Broadway Junction station only serves as a transfer point between different transit services, and the walk to nearby residential areas and commercial corridors is desolate and uninviting.

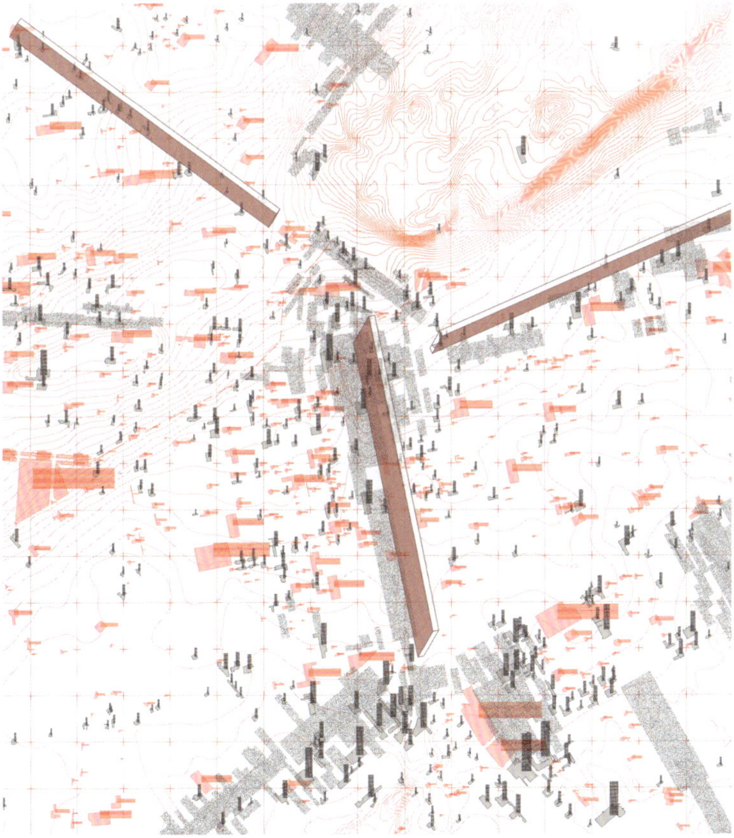

Figure 1: Analytical synthesis map of Broadway Junction.

The Broadway Junction studio took as a starting point the redevelopment framework adopted by the NYCDCP, which proposed to rezone the area for housing and mixed-use programs. In tandem with this proposal, the studio also incorporated the New York City Mayor's New York Works Initiative to create 100,000 jobs over the next ten years, and to align with the interests of the Brooklyn Borough Administration. This initiative proposed relocating the City's Human Resources Administration (HRA) from downtown Brooklyn to Broadway Junction to encourage new office growth by serving as an anchor program. This office/administrative hub is balanced by additional programs that address specific cultural, economic, and social issues of the neighborhood.

The studio adopted the HRA program from the NYCDCP plans and assumed that additional programs would occupy the remaining 50 percent, for a total program area of about 50,000 square meters (net). These additional programs were proposed to include commercial spaces, housing, amenities, entertainment (a movie theater, restaurants, educational spaces), parking, or institutional uses. The New York Works Initiative also includes major investments in cyber security, freight, life sciences, virtual reality, manufacturing, and other sectors with high growth potential to create good jobs and grow the middle class in New York City.

Operations

The studio was framed in terms of a series of operational approaches and phases that together form a pedagogical framework which embraces the inherent multivalence of the site and the design process, while rooting the outcomes within a clear analytical foundation of research and iterative design evaluation. These approaches include (1) analytical synthesis, (2) idea bombardment, (3) object/system, (4) programmatic alchemy, (5) ground dynamics, and (6) narrative and temporality. Through these lenses, the studio sought to maximize the spatial, functional, and social outcomes of the design projects. Complementing this approach was a site visit to document existing conditions, and to meet with representatives of the municipal government and other stakeholders and organizations that are actively involved in the development of East New York.

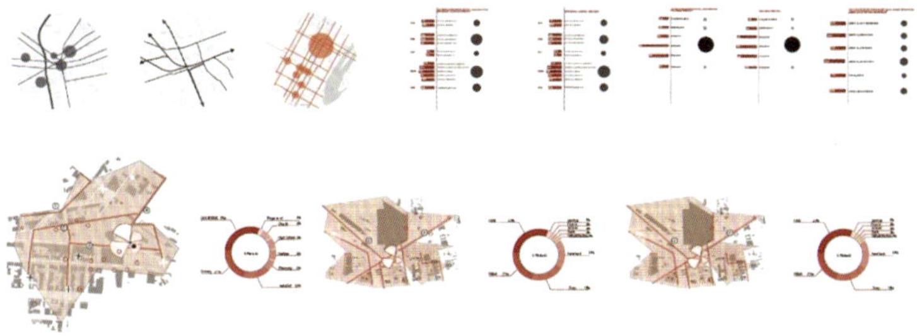

Figure 2: Analytical synthesis of site conditions including maps and diagrams integrating data and experience.

1. Analytical Synthesis

At its core, the studio initiates a research-based, empirical methodology that prioritizes analysis and synthesis of information about the site, its surrounding context, its program, and other parameters to generate an initial design intuition, as well as to form a range of potential design hypotheses and ideas. A key element of this approach is a foundation of analytical research that is iteratively contrasted with creative synthesis and interpretation, which relies on and develops design intuition. The research was directed toward developing an architecture that engages the physical and social context of Broadway Junction, including its geography, urbanism, and infrastructure. Visual documentation and analysis, including maps, diagrams, drawings, and models were essential tools for testing and communicating this work. Importantly, this process integrates data and experience at multiple scales: from strategic planning with respect to landscape, urban patterns, and infrastructure; to the program's organizational relationships; to ordering form and space; to material and construction.

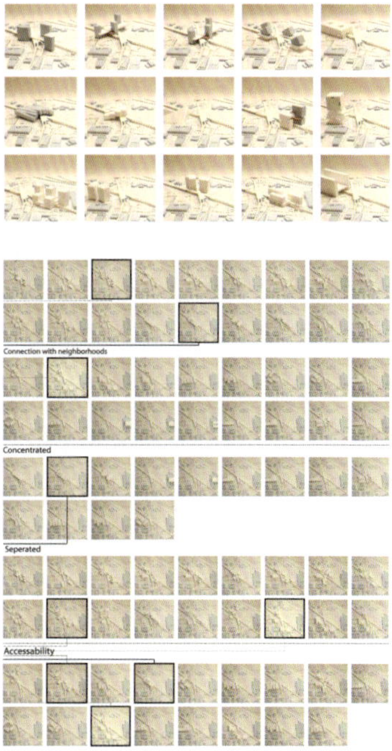

Figure 3: Iterative study models.

2. Idea Bombardment

An essential part of the design process was to work as a collective (in small teams) to rapidly generate and critique design iterations. This process of idea bombardment seeks to create an array of design proposals using multiple representational forms that include simple concept diagrams, massing models, collages, and program system diagrams. The resulting array is then evaluated and curated according to species and type, with an emphasis on identifying fundamental characteristics that will form a basis for evaluation and decision making. A continual process of creative synthesis and analytical evaluation is the key feature of this process. Selected ideas become the focus for successful iteration and refinement, while the archiving of discarded ideas provides a continual reference framework for future evaluation. For the bulk of the design process, teams developed their projects across multiple scales: from the urban to the detail, from interior to exterior, and from public space to infrastructure.

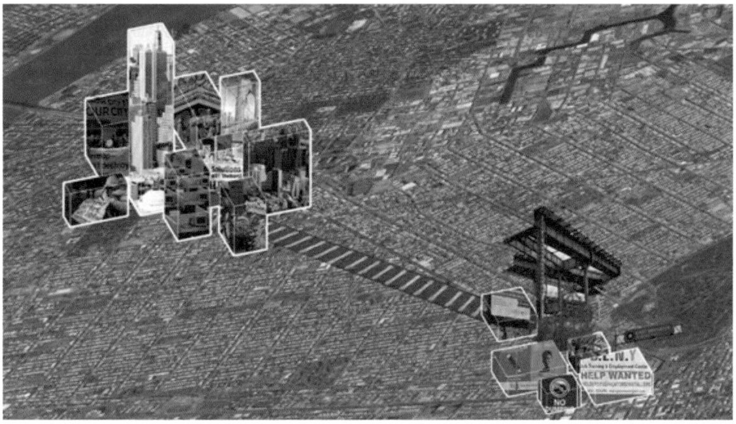

Figure 4: Architecture as urban organizational device.

3. Object/System

We seek to expand the domain of influence of the architectural project outward from the building envelope (building as object) to the domain of the city (building as organizational system). The large and complex site of Broadway Junction, and the studio's ambition to catalyze the transformation of the area, necessitated this approach. How can incorporation of existing elements and components of the site or the development of a clear relational spatial language lead to an expanded scale of influence? Historical precedents for large-scale "megaforms" range from Le Corbusier's Algiers project to the work of the Metabolists, midcentury American corporate architecture by Eero Saarinen and SOM, and mat planning by Candilis-Josic-Woods and others. Recent projects by OMA, Steven Holl, MVRDV, SANAA, and others have continued this ambition, revealing new possibilities for order through extending, amplifying, transforming, and inventing infrastructure.

4. Programmatic Alchemy

Programmatic composition and organization not only provide potential ways to establish functional relationships with the surrounding context, but also serve as critical means to guide the development of the form, scale, and spatial typology of an architectural project. By exploring and experimenting with programmatic types and their relational systems through adjacency, overlap, intersection, and functional capacity, the development of a clear program organizational strategy provides a means to evaluate overall spatial/massing strategies, and opportunities to mine the architectural tensions inherent in unexpected adjacencies. Simultaneously, such design constraints provide an opportunity to insert narratives within the overall design proposal (see Narrative and Temporality).

5. Ground Dynamics

The ground plane is the fundamental space for mediating between building and city, between indoor and outdoor, and between built and natural environment. Simultaneously, it is also the principal territory of "the public," as it serves as a relatively unregulated and universally accessible space as well as a theater for social interaction. Through its highly pliable and latent potential to redefine the linkage between architectural and urban scales, and the temporal contrast between the geologic and the transient, the ground plane is the key element in recontextualizing the architectural project within a city. It catalyzes human interaction through its endless material, spatial, and functional capacities, linking the scale of the body to those of infrastructure and ecosystems.

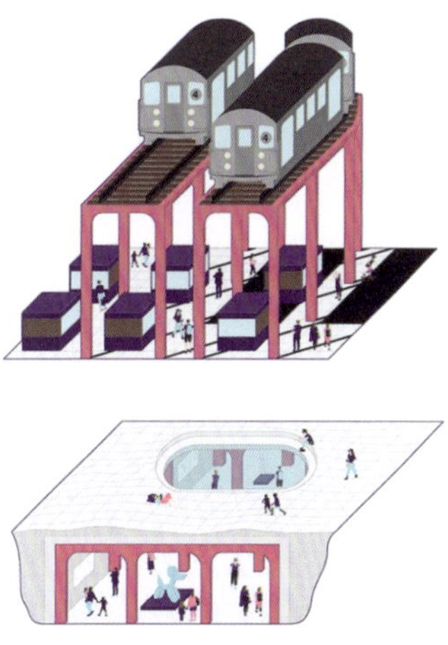

Figure 5: Repurposing infrastructure as public space.

6. Narrative and Temporality

Cities are continually in a state of flux. Multiple cycles of transformation occur—from the physical and spatial impacts of the ebbs and flows of commerce and development; to short-term environmental cycles that transform relationships between exterior and interior through ambient climate; to the much longer-term changes from climate change. Temporality is thus an essential component of the design process. Overlaid on this are the daily rituals of people and their continually changing behavioral patterns. Within the complex calculus of decision

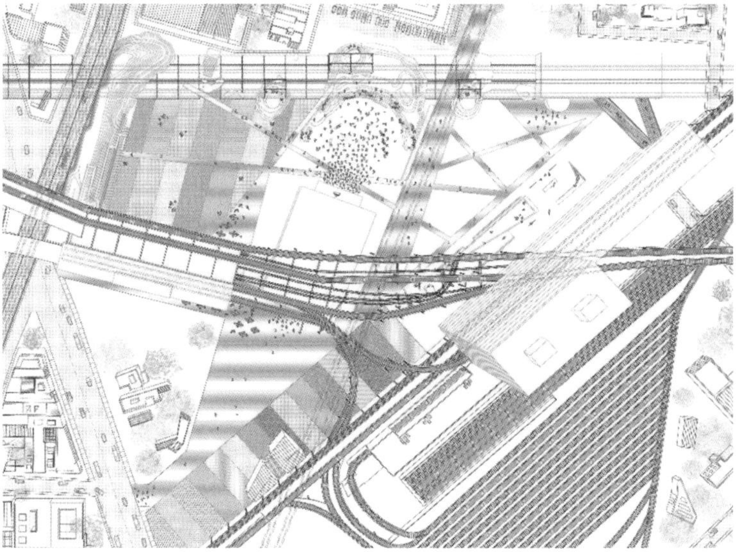

Figure 6: Site plan showing the latent potential of site's ground plane to host new public spaces.

making in the design process, there is a critical need to articulate and clarify both design logic and user-based experiential frameworks for evaluation and engagement through the development of visual narratives. Such a process foregrounds the editorial prerogative of the architect and the necessity for sequence and structure when articulating ideas. This process serves not only to communicate ideas, but also as a framework for an internal evaluation of design methodology.

Strategies and Outcome

One of the pedagogical challenges of the Broadway Junction studio was the absence of a specific site boundary. Although development areas were identified by the NYCDCP, students were asked to establish their own site boundaries and domains of operation. Complicating this effort were the large and complex infrastructural elements that extended physically across (and beyond) the immediate vicinity of the site. Through comprehensive site analysis and research, in addition to the site visit with stakeholders and community leaders, each student team developed a position and approach to the site based on the programmatic needs of the HRA office space and the additional programmatic elements they were asked to introduce, centered around cultural and educational amenities as well as public spaces. These included, for example, a performing arts school, a museum, a library, a swimming pool and exercise facilities, a market, retail space, and workspaces for small businesses.

Several key themes emerged from the studio projects. The first was a focus on linking the fragmented public spaces in order to improve pedestrian mobility in and through the vicinity of Broadway Junction. These projects sought to merge the architecture, public space, infrastructure, and circulation elements into a seamless experience of connectivity, attempting at times to make the massive physical infrastructure become essentially "transparent" through circulation, programmatic sequence, and materiality (see the project "Hip and Hop," for example). The second theme focused on the reuse of existing transit infrastructure as an integral component of the projects. This took the form of infrastructure as an orientation device for understanding position and movement, and as a means to challenge the notion of "ground." These approaches likely nucleated from the complex conditions on the site, where human and machine occupation occur simultaneously on multiple levels in a seemingly haphazard organization, distorting the notion of the physical ground. The result was a series of projects that prioritized above and below-grade spaces as ideal means of redefining movement and connection within and through the complex site (see "Infrastructural Intracultural" and "Collected Ground"). A third key approach to emerge was an increase of density and intensity in an already busy transport hub. This was accomplished through a combination of adjacent urban infill and the addition of new programmatic elements that could form cohesive connections with surrounding

Figure 7: Temporal vignettes from student projects.

manufacturing or educational needs. By bringing the cultural, economic, and social needs of East New York to a level of intensity and visibility, further opportunities for the growth of the community could emerge. At the same time, by making the neighborhood's potential visible and broadcasting it to the rest of New York through the transit hub as a communication device, this approach set up the possibility that Broadway Junction could become an urban destination and not simply a transit point (see "Infrastructural Intracultural Club").

As a site of experimentation for operational modes of architecture—vis-à-vis transfiguration—Broadway Junction served as an ideal laboratory. The neighborhood's lack of a coherent existing organizational structure and the complexity and scale of the infrastructure served to both challenge and destabilize the notion of architecture as an autonomous act, as adding one more "object" building to a large and complex infrastructural milieu would be destined for insignificance. This is where studio projects excelled—and where the heart of the studio pedagogy resided—in mining the latent potential of architecture to operate most powerfully to infiltrate, link, and catalyze existing urban spatial (or, in this case, infrastructural) potentials.

1
Momoyo Kaijima, Junzo Kuroda, and Yoshiharu Tsukamoto, *Made in Tokyo* (Tokyo: Kajima Institute, 2006), p. 10.

2
The expression used here implies both physical and perceptual transformation with the understanding that these are not mutually exclusive. See also "Mass Transfigured by Light: The Iconic Vision of an Orthodox Church," *Road to Emmaus* 16, no. 4 (Fall 2015): 17–57.

3
Nadia Alaily-Mattar and Alain Thierstein, "Urban Transformations through Exceptional Architecture: Introduction to the Special Issue," *Journal of Urban Design* 23, no. 2 (April 2018): 165–168. Rowan Moore wrote of the architect's reaction to the Bilbao: "When he got to Bilbao a month before it opened, says Frank Gehry, 'I went over the hill and saw it shining there. I thought: "What the fuck have I done to these people?"'" Rowan Moore, *The Observer*, October 1, 2017.

4
Rachel Stevens, "The High Line: Monument to Modern Ruin," *Afterimage* 38, no. 2 (September 2010): 4.

5
Winnie Hu, "A Tired Brooklyn Transit Hub Is Finally Getting Attention," *New York Times*, November 26, 2017, https://www.nytimes.com/2017/11/26/nyregion/a-tired-brooklyn-transit-hub-finally-getting-attention.html.

6
"Sustainable Communities East New York: Broadway Junction Subarea V." New York City Department of City Planning. (June 2014) 9. https://www1.nyc.gov/assets/planning/download/pdf/plans-studies/sustainable-communities/eny/east_ny_report/east_ny_broadway_junction_subarea.pdf.

Infrastructural Hybrids

Kathy Velikov and Geoffrey Thün

> Infrastructure networks are thus involved in sustaining what we might call "sociotechnical geometries of power" in very real—but often complex—ways. They tend to embody "congealed social interests."... The construction of spaces of mobility and flows for some, however, always involves the construction of barriers for others. Experiences of infrastructures are therefore highly contingent... We must therefore recognise how the configurations of infrastructure networks are inevitably imbued with biased struggles for social, economic, ecological and political power to benefit from connecting with (more or less) distant times and places.
> —Stephen Graham and Simon Marvin, *Splintering Urbanism: Networked Infrastructures, Technological Mobilities and the Urban Condition*

Infrastructure: Between Relations and Things

While physical urban infrastructures such as road networks, bridge structures, port complexes, or sewer systems have for millennia defined the anatomy and configuration of cities, the term "infrastructure" itself is a relatively modern one. Moreover, it is a word that historian Rosalind Williams has described as being "promiscuous," with no fixed meaning, and one that changes relative to the historical phenomena and sociopolitical contexts in which it is deployed.[1] Anthropologists Susan Leigh Star and Karen Ruhleder argue that "infrastructure is fundamentally always a *relation*, never a thing."[2] And yet, part of the potentially productive ambiguity of a term like "infrastructure" is that it can refer simultaneously to relations and material things, and also serves to put things into relational assemblages. Redefining this term has the capacity to transform the way we imagine and structure urban life.

The first use of the term "infrastructure" occurs in late-nineteenth-century technical literature in France and England related to railroad construction, where the word is used in reference to the logistics, planning, and subsurface preparations for tracks and other associated structures to deliver the physical system.[3] Here the term seems to be closely aligned with the relationally hierarchical connotations of the word, with the prefix "infra-" referring to the condition of being below or beneath, undergirding what is to come. "Infrastructure" remained a fairly obscure word until the post-war period, when it was appropriated by NATO in the 1950s as "a generic term to denote all those fixed installations which are necessary for the effective deployment and operations of modern armed forces."[4] In this open-ended definition, it included not only physical installations (highways, bridges, railroads, airports, military bases), but also facilities for communications, power, irrigation, and flood control, as well as warehousing, storage depots, fuel supplies, and the funding frameworks and coordination necessary to enable these installations.[5] With this new definition, the term became not only more expansive in its scope but also explicitly politicized, assembling these myriad interconnected things, practices, and protocols in the urbanization of military power and control within the context of urban production and reproduction. The new definition also illustrates the ability of the term to appropriate already existing systems and artifacts into new networks, hierarchically reconfiguring them in support of other objectives.

In the 1960s and '70s, the definition of "infrastructure" continued to expand and shift with contemporaneous societal transformations. By then, most usage had moved the term away from its military associations and began to be more closely related to government-sponsored economic and social development, often "treated as a synonym of social overhead capital, meaning capital goods like roads, schools, hospitals, and public parks that are broadly available to the public and typically provided by the government."[6] The word was also adopted into business and organizational vocabularies, where it carried its meaning in referring to sociotechnical networks. "Infrastructure" continued to be used in government terminologies: President Ronald Reagan referred to the "infrastructure of democracy—the system of a free press, unions, political parties, universities,"[7] and President Bill Clinton's Commission on Critical Infrastructure defined it as "a network of independent, mostly privately-owned, man-made systems and processes that function collaboratively and synergistically to produce and distribute continuous flow of essential goods and services."[8] Within the design disciplines of architecture, landscape, and urban design, "infrastructure" has most commonly been used to refer to the engineered systems of transportation, water, power, and communications. By the twentieth century, the design and implementation of these systems had become the specialist purview of the engineering professions. Increasingly, the term had begun to be synonymous with material objects as opposed to relational systems; in the United States, for example, the Office of Infrastructure sits within the U.S. Department of Transportation, and is responsible for structures and projects related to mobility.[9]

The fact that "infrastructure" has historically been a highly malleable term that refers to both relational systems and to actual things is not without consequence. "As a form of calculative reason, infrastructure promises to collect a heterogeneous, changing group of elements 'beneath' some higher-order goal," writes anthropologist Ashley Carse.[10] This enables the decoupling of the term from fixed meanings and relational schema, and privileges its use as a potent agent through which to construct new provisional assemblages with alternative goals.

Resilient Infrastructure

The 2000s witnessed a reengagement with the topic of infrastructural systems by the design disciplines, both at the building scale of mechanical and electrical systems and at the urban scale of mobility, energy, logistics, and landscape management.[11] One of the arguments behind this disciplinary expansion and renewed interest was that the roles of building and urban infrastructures needed to be rethought in response to new performance criteria related especially to energy conservation, renewable energy integration, water and resource conservation, environmental remediation, alternatives to personal vehicle-dominated mobility, and the rapid urbanization of city regions. Additionally, many existing large-scale physical structures built in the last century were reaching a critical end-of-lifespan condition, and designers recognized that the massive government capital that would be channeled to the replacement or rehabilitation of these structures could be leveraged to expand their environmental and social performance.[12]

The prevailing ontic paradigm that emerged from this period is one that privileges ecological and biological models, arguing that public works cannot be thought of within the siloed bounds of a particular system and these cannot continue to be designed through traditional mechanical models of singular optimization. Rather, public works should be recognized as

> dynamically intertwined with biophysical and human systems, exchanging matter, energies, and information beyond the artifacts that are present in these systems ... This precipitates a paradigm shift in how infrastructure is being conceived and implemented. As opposed to centralized, energy-intensive, monofunctional systems, designers, planners, and policy-makers are increasingly considering distributed, low-energy, multifunctional, and often redundant systems, which are believed to be more resilient to disaster and risk, and can be more adaptive over time.[13]

Architect Hillary Brown refers to this "interconnected, multipurpose, and synergistic" infrastructural ecology as "next generation infrastructure."[14] These types of infrastructural systems are also being rethought by industrial ecologists through the lens of urban metabolism, toward a redesign of sociotechnical systems aimed at supporting a transition to more resilient circular economies for food, water, energy, materials, and waste.[15] One of the attributes of a resilient, next-generation, or circular infrastructure is that biotic systems form an inherent part of the network of exchanges and flows. Environmentalist David Orr points out that "properly engaged, nature will in fact do a great deal of the work in engineered systems for free."[16] This concept is an important addition to the definition of "infrastructure." Whereas until recently "infrastructure" had explicitly referred to networks of human-made technologies and processes, landscapes and biotic systems are now being incorporated into an expanded definition that recognizes the intertwinements and interdependencies of human and biotic systems.[17]

Due to the complex and interrelated nature of these systems, their design and implementation can no longer be undertaken by the siloed capacities of engineers alone. Instead, new approaches require coordination and cooperation among diverse teams, where designers, with their ability to envision new futures and to think synthetically about how they may be realized, have a prominent role at the table along with engineers, computer scientists, biologists, planners, and community members and other stakeholders who bring expanded expertise. There is evidence that attitudes and processes are starting to change. After 2012's Hurricane Sandy, Rebuild by Design, an initiative of President Obama's Hurricane Sandy Rebuilding Task Force, included an international design competition that assembled cross-professional collaborative teams working with community feedback to develop environmentally resilient plans for the New York City area. The same organization launched the Resilient by Design | Bay Area Challenge for the San Francisco Bay Area in 2017, which again focused on resilient, community-engaged design propositions for wetland restoration and flood resilience, developed through the collaboration of complex teams of experts.

However, while some infrastructures, such as those designed for flood risk mitigation, have begun to be reconceived as hybrids that assemble built structures, landscapes, biotic systems, and public access, the priority of a majority of large-scale transportation and mobility infrastructure still remains largely limited, with a focus on instrumental performance of throughput and management of vehicles. The most significant transformation in this area has been the rethinking of urban street design to prioritize people, as has been promoted by Complete Streets policies, agencies such as the National Association of City Transportation Officials (NACTO), and in New York City through the work of Transportation Commissioner Janette Sadik-Khan, who famously transformed Times Square into a pedestrian-oriented public space, in addition to redesigning streets in Manhattan, Brooklyn, and the Bronx.[18] Larger-scale and especially elevated structures, such as highways and rail lines, have proved more challenging to reconceive, and even Manhattan's High Line elevated park still leaves extensive areas of the streetscape at grade neglected and unused by pedestrians.

New York City's Layered Infrastructural Typologies

Rethinking both the performance and the range of expertise assembled to define the goals of infrastructural systems in more synergistic and resilient ways has an impact on the physiology, form, materiality, and use of constituent structures. Intertwinement is a physical project as much as it is a conceptual and performative one. "Coupling," "bundling," and "layering" have been operative terms used by recent designers working infrastructurally with the aim of producing new typologies for alternative systemic ends.[19]

Mobility systems are physical and operational paradoxes: they both connect and separate.[20] While structures such as roads, railways, bridges, canals, airport terminals, and logistics zones are intended to enable increasingly unimpeded flow, their spatial footprint and configuration often constitutes a disruptive condition when they hit the ground of existing urban fabric. Operating at more elevated velocities, scales, and levels of security than their surroundings, they fragment local urban geographies, creating barriers, boundaries, and interstitial spaces. The resulting and marginal lands are not easily incorporated into urban uses or land markets, and often develop their own unmanaged ecologies.[21]

Radical separation and monofunctionality in service of frictionless flows are the characteristics of physical structures of conveyance. This paradigm has dominated mid-twentieth-century transportation planning, and was part of an overall ethos of the period in which scientific rationality and efficiency were identified with technological and societal progress. In the United States, massive amounts of federal and state funding before and after World War II were channeled toward the Public Works Agency, the Federal Works Agency, and the Federal Highway Administration to support the construction of the interstate highway system. Yet, these highways were often designed by state-level engineers whose primary focus was to relieve congestion and optimize vehicular throughput; their planning was typically undertaken with little input from local communities, and with seemingly no interest in integrating other functions such as public transit.[22] Moreover, many of these highways were additionally planned in alignment with the racialized goal to "facilitate slum clearance" within inner cities, and were designed to cut through and eviscerate poor and predominantly Black neighborhoods in cities such as Atlanta, Detroit, Chicago, Baltimore, and St. Louis, with often disastrous consequences for those communities.[23] In New York City, the Cross-Bronx Expressway, planned by Commissioner Robert Moses, displaced over five thousand residents from the Tremont neighborhood and precipitated the segregation and decline of the South Bronx.[24]

But even in the efficiency-focused urban constructions of the midcentury, there are rare examples of structures that coupled public spaces with transportation. The Brooklyn Heights Promenade, a public belvedere constructed over the cantilevered sections of the Brooklyn-Queens Expressway (BQE) in Brooklyn Heights, is one such instance. The promenade was the result of powerful lobbying by wealthy and influential residents of Brooklyn Heights in response to Moses's plans to run the new freeway through the space of residents' private gardens, which were constructed on top of warehouses creating an embankment and lining Furman Street below. The compromise reached with the Planning Commission in 1943 was to construct a cantilevered divided highway in the space of the embankment of the Heights, and to cover

Figure 1: Section through the Brooklyn-Queens Expressway. Circa 1950.

Figure 2: The Brooklyn Heights Promenade under construction, 1949.

Figure 3: Brooklyn-Queens Expressway, view of the triple cantilever from below

this with a deck that would become a public promenade, managed by the Department of Transportation (figures 1 & 2).[25]

The Brooklyn Heights Promenade has become one of the city's most well-known and cherished public spaces. From the belvedere, one is rarely aware of the freeway below. Brooklyn Bridge Park, designed by Michael Van Valkenburgh and Associates and completed in 2016, now extends along the riverfront in front of the cantilevered highway, providing further amenity to an area whose property values did *not* diminish after the construction of the freeway, and have risen quite dramatically in recent years. At the time we are writing, New York City has been in the midst of a heated series of public meetings on the necessary replacement of the deteriorated BQE decks, now an unwelcome backdrop to the waterfront park, and considering a very costly buried option, as well as even eliminating part of the freeway altogether (figure 3).[26]

The Brooklyn Heights Promenade and Expressway nonetheless presents a compelling typology of layered public landscape and mobility space, leveraging the sectional separation to provide social and spatial amenity. It additionally represents a typology of public space infrastructure that has been implemented in other parts of New York City, spatially layering pedestrian space onto and through its spaces of vehicular transportation, and providing vistas out over the density of the city. Recent public space projects like the High Line, designed by Diller Scofidio + Renfro with landscape architecture by James Corner Field Operations, and the East River Waterfront

Park and Promenade by SHoP Architects both exemplify this spatial and programmatic strategy. While the High Line in particular has been heavily criticized for being a catalyst for the runaway gentrification that has occurred in its proximity, social scientist Eric Klinenberg argues that these types of spaces nonetheless provide an important component of urban social infrastructure for residents, and are often realized only through strategic partnerships between cities, nonprofits, and civic organizations.[27]

Metropolitan Nodes and Knots

The spaces where systems cross, with transfers between networks, are referred to in network theory as "nodes." In the city, the nodes of transportation networks are its stations, terminals, and ports. Providing transfer between multiple flows, speeds, and trajectories, these structures also operate as gateways to cities, thresholds to other places, material artifacts of collapsed geographies made possible through the technologies of transportation. As buildings they also negotiate between speeds, scales, and atmospheres; between the apparatus of transportation and the pedestrian city street; between fleshy human bodies and large, noisy, fume-expelling mechanized vessels. The train stations of the late nineteenth and early twentieth centuries developed a hybrid typology, typically characterized by a grand civic building that faced the city (housing waiting halls, ticketing, baggage handling, etc.) onto which was grafted a large open-air shed, often of iron and glass, that collected the train tracks and organized them across access platforms.

In New York City, Pennsylvania Station, completed in 1910 by the firm McKim, Mead, and White, became the city's newest gateway for its recently electrified trains arriving in tunnels across the Hudson River. It was a grand neoclassical building of travertine and steel, covering four city blocks between 7th and 8th Avenues and 31st to 33rd Streets. Even though electrified trains would no longer require the large open-air shed to accommodate steam locomotives, the architects chose to roof the concourse and track levels in a conservatory space of vaulted wrought-iron and glass, reminiscent of European train sheds, where section was deployed not only to separate different classes of trains (local, suburban, regional), but to achieve a spatial condition of the spectacle of arrival and departure from the upper concourse similar to Paris's Orléans station.[28]

The architecture itself was explicitly intended to reference the ancient Roman "large, roofed-in areas adapted to the assemblages of people" such as the Baths of Caracalla, Titus, Diocletian, and the Basilica of Constantine.[29] The cutaway section-perspective drawn by architectural illustrator Harry M. Pettit in 1908 communicates the project's design intent as a grand, multilayered urban fragment, intertwined with the movements of the city. Its edges extend beyond the boundaries of the frame, and the inclusion of the railway levels in section emphasizes its networked condition as an architectural and urban ambition (figure 4). The activity and movement of the multitude that would come to define the modern democratic and capitalist city is also captured in the depiction of masses of people, occupying and flowing through every accessible space within this rendering of the civic complex.

Grand Central Terminal, completed in 1913 by the firm Reed and Stem in collaboration with Warren and Wetmore, takes the orchestration and spectacle of human movement even further. At Grand Central, the technologies that enable seemingly endless human flow are now suppressed into multiple levels of underground chambers, not visible or apprehensible from the concourse levels above. Here, "the crowd itself became an object to be aestheticized," collected in its ideal form within the singular monumental concourse and its overlooking galleries, and

Figure 4: Sectional view of the new Pennsylvania Railroad Station. Drawn by H. M. Pettit, 1908.

then dispersed among the intertwined halls, ramps, and walkways that weave the many trajectories of passenger trains back onto the grid of the surrounding city in a "theater of circulation."[30] The technologies of mobility and service were, however, entirely sublimated as infrastructure to a much more explicit spectacle of the official citizenry and multitude within modern society (figure 5).

Penn Station and Grand Central were more than just gateways; they were also conceived of and designed as microcosms of cities within themselves. Built by privately-owned railway companies, they presented a quasi-public civic space that, in addition to generous areas for waiting and circulation for the newly connected American workforce, also provided retail and amenities beyond the necessities of ticket offices, newsstands, and eating establishments. The 32nd Street wing of Penn Station housed an arcade of shops and stores that sold a variety of items, and the station included a drug store, bookstores, reading room, and even a hospital.[31] Grand Central Terminal was also described as being closer to a "bazaar" than a station, with its shopping, food, and exhibition spaces intended to make the terminal a destination for people without even needing to board the trains.[32] While at the time of its construction Pennsylvania Station boasted the largest waiting area in the world, it and Grand Central were also part of a new series of monumental and architecturally exuberant terminal structures throughout U.S. cities—such as the stations in Chicago, Detroit, Kansas City, Cleveland, Cincinnati, Minneapolis, Omaha, and

Figure 5: Section of Grand Central Terminal.
Drawn by H. M. Pettit. *Scribner's Magazine* v.52, 1912.

Washington, DC—constructed by railroad companies that were conscious of similar buildings being constructed in Europe.[33] As a type, these structures occupy the categories of both urban monument and urban node: a space of flows as well as a "space of appearance."[34] They cultivate an enactment of civic expression of the urban collective as a spectacle of mobility and commerce.

During and after the Depression era, New Deal funding through the Public Works Administration (PWA) was not directed toward the privately-owned railway companies, but focused instead on federally funded roads, bridges, dams, airports, hospitals, housing, schools, and electricity production and distribution. Increased personal vehicle ownership and road improvements meant that railway ridership declined drastically through the first half of the century. Amid financial turmoil, the Pennsylvania Railroad Company sold their air rights in Manhattan, and in 1963 Penn Station was demolished and redesigned as a much more utilitarian set of tunnels, passages, and waiting areas that sit underground below Madison Square Garden. While outcry against this decision was one of the linchpins in the foundation of the preservation movement, equally poignant were the arguments that the loss of the station also meant a loss of civic dignity. Architecture critic Ada Louise Huxtable bitterly noted that "we are an impoverished society ... that can't pay for these amenities."[35] Historian Vincent Scully also lamented the shift in metropolitan subjectivity produced by the difference between the old and the new Penn Station, writing of them, respectively, "Through it one entered the city like a god ... One scuttles in now like a rat."[36]

It is possible to be nostalgic for the architecture of the heroic metropolitan spaces of the early-twentieth-century railway terminals, and also easy to be nostalgic for the incredible volume of infrastructural spending and construction allowed through programs like the New Deal and the Federal-Aid Highway Act. It is at the same time important to situate these artifacts within their politico-economic contexts of global energy, resources, and colonization. Political theorist Timothy Mitchell makes a strong argument in his book *Carbon Democracy* that the economic model of the United States government between World War II and 1970 was only made possible by its control over the oil resources of the Middle East.[37] Similarly, the railroad companies profited immensely from the U.S. Congress's granting them thousands of acres of territory that lay within Indigenous Treaty lands, and through which they were able to build with impunity.[38] Today, massive infrastructure-building campaigns financed by cheap energy and imperialist extraction-based activity are no longer fiscally, environmentally, or morally possible.

Looking forward to future mobility infrastructures and interchange nodes in an already mature and densified city like New York, new structures will most often need to be conceived as adaptations, modifications, and grafts to what has previously been constructed. Designers and planners will also need to ask themselves important questions beyond the instrumentality of these works, such as for whom these infrastructures will be built, what kind of collective and social space will they produce, whose finances will build them, and what will be the politics of their architectural expression and materialization? As political theorist Langdon Winner has argued, "The issues that divide or unite people in society are settled not only in the institutions and practices of politics proper, but also, and less obviously, in tangible arrangements of steel and concrete, wires and transistors, nuts and bolts."[39]

Mobility Space as Social Infrastructure

> Social infrastructure is the network of physical spaces and institutions—from sidewalks to public parks, libraries to cafes—that, when robust, promote community-building activities among otherwise diverse clans ... The stakes are real: Weak social infrastructure breeds economic isolation, political misunderstanding, and the social divisions that fuel the most dangerous forms of xenophobia.
> —Eric Klinenberg, "Social Infrastructure"[40]

The urban condition of New York City, like that of many U.S. cities, is characterized by drastically uneven development, comprising large areas of dispossession and marginalization with highly asymmetrical distribution of urban services and uneven access across neighborhoods.[41] According to sociologist Saskia Sassen, these conditions of injustice and exclusion from core social and economic orders go beyond conventional discourses of inequality, implicating networks of systems, institutions, and instruments that operate through the logics of complexity.[42] Well before the 2008 financial crash, interacting systems of land use policies and development patterns have been leading to *increased* segregation by race and class, as well as the concentration and sharp growth of poverty in U.S. cities.[43] These systems are not only social, in terms of policies and services, but also spatial. They manifest in the urban practices of abandonment, lack of investment, impoverished public space, and lack of access to urban rights such as healthy and affordable food.

A growing body of research undertaken by human geographers, social scientists, and anthropologists makes a convincing case for the importance of *social infrastructure* as an essential component of an inclusive and democratic city.[44] Returning to the premise that "infrastructure" is a malleable term assembling things into interrelationships that serve higher-level goals, the idea of what social infrastructure comprises is expansive, and gathers the spaces where social life and public activities occur across public institutions (such as libraries or community centers), commercial establishments (such as coffee shops), recreational spaces, religious spaces, and transit spaces.[45] Beyond fulfilling their instrumental functions, "social infrastructures are necessary ... also for addressing and preventing some of the most pressing concerns of contemporary urban life: countering social isolation, negotiating difference, and creating places for all."[46] In times of environmental disaster, social infrastructure can impact community resilience, mortality, and social stabilization.[47]

The neoliberal playbook of urban redevelopment proves impotent when imagining how social infrastructure, access to needs, and the public realm can be improved without new market-driven housing and commercial development.[48] What this translates to on the ground is that communities living in an area of poverty are systemically disinvested in and neglected by cities, thus exacerbating inequality. In areas where market-based developments do occur, the circuits of capital and the ethos of land as "exchange value" tend to exclude existing residents and can increase spatial injustice, particularly for Black communities.[49]

Through our design work, we speculate on the potential to leverage funding directed toward the improvement of public transportation systems, as well as the space adjacent to transportation structures, as cooperative actors in new distributed socio-spatial assemblages that

Figure 6: Chicago's elevated Green Line through a neighborhood (top); street-level urban condition at the 95th Street Red Line Station (bottom).

aim to increase equitable public life in cities. This work reconceives the space of transit infrastructure as a physical platform that can be appropriated for the assembly of new social infrastructures, by engaging directly with community organizations, cooperatives, local programs associated with schools or with faith-based groups, NGOs, and local entrepreneurs, in order to provide access to a broader variety of urban needs beyond the provision of public mobility, while also facilitating emergent encounters, associations, and adjacencies.

In the city of Chicago, we developed combinatory mapping methods to identify areas in the city that most acutely lack access to the urban rights of access to food, health, and learning, and then identified high-use transit nodes within those neighborhoods that could be explored as prototypes for urban interventions at different scales and intensities.[50] These included spaces adjacent to high-volume bus lines, spaces where the city's elevated "L" line leaves abandoned and disused lands that fragment neighborhoods, and spaces such as the 95th Street Chicago Transit Authority (CTA) Terminal that spans the sunken Dan Ryan Expressway and where the at-grade urban space is poorly conceived, unwelcoming, and unsafe for pedestrians (figure 6).

In this work we think through design as a complex mobilization and assemblage of myriad forces: from the needs of the populations that are connected by and dwell adjacent to these nodes, to the community organizations that could be mobilized as partners in programming activity, to the sources of funding and enterprise that would provide resources for construction and operations, to the institutions and programs that would continue to care for and maintain these spaces and structures over time. The drawings we developed are intended to represent simultaneously the design proposition as a spatial and programmatic matrix, and the allied networked forces and mechanisms that might bring it into being, support it, and sustain it within the city. Proposals are developed typologically in their design elements, yet specifically in their assemblage of local actors, instruments, and urban strategies (figure 7).

The prototype developed for the CTA Green Line Garfield Station in Washington Park offers a lightweight urban model for rail-based transit stations with adjacent transit-owned and operated parking lots and/ or space beneath elevated rail lines (figures 8 & 9). The

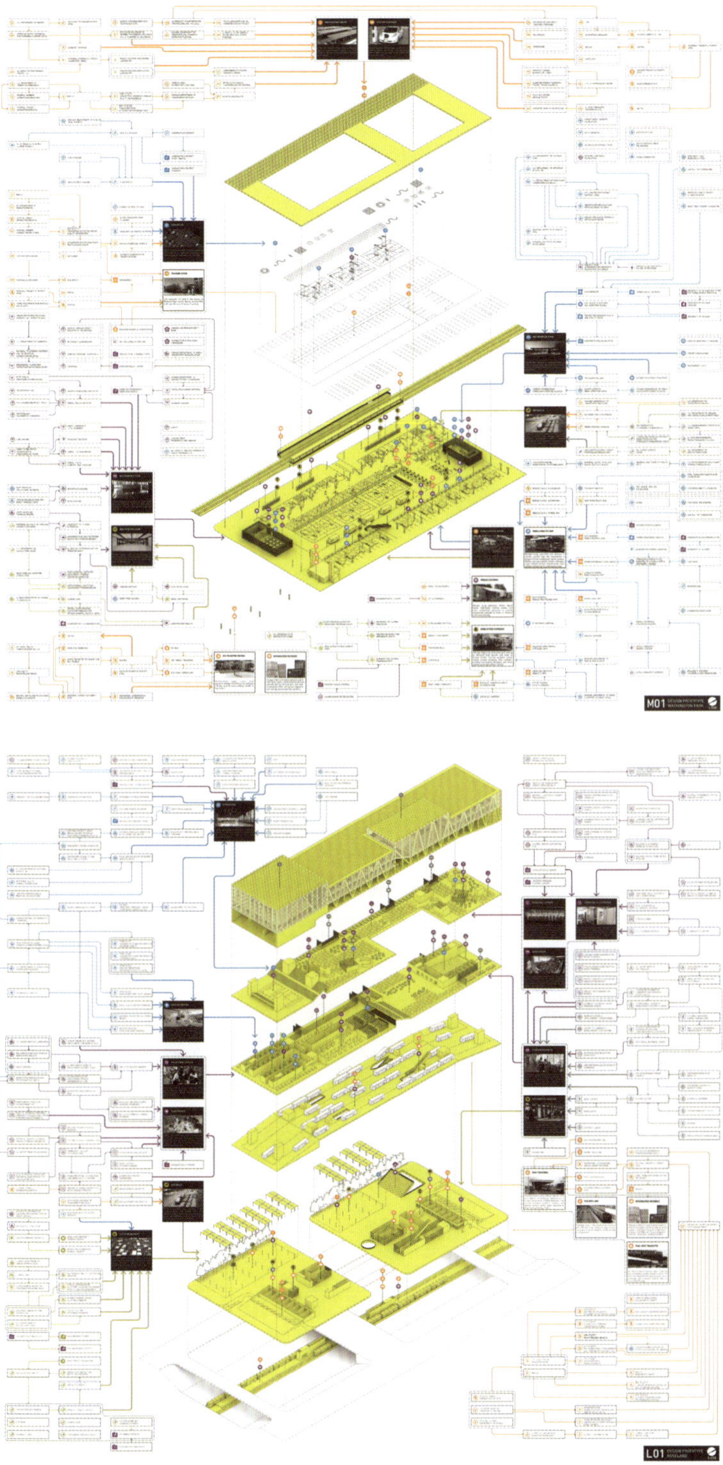

Figure 7: Prototype design proposals: medium intensity prototype at Washington Park / Garfield Station (upper), and high intensity prototype at the CTA 95th Street Terminal in Roseland (lower).

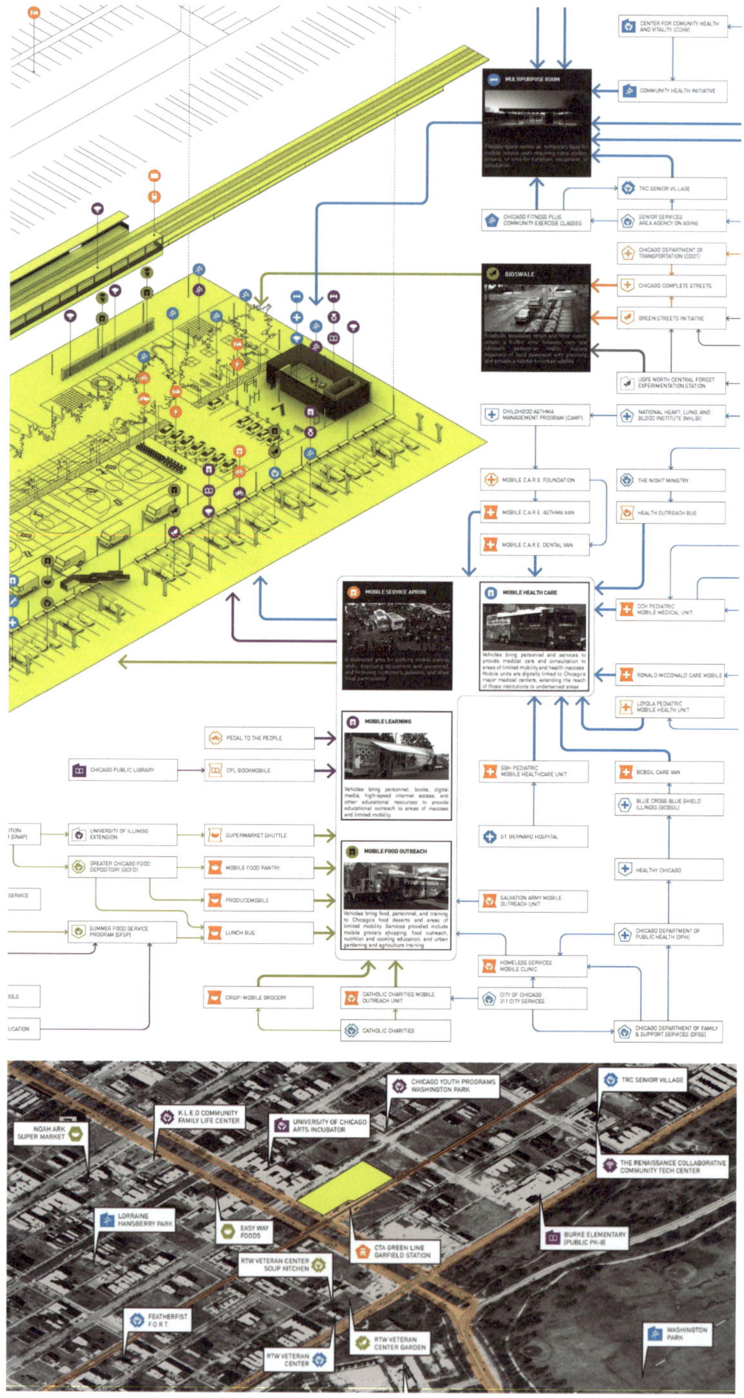

Figure 8: Detail from exploded axonometric of design scenario with networked Access-Enabling Instruments and Actors (top), and detail of the local Agents of Access to food, health, learning, and mobility at the Washington Park / Garfield Station prototype (bottom).

proposal reorganizes these spaces to assemble a mobile and itinerant public infrastructure that takes advantage of alternative spatial programming during times of low commuter use. The architectural elements consist of a perimeter roof structure that defines the street edge and provides shelter; curbside redesign to accommodate bike share, rideshare, and safe waiting; small-scale pavilions for community group-based education, classes, or meeting activities; landscaping for stormwater management and urban biodiversity; and a recodification of the ground plane that can enable mobile service delivery, temporary pop-up events, open-air markets, and play spaces.

In contrast to the "grand central stations" of the early twentieth century, the federally funded freeway programs of the mid-twentieth century, and the market-driven infrastructural developments since the 1990s, this work seeks an alternative model in crossbreeding mobility infrastructure with social infrastructure. This model is not centralized but distributed and multifold; it is not developed by top-down entities that view local communities as merely "stakeholders" but instead through contingent and imperfect collaborations that work in partnership with local groups and mobilize assemblages of multiple sources of funding. It also prioritizes everyday life and the use value of urban space over representation and exchange value. This work is offered not as a singular solution to the complex questions of urban inequality, but as a design-driven thought experiment of viable alternatives and hopeful possibilities.

As New York City embarks on realizing its Fourth Regional Plan, extensive upgrades and redevelopments of its rail and road networks and structures form a significant part of the plan.[51] This presents a timely moment when thinking differently about the role and possibility of these structures to do expanded work to address and even redirect systemic inequality in the city's neighborhoods. It would implicate new thinking from governments, planners, and community members on how to remake the city for its collectivity, and requires of designers a different kind of strategic agility, cooperative action, and imaginary.

A Next Agenda for Infrastructure

We write this chapter during the first peak of the COVID-19 pandemic, when the fragility of bodies, global supply chains, and the country's health infrastructure has

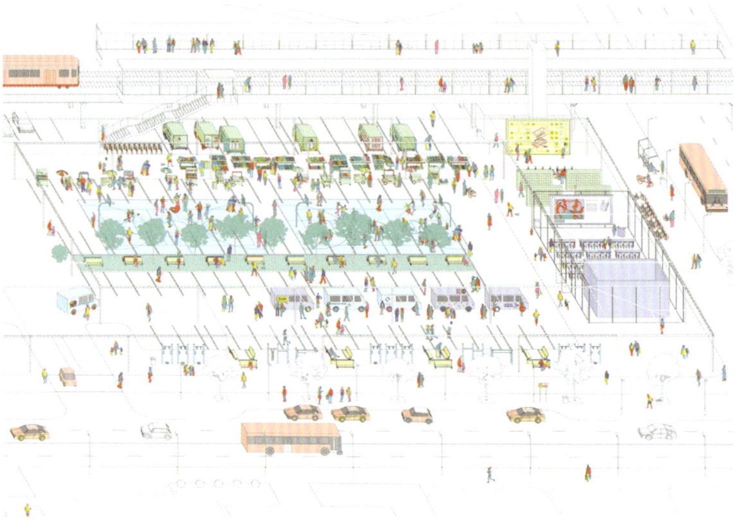

Figure 9: Urban axonometric detail of design scenario for Washington Park / Garfield Station during weekend public market.

become acutely apparent, when often invisible blue-collar workers have been rapidly elevated to the status of "essential workers" but with little improvement to their safety or wellbeing, when statistics show that systemically neglected Black and Latinx populations in the United States are far more vulnerable to serious complications from the disease, and as the killings of George Floyd, Breonna Taylor, and Ahmaud Arbery have reignited the Black Lives Matter movement with national and worldwide calls for systemic reform and an end to racial injustice. A new agenda for infrastructure must be articulated from an activist position to enable social change and an emancipatory alternative.

Because infrastructures can be conceived as relational networks that enable higher goals, a new agenda for infrastructure must reassemble flows, materials, and entities toward the needs and empowerment of communities that have been expelled from and ignored by contemporary and historic systems. Anthropologist Dominic Boyer calls for a "revolutionary infrastructure" that "may not resemble the familiar infrastructures of carbon modernity that currently encompass and enable us."[52] To this we would add that this infrastructure will assemble different actors and elements to produce alternative subjectivities and commons, and in doing so, may not resemble the familiar infrastructures of exploitative neoliberal economics and land market-driven urbanization.

A next agenda for infrastructure would aim to cultivate and "more fruitfully inform livable politics and ontologies in current life worlds" through partial, sometimes flawed, nonharmonious yet exuberant co-habitation, co-constitution, and contingency among humans and other species.[53] This infrastructure might leave aside the purely functionalist dynamics of current discourses of urban ecology to instead embrace a post-romanticist and post-capitalist environmental politics of urban nature.[54]

A next agenda for infrastructure would be conceived and materialized in the context of a changed and continually changing climate, where extreme weather, sea-level rise in coastal cities such as New York City, and the inevitable limits of material resources of the planet will require more pliable, lightweight, and adaptive infrastructures for social, mobility, energy, water, food, and waste systems. This will enable smaller, more localized circuits and exchanges that operate at multiple scales and intensities of built and biotic formation.

A next agenda for infrastructure will not find designers awaiting commissions conceived and funded by centralized sources of capital and power. New dialogues will need to be forged among disciplinary and design experts in collaboration with networks of institutions, organizations, enterprise, and advocates in shaping this agenda and working cooperatively to realize its goals. The flows mediated by public works that emerge from this new agenda will not be limited to management in service of instrumental control but will aim to structure and undergird new staging grounds for more just, heterogeneous, and resilient urban life.

Acknowledgments
The project in Chicago was made possible through seed funding from Alan and Cynthia Berkshire to Taubman College of Architecture and Urban Planning at the University of Michigan through its Research on the City program, funds from the University of Michigan Office of Research, and support by the U.S. Department of Transportation, Region V Center, Nextrans Project No. 163UMY2.2—*any opinions, findings, and conclusions or recommendations expressed in this material are those of the author(s) and do not necessarily reflect the views of the U.S. Department of Transportation.* Thanks to the project design team who assisted in the work: Dan McTavish, Susan Zielinski, Nick Safley, Anthony Pins, Andrew Wald, Komal Anand, and Ya Suo. We also thank Mona El Khafif and Seth McDowell for their editorial comments and suggestions on the chapter.

1
Rosalind Williams, "Infrastructure as Lived Experience," keynote lecture at Landscape Infrastructure Conference, Harvard University Graduate School of Design, March 23–24, 2012, https://www.youtube.com/watch?v=MfjkQjwoVHs.

2
Susan Leigh Star and Karen Ruhleder, "Steps towards an Ecology of Infrastructure," in *Proceedings of the 1994 ACM Conference on Computer Supported Cooperative Work* (New York: Association for Computing Machinery, 1994), 253.

3
William H. Batt, "Infrastructure: Etymology and Import," *Journal of Professional Issues in Engineering* 110, no. 1 (1984): 1; Ashley Carse, "Keyword: Infrastructure: How a Humble French Engineering Term Shaped the Modern World," in *Infrastructures and Social Complexity: A Companion*, ed. P. Harvey, C. B. Jensen, and A. Morita (London: Routledge, 2017), 29.

4
Carse, "Keyword," 31.

5
Batt, "Infrastructure," 2.

6
Carse, "Keyword," 33.

7
Batt, "Infrastructure," 5.

8
Paul N. Edwards, "Infrastructure and Modernity: Force, Time, and Social Organization in the History of Sociotechnical Systems," in *Modernity and Technology*, ed. Thomas J. Misa, Philip Brey, and Andrew Feenberg (Cambridge, MA: MIT Press, 2003), 187.

9
Office of Infrastructure, U.S. Department of Transportation, accessed July 1, 2020, https://www.fhwa.dot.gov/infrastructure/.

10
Carse, "Keyword," 35–36.

11
An incomplete list of design texts focusing on infrastructure would include Pierre Bélanger, *Landscape as Infrastructure: A Base Primer* (Abingdon, Oxon: Routledge, 2017); Neeraj Bhatia, Maya Przybylski, Lola Sheppard, and Mason White / InfraNET Lab, *Coupling: Strategies for Infrastructural Opportunism*, Pamphlet Architecture 30 (New York: Princeton Architectural Press, 2011); Keller Easterling, *The Power of Infrastructure Space* (London: Verso, 2014); Clare Lyster, *Learning from Logistics: How Networks Change Our Cities* (Basel: Birkhäuser, 2016); Kelly Shannon and Marcel Smets, *The Landscape of Contemporary Infrastructure* (Rotterdam: NAi Publishers, 2010); Geoffrey Thün, Kathy Velikov, Colin Ripley, and Dan McTavish, *Infra Eco Logi Urbanism: A Project for the Great Lakes Megaregion* (Zurich: Park Books, 2015).

12
Pierre Bélanger, "Landscape as Infrastructure," *Landscape Journal* 28, no. 1 (2009): 79–95.

13
Kathy Velikov and Geoffrey Thün, "Territorial Infrastructures: Recognizing Politico-environmental Ecologies," in *Infrastructure Space*, ed. Ilka and Andreas Ruby (Berlin: Ruby Press, 2017).

14
Hillary Brown, *Next Generation Infrastructure: Principles for Post-Industrial Public Works* (Washington, DC: Island Press, 2014), 7.

15
Peter Baccini, "Understanding and Designing the Metabolism of Urban Systems," in "Grounding Metabolism," ed. Daniel Ibanez and Nikos Katsiki, *New Geographies* 6 (2014): 28–37. See also Julie Marin's unpublished dissertation, "Circular Economy Transition in Flanders" (PhD diss., Katholieke Universiteit Leuven, 2018).

16
David Orr, foreword to Brown, *Next Generation Infrastructure*, xii.

17
Bélanger, *Landscape as Infrastructure*.

18
See National Association for City Transportation Officials (NACTO), accessed July 1, 2020, https://nacto.org/publications/design-guides/; National Complete Streets Coalition, Smart Growth America, accessed July 1, 2020, https://smartgrowthamerica.org/program/national-complete-streets-coalition/; and Janette Sadik-Khan and Seth Solomonow, *Streetfight: Handbook for an Urban Revolution* (New York: Viking Press, 2016).

19
See for example Bhatia et al., *Coupling*, and Thün et al., *Infra Eco Logi Urbanism*.

20
Stephen Graham and Simon Marvin, *Splintering Urbanism: Networked Infrastructures, Technological Mobilities and the Urban Condition* (London: Routledge, 2001), 11.

21
Whereas these lands are typically understood as abandoned and unproductive, Matthew Gandy identifies them as possessing unique urban biomes that need to be recognized as part of the urban metabolism. See Matthew Gandy, "Cities in Deep Time," in "The Urban Process under Planetary Accumulation by Dispossession," special feature, *City* 22, no. 1 (2018): 102.

22
Jeffrey Brown, "A Tale of Two Visions: Harland Bartholomew, Robert Moses, and the Development of the American Freeway," *Journal of Planning History* 4, no. 1 (2005): 3–32.

23
Raymond A. Mohl, "Stop the Road: Freeway Revolts in American Cities," *Journal of Urban History* 30, no. 5 (July 2004): 674–706. See also Brown, "A Tale of Two Visions," as well as Mark Benton, "'Saving' the City: Harland Bartholomew and Administrative Evil in St. Louis," *Public Integrity* 20, no. 2 (2018): 194–206.

24
Robert Caro, *The Power Broker: Robert Moses and the Fall of New York* (New York: Knopf, 1974).

25
Suzanne Spellen, "The Story of Brooklyn's Grand Stage, the Brooklyn Heights Promenade," *Brownstoner*, January 7, 2019, https://www.brownstoner.com/history/brooklyn-heights-promenade-history-robert-moses-bqe-repair-hezekiah-pierrepont/.

26
Emma G. Fitzsimmons and Winnie Hu, "Fix for a Hated N.Y.C. Highway: How About an $11 Billion Tunnel?," *New York Times*, February 24, 2020, www.nytimes.com/2020/02/24/nyregion/bqe-tunnel.html.

27
Eric Klinenberg, *Palaces for the People: How Social Infrastructure Can Help Fight Inequality, Polarization, and the Decline*

of Civic Life (New York: Broadway Books, 2018), 21–22.

28
W. Symmes Richardson, "The Terminal—The Gate of the City," *Scribner's* 52, no. 4 (1912): 407–409.

29
Ibid., 414.

30
Anthony Raynsford, "Swarm of the Metropolis: Passenger Circulation at Grand Central Terminal and the Ideology of the Crowd Aesthetic," *Journal of Architectural Education* 50, no. 1 (1996): 7.

31
Richardson, "The Terminal," 415.

32
Raynsford, "Swarm of the Metropolis," 9.

33
Samuel O. Dunn, "The Problem of the Modern Terminal," *Scribner's* 52, no. 4 (1912): 416–443.

34
George Baird, *The Space of Appearance* (Cambridge, MA: MIT Press, 1995).

35
Ada Louise Huxtable, "Architecture: How to Kill a City; Ours Is an Impoverished Society That Cannot Pay for the Amenities," *New York Times*, May 5, 1963.

36
Vincent Scully, *American Architecture and Urbanism* (1969; repr., San Antonio, TX: Trinity University Press, 2013), 143.

37
Timothy Mitchell, *Carbon Democracy: Political Power in the Age of Oil* (London: Verso, 2013).

38
Manu Karuka, Empire's Tracks: *Indigenous Nations, Chinese Workers, and the Transcontinental Railroad* (Oakland: University of California Press, 2019).

39
Langdon Winner, "Do Artifacts Have Politics?," *Daedalus* 109, no. 1 (1980): 128.

40
Eric Klinenberg, "Social Infrastructure," *Foreign Policy* (January/February 2017): 76.

41
Geoffrey Thün and Kathy Velikov, "Protean Prototypes: Urban Platforms for Appropriation," *OASE*, no. 96 (2016): 100.

42
Saskia Sassen, *Expulsions: Brutality and Complexity in the Global Economy* (Cambridge, MA: Harvard University Press, 2014).

43
Paul A. Jargowsky, "The Architecture of Segregation: Civil Unrest, the Concentration of Poverty and Public Policy," 2015, The Century Foundation, accessed 8 August 2015, http://apps.tcf.org/architecture-of-segregation.

44
See, for example, research by Eric Klinenberg, Alan Latham, Shannon Mattern, and Helen F. Wilson, among others.

45
Alan Latham and Jack Layton, "Social Infrastructure and the Public Life of Cities: Studying Urban Sociality and Public Spaces," *Geography Compass* 13, no. 7 (2019): 6.

46
Ibid., 2.

47
Eric Klinenberg, *Heat Wave: A Social Autopsy of Disaster in Chicago* (Chicago: University of Chicago Press, 2002).

48
Jason R. Hackworth, *The Neoliberal City: Governance, Ideology, and Development in American Urbanism* (Ithaca: Cornell University Press, 2006).

49
Themis Chronopoulos, "African Americans, Gentrification, and Neoliberal Urbanization: The Case of Fort Greene, Brooklyn," *Journal of African American Studies* 20, nos. 3/4 (2016): 294–322.

50
Thün and Velikov, "Protean Prototypes." See also RVTR, "Projects: Protean Prototypes, Chicago, IL," accessed July 2, 2020, http://www.rvtr.com/projects/protean-prototypes.

51
New York Regional Planning Authority (RPA), *The Fourth Regional Plan*, accessed July 2, 2020, http://fourthplan.org/.

52
Dominic Boyer, "Infrastructure, Potential Energy, Revolution," in *The Promise of Infrastructure*, ed. Nikhil Anand, Akhil Gupta, and Hannah Appel (Durham, NC: Duke University Press, 2018), 221.

53
Donna Haraway, *The Companion Species Manifesto: Dogs, People, and Significant Otherness* (Chicago: Prickly Paradigm Press, 2003), 64.

54
Matthew Gandy, "Urban Nature and the Ecological Imaginary," in *In the Nature of Cities: Urban Political Ecology and the Politics of Urban Metabolism*, ed. Nik Heynen, Maria Kaika, and Erik Swyngedouw (London: Routledge, 2006), 63–74.

From Industrial Land to Public Infrastructure

SHoP Architects

Before there were railways, subways, and junctions, and before there were bridges, tunnels, airports, streets, and all of the other networks and facilities we think of as the city's essential infrastructure—New York had its rivers. The Hudson, giving ready access to the exploitable resources of the upstate hinterlands (and later, after the completion of the Erie Canal, to the continent via the Great Lakes), and the East River, a critical link for both coastwise regional trade and distribution within the city itself. Opening into a singular natural harbor, among the largest and best-protected in the world, this system of waterways begot and sustained the city from its earliest days as an outpost of Dutch colonialism until the mid-twentieth century when, abruptly, containerization displaced break-bulk cargo handling and New York City declined as a maritime port.[1]

With the single exception of the Red Hook Terminal, which is often threatened by plans for redevelopment but still in operation today, none of New York City's pier facilities could be adapted for use by the new container cranes, ships, and expansive handling and storage yards that increasingly became the norm for global trade through the 1960s and 1970s.[2] The ensuing abandonment and neglect of Manhattan and Brooklyn's riverfronts is a well-rehearsed story; one that parallels the contemporaneous fate of a host of other industrial infrastructures throughout the city such as its railyards. Absent from their original, industrial animus, increasingly throttled by highways, and suffering as well from the collapse of both transatlantic liners and local waterborne transportation, the city's piers were largely repurposed for the type of non-maritime uses suitable for an undesirable edge (tow lots, sanitation, electrical stations) or simply gated off and forgotten by local authorities.

Where those chain-link fences could be breached, however, the public increasingly made a case for a radical new use: recreation. This portent of the current state of the waterfront could be seen early at locations such as the Greenwich Village piers or, twenty blocks south along the condemned viaduct of the West Side Highway, on the expanse of World Trade Center excavation debris that would soon be developed as Battery Park City, at a guerrilla urban amenity known as The Beach. There, and at hundreds of smaller, less well-known but equally opportunistic points around the city, the once-working waterfront began to be reborn as a network of informal sites for leisure.

The East River Waterfront Park and Promenade, a master planning and design commission that SHoP Architects won through an open competition in 2004, is a product of the formalization of that new use (figure 10). With the ongoing work to transform the entire Hudson River shore as an interconnected series of landscapes for play and relaxation, as well as the recent completion of the Brooklyn Bridge Park directly across the East River in Brooklyn, that project represents the codification at the city scale of formerly industrial waterfronts successfully reborn as an infrastructure of recreational public spaces. Each of these projects was instantiated and moved forward by city officials during the three-term mayoralty of Michael Bloomberg from 2002 through 2013.[3] SHoP's park was a component of an overall vision for the city during those years that focused on greening and non-automotive mobility. The transformation included the calming and pedestrianization of streets, the implementation of bike sharing and the establishment of a network of dedicated paths, as well as the controversial plan, not yet implemented, to significantly reduce car traffic in Manhattan through a program of congestion pricing.[4]

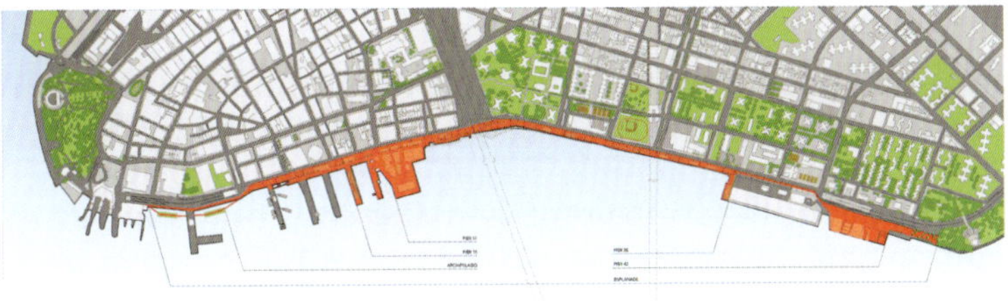

Figure 1: East River Waterfront Master Plan
The East River Waterfront master plan comprises 14,000,000 square feet of public space along 1.5 miles of Manhattan riverfront.

Bloomberg-era priorities were generative in our design for the area, which comprises 14 million square feet of new public terrain, as evident in its ambition to achieve a more livable city as well as the prominence of circulation for bicycles, runners, and pedestrians throughout. SHoP sought as well to ensure the utility of this new resource by including a suite of "everyday" amenities, such as dog runs, restrooms, and public exercise-machine stations. These amenities were installed at strategic locations in the liminal space beneath the elevated structure of the four-lane FDR Drive that continuously defines the landward edge of the site (figure 2). Programs inhabit the space beneath the highway opportunistically, frequently taking advantage of its broad cover for shade or protection from the elements. Our intention was not to obscure but to highlight the strong urban feature that so decidedly marks this place as an example of a new urban landscape typology native to our century—in contrast to the French, English, or Olmstedian norms seen in parks throughout New York City (figure 3).

Figure 2: East River Waterfront, dog run. Specialized sites provide everyday amenities tuned to the specific needs of each neighborhood abutting the park.

Program selection and placement were fine-tuned to the specific needs of each adjacent neighborhood. SHoP learned and assessed these priorities through a protracted and fruitful engagement with dozens of civic agencies and grassroots groups representing the great variety of communities situated along the park's 1.5-mile run from Wall Street to the Lower East Side. Public consultation also shaped the commercial programming of the East River Waterfront, including sites for dining and shopping, a feature we felt was critical to maintain the dynamism of the new park through different seasons and times of day (figure 4). We welcomed the inclusion of those ordinary programs to maintain an overarching sense of utility in the park, seeing them as features that would both suit what the city had so quickly become—a global capital of leisure and consumption[5]—and honor, in the era of the service economy, the quotidian nature of the transshipment work that once took place there.

Those factors all come together at Pier 15, completed in 2011, the first of the special-use areas in our East River plan (figure 5). The design took advantage of an existing zoning condition that allowed for public occupation on two levels—a legacy of the nearly forgotten elevated waterside viewing pavilions that punctuated the activities of the port at this and several other locations in Manhattan in the late nineteenth through early twentieth century. Pier 15 works to balance those traditions. It serves as a working pier, at present a berth for several ships operated by Hornblower Cruises, with the ground level also giving access to the cruise-line offices, simple visitor services, and, at the far end, a restaurant that activates the distant pier head with the combined press of both tourist and Wall Street lunchtime crowds. Above, there is an unprogrammed open space, centered on the planted roofs of the structures below. Dual means of access, a broad ramp, and a smaller, somewhat more secretive stair suspended over the river connect back to the promenade and continue in their variety its spirit of purposeful ambling.

In its program, and the infrastructural air of its concrete and steel structure, Pier 15 reflects its exact position on the sliding scale of urban needs that defines the many public uses of the park and determined the design of each. Its doubled nature was intended to reflect the demands of its location, just south of the intensely touristed blocks of South Street Seaport and just north of the city's major public ferry hub at Pier 11, which today offers not only dramatically scaled-up service to points in Manhattan, Brooklyn, Queens, and the Bronx, but also regional boats to New Jersey (and, seasonally, as far as Massachusetts). It needed to be a way-station for tourists, but also a place that New Yorkers would seek out and use (figure 6).

About a mile north, Pier 35 was shaped by the popular demands of its very different neighborhood. There, representatives of the Chinatown community expressed a desire for a waterfront-specific, all-ages educational component, resulting in the installation of a restorative tide-pool ecosystem and observatory known as Mussel Beach, as well as open grounds on which group exercises, such as morning tai chi, might take place (figure 7). With the addition of a monumental planted screen to shield it from an adjacent warehouse (beyond the bounds of the

Figure 3: East River Waterfront, rail seating. High seating and a wide, flat rail invite intensive use by lunchtime crowds.

Figure 4: East River Waterfront, restaurant pavilion. Industry Kitchen, a popular restaurant and bar, occupies a purpose-built pavilion that embraces the structure of the elevated FDR Drive.

Figure 5: East River Waterfront, Pier 15. View from promenade. The structure on Pier 15 combines spaces for leisure with the facilities necessary to serve continued use as a berth for tour boats and pleasure craft.

park), and a series of hanging loveseat swings (another strategy to activate the extremities of the pier), Pier 35 was shaped one-to-one as an infrastructural reflection of its neighborhood's specific needs (figure 8).

After completing the master plan and working for some time to realize the park under its city contract, SHoP was also hired by the owners of the South Street Seaport, based on the strength of our relationships with local stakeholders. This relic of eighteenth-century Manhattan fabric had been forgotten, rediscovered, preserved, then reborn in the 1980s in the festival marketplace mode. Among several projects in the area, including the renovation of the historic Tin Building (once home to the storied Fulton Fish Market), SHoP was asked to replace the maligned pavilion on Pier 17 that had been raised in 1983 by James Rouse. The project gave SHoP the opportunity to extend creative control of the East River Waterfront design through what might otherwise have become a jarring commercial ellipsis. Paving, planting, seating, and rail details are continuous now across the publicly and privately owned sectors—allowing SHoP to reconfirm the respectful introduction of waterfront play into what was once so decidedly a domain of work, and connecting the network of waterfront public space infrastructure that now nearly bounds the entirety of Manhattan Island.

Figure 6: East River Waterfront. Pier 15. Lower level seating. Visitors take advantage of the shade at a step-down to the river.

Figure 7: East River Waterfront. Pier 35. View from promenade. Fine-tuned to the needs of its Chinatown neighborhood, Pier 35 balances a multitude of uses.

Figure 8: East River Waterfront, Pier 35. Swing seating. Activating the pier head is a proven strategy for creating vibrant public infrastructure along the water's edge.

Completed in 2019, Pier 17 leverages a broad mix of uses to create a focal point for the park and an all-hours destination of value to tourists and New Yorkers alike (figure 9). On the ground level, elevated above the post-Superstorm Sandy floodplain, the open pavilion is occupied by new shops and restaurants, and set back from the water's edge to allow free public passage. Above, two commercial floors (home now to ESPN offices and studios) are topped by a public park that hosts events ranging from ice skating to fashion shows to pop concerts. The frank steel structure of the whole is wrapped by an operable channel-glass facade that evokes the gray-green hues of the river; select panels slide down to provide wind protection as necessary to the open spaces of the ground floor. A wide notch in the pier end, straddled by the outboard edge of the building, allows the river into the covered spaces. An early plan to accommodate embarkation in that slip was not carried out, but the building retains a hybrid sense of infrastructural utility. It increasingly serves as a gantry on which a series of recreational and performance-driven

Figure 9: East River Waterfront, Pier 17. View from promenade. Evoking the architecture of the East River's industrial era, Pier 17 is home to a wide variety of retail, dining, workplace, and entertainment uses.

substructures are mounted and remounted as suits the clients' needs (figure 10).

In the sixteen years since receiving the first commission for the park, SHoP has completed two other major projects along the East River, each of which seeks to reflect and enhance the new identity of that increasingly urbane waterway. Our master plan for the Domino Sugar site in Brooklyn's Williamsburg neighborhood hinged on our knowledge of city processes to increase the available public space by 60 percent, adding several acres to the popular new park that now borders the water there, while contributing significantly to that neighborhood's stock of both market-rate and affordable housing. Across the river in Manhattan, the firm's American Copper Buildings dramatically signpost an adjacent busy ferry stop (figure 11). The ground plan of the complex is optimized to direct foot traffic across the site to reach that lively new access point.

Work at a third major site, underway as of September 2020, will cement the transformation of the East River waterfront at a much greater scale, and confirm the role of SHoP in helping to prepare urban shores for the way we live today. In Long Island City, Queens, the Riverlinc project will adapt a 6-acre area of industrial riverfront opposite the southern end of Roosevelt Island and bound on the landward side by Vernon Boulevard; immediately adjacent, in the area that was once slated for the future Amazon HQ2, SHoP is leading the effort to integrate an additional 20-plus acres with multiple stakeholders into

Figure 10: East River Waterfront, Pier 17 Head.
A wide, covered slip in the end of Pier 17 was originally intended as a maritime berth.

a single master plan that puts the preservation of public access to the river as its shared and highest goal. The architecture of this new neighborhood, centered on the ingress of the river known as Anable Basin, will comprise a diversity of infrastructures for living, working, and the particular forms of play that New Yorkers have now come to expect from such locales.

In the spirit of all of the waterfront work the firm has engaged in along the East River and elsewhere, and reflecting the focus and discoveries of the Broadway Junction studio, SHoP understands that developments like Riverlinc in Queens will not be complete if they become only places to live, work, and play. Sites along the water's edge, atop railyards, and underneath highway overpasses—where the rigor of the city grid is broken by centuries-long patterns of functional use—must also succeed in realizing something more subtle and rare, and far more likely to be overlooked: the return of a sense of infrastructural utility to the site, and the leveraging their native assets and location to serve in silent support of city life.

Figure 11: American Copper Buildings. View from ferry landing. The distinctive form of the American Copper Buildings serves as a landmark on the city's network of public ferries.

1
Marc Levinson. "Container Shipping and the Decline of New York, 1955–1975." *Business History Review* 80, no. 1 (2006): 49–80. doi:10.1017/S0007680500080983.

2
Ibid.

3
"Mayor Bloomberg Announces Approval of Development That Will Allow for Expansion and Funding of BBP" *The City of New York Office of the Mayor*. (July 31, 2013). https://www.brooklynbridgepark.org/press/mayor-bloomberg-announces-approval-of-development-that-will-allow-for-expansion-and-funding-of-brooklyn-bridge-park.

4
"New York City Mobility Needs Assessment: 2007–2030." *PlaNYC 2030*. June 12, 2007. Accessed September 27, 2020. http://www.nyc.gov/html/planyc2030/downloads/pdf/tech_report_transportation.pdf.

5
Karrie Jacobs. "The Rise of New York's New Leisure Waterfront." *Curbed NY*. (August 31, 2018). Accessed September 27, 2020. https://ny.curbed.com/2018/8/31/17797174/nyc-parks-waterfront-architecture-design-brooklyn-bridge.

Infrastructural Intracultural Hub

Student Team
Darcy Engle
Samuel Johnson
Christopher Weimann

Instructor
Matthew Jull

Infrastructural Intracultural Hub negotiates the tension between an expanding city and a neighborhood in need of re-contextualization by connecting a series of existing parks, empty/vacant spaces, and rail infrastructure to create a new "Central Park" cultural hub for East New York. The project acts as an incubator of activity and provides a network of multi-scale spaces within which the community can utilize and develop its cultural capital. An array of cultural, commercial, and educational buildings, including a market, theater, performing arts school, and city offices (human resources), is tied together through a landscape of informal performance and gathering spaces, and a circulation system prioritizing neighborhood-scale pedestrian movement.

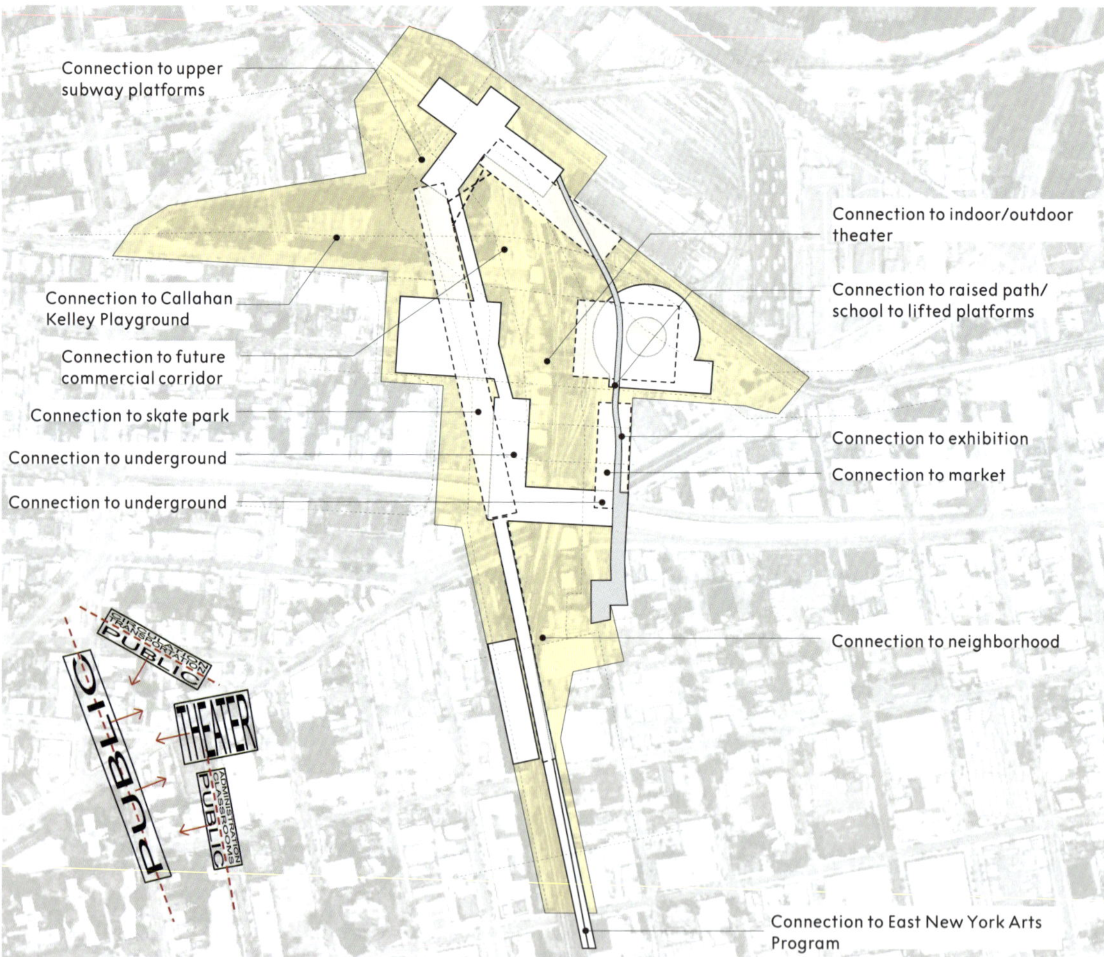

Site plan and parti diagram showing key urban and programmatic features

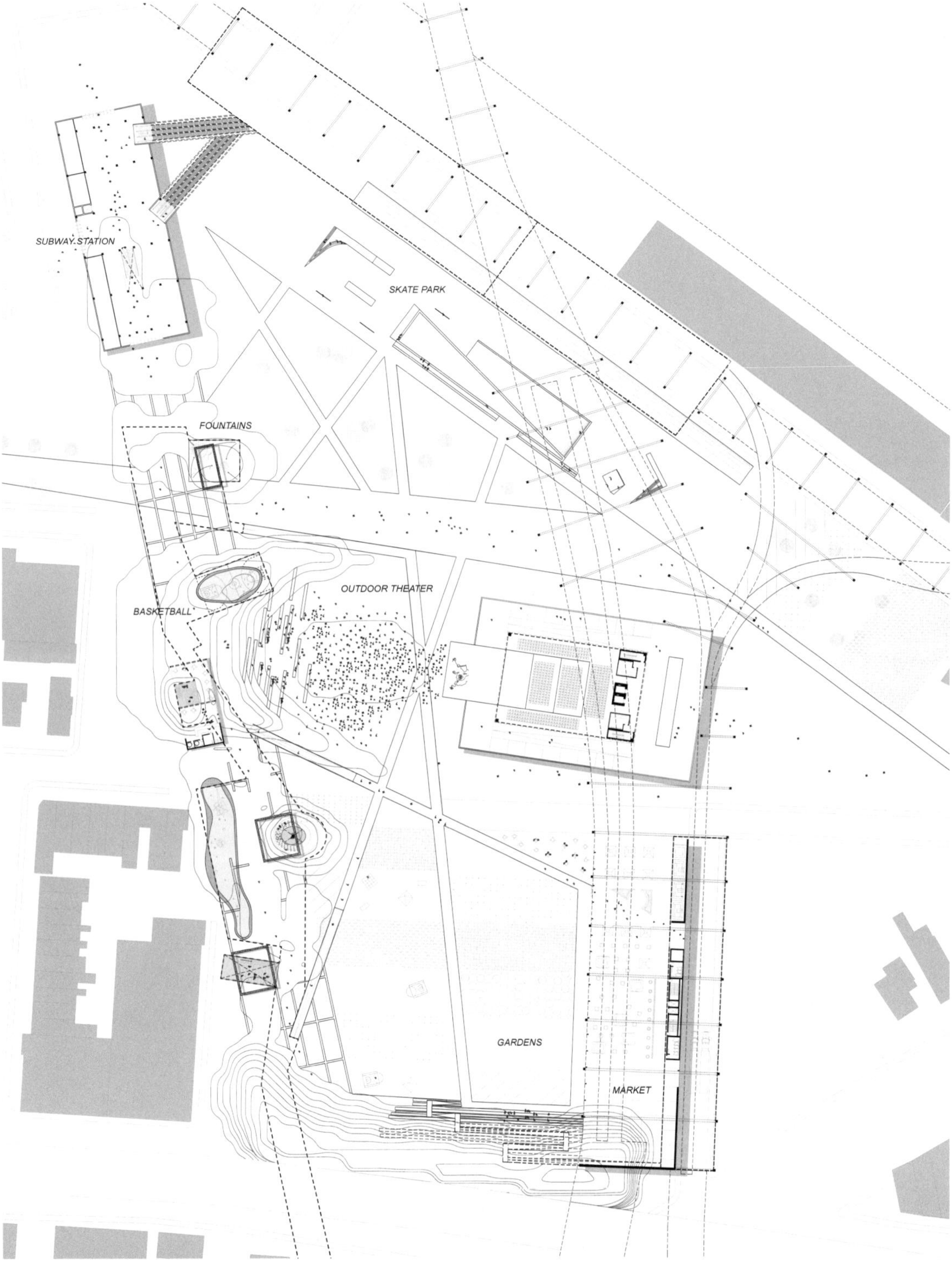

Ground floor building plan

1:200 model, "Infrastructural Intracultural Hub"

Hip and Hop

Student Team
Monisha Nasa
Matthew Reger

Instructor
Matthew Jull

Hip and Hop aims to redress the panoply of physical barriers in the urban fabric around Broadway Junction by re-configuring the existing transportation hub into a multi-functional ordering device. The primary office program, efficiently organized as a linear array along Broadway avenue, is intersected by a series of larger and more flexible education, performance, recreation, and circulation elements. By re-conceptualizing pedestrian movement, the project not only creates a strong urban identity for arts education, but also increases community visibility, interaction, communication, and safety.

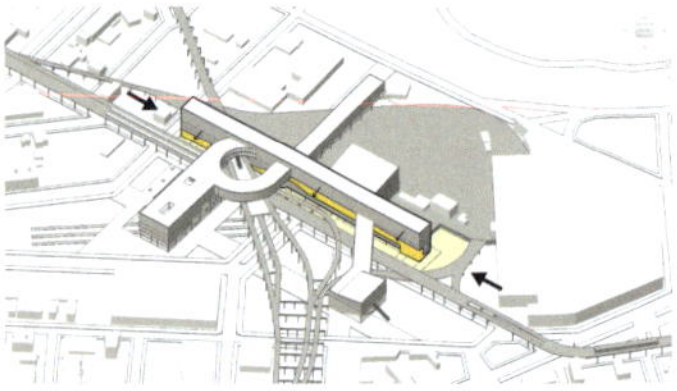

Learning space

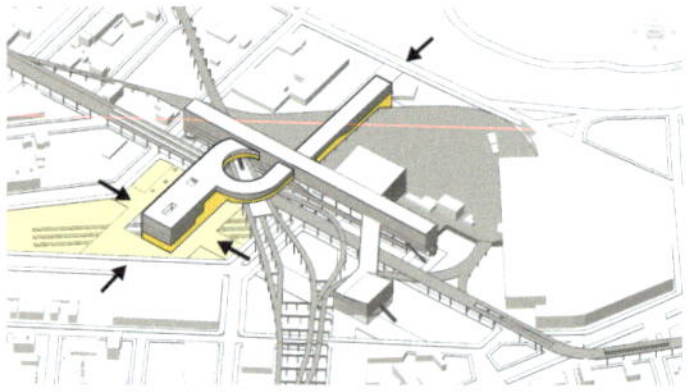

Practice space

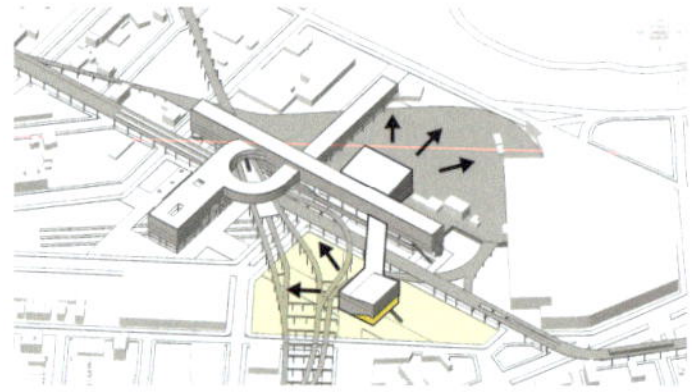

Performance space

Site analysis map

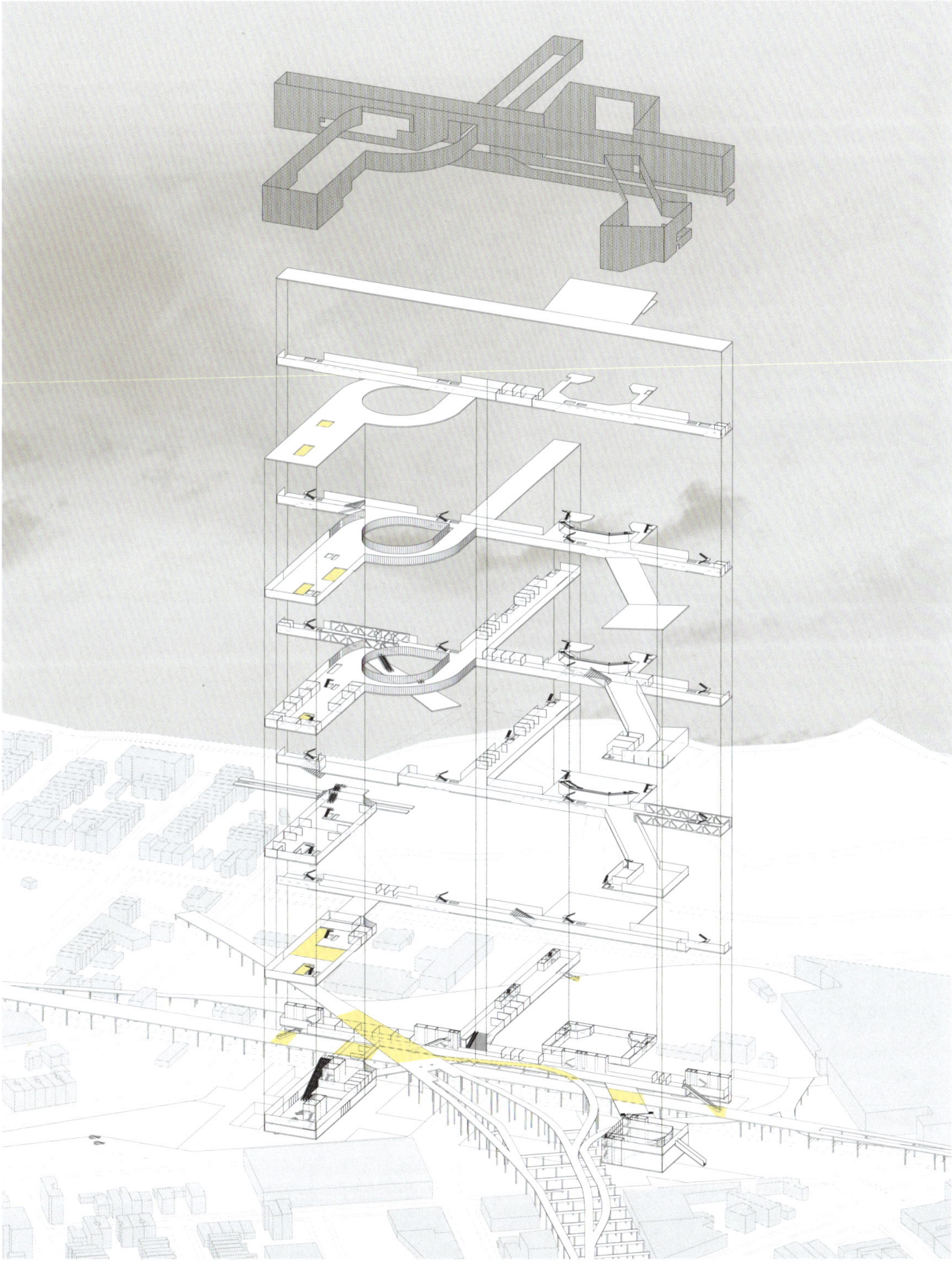

Delayered isometric drawing showing programmatic distribution across site

Interior perspective view of ground floor public atrium

Perspective view down Broadway alongside main program bar

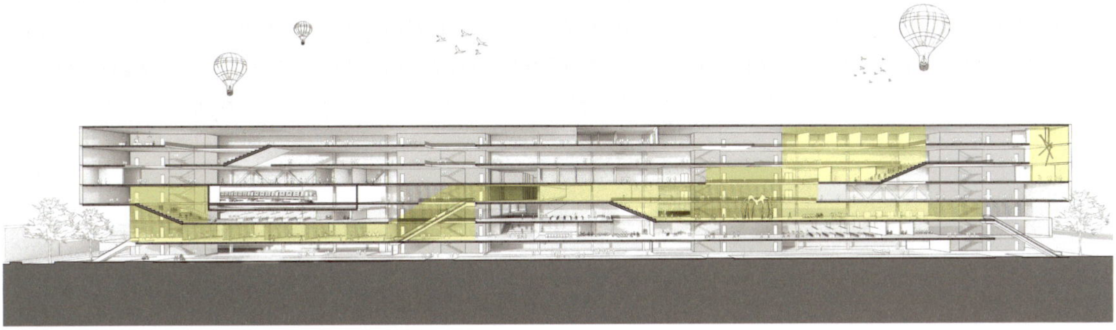

Longitudinal section showing performing arts school woven through HRA office space

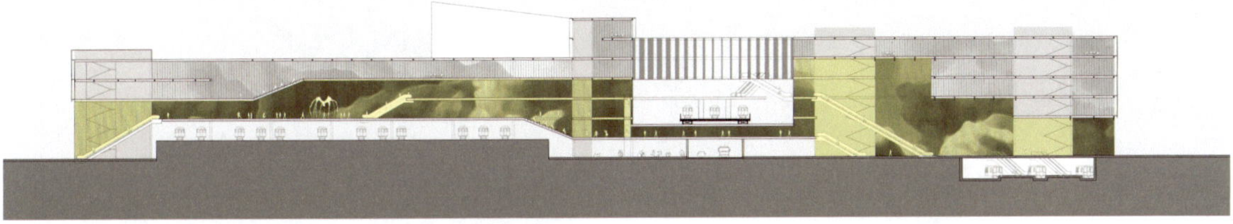

Longitudinal section through contiguous multi-level public atrium

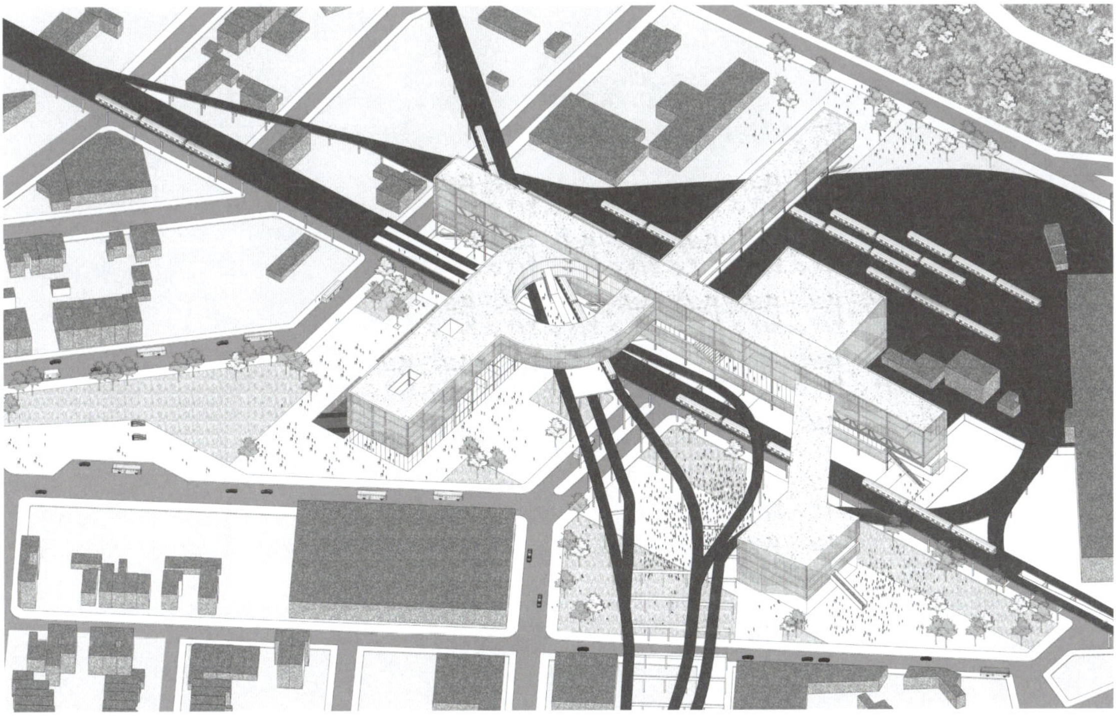

Isometric aerial view of site

1:1000 model, "Hip-Hop Urbanism"

1:200 model, "Candy Campus"

1:200 model, "Candy Campus"

Candy Campus

Student Team
Weiran Jing
Samantha Kokenge

Instructor
Mona El Khafif

Candy Campus re-imagines Broadway Junction as a field condition of typological building units, each permutation generated by parametric inputs such as FAR, and organized about the site via a multi-level system of paths. While the campus is open to the public at ground level, the individual building masses housing the HRA offices are also connected to nearby rooftops through an elevated network of public platforms and bridges. Embedded within the building masses are special "candy" programs: unique spatial moments designed to enhance the core office program and encourage community life.

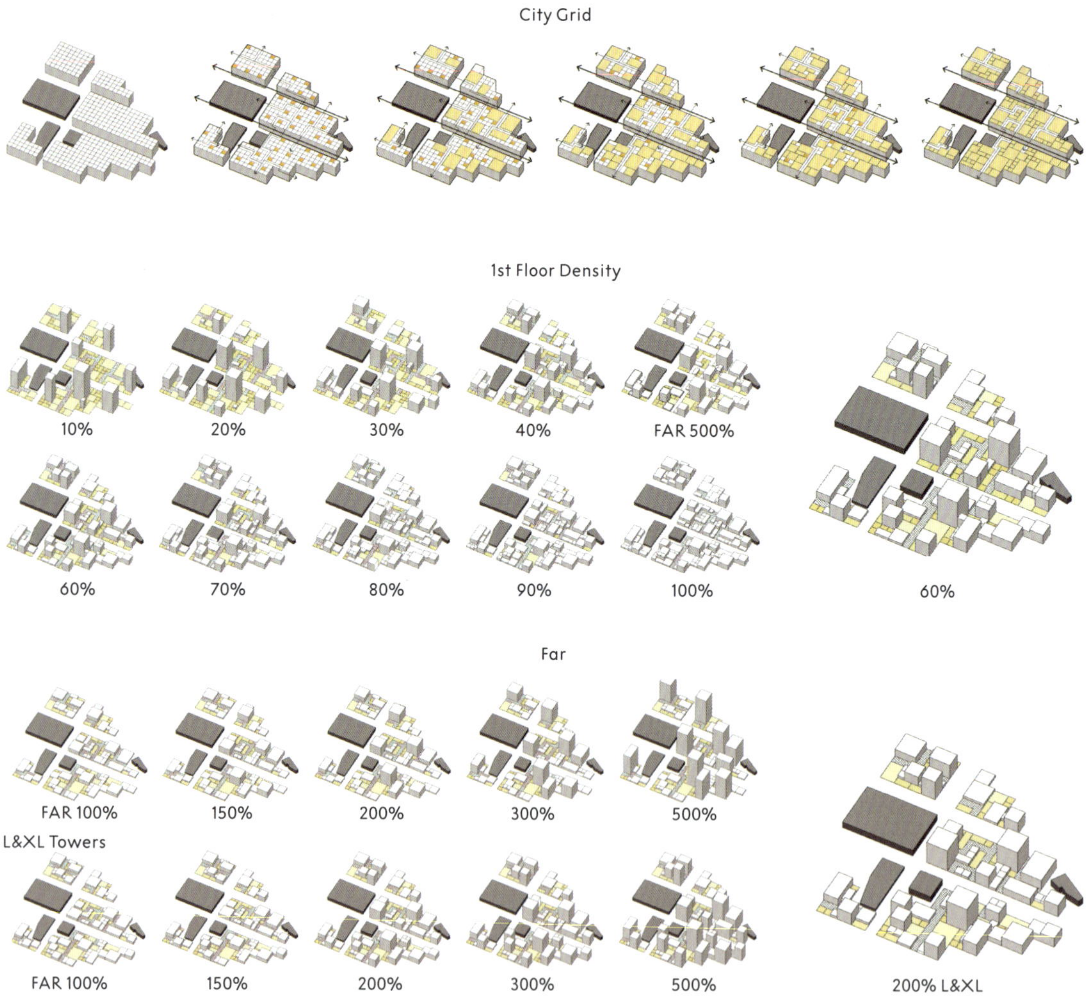

Typological diagram illustrating parametrically derived urban fabric permutations

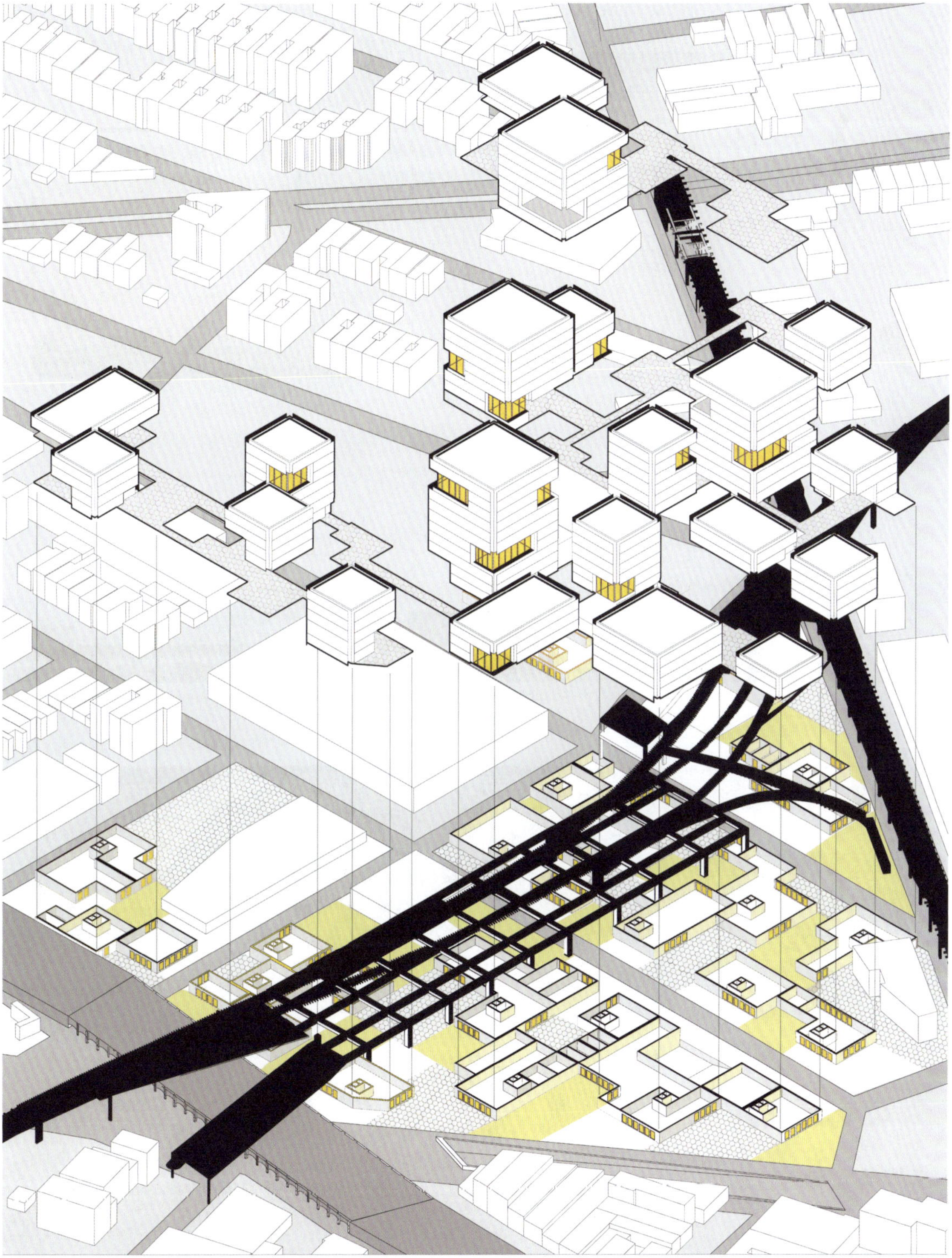

Exploded site isometric drawing showing distribution of campus block typologies

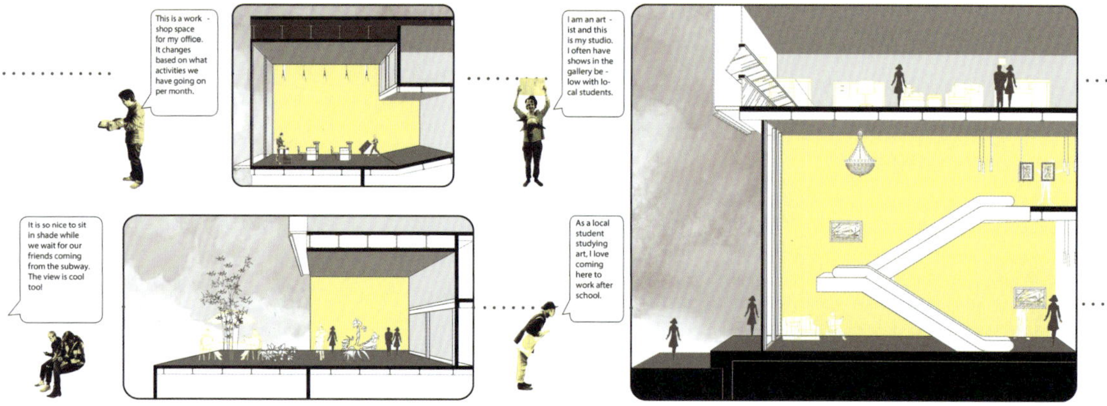

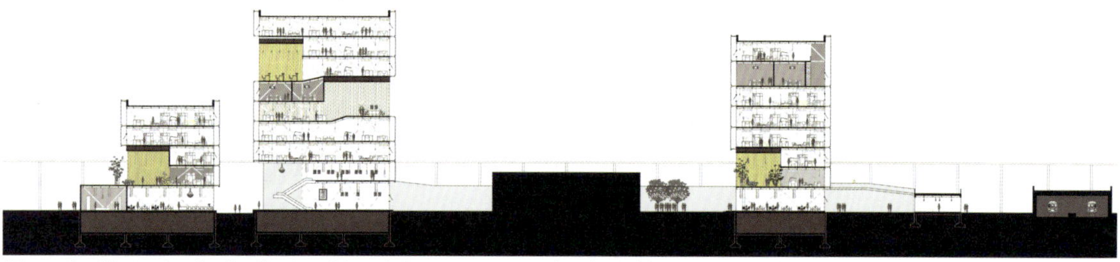

Site section illustrating the distribution of "candy" programming within the field of HRA office blocks

Night perspective scene showing temporally activated public space

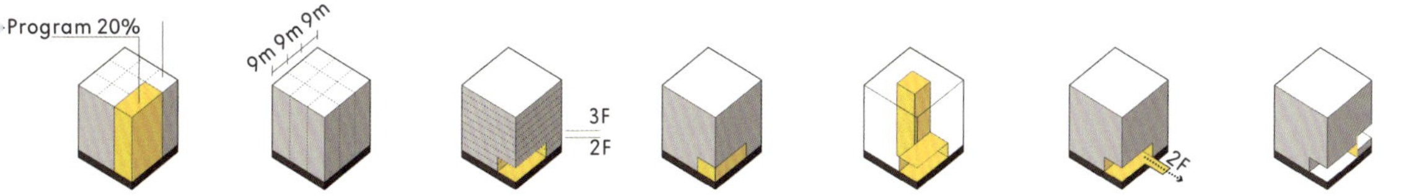

Rule 1
Void is 20%
of the tower

Rule 2
Void uses the
9Mx9M grid

Rule 3
Void is two
floors high

Rule 4
Void touches only
two facades

Rule 5
Void connects
to the core

Rule 6
2nd floor void links
to public circulation

Rule 7
Voids join through
a line, not a point

Ground floor site plan showing distribution of building masses

Five-Minute City

Student Team
Jing Huang
Sihan Lai
Mengzhe Ye

Instructor
Mona El Khafif

Five-Minute City develops a methodology of urban analysis and place-making based upon a temporal interpretation of Guy Debord's Dérive map. Here, the psycho-geographical "Five-Minute City" radius is generated not only by physical distance, but also by the compressive effect of deliberately curated building densities and street activation schemes. The proposal is centered around a re-articulated subway system, communal farmers market, assembly space, and multi-level network of pedestrian ramps which collectively generate an array of radiating urban corridors: connecting clusters of HRA offices, improving the infrastructural systems, and containing a variety of housing, hotel, and retail spaces.

Film reel storyboards illustrating the density of urban activity and space along radial walks

Concept dérive map illustrating the five-minute radius of Broadway Junction

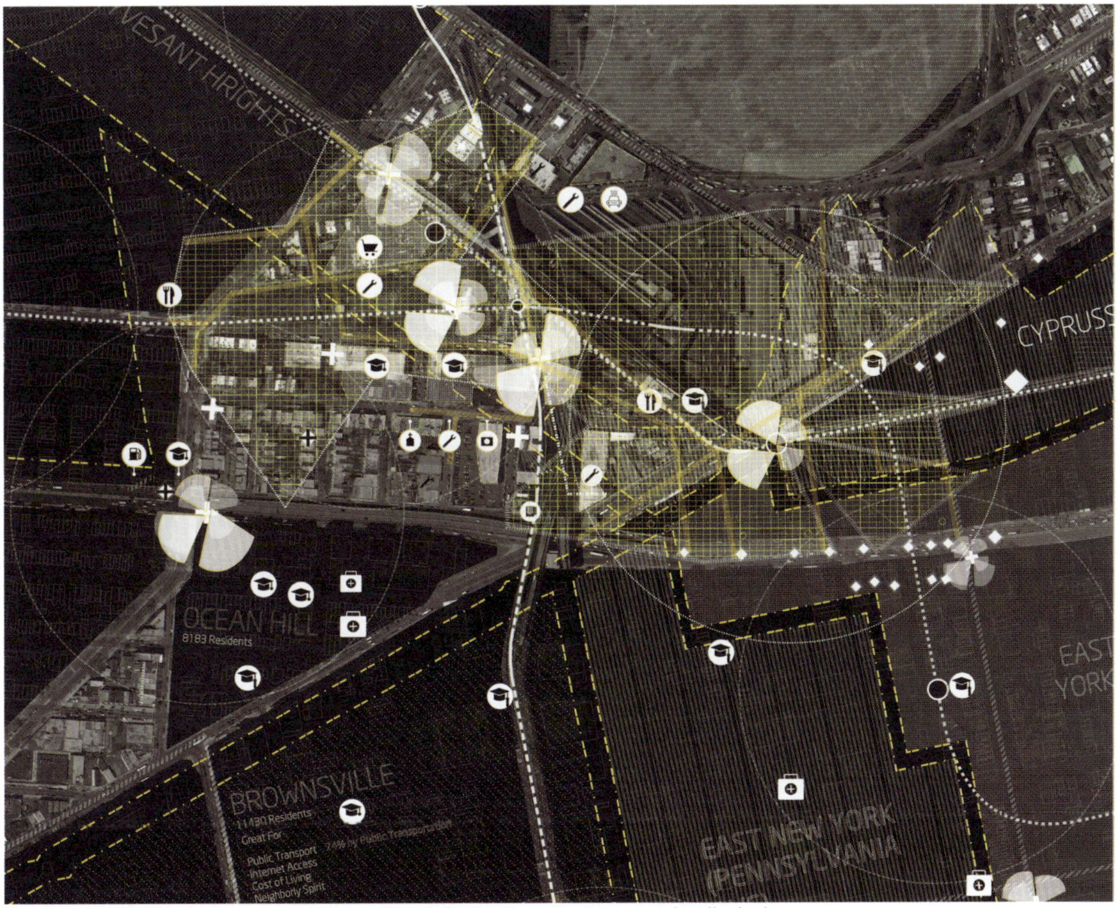

Site map showing nearby urban amenities and their radiating five-minute view and walk-sheds

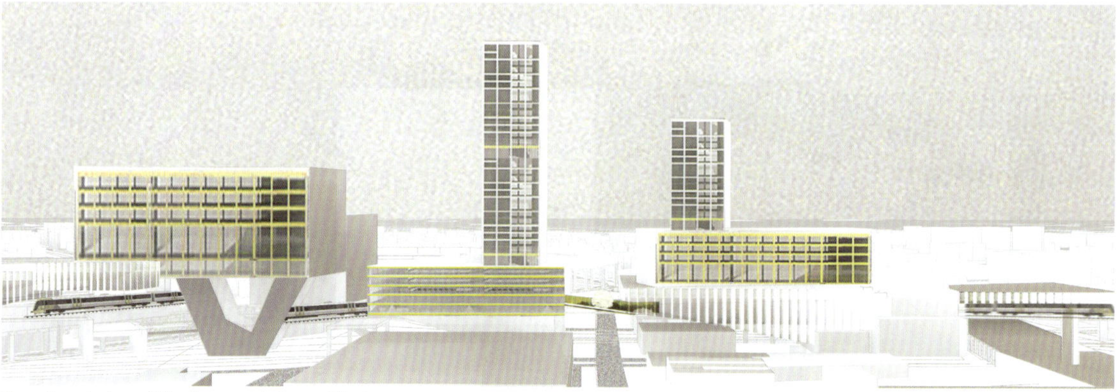

Elevational view of the three main tower blocks

Key site features

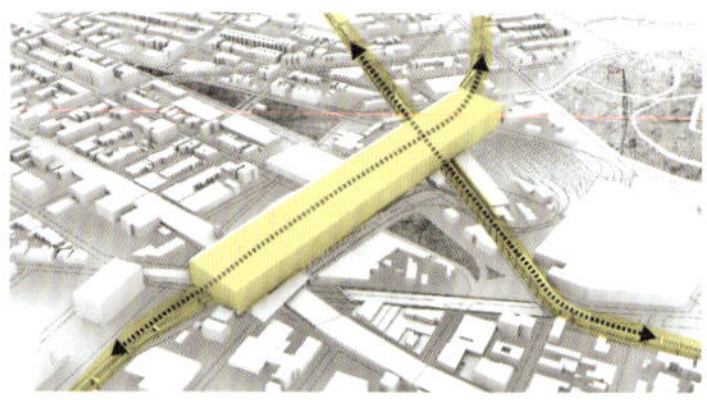

Primary transit connection

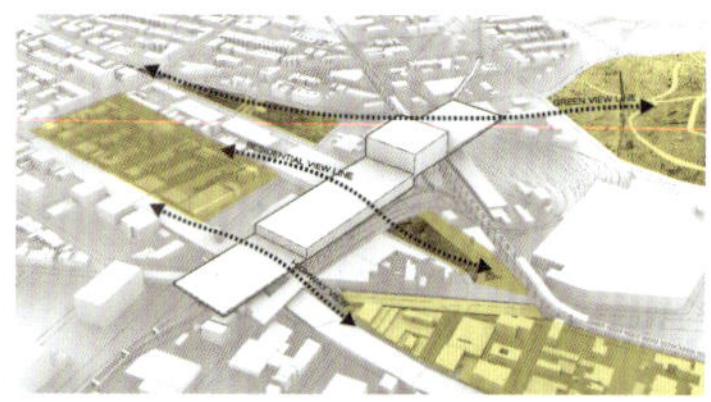

Transverse view corridors

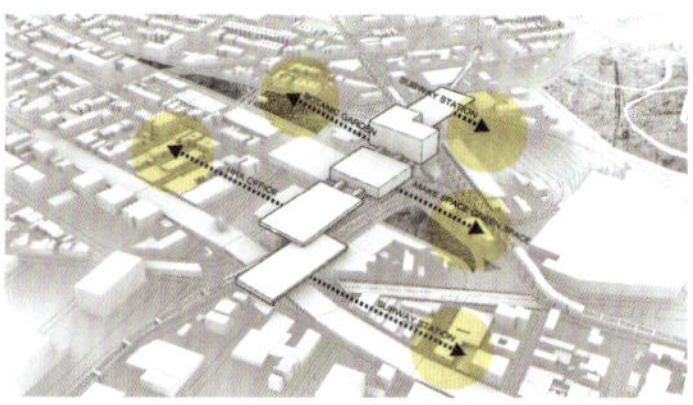

Programmatic distribution

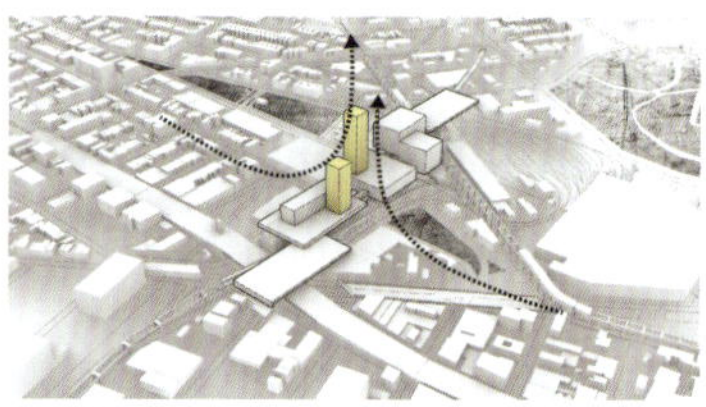

Building massing

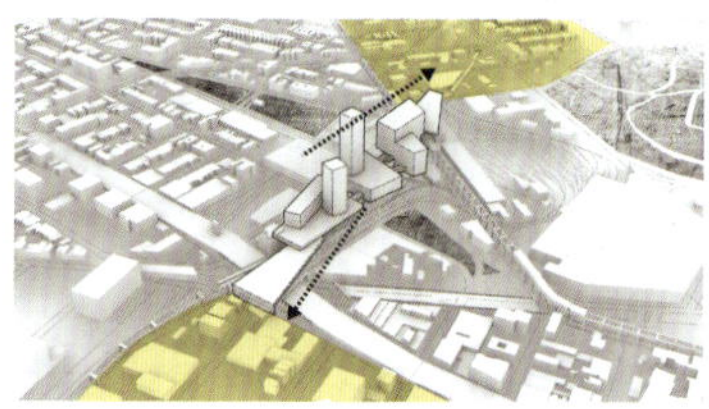

Tower orientation

Perspective view of office hub towers at night

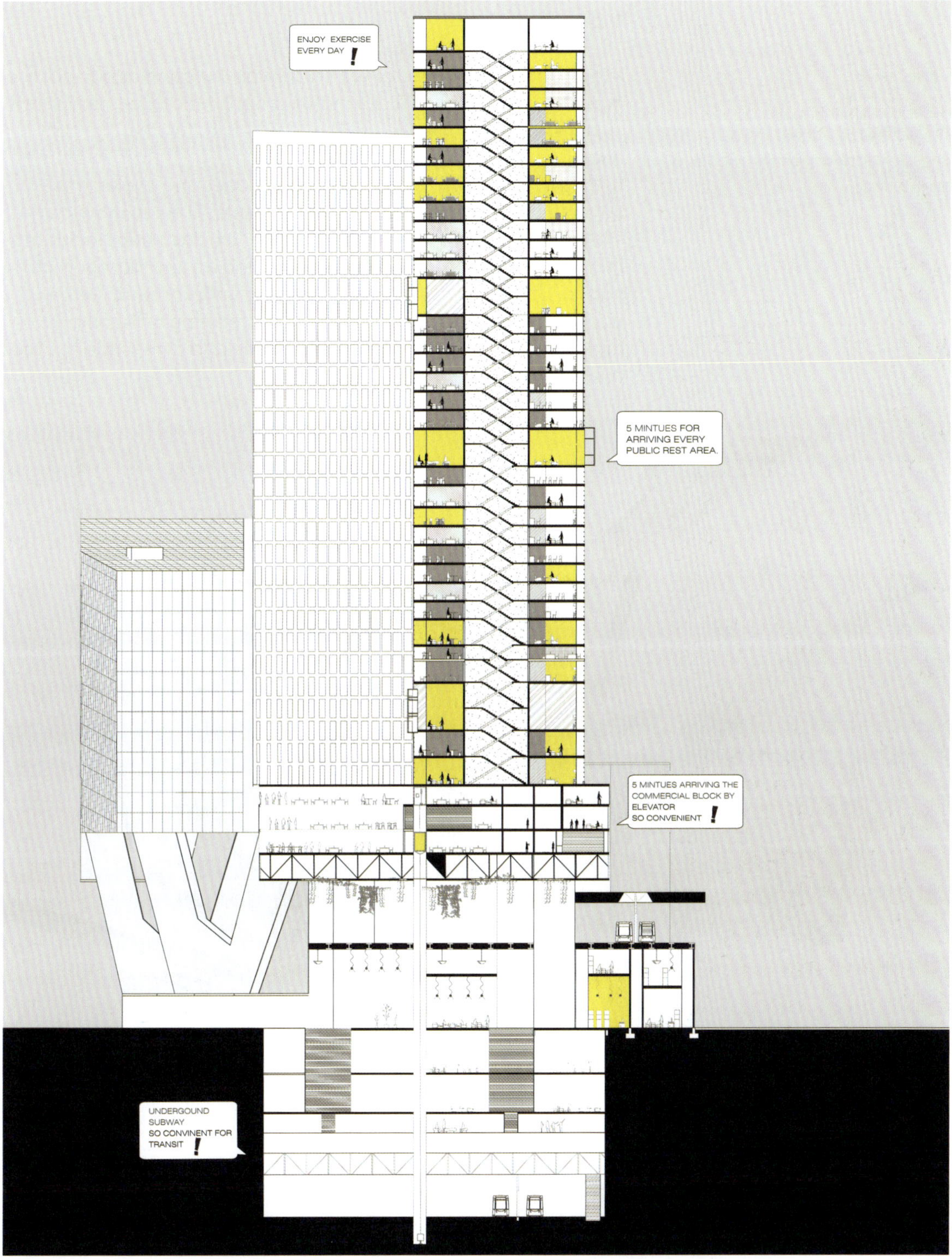

Cross-section of tower, including HRA office hub, public programming, and subterranean transit infrastructure

Make_Play_Die

Student Team
Nicholas Grimes
Hutchins Landfair
Sherry Ng

Instructor
Mona El Khafif

Make_Play_Die re-imagines Broadway Junction as a tripartite massing consisting of three major programmatic centers, each occupying a building block. The first block, "Make," reconnects the site to the industrial zone south of Atlantic Avenue through the establishment of makerspaces and cooperative housing for area businesses and residents. The second block, "Play," adds community amenities to the transit hub, including HRA offices, a library, supermarket, and an underground bath house. The third block, "Die," pairs an underground columbarium and research center with a performing arts complex, making end-of-life services sustainable and accessible to area residents.

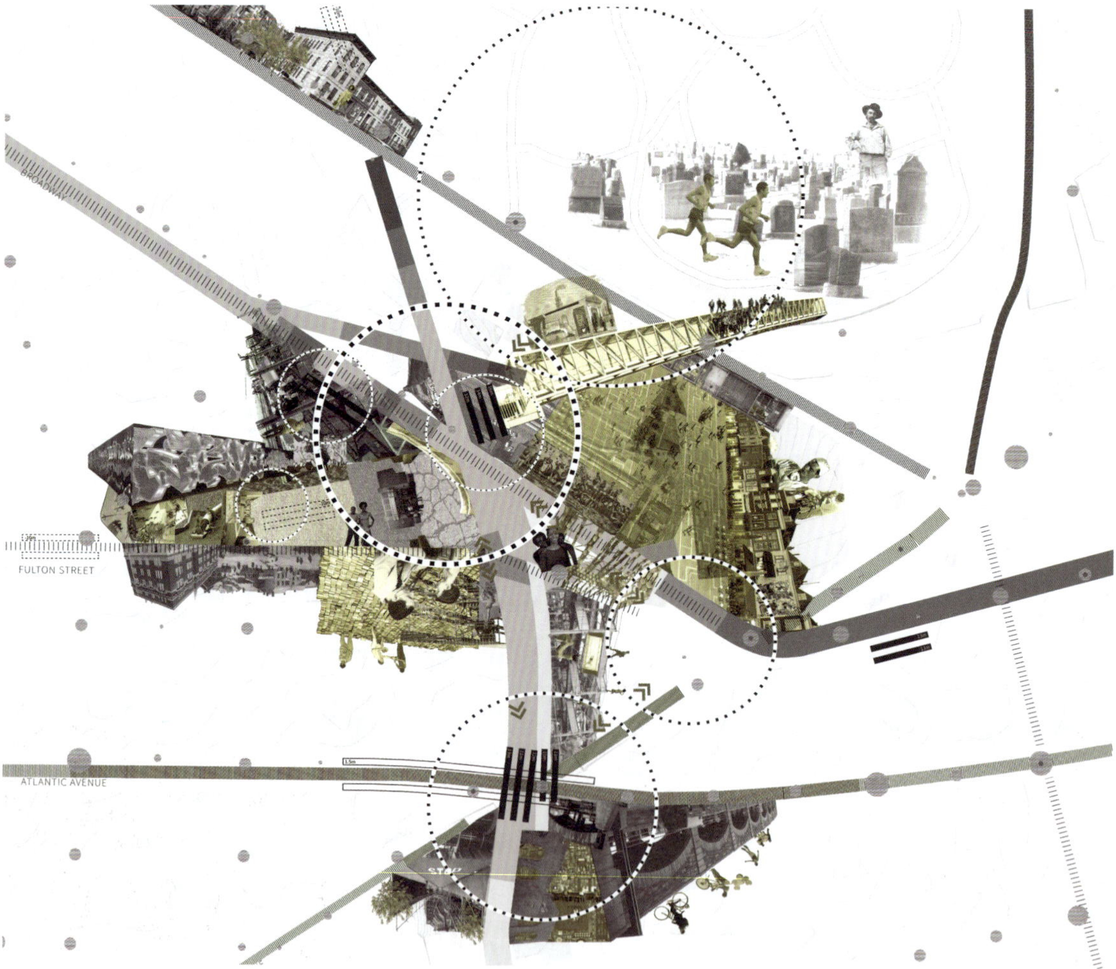

Site concept map illustrating the three major programmatic blocks, from South to North: "Make," "Play," "Die."

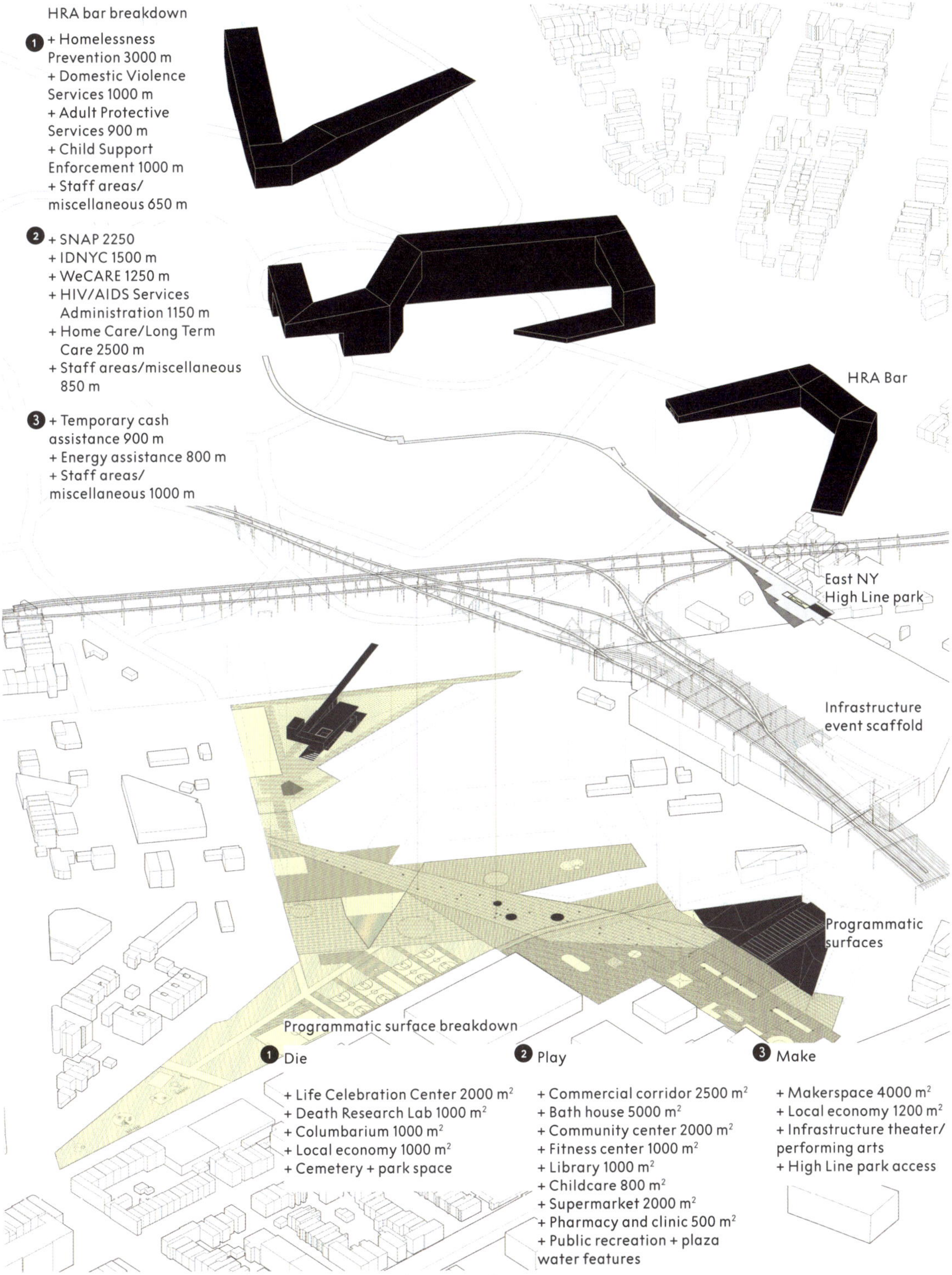

Delayered isometric site drawing of the main programmatic components

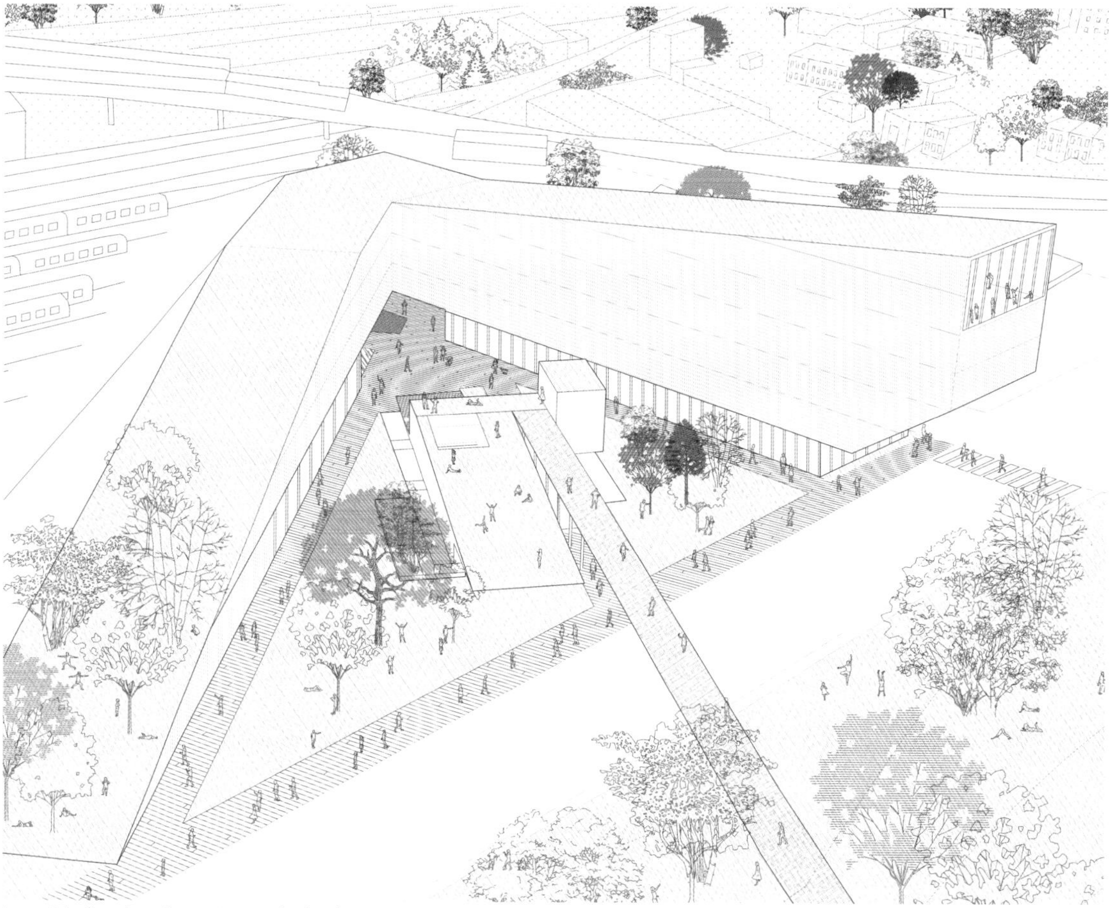

Isometric drawing of cemetery and columbarium ("Die")

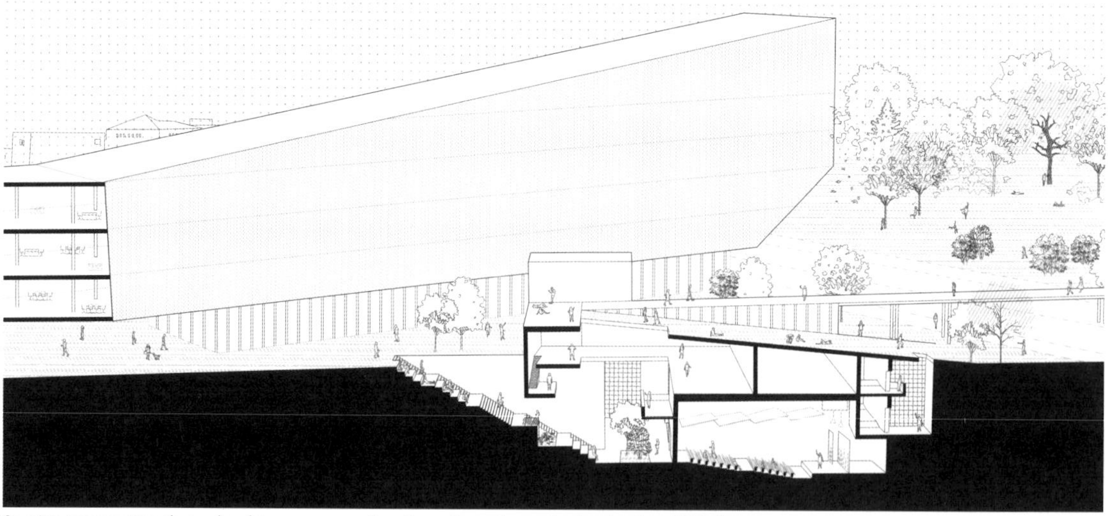

Section perspective through subterranean performing arts center and columbarium ("Die")

Perspective view of food market along pedestrian promenade ("Play")

Pedestrian view of public recreational space and retail commerce ("Play")

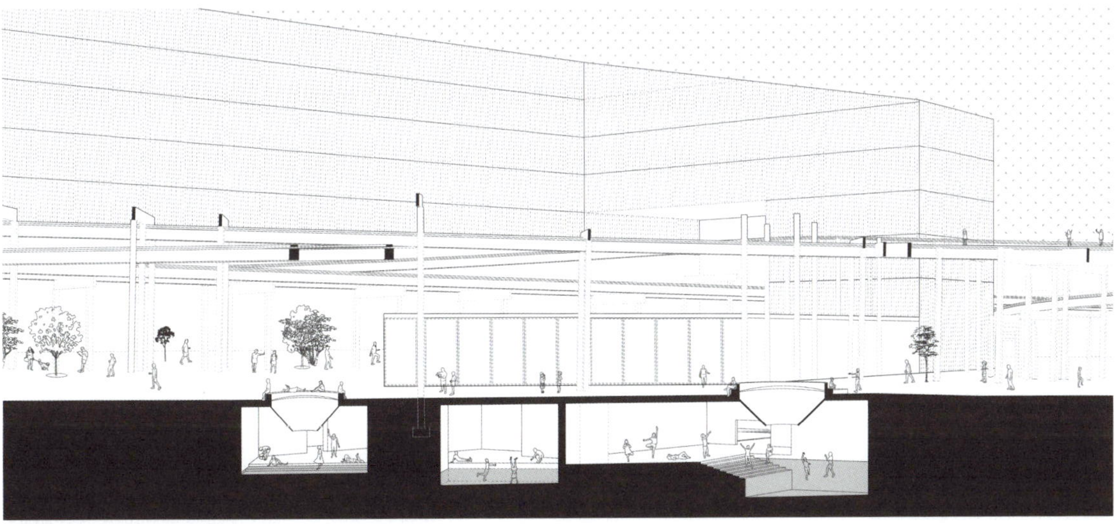

Section perspective through community and transit programming ("Play")

1:1000 site model showing tripartite massing, "Make_Play_Die"

1:200 model, "Make_Play_Die"

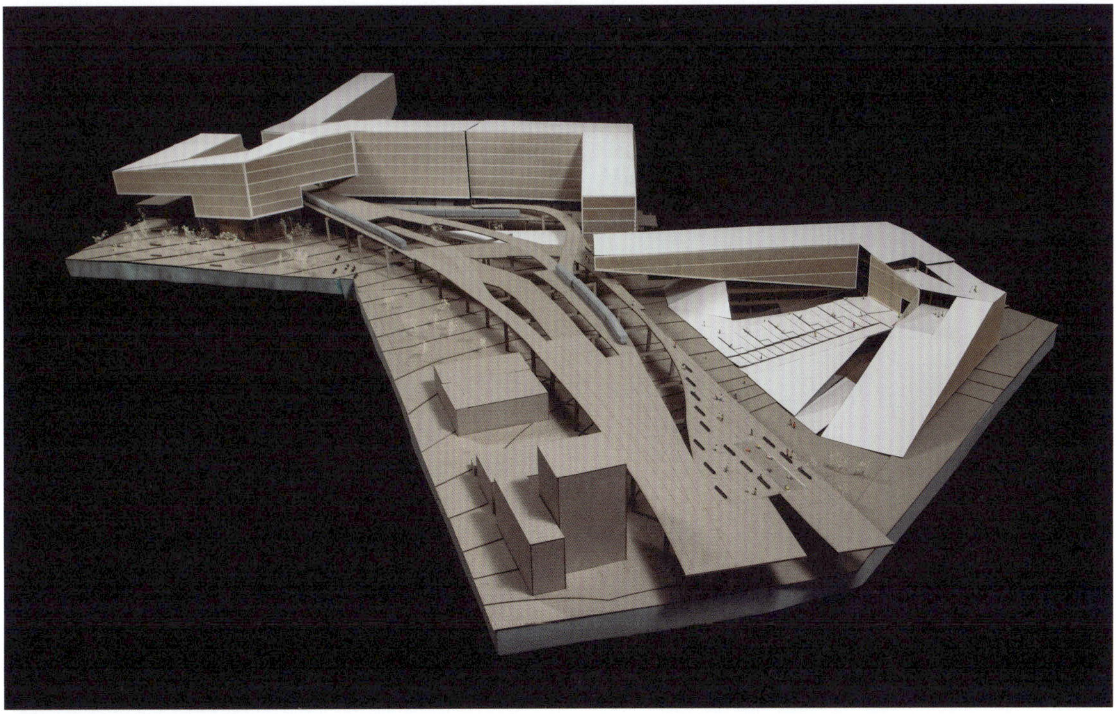

1:200 model, "Make_Play_Die"

Community Conjunction

Student Team
Theodore Bazil
Mark Meiklejohn
Wan Ziyu

Instructor
Seth McDowell

Community Conjunction's bi-axial site strategy links adjacent, yet disconnected neighborhoods by re-purposing aging and under-utilized railway infrastructure as newly occupiable landscape. Additionally, it encourages the growth of the industrial zone South of Atlantic Avenue by revamping its connection to transit amenities and embedding jointly occupied and operated community spaces into the multi-level infrastructural topography. These programs, such as a rec center, public pool, food market, makerspace, and job training center, fill in the variegated gaps below the tracks at street-level, while the HRA administrative offices are housed above within three bent slab-shaped towers.

Urban map and parti diagram showing key urban features and potential neighborhood connections established through new infrastructre and green space

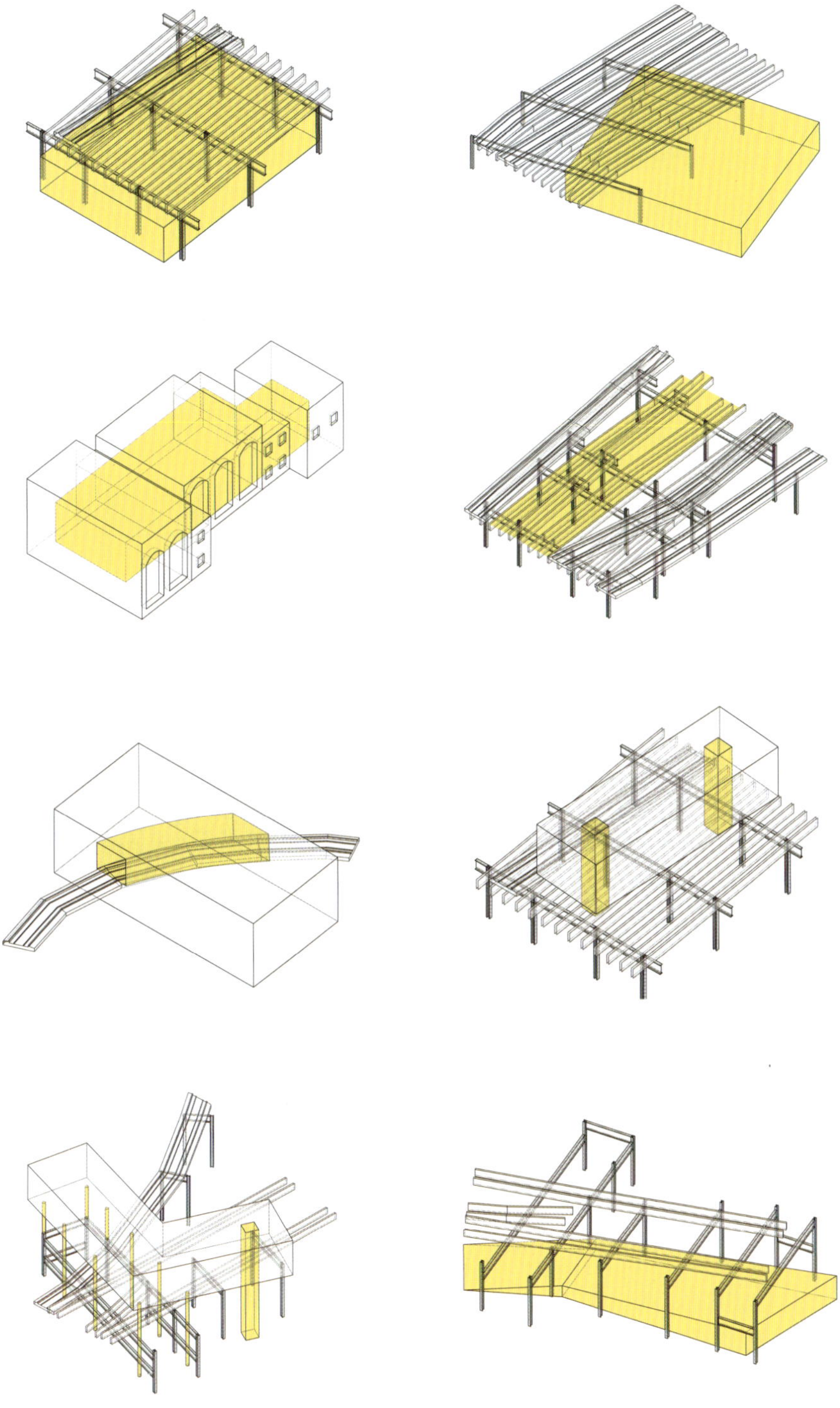

Operational diagrams illustrating strategies for working with existing infrastructure

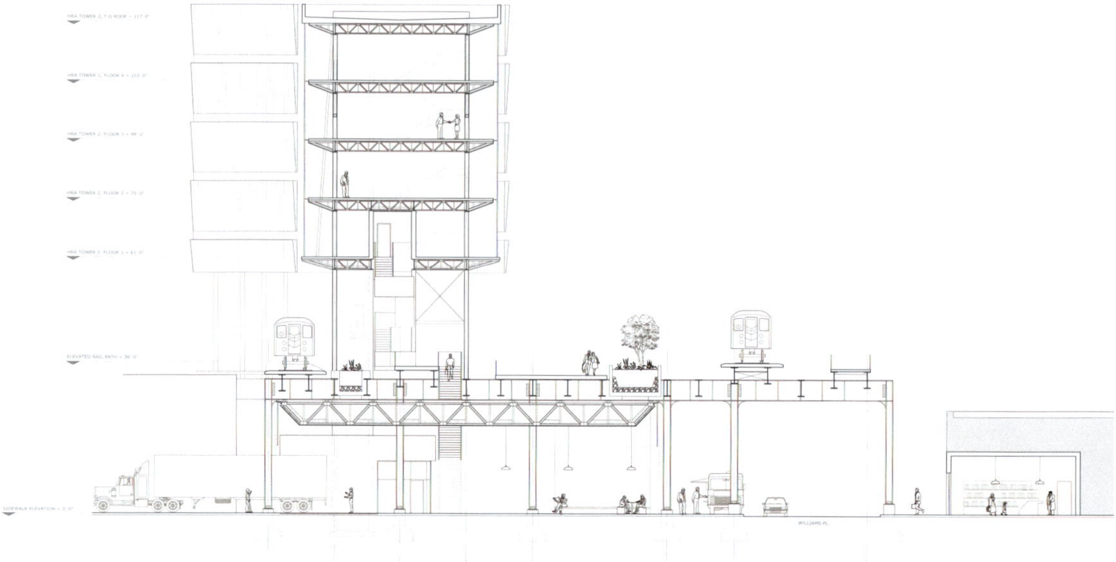

Cross-section through public food market and HRA office tower

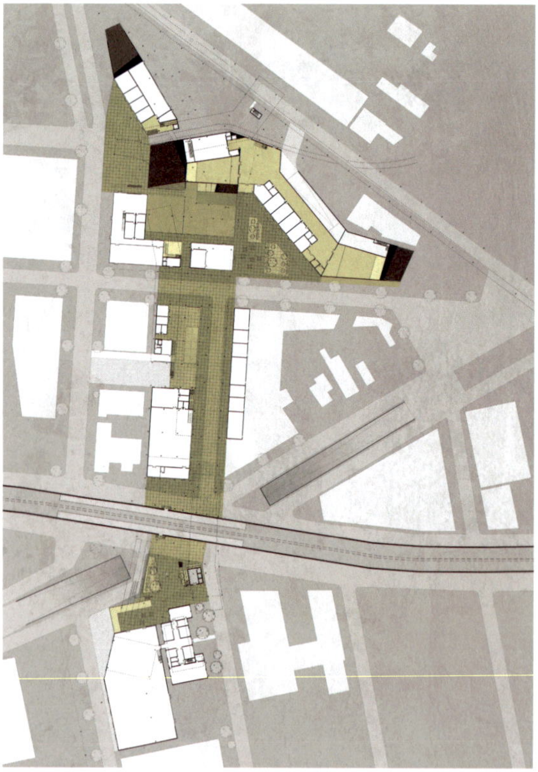

Ground floor plan

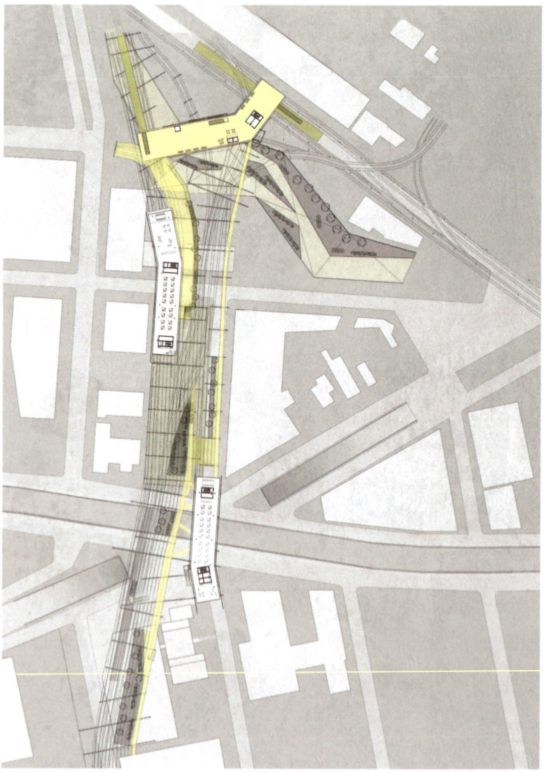

Elevated ground and tower plan

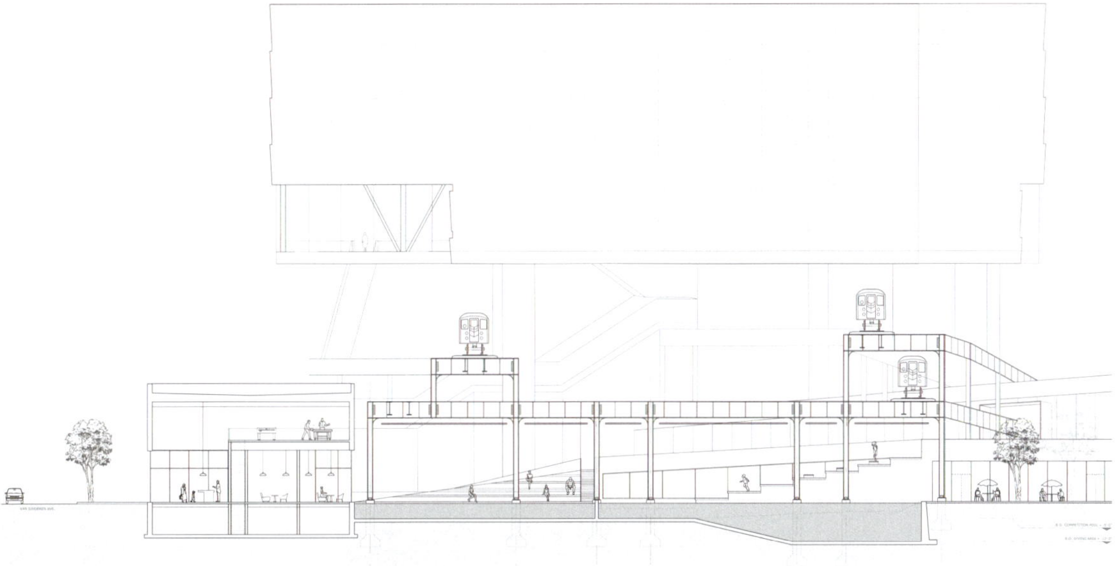

Cross-section through community pool, recreational center, and transit hub

Perspective view through community pool

1:1000 model, "Community Conjunction"

Collected Ground

Student Team
Anna Morrison
Yin Yu Fong
Zazu Swistel

Instructor
Seth McDowell

Collected Ground proposes that all site structures be sunken underground in order to maximize open space and highlight the striking visual and sensory effect of the site's looming elevated railways. Materially, the project relies on re-utilizing the existing: fill from site excavation, for instance, informs the design of ground level landscape elements, while the elevated rail trestles are repurposed as public viewing platforms. Below grade, building masses wrap around sunken, verdant courtyards, whose tapered vertical edges help bring light down to the HRA offices and other public-interfacing programs such as artist studios, fabrication spaces, and galleries.

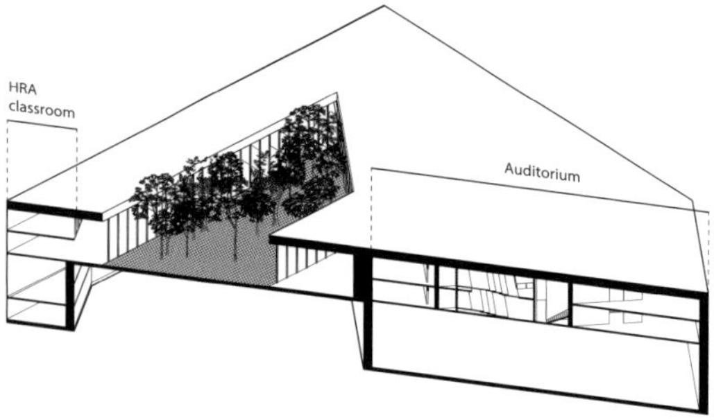

Sunken courtyard solar study, sunny weather

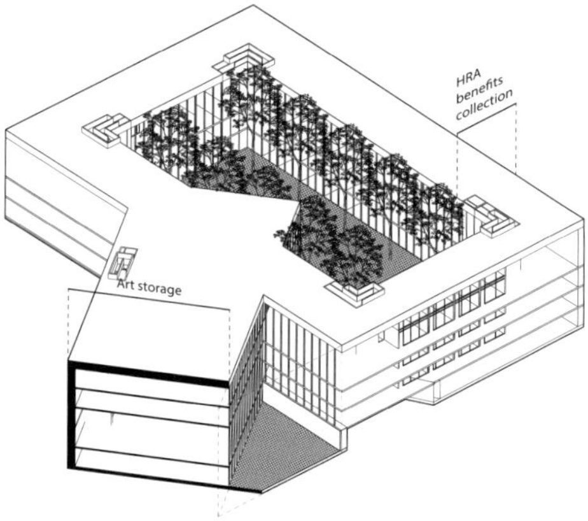

Sunken courtyard solar study, cloudy weather

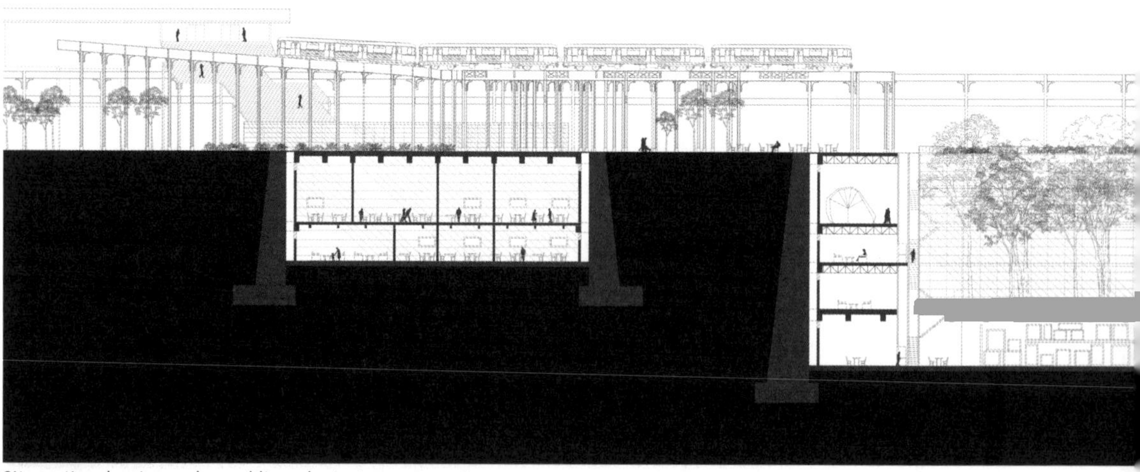

Site section showing sunken public and private programming

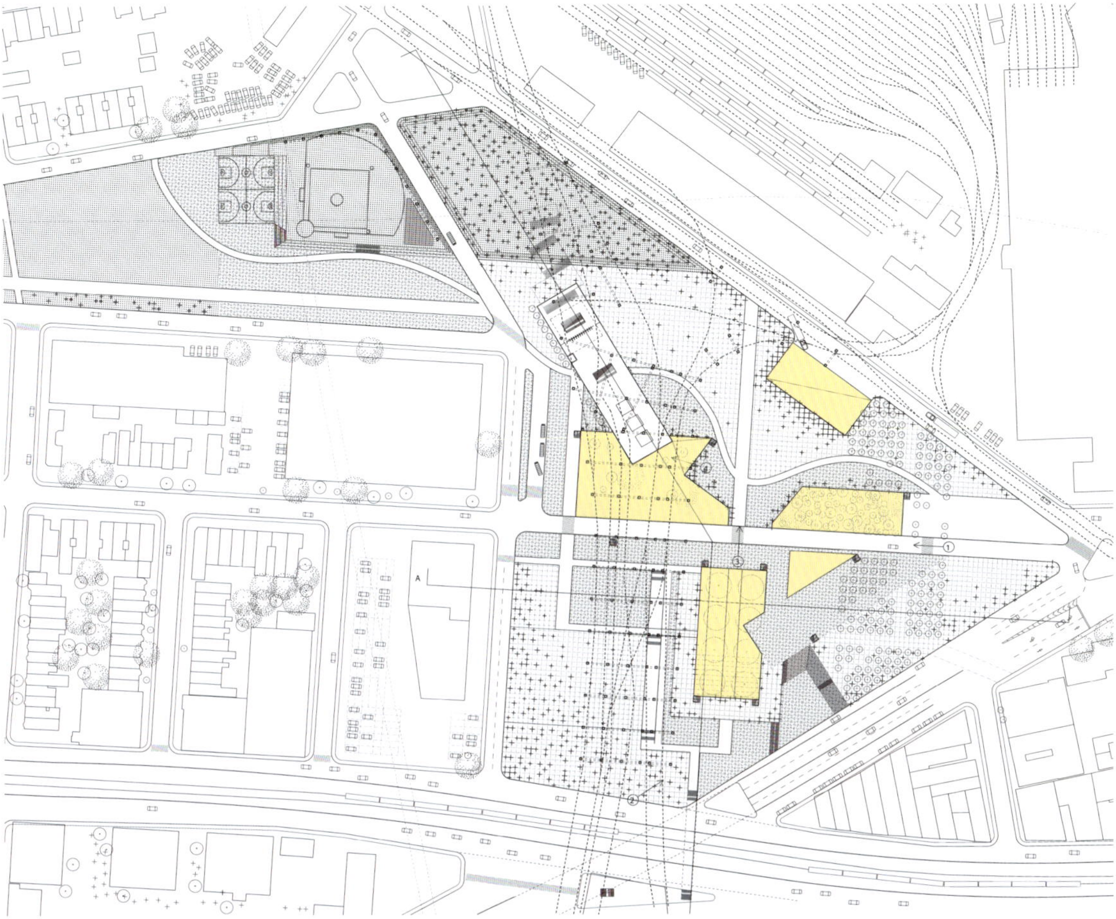

Ground floor site plan showing sunken courtyard spaces

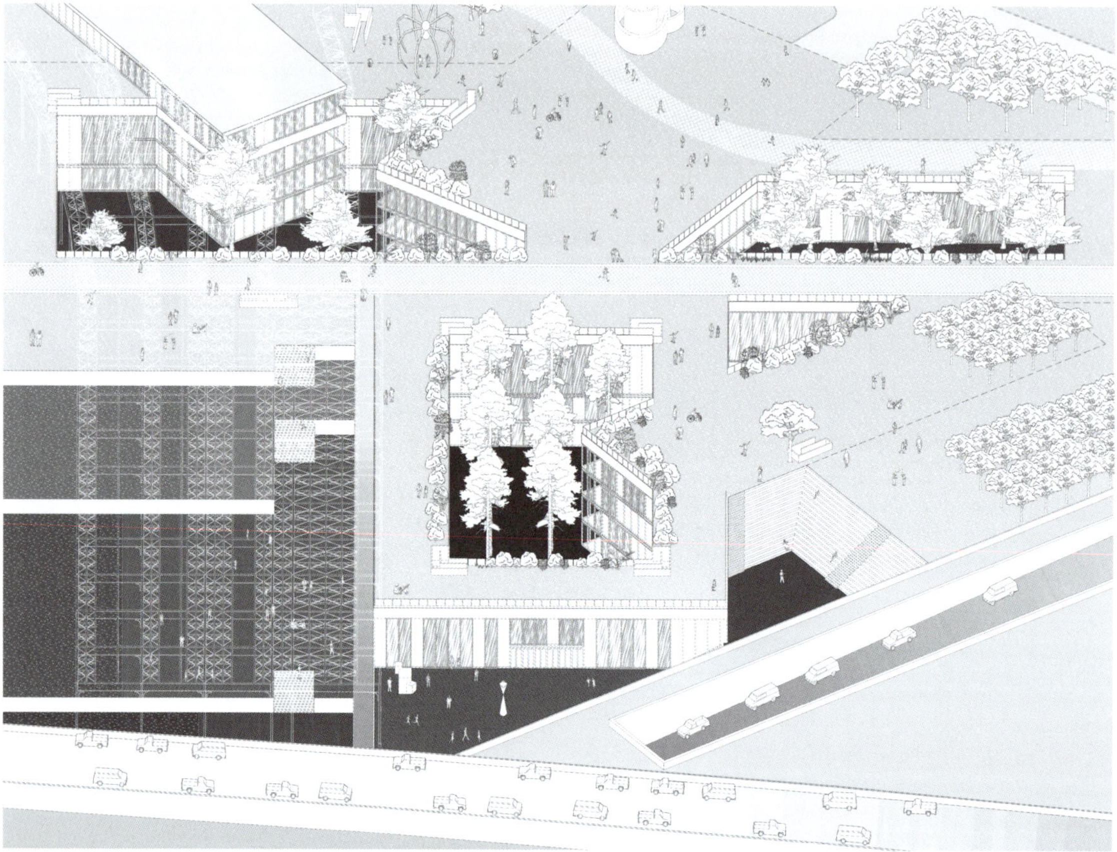

Isometric view of site showing at-grade circulation and sunken building masses

Perspective at Herkimer Street showing uninterrupted ground plane

Isometric section through sunken courtyard and subterranean building program

Perspective view at grade looking down toward sunken courtyard

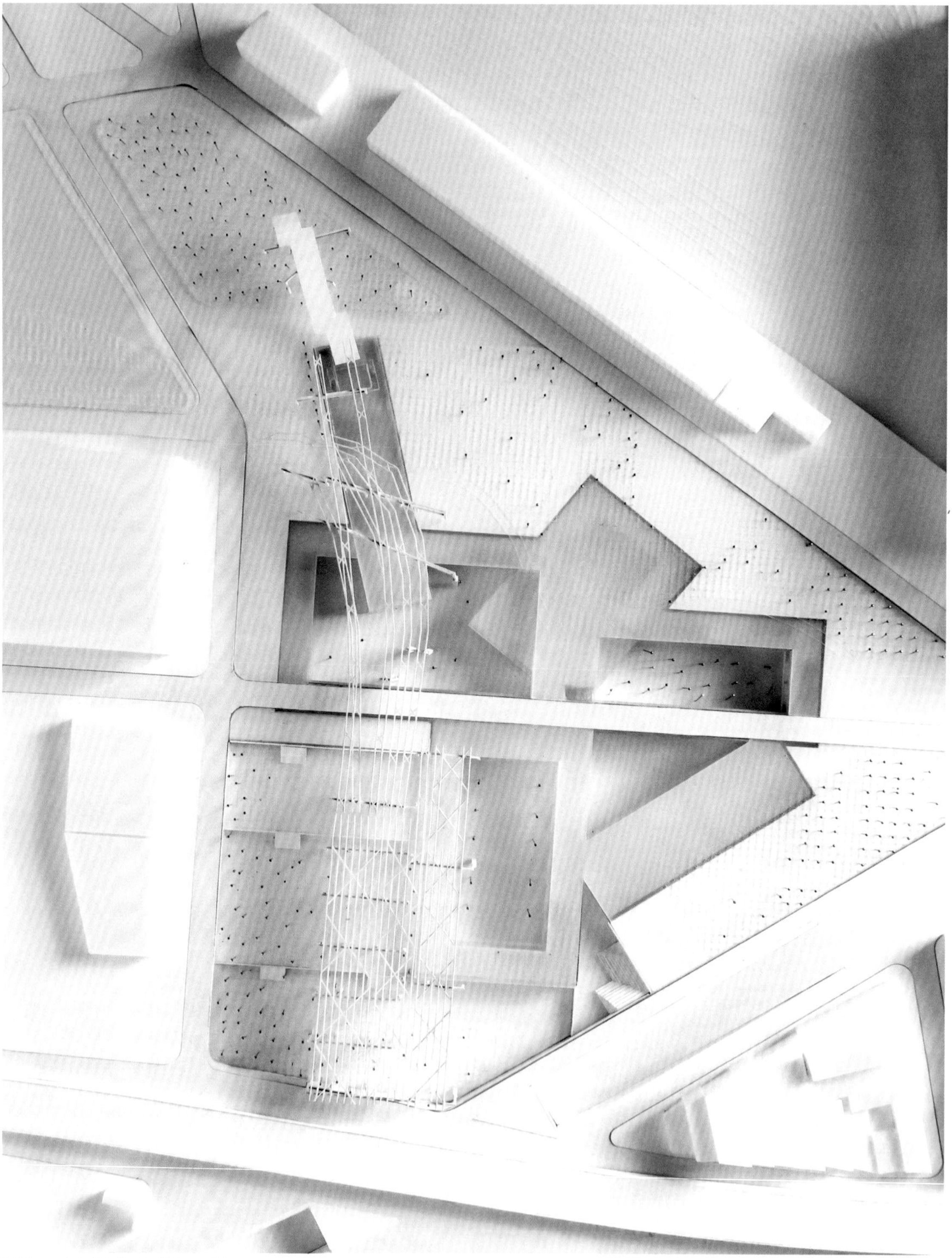

1:200 model, "Collected Ground"

1:200 model, "Collected Ground"

1:200 model, "Collected Ground"

Active Idling

Student Team
Colin Gilliland
Ginny Lee
Katherine Rush

Instructor
Seth McDowell

In addition to its illegible and visually chaotic array of transit infrastructures and leftover spatial fragments, Broadway Junction is also a site defined by people aimlessly waiting around. Active Idling addresses these two conditions in tandem: first by appropriating the site's many shards of leftover space and reconfiguring them into a clear parti strategy of three tall and thin towers connected by subway lines; and second, by articulating each tower as a diverse and variegated tapestry of spaces and facade conditions devoted to facilitating more deliberate, enjoyable, and experiential forms of temporal activity: lingering, spectating, conversing, gathering, and resting.

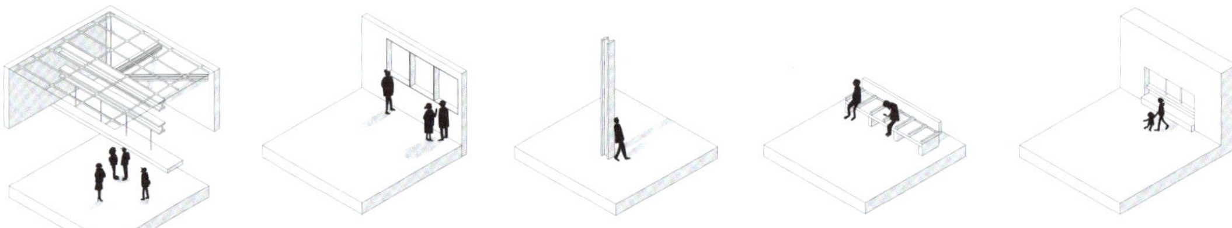

Waiting typologies

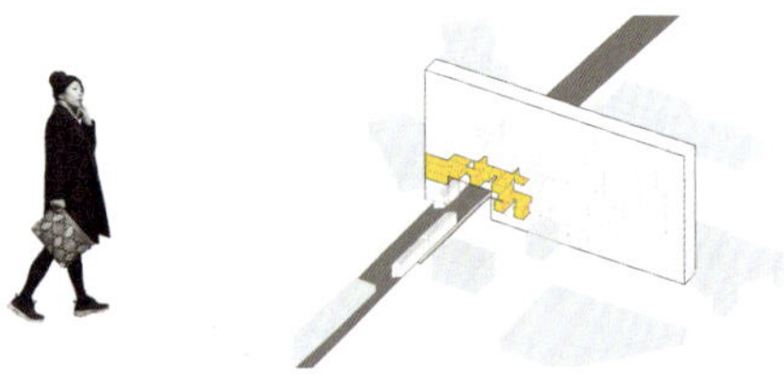

Commuter

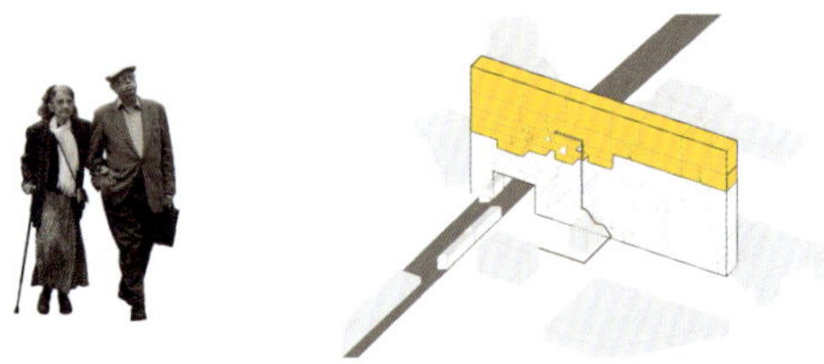

HRA visitors

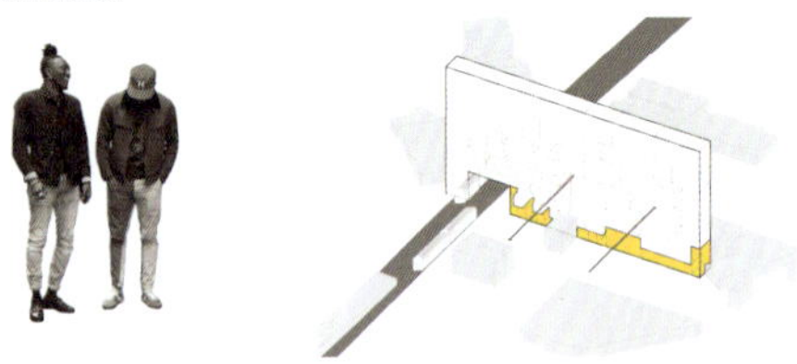

Passerby

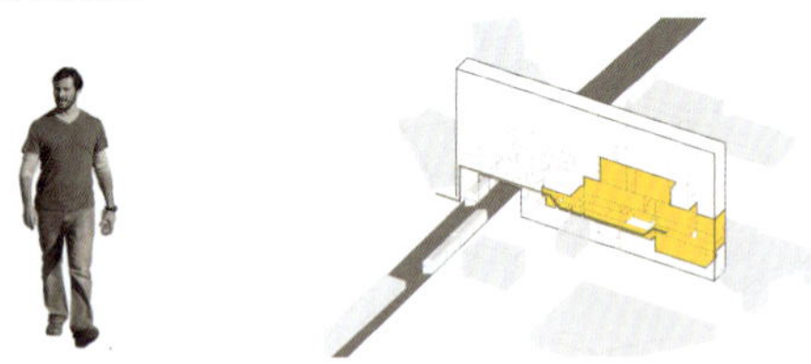

Guy getting car fixed

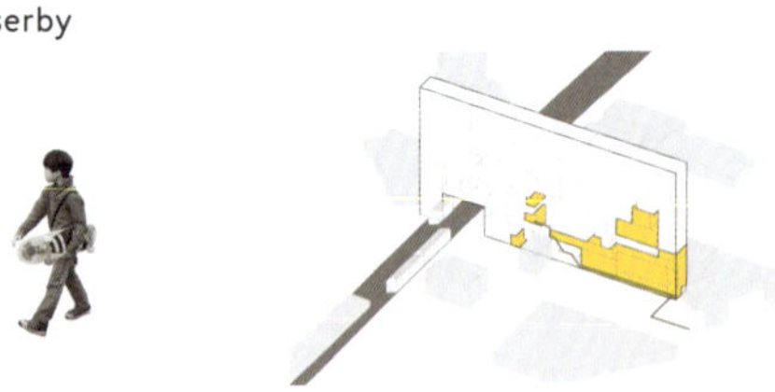

After-school kid

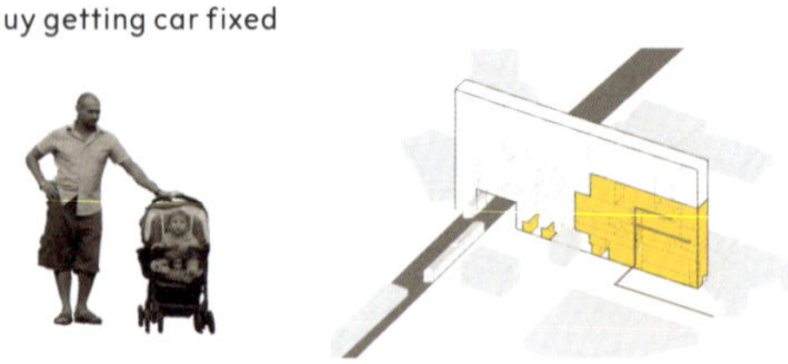

Community family

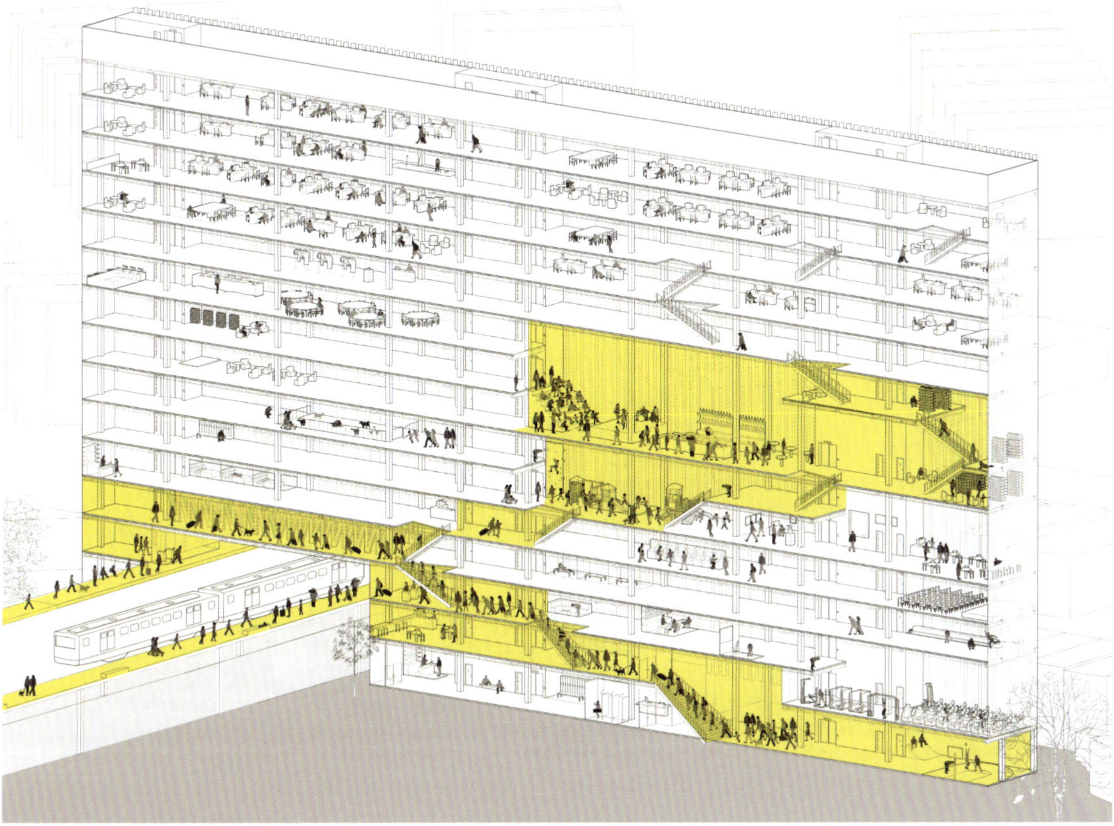

Isometric section through tower slab

Interior perspective view: performing

Interior perspective view: congregating

Perspecive view looking north along elevated subway tracks

Building elevation

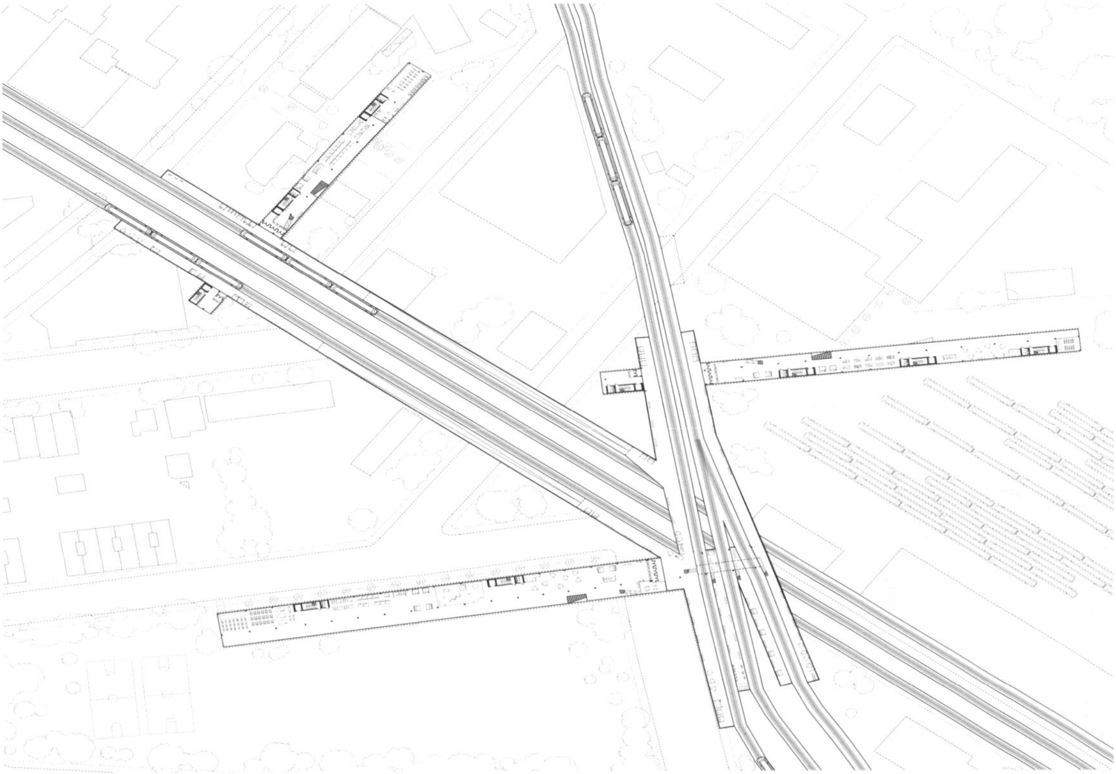

Site and tower floorplans

1:200 model, "Active Idling"

Final review models, May 2018

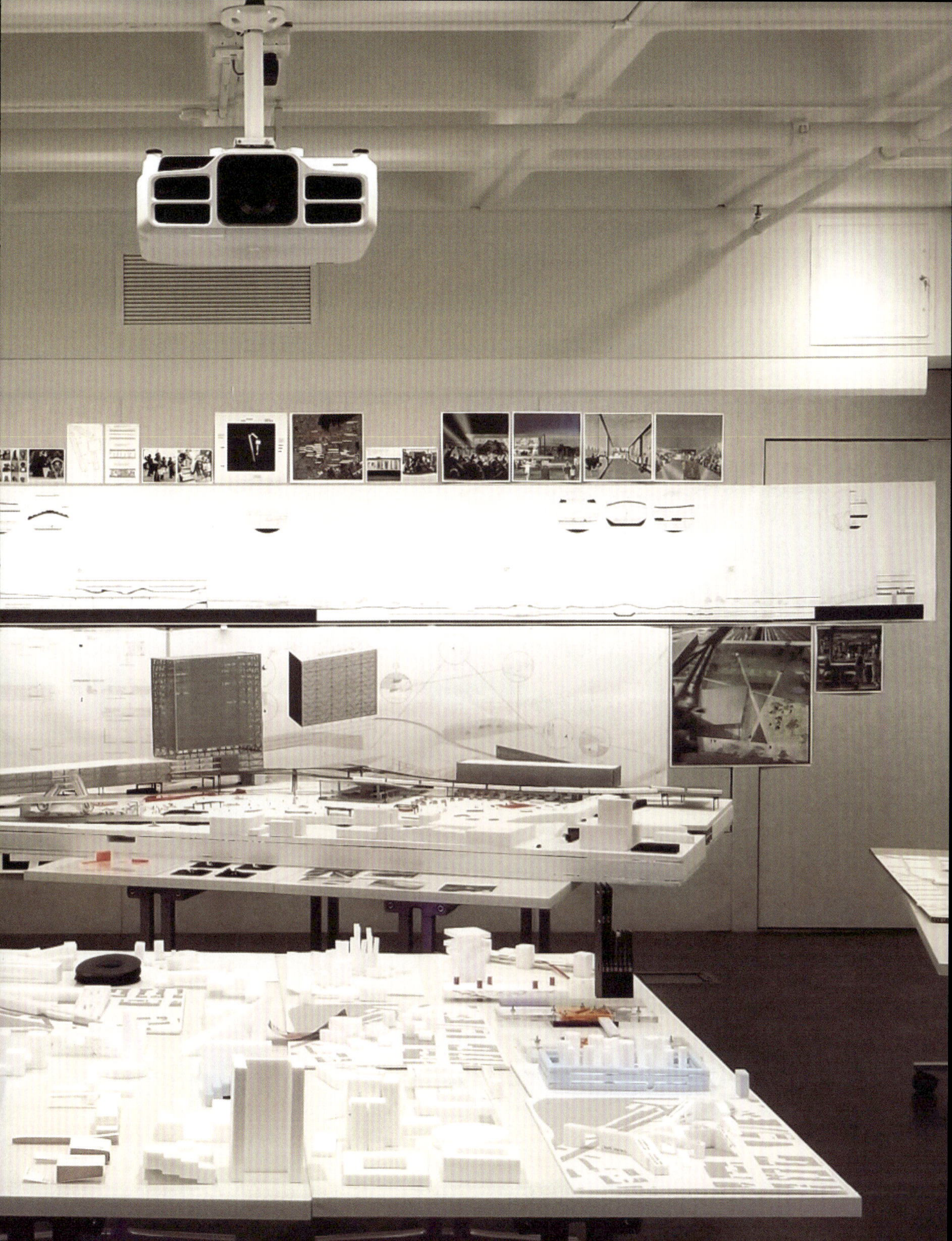

Shared amenities and jointly operated open spaces that can simultaneously serve the schools and the neighborhood emerged as important architectural spaces to construct physical, programmatic, and organizational relationships. Here spatial negotiation is understood not only as an act of legal negotiation framed through a PPP, but as an act of architectural design that facilitates hybrid and time-based spaces.
—Mona El Khafif

If the grid is both urban plan and ground plane for the commodification of New York City, a foreshadowing of urban growth, and a reduction of that growth to the economy of real estate speculation, the prototype school building both configures itself to these logics and reforms them. It enables mid-block school buildings on less expensive lots and returns these sites to the public realm.
—Sharon Haar

The role of an architect in complex projects such as this, where priorities can be divergent between each partner, becomes much more than just design thinking—it is one of facilitator, analyst, and advocate that can yield outcomes that are not obvious at the onset and are transformative in their resolution.
—Carrie Moore

Partnering

Spatial Negotiations: Can Public-Private Partnerships Operate as Spatial Machines?

Mona El Khafif

> From City Hall to Trump Tower, public space does not exist because parks, plazas, sidewalks, and streets exist. For a space to be public space, people who talk about, use it and re-imagine it must tie it to the nonphysical processes that bind it to our public life: to patterns of law, speech, representation, policy, distribution, and economics. Design as a way of considering, representing, and constructing relationships between people and space can play a role in reforging these connections.
> —Kristine Miller, *Designs on the Public*

The city, as both a material artifact and an immaterial phenomenon, is defined by processes of making and acts of negotiation. New York is no exception—rather, it is a prime example of how market forces and real estate dynamics shape the physical city and impact the production of public spaces. Additional conditions, as highlighted in Kristine Miller's book *Designs on the Public: The Private Lives of New York's Public Spaces*, further call out the heavy burden of public spaces in a city like New York, where openness and accessibility, as well as public ownership, are often only temporary phenomena bounded by regulations and codes of conduct.[1] At a moment when Public-Private Partnerships (PPP) are redefining those ongoing temporal and more permanent negotiations, design needs to unleash typological strategies at the scale of the urban block. In "Typological Urbanism," Christopher C. M. Lee and Sam Jacoby[2] reengage architecture with the city through these operations and argue that the domains of urbanism and the architectural object are not oppositional, but instead exist in a synthesis with one another. In this context, programmatic and architectural typologies serve as infrastructural devices to facilitate public life and strengthen the city's environment by encouraging social interaction and curating dynamic relationships between public and private spaces. Here, the architectural project operates at the scale of the city and becomes a negotiator between public and private spaces and interests.

The two foundation studios offered in fall 2018 and 2019 addressed the architectural object at the scale of the urban block. The studios questioned how architecture and urban typologies can respond to—and strengthen—their social, urban, and environmental contexts. Framed around an existing PPP, the studio brief re-imagined one of New York's most compelling legal mechanisms of revitalization: the partnership between public and private investments.

Public-Private Partnerships: A Means of Negotiation?

New York, as described in Carrie Moore's essay, is one of the best places in the United States to study and understand the impacts of PPPs on the built environment. PPPs are projects where capital-intensive, long-lived infrastructures are built using a complex combination of government and mostly private financing. A private entity then operates these projects under a long-term contract or lease with the city. The payments are usually spread over an extended period and cover construction, operation, maintenance, and capital costs. Typical PPP projects are urban infrastructures like roads, bridges, airports, water systems, and power plants, but public institutions like schools and municipal buildings have also been developed through this method.[3]

While New York has realized a series of PPPs that fit the above definition and developed partnership organizations for some of its larger public parks, such as the Central Park Conservancy, the city is best known for the land transaction invention, inaugurated in 1961 as part of a new series of zoning regulations, that facilitated the creation of "privately owned public spaces" (POPS).[4] The 1961 zoning resolution, which was introduced to replace its predecessor from 1916, adjusted regulations to address height and land use challenges and defined a maximum building bulk in the form of FAR regulations on a parcel. The lack of investment in public spaces caused by the 1916 zoning law was further addressed through a new incentive zoning provision that allowed the city to offer floor-area bonuses to office and residential developers in exchange for interior or exterior public spaces located on the private lot. As cities across the United States and North America followed New York City's lead, countless smaller-scale privately-owned public spaces have subsequently been erected. This PPP has now existed for nearly sixty years and has accumulated, as of this writing, 592 sites in New York City.[5]

While privately-owned public spaces are the result of the city's comprehensive plan and its embedded zoning tools, it was Mies van der Rohe's Seagram Building of 1958 that served as the ultimate prototype for such new incentive zoning regulations. Famously, the tower occupies less than 25 percent of its lot, while its deep setback offers a substantial public space at street level. The authors of this new zoning resolution understood the immense value of this new architectural typology, and utilized incentive zoning measures as a effective regulatory tools in realizing and propagating a new modernist vernacular across the city.[6] This novel typology of a tower on a plaza soon encouraged the emergence of a new PPP, one which proved to be one of the most effective regulations to promote specific design outcomes.[7]

As further discussed in this chapter, the City of New York also developed a PPP that leverages publicly-owned land and allows for a private, mostly residential program on these sites in exchange for the renovation or complete replacement of the site's existing public program. This chapter, and the two studios dedicated to the topic, investigate the design potential of an ongoing and controversial PPP marrying city-owned land occupied by public schools with private residential development.

PublicSURplus@nyc.edu

While initiated with the intention of helping to upgrade the city's public schools, this particular PPP has also generated significant economic and social impacts on its various urban contexts. As stated in a 2016 real estate analysis of institutional landownership in New York City,[8] the Department of Education ranks second among public landowners in square footage of land, topped only by the Housing Department, and ranks first in real estate land value. Sitting atop this dramatic real estate portfolio, the city could make over $18 billion today if its public schools were to be liquidated for private development. Considering that the New York City public school system educates more than 1.1 million students—the largest number in the world—this is not astonishing. The city owns 1,700 public schools, 21 elementary schools, 63 high schools, and 21 middle schools in Manhattan alone, and many of these sites are located in high-pressure market areas that are currently under-zoned.[9]

While this real estate wealth gives the Department of Education an economic advantage, the yearly city budget for education is not sufficient to maintain or upgrade these properties, many of which were built in the 1970s and 1980s. The lack of funding to bring these facilities up to twenty-first-century standards is accompanied by a growing crisis in the housing market, as the city—and specifically Manhattan—needs to develop new affordable housing strategies to balance out a market currently catering to primarily high-income demographics.

As Carrie Moore discusses with greater depth in her essay, to address this situation, the city developed a new PPP that has generated a series of precedent cases. To save the city schools and libraries, government-financed agencies are now offering their public lands for sale to the developer with the best bid. To participate, developers are required to replace the existing public program with new, modern facilities; in return, they receive the rights to erect mixed-used housing projects on the same site, often facilitated through floor-area bonuses. Although this transaction is potentially a win-win situation for both the developer and the city, it has generated significant local resistance due to fears of a sole developer's gain and a loss of community identity for the school.[10]

Two recently developed projects are the Riverside School for Makers and Artists at West 61st Street, which opened its doors in 2017, and the High School of Art and Design on East 56th Street from 2012. Although both developments offer state-of-the-art educational facilities and have received architectural awards, they lack programmatic synergies or contributions to the neighborhood in the form of new open spaces and social infrastructures that would balance out the increased density. Further, the residential programs in the same building as the two schools primarily serve the upper-income housing market, thus failing to address the demand for more affordable housing.

The question raised in this studio was how architectural design and its integrated systems could accommodate increased residential density, while simultaneously expanding the amount of open space these schools currently provide. Further, students were encouraged to invent new programmatic synergies between learning environments and housing, to experiment with new forms of affordable housing typologies, and to integrate shared open spaces that contribute to the neighborhood's identity. These programs could serve as essential connectors and thresholds between the residential program, the educational program, and the surrounding community.

PublicSURplus@NYC.edu, therefore, addressed three critical challenges that the city is currently facing: the need to upgrade public school facilities; the necessity for affordable mid-market housing; and the need for investments in neighborhoods in the form of public spaces, parks, and public facilities. As such, the studio invited students and faculty to radically rethink the existing partnership in support of a public (rather than a private) surplus.

How Can We Learn to Negotiate and to Collaborate?

Translating often-competing stakeholder objectives into architectural projects that balance the need for density and housing, but also contribute a public program to surrounding neighborhoods, is a process of spatial negotiation. As such, the PPP stands in for a prototypical situation of our profession in which profitability has to be negotiated with social and environmental sustainability, conceptual clarity, and novel approaches to rethink our cities. How can a studio brief be structured to allow students to understand processes of negotiation and collaboration? The syllabus established a series of scaffold assignments which ultimately led to the design of a detailed architectural proposal. These preliminary assignments ranged from an urban analysis at the scale of Manhattan to the iterative study of typological massing strategies at the scale of the urban block. This encouraged students to work flexibly across multiple scales and to understand the architectural project as a contextual contribution to the city.

The studio further emphasized an iterative design process to help clarify design objectives. Students worked in teams of different formations to encourage a process of collaboration, while round table discussions, gallery reviews, and debates worked to establish a culture of discussion.

Drawing the City: Understanding Context

A fictional feasibility study set the stage to explore the location of all public school sites and their capacities to impact their immediate urban contexts through the PPP. This comprehensive approach rejected the case-by-case nature of development as it often exists in practice. Instead, it provided an overview of how different school developments could transform areas of the city and better serve their neighborhoods by generating a broad inventory of locations, typologies, characteristics, and urban contexts.

Working collectively, the cohort reviewed all the school sites through specific conceptual lenses, and produced thematic maps unveiling latent spatial, social, and economic relationships. Among the many city layers analyzed for each site were green space, open space, mobility and public transit, demographics, zoning regulations, climate and environment, history and narrative, real estate values, public program, population density and growth, urban fabric and massing, energy and urban metabolism, and the performance and needs of the individual schools. Each studio produced twelve analytical maps at the scale of Manhattan which individually investigated one of the above agendas before synthesizing the findings into a more complex site-specific analysis. The results were presented in the form of gallery reviews to exchange findings, data, and conclusions (figure 1).

Figure 1: Gallery review A1, UVA Fall 2019.

The city-wide analysis further helped to select prototype sites that would best show the capacity of the PPP, not only to benefit the educational and residential programs, but also to support city-wide agendas and neighborhood interests. In addition to featuring the locations of public schools and green spaces, for example (figure 2), the analysis also placed them in relation to the as-yet-unfinished waterfront green network outlined by the 2011 Comprehensive Waterfront Plan.[11] Specifically, schools located in state-owned public housing projects along the eastern waterfront could regenerate the public housing neighborhoods while simultaneously reshaping the waterfront as one continuous public space.

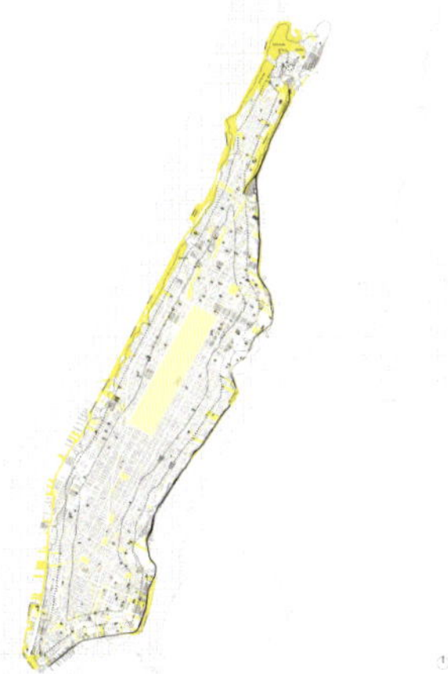

Figure 2: Schools and open space.

The historic analysis generated a comprehensive inventory of Manhattan's public schools and their cultural relevance, and identified sites desperately in need of renovation (figure 3). The typological inventory extracted from this analysis was enriched through a deeper understanding of the impact of Charles Snyder, who served as a city architect from 1891 to 1922. To ensure light and air, Snyder developed a school typology that explored a through-block H-plan, which became his signature design.[12] The real estate analysis, without doubt an important lens in the context of the PPP, identified the sites with the highest capacity for profit, but also showed that those neighborhoods most in need of investment would not necessarily benefit developers. The program analysis, in contrast, investigated the synergies for sharing programs across the neighborhood within a five-minute

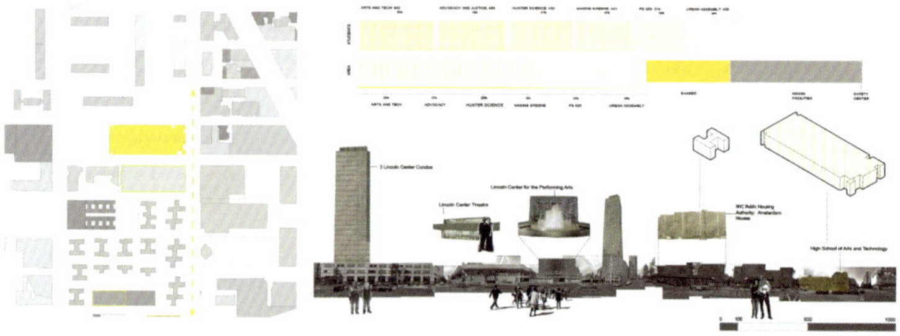

Figure 3: Schools and history, H-Type.

walking shed around public school sites (figure 4). These findings offered opportunities—as called out in Sharon Haar's essay—to rethink the school as a networked institution that offers shared after-school programs for a larger audience and simultaneously takes advantage of existing resources within its walking shed.

Typological Inventory: Iterating Site Strategies

The design process started with a typological study investigating urban block potentials for the selected prototype sites. Following the example of the Seagram Building, the goal of this design process was to strategically rethink the current PPP through the framework of a prototypical design. Starting with the zoned FAR, an iterative study was initiated to test massing strategies based on typological, morphological, and programmatic parameters. These were documented through physical models, 3D digital models, and a series of diagrams focusing on how separate parameters (density, open space, light access, vegetation, neighborhood context, program requirements, circulation) inform the formal and experiential identities of the types in question. The iterative results were recorded through evolutionary taxonomy diagrams (figure 5), which allowed students to comparatively analyze how different typologies might respond to a range of block densities. In all iterations, the existing school buildings on the sites were replaced, neighboring buildings on the given block were integrated or likewise redeveloped, and new residential and community-based programs were added. The developed inventory, then, produced a vocabulary of different formal operations, established a clearer idea of urban design objectives, and allowed for stronger typologies to rise. Similar to investigations featured in *Why Density?*,[13] these iterative studies showed that generic typologies are less capable at addressing complex urban environments and absorbing higher densities than hybrid ones. Such hybrid typologies, furthermore, were much better able to support and accommodate the varied programmatic needs of the school facilities, as they require considerably different massings from their accompanying residential programs. This twofold condition often produced a form of plinth strategy, featuring an elevated second ground and an upper level residential massing.

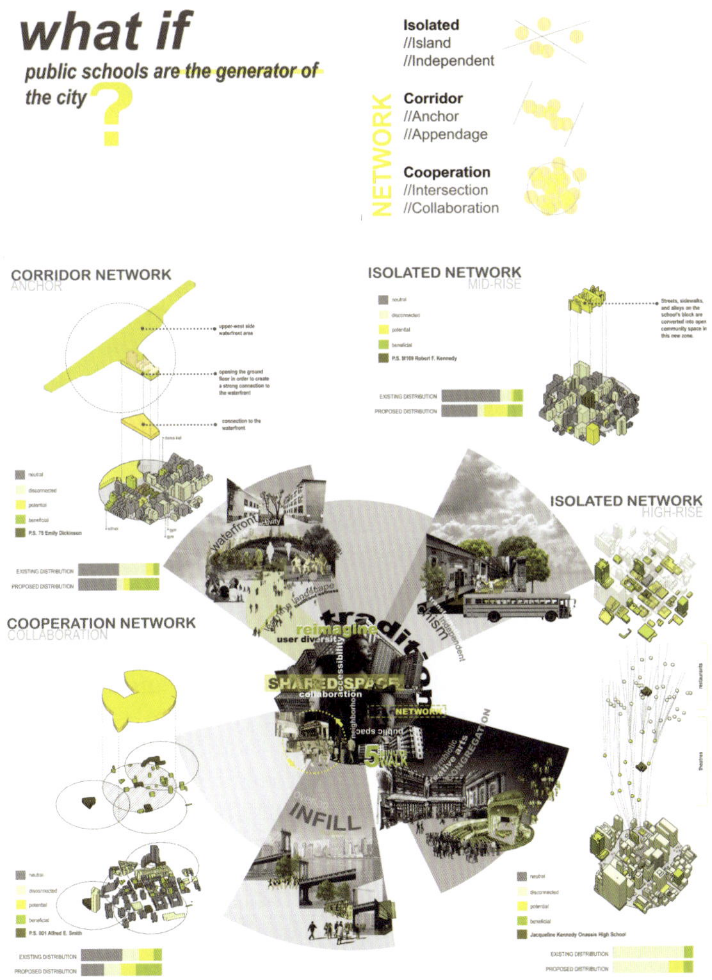

Figure 4: Schools and program.

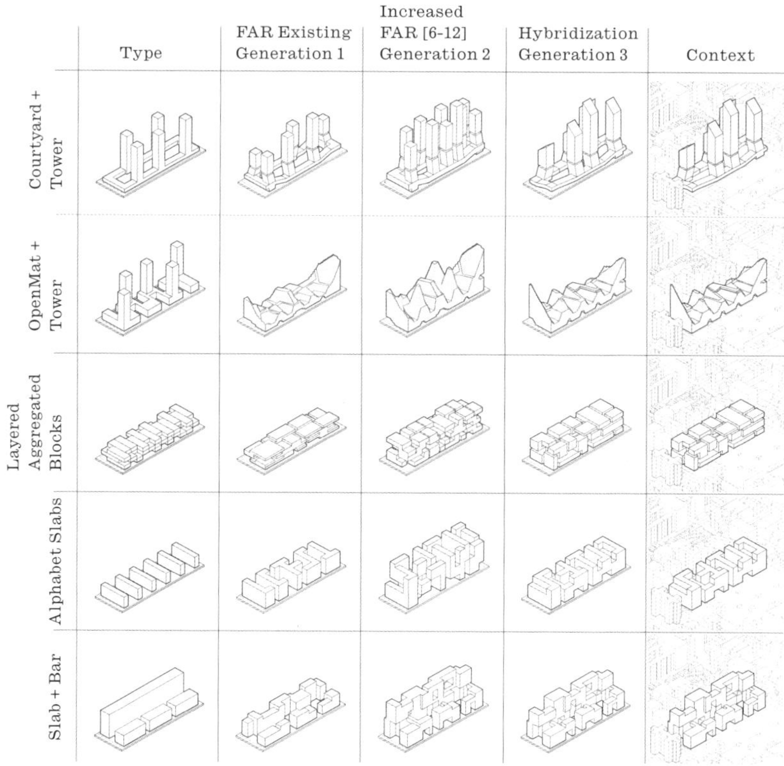

Figure 5: Typological taxonomy.

PPP: Negotiation Across Programs and Disciplines

With this understanding of potential massing strategies in mind, students and faculty traveled to New York to conduct "reality checks" on site. Discussions and site visits led by the Educational Construction Fund and SOM, who realized 252 East 57th Street, were tremendous aids to help the students understand the economic and legal constraints of these partnerships.

Working with education, housing, a community-based "plus" program, and open spaces, the students' schematic designs emerged from their interpretations of how public and private interests could be negotiated through the architectural project. Teams then carried their individual theses forward toward greater architectural resolution. Hands-on feedback was facilitated through two expert workshops addressing open space design and building structure. These workshops allowed students to negotiate the public and private economic interests and ecological necessities of their projects (figure 6).

Hybrid Types: Compositional Aggregations, Contextual Objects, and Distributed Fields

A series of critical topics were raised and discussed in the studio. First, how can Bigness, as defined by Koolhaas,[14] be avoided in favor of a dense, block-scaled project that does not foster a competition between the city and the architectural object but, in contrast, establishes relationships across the urban fabric? Furthermore, is it possible to interpret school sites as assets for the city, rather than as fenced off enclaves?

Lastly, it seemed critical to investigate how architecture and, ultimately, a shared community-based program can strengthen vulnerable neighborhoods. The socio-economic and demographic histories of many of the school sites made such discussions equal parts delicate and necessary. How can, if at all, architecture address the gentrifying effects often caused by increases in market-rate housing?

The history of New York City Public Housing, notable for its failures since the turn into the twentieth century,[15] was a critical socio-political context. All six test sites were located either in vulnerable neighborhoods (Success Academy in Harlem, P.S./M.S. 57 James Weldon Johnson in East Harlem, Shuang Wen School, P.S. 33 in Chelsea, Lower School) or near public housing (Manhattan/Hunter Science High School, Lincoln Center, East Side, and Murry Bergtraum High School for Business Careers), where the schools' future facilities could potentially support the surrounding neighborhoods with essential infrastructures.

The projects developed in these two studios offered a variety of hybridized solutions addressing the challenges raised in the studio brief. These typologies proved their capacities to absorb higher densities while simultaneously offering a variety of open spaces and addressing programmatic requirements. Among the projects featured in this chapter, three dominant spatial approaches can be extracted.

First, Compositional Aggregations can be described as the combination of two or more generic typologies within one urban block. Here, the school program was predominantly placed within a two- to three-floor plinth with access to the street, allowing for very deep building volumes. Such plinths were variously explored as mat slabs, courtyards, or even programmed ground schemes with shared open spaces located laterally as dividers between programs. The residential portions were then placed in tower typologies or slabs, either

Figure 6: Professional workshops.

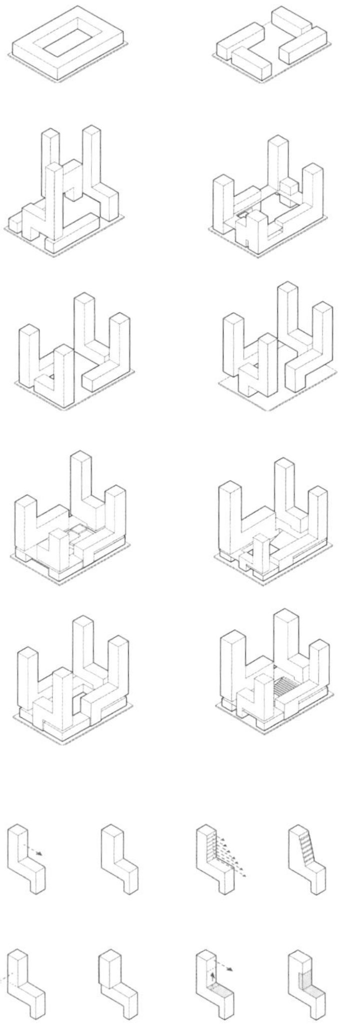

atop or puncturing through the plinths. The elevated second grounds were furthermore articulated as publicly accessible open spaces or parks connected to the street, and additional common spaces were offered as residential and neighborhood amenities. Infrastructures such as community art spaces, galleries, workshops, or computer labs were often located at the street level. During school hours, these infrastructures serve the educational program, but on weekends and evenings, they could be opened up to the neighborhood and organized in relation to the proposed circulation systems so as to allow dual access and use. Such jointly operated infrastructures could be identified as public surpluses as they effectively give back to their surrounding communities.

Compositional Aggregation strategies are most evident in projects like "Circulating through Scale" (page 254), "Vertical Commons" (page 248), or "Courtyard Unleashed" (page 256). Yet, the invention of new typologies within this context was often just as critical as the hybridization of types. "The Giraffe Towers" (figure 7), for example, allowed the traditionally vertical element of the tower to bend, creating an open and perforated courtyard system that enables deep connections with the neighborhood. The horizontal part of the Giraffe, furthermore, offered adequate spacing for elevated row houses, expanding the residential unit typologies. "Street Lives in a Block," on the other hand (page 270), developed an urban alphabet of layered, bar-like typologies suggesting a neighborhood above an elevated street, distinguished the residential program from the school, and articulated the public social infrastructures as if emerging from the landscape and the neighboring park. Not unlike Steven Holl's *Alphabetical City* from 1980,[16] this project generated a typological system for the residential program that facilitated the creation of a new urban neighborhood with shared open spaces and a highly programmed ground partly accessible to the public.

The attempt to occupy the urban block with a single object is a modernist concept, and uncountable sites in New York are evidence of the tower or slab in the park concept. However, the lessons learned cannot be ignored, and projects that suggested an architectural object also invested in contextual maneuvers. The project "Objection@NCY.edu" (page 276) drew a line across its Chelsea site with a diagonal slab residential structure, while simultaneously offering a generous new park below. To accommodate the pedestrian experience along the sidewalk, the project articulated a programmed landscape perforated with light wells and tectonic

Figure 7: The Giraffe Towers.

human-scale landscape architecture elements. Providing access to the school, this programmed landscape also continued into the interior of the slab, serving as an armature for common and shared infrastructures. "Life | Learning | Leisure in the Voids" (page 238) offers a similar attempt to connect a thickened ground to the urban context, but further interprets the usually horizontal conditions of urban courtyards as vertical perforations for the slab buildings. Here, interconnected interior public spaces and shared programs counterbalance an otherwise dense system of unit typologies and school programs.

Similar strategies were implemented in projects like "Extended Horizons: Vertical Density" (page 292), where three residential towers were proposed for a site surrounded by dividing infrastructures. Expanding upon the initial property boundaries, the school program was located within a tectonic plinth consisting of rotating courtyards and spanning the first three floors. The open spaces, located atop the terraced plinth, are connected back to the street level through a system of ramps, elevators, and stairs. Adjacent underutilized areas were occupied and taken over for outdoor activities and parks as a means of connecting with the site's surrounding neighborhoods. This horizontal ground strategy was also adopted vertically, offering a system of shared amenities and semi-public spaces within the towers as well. Such amenities were strategically located at moments where the towers could benefit from views across the bay, or back into the city.

Understanding the urban block as neither a contextual object nor a hybrid type, a third approach—the distributed urban field—articulates the urban block not as a bounded unit, but as an open system. The most radical interpretation of this concept is offered in "Micro City in New York" (page 244). By atomizing the program, the project established a system of micro towers for both the school and the residential program where pedestrian connections and plazas replace conventional interior circulation infrastructures. "Common Stage" (page 280), similarly, distributed its residential program throughout a series of point towers with different residential-unit typologies atop a second ground. This second ground extended deep into the neighborhood to connect with nearby schools and the East River waterfront, offering a highly connected system of public and shared spaces. On the other hand, "Voxel Grounds" (page 298) established a superstructure for high-density development, allowing the tower to be articulated as a pixelated field flexible enough to address site constraints and view relationships, while simultaneously allowing for vertical neighborhoods with distributed social infrastructures and open spaces.

Lastly, some projects did not clear the sites of their existing fabrics, but instead, after thorough analysis, maintained or retrofitted them. One project at 375 Pearl Street, for instance, was first developed as an early PPP of the Educational Construction Fund (ECF), established in 1966. In 1975, the Murry Bergtraum High School, at 411 Pearl Street, and an adjacent tower at 375 Pearl Street were constructed at the base of the Brooklyn Bridge through a partnership between the ECF and the New York Telephone Company, a deal which funded not only the school but also the budgets for several other projects throughout the city. "375 + 411 Pearl Street" (page 304) argues that high demolition costs would make retrofitting the existing structures a compelling alternative. Working with the structure of the existing tower, the new architectural strategy unfolds in the design of a thickened skin that perforates the tower's skeleton and adds new cultural and public programming.

Prospect

PublicSURplus@NYC.edu offered a fictional, yet realistic setting to investigate the spatial and programmatic potentials of an alternative PPP. Such an arrangement would allow for higher-density affordable and market-rate housing and enable critical upgrades to public education facilities, while also investing in surrounding neighborhoods. Shared amenities and jointly operated open spaces which simultaneously serve the schools and their neighbors emerged as important architectural spaces to construct physical, programmatic, and organizational relationships. Here, spatial negotiation is understood not only from a legal standpoint through the framework of a PPP, but also through acts of architectural design such as the facilitation of programmatically hybridized and temporally conditional spaces.

While the projects effectively explored a wide range of programmatic and typological responses, the spatial solutions were less effective at addressing questions of equity and social justice. For a city like New York, currently in the throes of an affordable housing shortage that the Department of Housing maintains has reached a crisis point not seen before, a new meaning of "public" and "housing" has to be developed through an ongoing dialogue between public administration, private development, interdisciplinary practice, communities, and academic institutions.[17]

Whether challenges raised in the studio brief have been comprehensively resolved by the student projects is up for debate; however, academic assignments like this one are important because they allow students to understand the roles that their discipline can play in the negotiation of public and private interests. While grounded in reality, they also provide speculative laboratories for experimenting with, and developing strategies for challenging the prevailing mindset around Public-Private Partnerships and the effects they have on the shape of our cities. Ultimately, these assignments equip our students with the tools and intellectual discourse to design better cities.

1
Kristine Miller, *Designs on the Public: The Private Lives of New York's Public Spaces* (Minneapolis: University of Minnesota Press, 2007), xxii.

2
Christopher C. M. Lee and Sam Jacoby, "Typological Urbanism and the Idea of the City," *Architectural Design* 81, no. 1 (2011): 14–23, https://doi.org/10.1002/ad.1184.

3
Emanuel S. Savas, *Privatization and Public-Private Partnerships* (New York: Chatham House Publishers, 2000).

4
Savas, *Privatization*.

5
"New York City's Privately Owned Public Spaces: Overview," *Department of City Planning*, accessed June 18, 2020, https://www1.nyc.gov/site/planning/plans/pops/pops.page.

6
Jerold S. Kayden, The New York City Department of City Planning, and The Municipal Art Society of New York, *Privately Owned Public Space: The New York City Experience* (New York: John Wiley & Sons, 2000).

7
Kayden et al., *Privately Owned*, 1.

8
Aleksey Bilogur, "Who Are the Biggest Landowners in New York City?," Aleksey Bilogur </>, blog post, May 27, 2016, accessed June 10, 2020, http://www.residentmar.io/2016/05/27/biggest-landowners-nyc.html.

9
Bilogur, "Who."

10
Joseph Berger and Al Baker, "Saving Schools and Libraries by Giving Up the Land They Sit On," *The New York Times*, March 17, 2013, New York sec., https://www.nytimes.com/2013/03/18/nyregion/public-agencies-needing-money-give-up-land-and-buildings.html.

11
"Vision 2020: New York City Comprehensive Waterfront Plan," *Department of City Planning*, accessed June 23, 2020, https://www1.nyc.gov/site/planning/plans/vision-2020-cwp/vision-2020-cwp.page.

12
Christopher Gray, "Streetscapes/Charles B. J. Snyder; Architect Who Taught a Lesson in School Design," *New York Times*, November 21, 1999, Real Estate sec., https://www.nytimes.com/1999/11/21/realestate/streetscapes-charles-b-j-snyder-architect-who-taught-a-lesson-in-school-design.html.

13
a+t Research Group, *Why Density?: Debunking the Myth of the Cubic Watermelon* (Vitoria-Gasteiz, Spain: a+t Architecture Publishers, 2015).

14
Tine Cooreman, "On Bigness and the City," in "Urban Formation and Collective Spaces," *OASE* 71 (2006): 72–77, accessed June 24, 2020, https://www.academia.edu/36647255/Tine_Cooreman_On_Bigness_and_the_City.

15
Luis Ferré-Sadurní, "The Rise and Fall of New York Public Housing: An Oral History," *New York Times*, June 25, 2018, New York sec., https://www.nytimes.com/interactive/2018/06/25/nyregion/new-york-city-public-housing-history.html.

16
Steven Holl, *The Alphabetical City*, Pamphlet Architecture 5, 1st ed. (1980; repr., Princeton, N.J: Princeton Architectural Press, 1997).

17
Reinhold Martin et al., "The Housing Question," *Places Journal* (June 2012), https://doi.org/10.22269/120625.

Liquid Knowledge: Spaces for Pedagogy in the Speculative City

Sharon Haar

> Knowledge is no longer an immobile solid; it has been liquefied. It is actively moving in all the currents of society itself.
> —John Dewey, "The School and Social Progress"

In 1937 the University of Pittsburgh dedicated one of the most iconic college campuses in the United States, the forty-two-story Cathedral of Learning designed by Charles Klauder, one of the country's leading collegiate architects in the period before World War II. Standing atop a hill in the center of Pittsburgh's Oakland neighborhood, the building celebrates pedagogy, the attainment of knowledge, the capacities of modern building technology, and a land-poor university's ambitions (figure 1). If, thanks to Rem Koolhaas, New York's Downtown Athletic Club (Starrett and Van Vleck, 1930) is the better-known hybrid building, the Cathedral is a purer skyscraper and, perhaps, contains the more compelling, publicly available interior. Its mix of programs includes a soaring commons space built of load-bearing stone, thirty-one "nationality rooms" designed in conversation with local ethnic communities, (originally) the main stacks of the university library, a theater, a food court, lounges, labs, more than twenty floors of classrooms and lecture halls, and departmental and faculty offices, all made possible by steel-frame construction, elevators, and electric lighting, if not central air conditioning (figure 2). It is the predecessor of contemporary educational buildings such as Diller Scofidio + Renfro's Roy and Diana Vagelos Education Center for the Columbia University Medical Center in New York. There is one important difference: the latter's inversion of the logic of the Gothic revival uniform—concealing the precocious, complex body—in favor of an architecture of programmatic over-articulation—letting it all hang out.

Despite being buildings for higher education, the Cathedral of Learning and the Vagelos Education Center set the stage for thinking about the place and space of public education in the city. First, they challenge the notion that education is largely a project of horizontality, the section somehow anathema to both physical and educational

Figure 1: Cathedral of Learning, exterior

Figure 2: Cathedral of Learning, interior

mobility. Second, they project differing visions of identity and identification. Finally, they demonstrate distinct positions on the relationship of modern building technology to hybrid programs, the former largely subsumed within a gridded steel frame set behind a neo-gothic limestone facade, the latter revealing contemporary ideas of educational space made possible by a complex, custom concrete structure behind a glass curtain wall. Each of these issues plays out as we contemplate the history of pedagogical space in New York City and its relationship to larger questions of real estate and urbanism (figure 3).

In the context of contemporary mass customization, the prototype is a leftover of modernism, the resultant of the combination of mass education with infrastructural need. The zenith of the prototypical school building in New York City—three decades, beginning in 1891—aligns with the celebration of education by American philosopher and

Figure 3: Roy and Diana Vagelos Education Center

educator John Dewey. As he noted at the time: "Learning has been put into circulation."[1] With Charles B. J. Snyder's still-respected base models of H, U, E, and later M buildings, New York "put into circulation" over four hundred new schools in an effort to resolve the problems of unhygienic, overcrowded, and underserved spaces, as well as in response to the pressure created by the threefold increase in population in the first three decades of the twentieth century. These results of industrialization and mass immigration brought with them the progressive intellectual revolution desired by Dewey, even if the prototype itself seemed antithetical to his quest for a child-focused experiential education (figure 4).

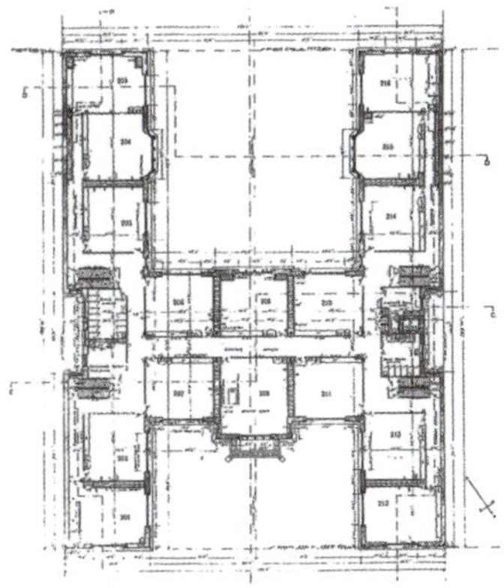

Figure 4: P.S. 90 Plan

Snyder's schools are the schools of Steven Holl's figure-ground Alphabetical City, itself a product of the 1811 Grid of Manhattan and its extrapolation into adjacent boroughs. If the grid is both urban plan and ground plane for the commodification of New York City, a foreshadowing of urban growth, and a reduction of that growth to the economy of real estate speculation,[2] the prototype school building both configures itself to these logics and reforms them. It enables mid-block school buildings on less expensive lots and returns these sites to the public realm. A product of the Progressive Era city, the prototypical alphabet school building also disciplined it, turning in from the street, offering a hygienic alternative to crowded tenements, and acting as an agent of Americanization. While the schools are buildings for public use, representing the institutionalization of education, in their repetition of similar elements dictated by access to light and air, they are not dissimilar to Holl's catalogue of "unmonumental urban buildings."[3] Given these logics, we should not be surprised that Snyder's alphabet-type schools operate equally well when converted to domestic use, as can be found in the recent conversion of P.S. 90 and P.S. 109 in Harlem (figure 5).[4] Holl's examples are buildings of largely repetitive units—apartment buildings, hotels, offices—in which the floor plate is carved out to allow for the maximum depth possible for the given program to have access to light and air.

Figure 5: P.S. 109 under renovation

It is no longer the alphabet school that concerns us as we consider urban surplus, but the hybrid building, what Holl refers to as the "anti-typology."[5] He notes: "In the hybrid, form may remain absolute while function is changing and in conflict," and the base can respond to any variety of public need.[6] If we accept Rem Koolhaas's assertion that "the Grid's two-dimensional discipline also creates undreamt-of freedom for three-dimensional anarchy,"[7] then we are only a step away from the real estate logic that is producing many of today's public school buildings in New York City. Whether the city is offering its own land to developers or negotiating for space in new development, schools are no longer the exception to speculation, they are the product of it. And while these real estate deals might look like the product of Mayor Bloomberg's New York, their history predates the fiscal crisis of the 1970s.[8] In "The Private Lives of Public Schools," Suzanne Schindler delineates the origins of the Educational Construction Fund (ECF) in 1966, a still-extant public benefit corporation designed to allow the city to lease unused air rights to developers in exchange for the construction of a new school on publicly owned land. This practice went dormant until brought back to life during the Bloomberg administration. What made the ECF of the early 1970s powerful, Schindler notes, was that "the grand scale [...] was generally seen as a vehicle for local residents' interests." Moreover, the ECF had an interest in studying new models for educational space and strong control over the choice of architects. Nonetheless, the model worked best when sites were in areas of high land values, even if the need for a new school building might be elsewhere.[9]

As the city emerged from its fiscal crisis and the population began to revive in the late 1980s, the establishment of the School Construction Authority (SCA) brought about a period of repair and new building. In 1989 the Architectural League of New York worked with the Public Education Association on a large-scale research project, New Schools for New York, aimed at informing the SCA on the rehabilitation of existing buildings and the creation of new, often hybrid, construction designed to promote the reorganization of mass education into "small schools."[10] An open call to architects to consider six sites across four boroughs, meetings with community stakeholders, exhibitions, and eventually a publication brought forth a series of progressive proposals for redefining the space of public education across the city. As Rosalie Genevro notes, the goal was unique in that it incentivized "urban opportunism": the "insertion, renovation, and combination with other facilities as building and development strategies."[11] Critical to the project was the idea that new schools would go beyond the pedagogic imperatives of the K-12 space to engage the larger programmatic needs of

Figure 6: Gans, McGrath, Robbins, and Mosseri Flushing proposal for New Schools for New York

their neighborhoods. The site in Sunset Park was to incorporate a new public library; in Harlem, a renovation of the existing P.S. 180 would include a new community center. Notably, in Flushing, architects were asked to insert a small middle school into a proposed commercial building, raising the important question of identity: should the academic program be subsumed within the building block or express itself as a distinct entity? The team of Deborah Gans, Brian McGrath, Mark Robbins, and Shauna Mosseri opted to carve out the base of the speculative building to create a public plaza holding a suspended classroom cube, accessed by ramp from the sidewalk below (figure 6). The project illustrated three key ideas: the expression of the building's hybridity; the engagement with Flushing's busy, immigrant streets; and public-facing spaces intended to be shared with the community. While those who tackled the Harlem site, for instance, contended with how to planimetrically add or subtract from the figure-ground of one of Snyder's notable H-plan schools (P.S. 90, which as noted above has since been converted to residential space), those contending with the Flushing site both looked back at the imperatives of the ECF program and looked to the future: how could the program of the public school be built into the sectional city, and to what extent could it be subsumed within the "three-dimensional anarchy" retroactively foretold by Koolhaas?

In reality, the desire to produce "small schools" played out at fairly mundane levels, at least from an architectural perspective. In "Schoolhouse Shuffle," A+A+A and Gail Robinson describe the complexities of co-locating four discrete schools within the body of the existing, landmarked Standard Oil Building in lower Manhattan. Here issues of entry—students may not enter through the office building lobby, and they share a congested bank of elevators at the rear of the building—and tensions around which schools can and which can't afford to hang a banner declaring their presence are the day-to-day reality of access and identity before even getting to questions of access to social services, libraries, and other community features.[12] While locating an all-female high school focused on business in the building that once contained the offices of several Rockefellers may make sense, other schools are co-located as the result of overcrowding in nearby schools—a consequence of the expansion of residential development in the financial district. Such reorganizations of urban development place multiple challenges on the relationship of existing school building stock to areas in need of the colloquial "seat."[13]

But to what extent has the enterprise of New York City school building attended to the construction of the city's urban realm? Here we might distinguish the urban realm from urban infrastructure. This was certainly a question that undergirded the New Schools for New York program in its attempt to consider hybrid programming that included community centers, public libraries, and even new curricular imperatives. How typologically specific should these new schools be? In her accounting of the development of schools in New York City, Anne Rieselbach covers a shift in the typological approach—in particular, the ways in which post-war schools valued a typological catalogue of parts over a typological approach to the urban site—as well as how educational innovations of the 1960s and 1970s brought innovations in internal space design, including flexible classrooms, more informal teaching areas, new gathering areas for students, and more experiential learning areas.[14] Susana Torre, in her comments as part of the New Schools for New York jury, describes the internal organization of the school as producing "'the model of society' and the world that the school's plan and environment suggests to a child."[15] Rieselbach points to innovations in programmatic sharing as well, for instance the combination of the High School of Art and Design and P.S. 59 in Manhattan (William Lescaze with Kahn and Jacobs, 1959-1960), and highlights the private Acorn

School consolidated into the base of the affordable housing development Phipps Houses. Her examples bring to mind Dewey's conception of the individual mind, which "is important because only the individual mind is the organ of modifications in traditions and institutions, the vehicle of experimental creation."[16] To Dewey, an individual is one "who evolves and develops in a natural and human environment, an individual who can be educated."[17] An individual, perhaps, who participates in the life of the city, capable of negotiating complex building arrangements and programs, perhaps thriving on such hybridity.

If the block archetypically lacks "articulation and differentiation," then, as Koolhaas notes, "it forces Manhattan's builders to develop a new system of formal values, to invent strategies for the distinction of one block from another." At the same time, "architecture is no longer the art of designing buildings so much as the brutal skyward extrusion of whatever site the developer has managed to assemble."[18] How might we reconcile Koolhaas's concept of urban individuation with Dewey's individual mind in the urban space of the city in light of the city's need for both sites for schools and the budget for building them? Koolhaas's individuation is the result of pure capitalist speculation, Dewey's of social life. The SCA describes its own approach to this speculative necessity as follows:

> Because locating space for new schools becomes more and more challenging in a dense city like New York, creative ways to build new schools have to be found. The Mixed Use Facilities program was born from this need. In this program, the SCA seeks out developers and presents the option of co-developing the property, where the lower floors would offer space for educational programs. For the developer, this helps defray development costs. It also eliminates the need for developers to sell space on the lower floors, which is considered less desirable to buyers.[19]

Not occupying the full allowable building envelope is seen as under-utilization of the lot(s) such that even a public building can be considered as underperforming the speculative potential of New York real estate; this is what compels contemporary public-private partnerships, and how in various ways the cubic footage created by the extrusion of the grid translates into the funding required to create public

Figure 7: Spruce Street Educational Campus

infrastructure. Two projects exemplify this principle in hybrid public school/residential buildings. 250 East 57th Street, a product of the ECF, creates new school buildings for the High School of Art and Design and Beekman Hill International elementary school (P.S. 59)—discussed above as an innovative campus of the mid-twentieth century—as part of a fifty-nine-story luxury housing project by SOM (Moore, figure 6). The Spruce Street Educational Campus (P.S. 397), designed by Swanke Hayden Connell & Partners, forms the base of New York by Gehry, a seventy-six-story, stainless steel clad, rental high-rise, and is the product of a negotiation for approval to build that building (figure 7). While the two schools are products of different models—the former is a lease of school air rights to a developer, the latter a "conventional orange brick"[20] shell for a new school in exchange for tax-exempt bonds and other incentives—the architectural results are similar. In each, the school buildings are constructs distinct from the formal and material articulation of the residential towers, the products of two distinct financial and architectural logics, accidental co-inhabitants of an island on Koolhaas's and Zoe Zenghelis's "City of the Captive Globe." Both fill the maximum volume available with programmatic content, but unlike, for instance, the Cathedral of Learning, constructed of a "thematic program," they are clearly the result of a "disparate program," and articulated as such.[21] Whereas the earlier generation of ECF projects asked whether the combination of school and housing or school and commercial development could create surplus beyond the capacity of either, contemporary projects are increasingly transactional. Architecturally, neither produces the type of hybrid building described by Holl and documented by Joseph Fenton in the volume Hybrid Buildings.

Public-private partnerships come about as the result of density, real estate speculation, and, perhaps most importantly, the costs of building new schools or, more accurately, the city's inability to adequately budget for them. Combined, these factors turn the extrusion of the ground plane into a commodity to be leased or negotiated. The role that school buildings now play in the real estate economy of the city is made clear by the rollout of ECF "Requests for Expressions of Interest" for redevelopment of school sites. One recent example is the site of the New York City iSchool and the Chelsea Career and Technical Education High School, which is marketed as "a prime opportunity to capitalize on an area with a strong residential, office and retail market in one of the most highly desirable neighborhoods in Manhattan...[in] an area where there are few remaining opportunities."[22] Given the current building's listing in the state's database of National Register-eligible properties, interested parties are encouraged to consider the incorporation of the building's facade into the resulting building, a twist on Genevro's notion of "urban opportunism." This begs the question: is the ability to provide the infrastructure for quality public education today only made possible by the real estate machinations of an inherently unequal urban landscape?

School projects such as those at 250 East 57th and New York by Gehry, contained within the bodies of their hosts, do not incite much opposition, even if the buildings themselves are occasionally controversial. This is less the case with larger complexes of buildings such as two current ECF projects in Harlem and Brooklyn. Although the projects are different in many respects, public opposition to both hinges on larger concerns about densification, gentrification, and the potential loss of public space.[23] This is unfortunate. If thought through as a coherent whole, the East Harlem full-block site offers opportunities to move beyond a hybrid building model and toward the integration of new educational spaces into a larger piece of urban design. The Brooklyn project creates density at an important infrastructural node. By contrast, residents of the Lower East Side have been fighting to get a new school building built as part of the new, mixed-use Essex Crossing, a project threaded through nine blocks of the Seward Park Urban Renewal Area, which includes mixed-income residential, office, retail (the new Essex Market), public, and cultural space (the relocated Institute for Contemporary Photography).[24] At the very least, the project contains a site slated for a new school, although funds for it are not yet allocated in upcoming budgets, with the Department of Education claiming that community capacity does not warrant a new school. Nonetheless, the incorporation of the school site into the master plan by SHoP and Beyer Blinder Belle, along with community-based centers and spaces for educational programming and work-force development, suggests an overall sense of urbanism, a way forward for contemplating educational space as inherently part of city planning.[25]

As I have argued elsewhere,[26] the city itself is a pedagogical space, or as Shadrach Woods put it fifty years ago:

"Teaching and learning are also performing arts, and the city is the theatre of these performances."[27] Giancarlo de Carlo went further: "The school should not be an island"; rather, it should be "disaggregated and dispersed."[28] For architects of educational space during the student revolts of the 1960s, education and urbanism could not be separated. While many were speaking of higher education, their ideas are worth considering today even in the K-12 environment if we are to realize school buildings that are more than the provision of seats and are capable of providing an urban realm that exceeds or perhaps mitigates the financialization of public resources. Indeed, as one encounters groups of New York City teenagers interacting in the subways of the city in the hours after school dismissal, or recognizes the disconnect between where students live and where they attend school, or considers the multitude of curricular options available to students as they move into middle and high school, Dewey's notion of knowledge as liquid has a counterpart in the physical encounter of student and city. Beyond the school as part of a hybrid building or campus, or integrating the public realm of libraries and community spaces into school buildings, might the resources available throughout a neighborhood (for elementary schools) or the city as a whole (for middle and high schools), workforce housing, and public space become the larger substrate upon which educational space is grown? This would require an infrastructural dimension as well as coordination across multiple private interests, public institutions, and civic organizations. But this SurPlus is nascent in the city we already occupy and stands ready to be recognized as such.

1
John Dewey, "The School and Social Progress," in John J. M. McDermott, ed., *The Philosophy of John Dewey* (Chicago: University of Chicago Press, 1981), 465.

2
See Hilary Ballon, ed., *The Greatest Grid: The Master Plan of Manhattan, 1811–2011* (New York: Museum of the City of New York and Columbia University Press, 2012).

3
Steven Holl, *The Alphabetical City*, Pamphlet Architecture 5 (New York: Pamphlet Architecture Ltd.; San Francisco: William Stout Architectural Books, 1980), 3.

4
See "From the Archives: Harlem's PS90," *Urban Omnibus* (March 2, 2011), accessed February 16, 2020, https://urbanomnibus.net/2011/03/from-the-archives-harlems-ps90/. The P.S. 90 conversion created market-rate condos, middle-class apartments, and space for a nonprofit community organizations. See El Barrio's Artspace PS109, accessed April 13, 2020, https://www.artspace.org/ps109. The P.S. 109 conversion created affordable live/work housing for artists and space for art organizations.

5
Steven Holl, foreword to Joseph Fenton, *Hybrid Buildings*, Pamphlet Architecture 11 (New York: Pamphlet Architecture Ltd.; San Francisco: William Stout Architectural Books, 1985), 3.

6
Holl, *Alphabetical City*, 6, 7.

7
Rem Koolhaas, *Delirious New York: A Retroactive Manifesto for Manhattan* (1978; repr., New York: Monacelli Press, 1994), 20.

8
See Kim Phillips-Fein, *Fear City: New York's Fiscal Crisis and the Rise of Austerity Politics* (NY: Metropolitan Books, 2017).

9
See Susanne Schindler, "The Private Lives of Public Schools," *Urban Omnibus* (March 13, 2019), https://urbanomnibus.net/2019/03/private-lives-public-schools/. As of early 2020, the ECF has created 18,000 "seats" in school buildings, 4,500 units of housing, and 1.2 million square feet of office space; see City Department of Education, accessed February 15, 2020, https://www.schools.nyc.gov/about-us/planning-and-buildings/school-construction.

10
See The Architectural League of New York and Public Education Association, *New Schools for New York: Plans and Precedents for Small Schools* (New York: Princeton Architectural Press, 1992).

11
Rosalie Genevro, introduction to Architectural League and Public Education Association, *New Schools*, 10–11.

12
A+A+A and Gail Robinson, "Schoolhouse Shuffle," *Urban Omnibus*, June 26, 2019, https://urbanomnibus.net/2019/06/schoolhouse-shuffle/. See also Caroline Spivack, "Parents Fear New Charter School Is a 'Disaster Waiting to Happen,'" *Patch*, August 7, 2018, https://patch.com/new-york/downtown-nyc/parents-fear-new-charter-school-disaster-waiting-happen.

13
Gregory Beyer, "For Downtown Primary Schools, Ever Less Wiggle Room," *New York Times*, October 3, 2008, https://www.nytimes.com/2008/10/05/nyregion/thecity/05scho.html. Ultimately, the elementary school did not move to 26 Broadway, as buildings with elevators were deemed inappropriate for this demographic.

14
Anne Rieselbach, "Building and Learning," *New Schools*, 179–180.

15
Susana Torre quoted in Genevro, introduction, *New Schools*, 29.

16
John Dewey, "The Development of American Pragmatism," in John J. M. McDermott, ed., *The Philosophy of John Dewey* (Chicago: University of Chicago Press, 1981), 57.

17
Ibid.

18
Koolhaas, *Delirious New York*, 20, 88.

19
Julia van den Hout, *Building Great Schools for a Great City* (Novato, CA: ORO Editions, 2019), 26.

20
Ibid., 160.

21
Fenton, *Hybrid Buildings*, 6.

22
CBRE, "131 Avenue of the Americas RFEI," undated, accessed February 20, 2020, https://infohub.nyced.org/reports/financial/educational-construction-fund/proposed-projects.

23
See Alexandra Lange, "Is America's Densest City Ready to Make Room? Our New York-based Architecture Critic Says, 'Yes, in My Backyard,'" *Curbed New York*, September 12, 2018, https://ny.curbed.com/2018/9/12/17841844/downtown-brooklyn-80-flatbush-building-yimby, and Schindler, "The Private Lives of Public Schools."

24
"Assembly Member Niou, Colleagues Renew Push for School at Essex Crossing," *The Lo-Down: News from the Lower East Side*, November 2017, http://www.thelodownny.com/leslog/2017/11/assembly-member-niou-colleagues-renew-push-for-school-at-essex-crossing.html; James S. Russell, "Why Essex Cross Is a Model Mega-Development," *Citylab*, September 12, 2019, https://www.citylab.com/design/2019/09/essex-crossing-development-nyc-real-estate-lower-east-side/596818/.

25
The *New York Times* architecture critic refers to Essex Crossing as the "Anti-Hudson Yards." See Michael Kimmelman, "Essex Crossing Is the Anti-Hudson Yards," *New York Times*, November 7, 2019, https://www.nytimes.com/2019/11/07/arts/design/essex-crossing.html.

26
Sharon Haar, *The City as Campus: Urbanism and Higher Education in Chicago* (Minneapolis: University of Minnesota Press, 2011).

27
Shadrach Woods, "The Education Bazaar," *Harvard Educational Review* 39, no. 4 (December 1969), 119.

28
Giancarlo de Carlo, "Why/How to Build School Buildings," *Harvard Educational Review* 39, no. 4 (December 1969): 22, 29.

Partnerships for Transformational Development in New York City

Carrie Moore

Figure 1: 252 E. 57th Street, Skidmore, Owings & Merrill.

On its surface, the undulating glass tower at 252 East 57th Street appears to be yet another residence for affluent New Yorkers on an eastern extension of what is sometimes called "Billionaires Row." What is not immediately evident is that the sixty-five-story building is just one component of a successful public-private partnership that, after years of planning, also includes two state-of-the-art public school facilities next door at 250 East 57th Street (figure 1). Public-private partnership arrangements such as this, involving the public school system and a private developer, have become the new local model for redeveloping failing public school buildings when additional zoning air rights are available. This development model represents a synergy between the investment potential of New York

City real estate for private gain and the regeneration of public service infrastructure critical to sustaining local neighborhoods and the economic growth of the city. The completed development responds creatively to economic constraints and addresses programmatic needs with durable construction techniques—achieved through a dynamic collaboration facilitated by SOM with the New York City School Construction Authority and private developer World Wide Group. The role of an architect in complex projects such as this, where priorities can be divergent between each partner, becomes much more than just design thinking—it is one of facilitator, analyst and advocate that can yield outcomes that are not obvious at the onset and are transformative in their resolution. By playing a multifaceted role in this complex project, SOM's team was essential to the project's successful completion.

New York's 1,840 public schools are managed by the city's Department of Education (NYCDOE), which in 1988 surrendered control of the Board of Education's capital projects to the New York City School Construction Authority (SCA), a public-benefit corporation that manages the design, construction, and renovation of school facilities and is funded through city hall's budget. But the task of partnering with private developers in order to finance new public school projects is taken on by an older, recently revived state public-benefit corporation, the New York City Educational Construction Fund (ECF). Chartered in 1966, the ECF was a pioneering experiment in financing new public schools by selling tax-exempt bonds to raise capital for land, predevelopment, and construction costs for mixed-use developments anchored by new and much-needed public schools, paying back bond-holders with rents generated from its unique portfolio. Early ECF projects included low- and moderate-income housing thanks to a variety of available public subsidies, and included schools such as P.S. 126 in the Bronx (the ECF's pilot project) as well as Confucius Plaza in Manhattan's Chinatown. But, following President Richard Nixon's moratorium on federal housing programs in 1973 and a state-wide economic downturn, ECF ultimately had to be bailed out by New York City in 1975 in order to avoid defaulting on its bonds.[1] Dormant until the Michael Bloomberg administration reintroduced it in the early 2000s, the ECF is back and issuing Requests for Proposals (RFPs) on city-owned land in order to generate interest from developers—an arrangement that provides funds for the construction of combined occupancy structures on city land when additional zoning air rights are available for development. The school component of any such project is financed through tax-exempt bonds as well as the rents, leases, and tax-equivalency payments collected by the ECF, while future revenues are used to pay off the school facility's debt. The construction of these projects is overseen by the SCA to ensure that each new school facility meets the standards of its entire portfolio. The first such example under Bloomberg—and the first new public school to be privately financed since the 1980s—was East Side Middle School, which opened in 2010 through a partnership with developers, the DeMatteis Organization and the Mattone Group. Located in Manhattan on 91st Street and 1st Avenue, the project included a building with retail and 120 residential units, all under a seventy-five-year lease from the city, with the purpose of paying off the school's $45 million construction cost via annual payments from the developers.[2] In the case of the 250 East 57th Street project, that meant allowing World Wide to build luxury residences and retail in return for constructing a new facility for an expanding P.S. 59 (pre-kindergarten through grade 5; enrollment: 638 students) and the High School of Art and Design (grades 9 through 12; enrollment: 1,466 students), which opened in 2012 as part of Phase One. (The residential tower opened in 2016.) This partnership resulted in 300,000 gross square feet (gsf) of school space and 30,000 gsf of retail space (a Whole Foods Market) in Phase One, followed by 470,000 gsf of residential space (condominiums), 3,000 gsf of loading space, and an additional 80,000 gsf of residential space (market-rate rentals) in Phase Two.

The three most critical elements of the arrangement were the understanding that the city would not give up control of the land (which was provided in a ninety-nine-year land lease to World Wide), that the schools had to remain in continuous operation and open prior to the construction of the residential portion, and that the city had the right of approval for the design of the school—which was accomplished through a collaboration with the SCA.

These two existing schools, located inside a utilitarian mid-century structure on the corner of East 57th Street and 2nd Avenue since 1960, were identified by the city as being most in need of upgrades. Through the ECF, World Wide was able to apply land use rights in exchange for building a new school facility. Unique to New York, this financing model makes it possible for underfunded schools to receive new investments that would be almost impossible to arrange with public funds alone. In order to move this public school project forward, SOM and World Wide were required to follow the SCA's Design Standards, including compliance with standard specifications and details, room-planning standards, and the Green Schools Guide (the SCA's equivalent to LEED for Schools). A project of this kind, however, must also meet the developer's pro forma in order to be financially viable during the extended period of time in which only retail rental revenue was available during Phase One.

In 2005 World Wide Group and the ECF secured the project with a different architectural concept, but immediately ran into challenges with the complexity of its phasing. SOM was brought on board the following year, developing a new concept and helping to restructure it after the Great Recession of 2008 made financing for the first concept impossible. While the residential tower had to be redesigned and the total amount of retail reduced, the school concept essentially remained the same throughout.

Efficiencies from the updated project scope included a shared school kitchen and the elimination of single-loaded corridors. A reduction in the size of the Whole Foods eliminated significant loading-area requirements, including truck elevators and turntables, that would have involved major structural transfers, costly equipment, and an inefficient below-grade layout. The height of the Phase Two residential tower was maximized as well.

Unlocking density and height through the design was critical to the project's success. So, rather than treat the entire lot as one development, a lot line was established at the western side of the existing seven-story school, forming a street wall with sky exposure plane massing for the Phase One development in order to use the remaining air rights for a tower on a base zoning massing for Phase Two (figure 2). Every zoning square foot saved from Phase One meant greater development area for Phase Two. With a corner site, the Phase Two retail and residential portion benefits from the exposure provided by three street frontages, and the location of the school development mid-block allowed for access to light and views. This is often overlooked in mixed-use developments where schools are placed at the base of the building to respond to the pragmatic requirement of easy access and net to gross efficiencies that encourage less circulation space. In a vertical

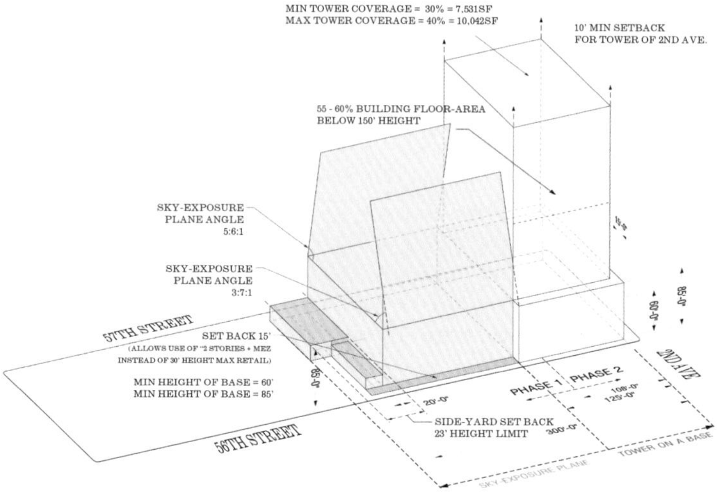

Figure 2: 250 E. 57th St, zoning envelope diagram. Skidmore, Owings & Merrill.

school the circulation serves the functional need to connect spaces and acts a platform for social interaction. As a school gets taller, it is the connective tissue of circulation that becomes the opportunity to blur the lines of what a teaching space should be and where it can occur.

Phase One delivered the school building for P.S. 59, the High School of Art and Design, and Whole Foods all at the same time. The structure of the deal drove a complex phasing scenario, requiring design and technical creativity. Prior to Phase One, P.S. 59 students were relocated to a temporary school on East 63rd Street, which later became the permanent home of P.S. 267. The high school portion was consolidated into a smaller building footprint on the existing site. In this make-ready phase, the existing seven-story high school remained, while the primary school portion—which included the shared kitchen, cafeteria, gymnasium, and auditorium—was demolished. As a result, storage rooms in the high school were renovated to become exercise and yoga rooms, administrative offices were converted into a warming kitchen and servery, lunch periods were expanded so fewer students could occupy a smaller cafeteria, the library was consolidated to accommodate administrative offices, and new mechanical systems were installed because windows were removed from the entire west side of the building to comply with code requirements for the new imaginary lot line to the adjacent Phase One development. The optimization of existing spaces was achieved primarily by removing a defunct escalator in the center of the floorplate and converting this space into new mechanical, electrical, and plumbing risers to serve new equipment on the roof that provided ventilation, heating, and cooling. Because the renovation work and the construction of the new facility would take up an entire four-year high school term, the renovation required additional upgrades in order to enhance the student and faculty school-day experience. This included new equipment, lighting, and shared program spaces. This entire first phase of construction occurred over two summers and one school year before Phase One could even begin. Phase One took place the following three years, during which the existing high school's masonry wall—its windows now infilled with CMU block—established the necessary separation between old and new. For Phase Two, students from both schools were moved into their new facility while the demolition of the original seven-story high school building took place, allowing for work on the Phase Two residential tower to proceed.

There were many conversations and studies related to the project's proper separation of all the facilities. How would the schools and retail co-exist? How would one party deal with damages or interferences from the other? The Phase One building was optimized through verticality and became a shrink-wrapped volume following the permitted zoning envelope (figure 2). With one point of entry to the

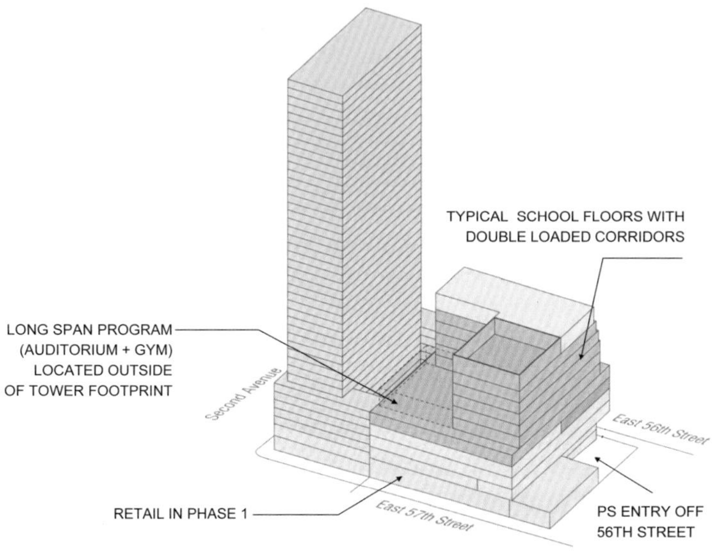

Figure 3: 250 E. 57th St, phase 1 and II massing. Skidmore, Owings & Merrill.

Figure 4: Rooftop outdoor playspace at P.S. 59. Skidmore, Owings & Merrill.

site for utilities, shared service rooms were created and sub-metered for both user groups. As a result, the retail portion required easements to access the air-handling units and cooling towers on top of the school that serviced the entire facility. Double structural slabs with waterproofing were constructed, separating school floors above retail and retail above school programs (figure 3). Horizontal plumbing, electrical, and mechanical distribution had to remain within the facility it was serving. This meant that within the usable area of the floorplates, no corner could go without optimization on the retail floors in order to increase rent dollars to square footage. The egress stairs from the school tower were required by code to exit at-grade along East 57th Street, and the orientation of any non-retail program along the street frontage had to be minimal. This required a fire-rated enclosure and stair configuration that twisted and offset to clear as much usable area as possible for the ground-floor retail. Numerous agreements were folded into the final contract once Whole Foods was officially on board, detailing everything down to permitted delivery hours, truck size limitations, and exhaust volume and locations. The retail component was given East 57th Street frontage due to its high pedestrian traffic. The quieter East 56th Street side was given delivery access as well as separate entrances for P.S. 59 and the High School of Art and Design. Divided by a lot line, the Phase One and Two buildings also had design issues to solve, with conversations taking place with the developer about residential unit views and their proximity to the primary school's outdoor play space on the sixth-floor roof (figures 3 & 4).

SOM's active role in the design process also led to concessions from the SCA for the sake of a better and more affordable building. SOM's team persuaded the authority to reconsider its standard masonry cavity wall in favor of a metal panel on engineered cold-formed steel. As designed, the metal panel on engineered cold-formed steel framing had better thermal performance than the SCA standard masonry cavity wall, as well as lighter wall assembly which reduced structural loads. A metal panel assembly achieved greater quality control during erection than a masonry cavity wall would have had, resulting in shorter installation time. This change allowed for the cost savings the developer needed while providing a better-performing exterior wall for the school that requires less maintenance over the life of the building.

Figure 5: High School of Art and Design, interior.
Skidmore, Owings & Merrill. Photo: Eduard Hueber

Beyond the key decisions made on material selection and construction scheduling, the school building, like any other public building in New York City since 1983, came with a public art component. Thanks to the Mayor Ed Koch-initiated Percent for Art program, in which 1 percent of the budget for city-funded construction projects is spent on artwork, students inside P.S. 59 and the High School of Art and Design now get to experience high-quality visual works. Some of these pieces are even made by graduates of the same school. While an architecture firm's role in the art selection of a New York City public work varies from commission to commission, SOM was invited to be a voting member of 250 East 57th Street's art selection committee, which included people from the school system, the Department of Education, and three independent art professionals.

The two artists selected, Art Spiegelman and Lawrence Weiner, are both graduates of the New York City public school system. Spiegelman, in fact, graduated from the High School of Art and Design in 1965 before embarking on a successful career as a cartoonist and editor. His most celebrated work, *Maus*, was the first graphic novel to win a Pulitzer Prize. Weiner, a Stuyvesant High graduate, is best known for his conceptual, typographic art which has been exhibited around the world over the last fifty years. Inside the SOM-designed school building, Spiegelman's contribution is a stained-glass piece along a hallway that looks down into the cafeteria (figure 5). The 60-foot-wide work, displayed as a series of frames, depicts the development of a young robot's brain and the professional outlets it (and the students looking at the piece) can pursue through education. Weiner's piece spells out "ONE WAY & ANOTHER… CUSPED" in a modern, industrial font not unlike his other typographic works, while the wording defines the placement of complementary curved lines. This work is laid out on the floor of the main entrance to the school in plain view for all visitors, staff, and students to see upon entering.

SOM's team added another layer of art inside the building, creating large-scale mosaics of selected works by graduates of the high school in the floor of each corridor with a corresponding wall plaque referencing the original art. The architects, along with a committee of students, teachers, and administrators, chose works including the depiction of DC Comics superheroes (created by alumni Ralph Bakshi, Neal Adams, and Jimmy Palmiotti) to install along the eighth floor, and a piece on the eleventh floor by figurative artist Steven Assael (class of '75) that depicts a group of firemen outdoors observing a massive plume of smoke. The end result provides an added layer of purpose and inspiration by design.

The success of 250 East 57th Street after years of planning and flexibility in the face of changing circumstances demonstrates the resilience and creative nature of New York's most competitive real estate developers. It also demonstrates an awareness among the city's public school agencies that while they have many pressing needs, they also have assets that can be leveraged from a position of great strength. SOM's role demonstrates the value of an architecture firm's active participation in a public-private partnership due to its understanding of materials, construction logistics, and the varied needs of users—from

Figure 6: 321 East 96th Street, Skidmore, Owings & Merrill.

delivery driver to student—that the partnerships may not always fully grasp (figure 6).

The ECF continues to develop P3 project sites, such as 321 East 96th Street in East Harlem (a 1.3-million-square-foot development comprising a sixty-eight-story residential tower); new facilities for the School of Cooperative Technical Educational vocational trade school, Heritage School, and Park East High School; as well as renovation of the existing Marx Brothers Playground, managed by the NYC Parks Department. Ambitious projects such as these, however, are still subject to the scrutiny of the local community, which often has divergent thoughts on what the neighborhood needs and, ultimately, who benefits from such developments. Vacant sites are disappearing in New York City, but creative designs that tackle the issues of preservation and expansion raised by complicated sites are increasingly the norm, due not only to the city's great density but to a rising awareness of the environmental impact of large-scale demolition, new construction, and carbon emissions. These are issues that architecture and construction firms will continue to grapple with for years to come.

In a city with high land costs, New York's most vulnerable public schools can, under the right circumstances, provide opportunities that benefit both developers' bottom line and the expanding minds of young students. Creating these circumstances will require steadfast oversight that protects the interests of the school system through ironclad agreements with private-sector partners before shovels hit the ground. The partnership between the ECF and World Wide benefited from its location, yet we continue to see an appetite from developers to take on more complex project sites to invest in equally desirable locations. Challenges remain for similar projects in areas segregated from New York's prosperity. Can we as architects demonstrate what is possible and encourage development on less-established sites that have the potential to positively impact the local community while also providing the financial incentive for developers to keep taking these risks? What needs to happen in order to make these sites advantageous for development while serving neighborhoods with the greatest needs?

The final result of the 250-252 East 57th Street project gives the perpetually cash-strapped public school system a tremendous facility in exchange for the astronomically valuable land and air rights around it that World Wide now benefits from through its residential tower. SOM's active participation led to important breakthroughs in material use, spatial arrangements, logistics, public art, and economic efficiencies that brought the project to life.

These public-private developments in New York City could alter the way we look at densification in our cities. If long-standing contract agreements with various NYC public school entities that oversee programming and services—such as school meals and community-based events—were abandoned, tremendous opportunities would be available for the private component to be of continual benefit to public schools. The result could be meal contracts with grocery and food-service tenants that provide healthier and fresher food, and could even go so far as to incorporate educational gardens with urban farming. The public schools could collaborate with fitness and performing arts entities, enriching school programming by utilizing school theaters, gymnasiums, and exercise rooms, extending into programming beyond the school year. Strengthening the link between the public and private users, this approach could ultimately streamline a building's program spaces to incorporate more shared programming like kitchens and assembly spaces, allowing for even greater development potential. And with an increasing portfolio of public-private partnership developments in the city, development could be increased on a single site to free up space on existing school sites for green space or renewable-energy generation. By encouraging circular economies in what are currently linear production processes, urban densification can be focused less on building and more on maximizing developments in ways that can contribute to reducing waste, energy usage, and our carbon footprint. The role architecture plays to provide transformational change in our communities can be realized in ways that are beyond the built form. As architects we should seize these opportunity to realize our work with meaningful impact to our culture and environment to enhance the way we live, work, and learn.

1
Susanne Schindler, "The Private Lives of Public Schools," *Urban Omnibus*, March 13, 2019. The 1967 *New York Times* article on the opening of P.S. 126 can be found at https://timesmachine.nytimes.com/timesmachine/1967/07/02/issue.html.

2
Stephen Ceasar, "City Opens East Side's First New Public School Building in 50 Years," *New York Times*, June 18, 2010, https://www.nytimes.com/2010/06/19/nyregion/19school.html.

Site 1
P.S. 30 Hernandez/Hughes | Harlem
Site 2
P.S. / M.S. 57—James Weldon | East Harlem
Site 3
Manhattan-Hunter Science High School | Lincoln Center
Site 4
P.S. 33 | Chelsea
Site 5
Shuang Wen School | Lower East Side
Site 6
Murry Bergtraum High School For Business Careers | Civic Center

Site 1

P.S. 30 Hernandez/Hughes | Harlem

Site 2

P.S. / M.S. 57—James Weldon | East Harlem

Site 3

Manhattan-Hunter Science High School | Lincoln Center

Site 4

P.S. 33 | Chelsea

Site 5

Shuang Wen School | Lower East Side

Site 6

Murry Bergtraum High School For Business Careers | Civic Center

Life | Learning | Leisure in the Voids

Student Team
Andres Soria G.
Taylor Kitchens

Instructor
Mona El Khafif

Harlem's Hernandez/Hughes public school (P.S. 30) site sits at the intersection of two under-leveraged urban corridors: one of pedestrian circulation to and from the 125th Street transit station on Lexington Avenue and the other a series of connected green spaces along 3rd Street. This project amplifies the convergence of the two, and forms a new community nexus by adopting a massing strategy of two vertical slabs separated by a large, shared, open space. To draw the public further into the site, both slab buildings—featuring residential units, a new elementary school, and an adult vocational training center—are punctuated by a multi-scalar array of interior void spaces shared between the major program elements, the surrounding community, and the greater public.

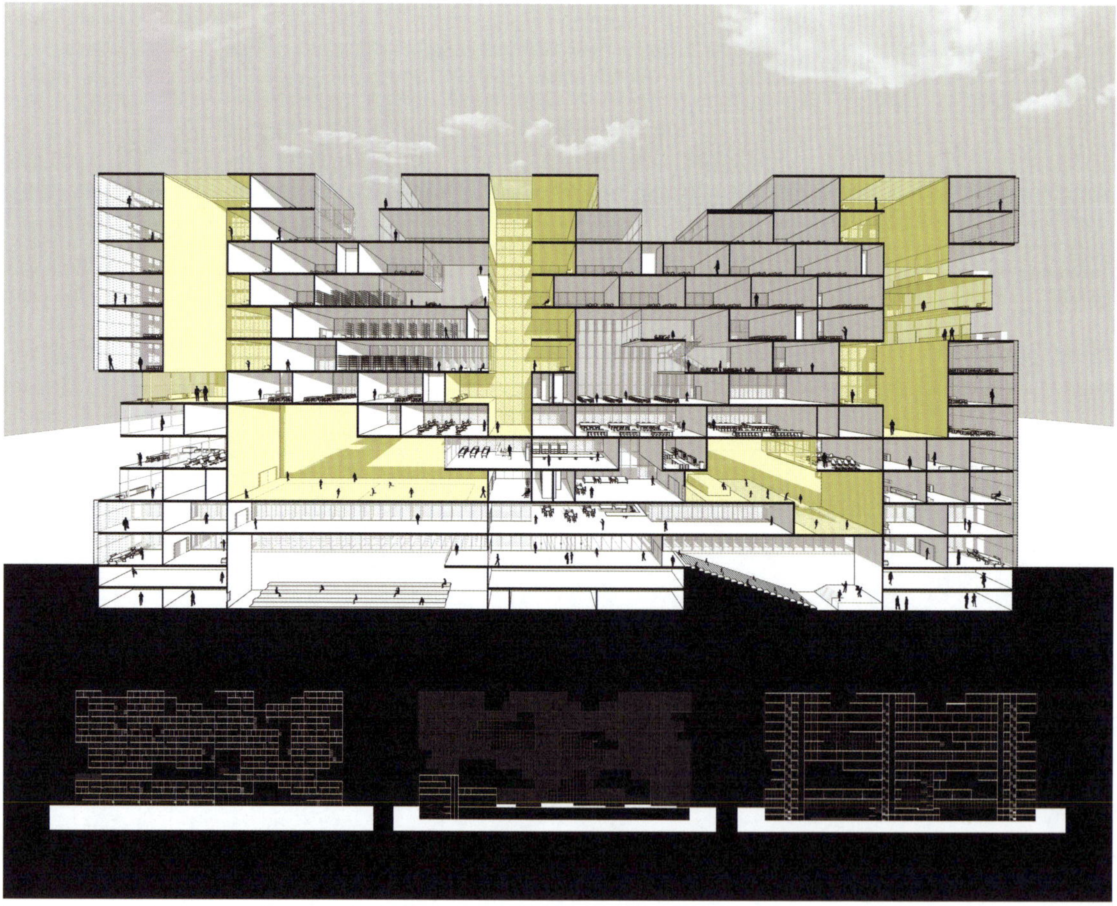

Section perspective through public space voids (yellow)

Perspective view

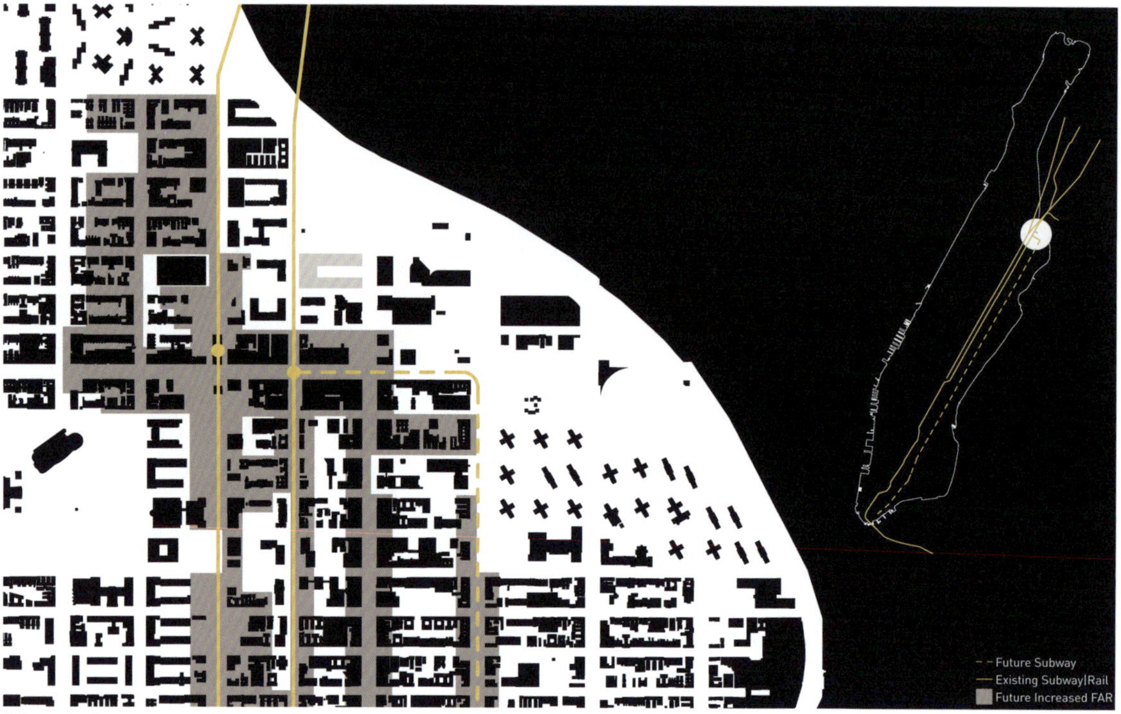

Site context map

Building section illustrating mass and void facade strategy

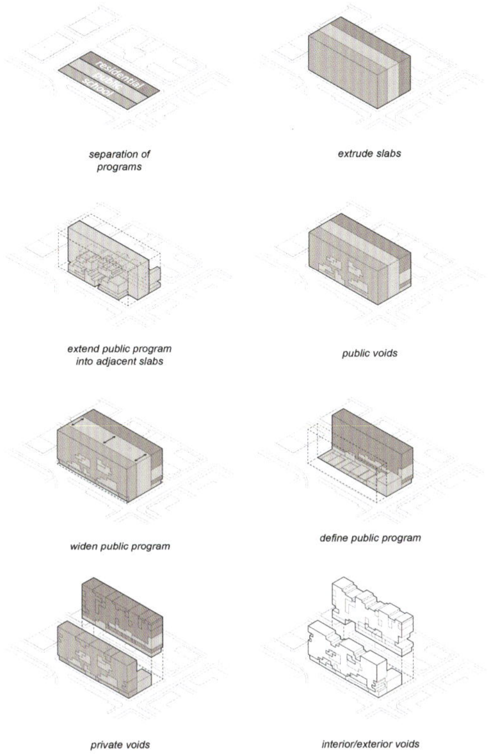

Operational diagrams

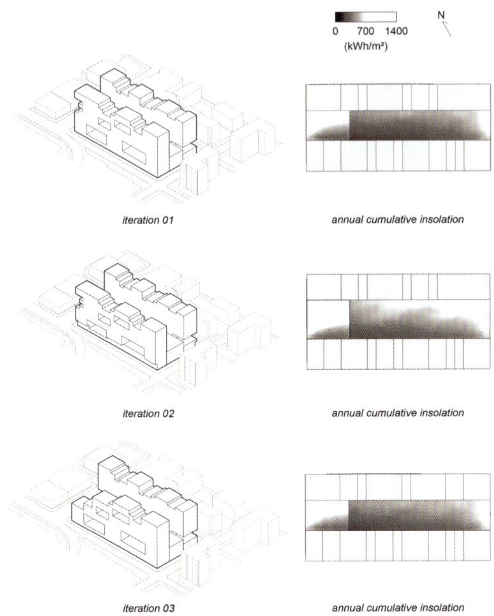

Solar studies

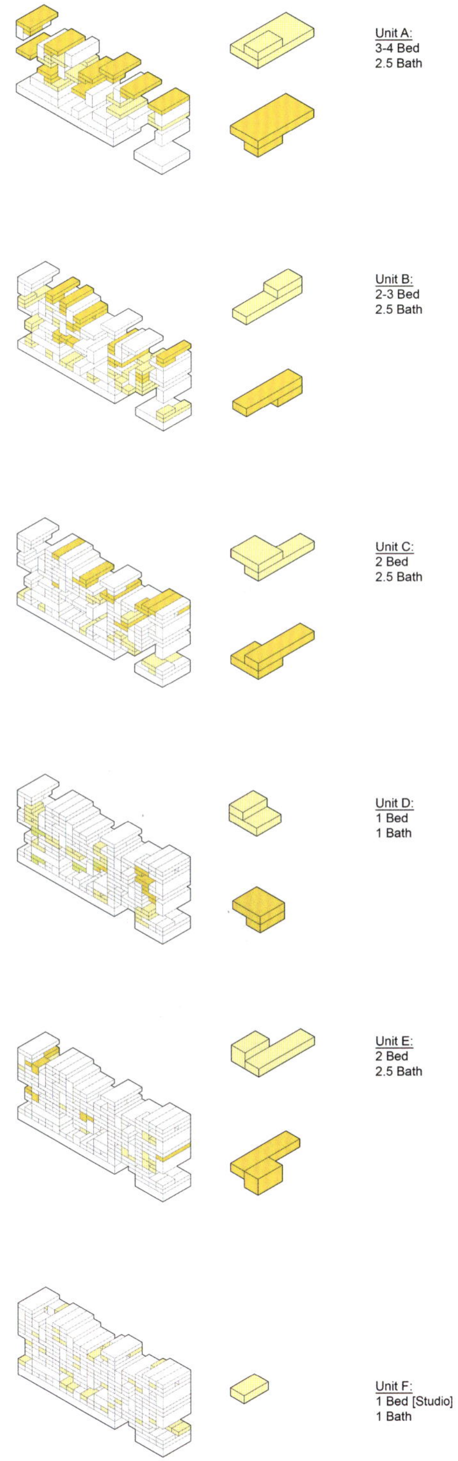

Residential unit typologies

1:200 model, "Life | Learning | Leisure in the Voids"

1:200 model, "Micro City in New York"

Micro City in New York

Student Team
Shan Zhu
Jiawei Luo

Instructor
Matthew Jull

This project challenges the notion of scale in a city that is defined by a relentless 264' × 900' rectangular city block. By introducing a new city fabric within the larger one, diverse programmatic elements such as a church, climbing club, aquarium, library, gym, office, museum, and shops can be mixed and combined with housing and the existing public school to create a compact, dense, neighborhood of low to mid-rise towers. Altogether, fifty-five unique mini towers create a microcosm of individual expression, circulation, exchange, and interaction for residents and public within the anonymous Manhattan street grid. Linked together by a sloping plinth containing the redesigned public school, the site is not only functional and efficient, but it also critically engages the relevant issues of digital communication, navigation technology, and the role of shared spaces within an increasingly anonymous urbanity.

Perspective view of micro-city skylne

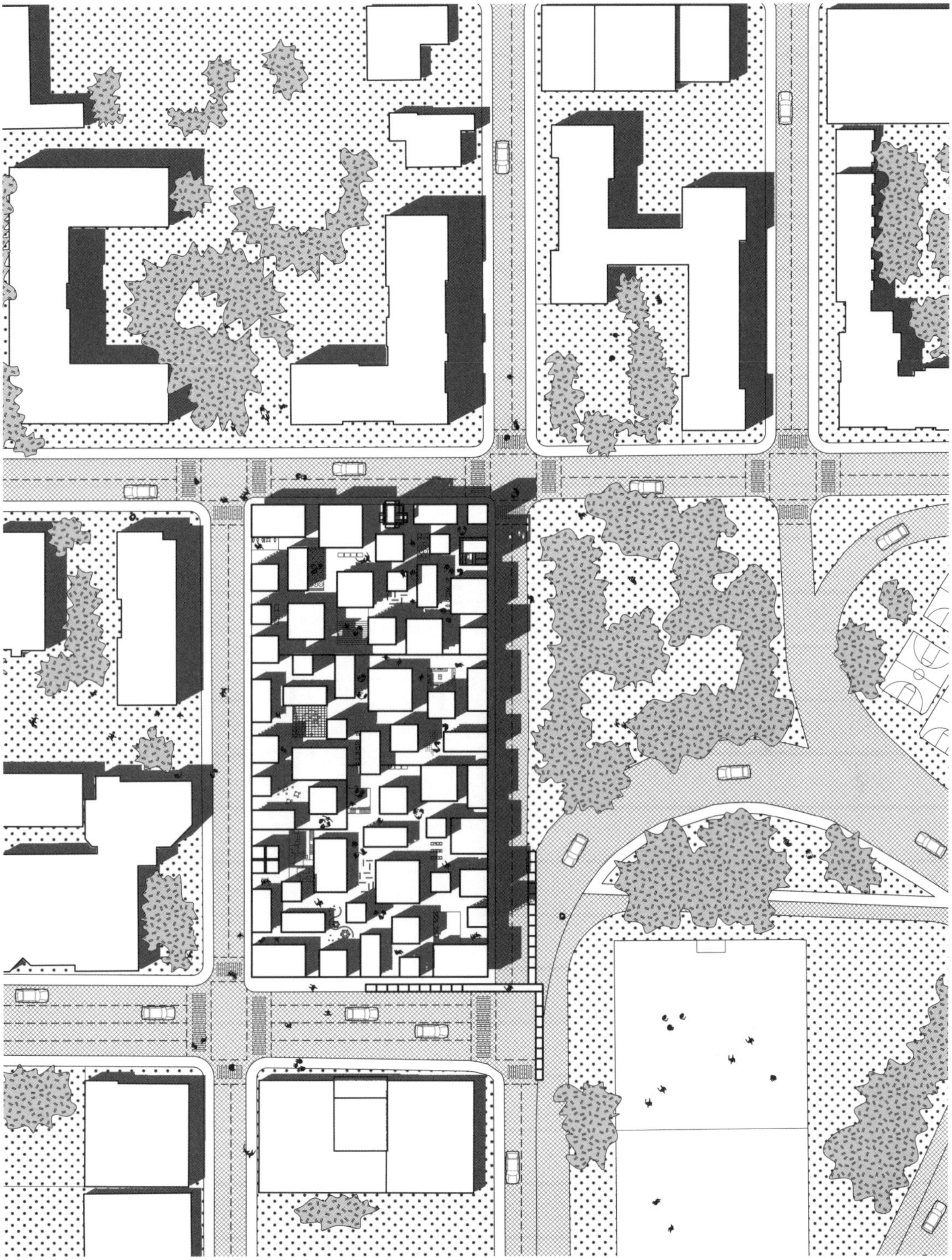

Site and urban context plan

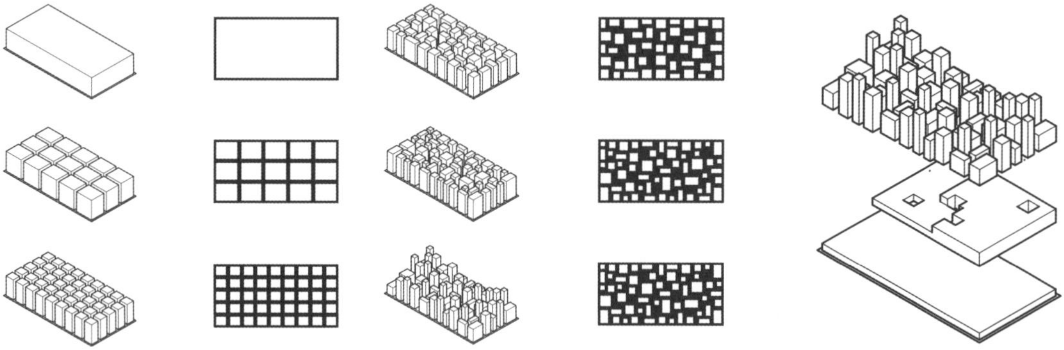

Urban concept / operation diagrams

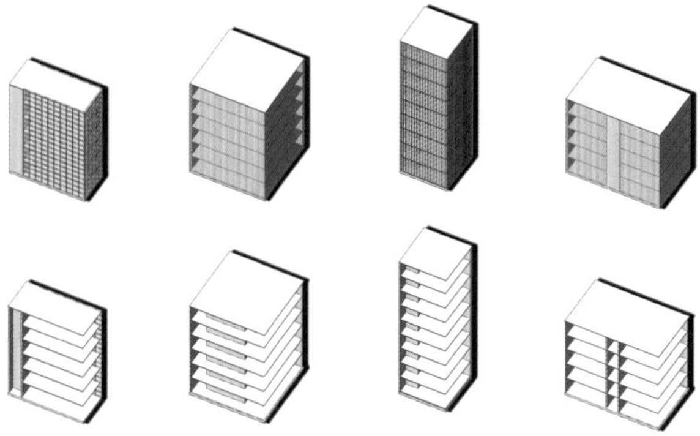

Residential typologies

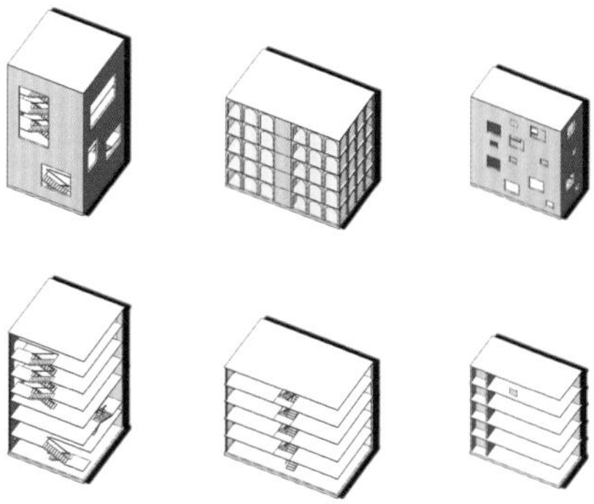

School auxiliary typologies

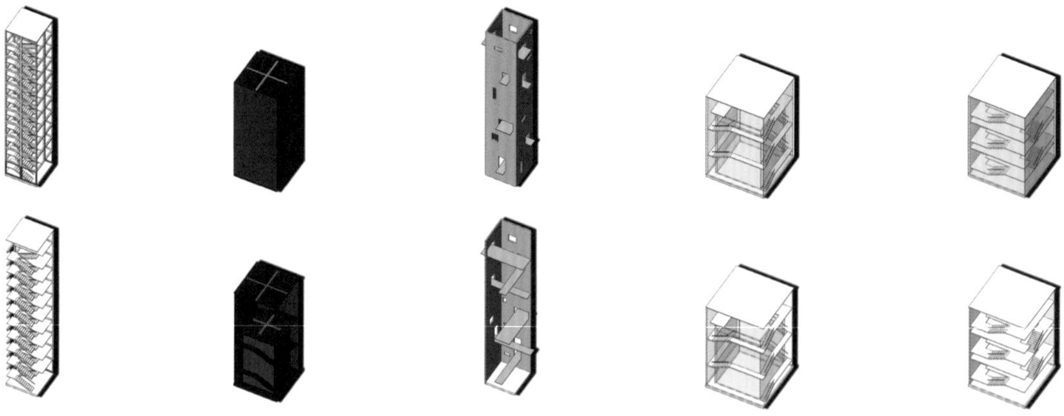

Public space typologies

Urban isometric drawing, southeast view

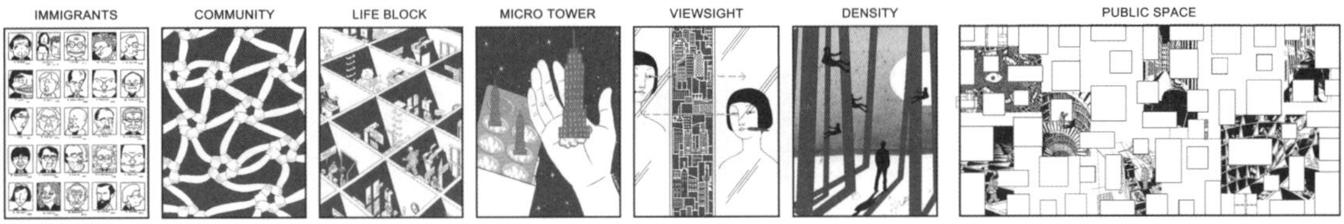

Micro-city concept narrative panel

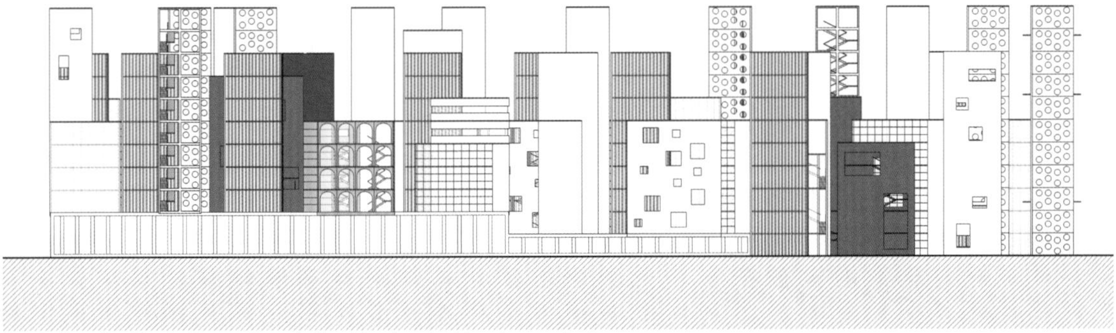

South elevation illustrating scalar relationship of project to urban context

Vertical Commons

Student Team
Haitong Yu
Linxi Lu

Instructor
Mona El Khafif

Unlike most of Manhattan, the area around P.S. 030 in East Harlem (site 1) is characterized by low and mid-rise residential buildings, and features a limited amount of desirable public space. Vertical Commons argues that a significant increase in verticality and programmatic density on the site would maximize the land area available to serve as new, public, open space. Accordingly, the site strategy is organized around a central, multi-level courtyard, encircled by a wide range of public and semi-public spaces relating to the major programmatic elements of the site: a school, residences, and community programs including a library, a gymansium, auditoriums, and rooftop gardens. These perimeter spaces are stacked vertically within a staggered series of bands: encouraging the project's vertical growth, and generating apertures and moments of slippage in the exterior massing which yield a granular series of open spaces such as terraces and public viewing platforms.

Section perspective through interior courtyard and staggered massing layers

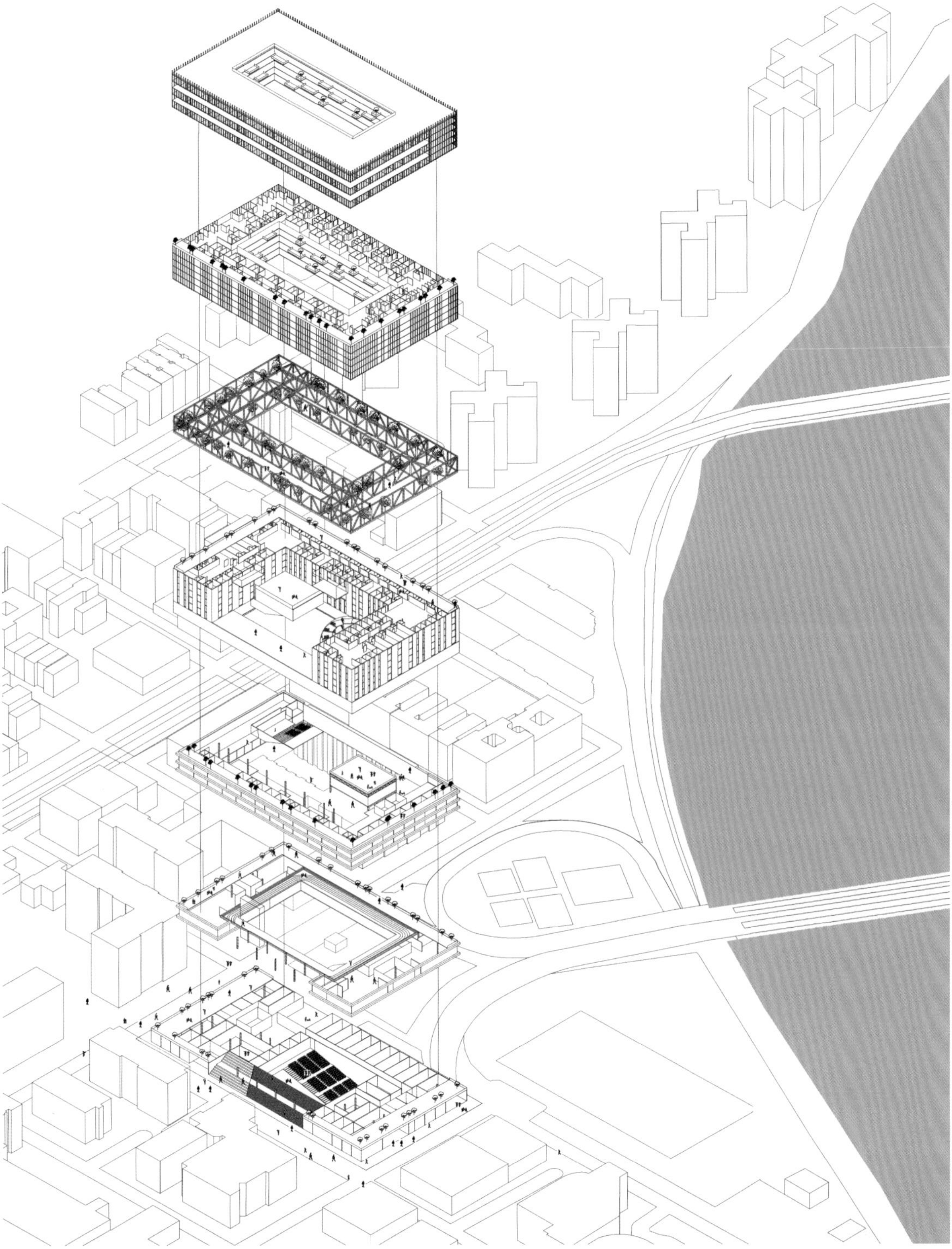

Delayered isometric view of staggered massing layers, southeast view

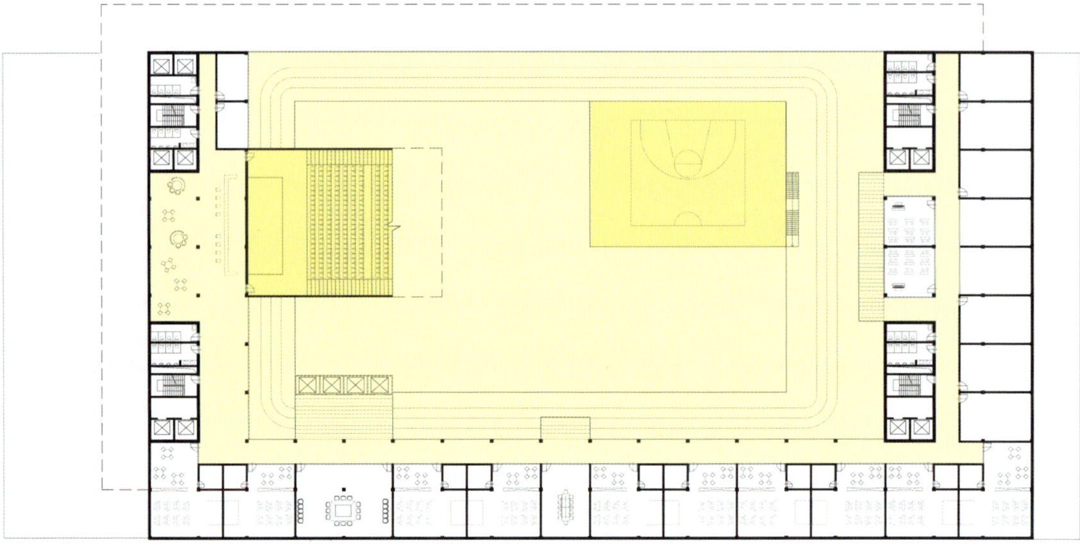

Upper level floorplan at viewing terrace

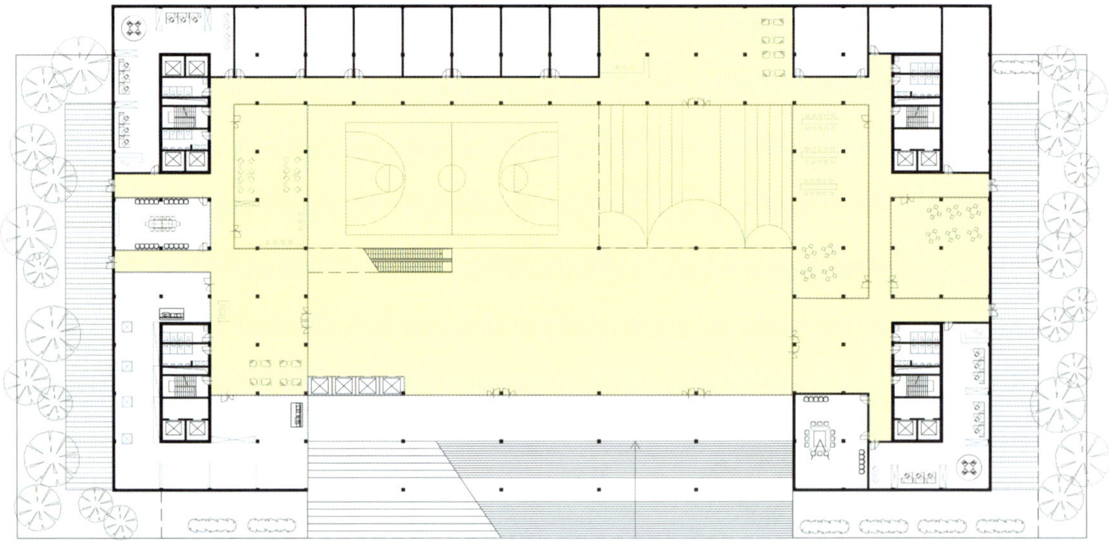

Ground floor plan

Exterior perspective view and concept diagrams

Common Ground

Student Team
Barrett Weaver
Rita John

Instructors
Kyriaki Kasabalis

The East Harlem triangle (site 1) is located at both the physical and perceived edge of Manhattan island. Common Ground aims to push back on this sense of physical, economic, and social marginality by fusing residential, educational, and library programming to create a new, neighborhood-centric live/work/learn campus. The site strategy embraces porous pedestrian circulation, programmatic hybridity, and the urbanist need for multi-scalar, "in-between" spaces. At the scale of the individual classroom unit, for instance, the vibrancy of the project is not driven by the building masses themselves but the symbiotic relationships they share with adjacent, shared amenity spaces. At the block scale, an urban landscape extends beyond the site boundaries toward the East River, transforming two currently isolated traffic islands into new pocket parks with complementary public programming.

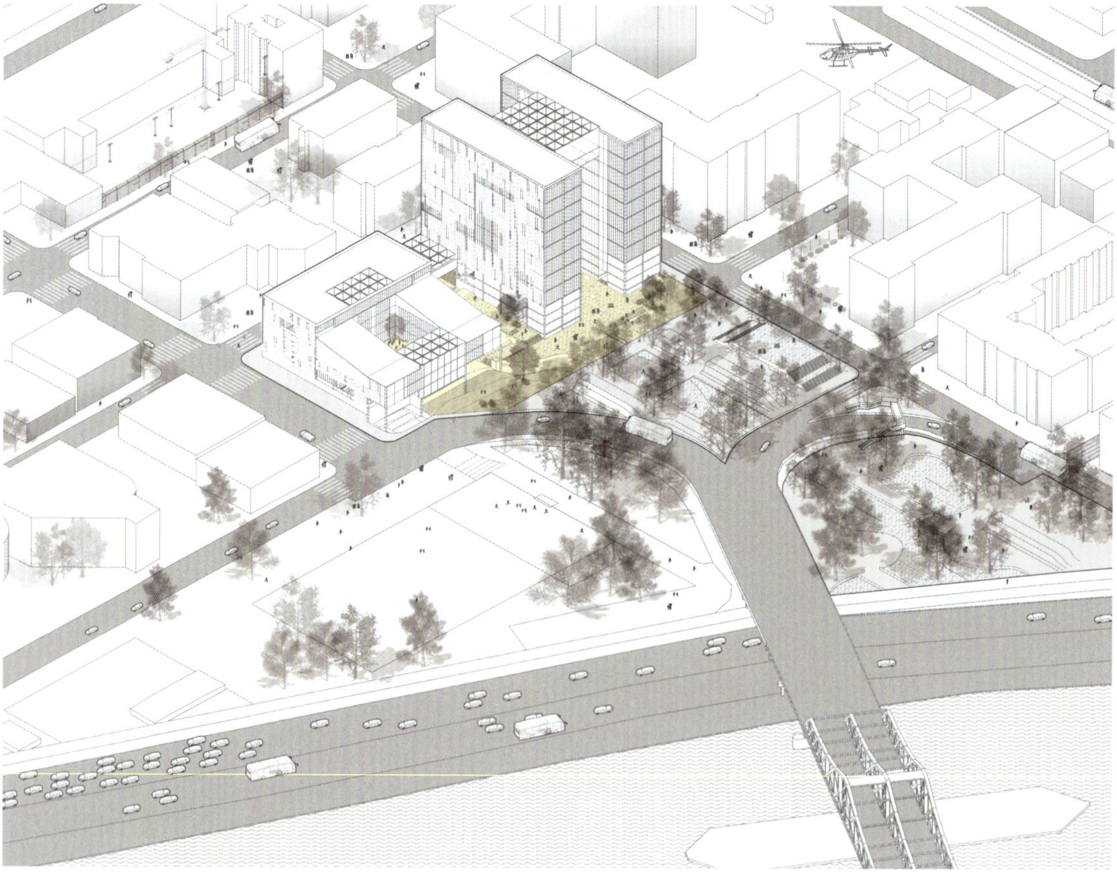

Isometric view showing site and surrounding publically used lands

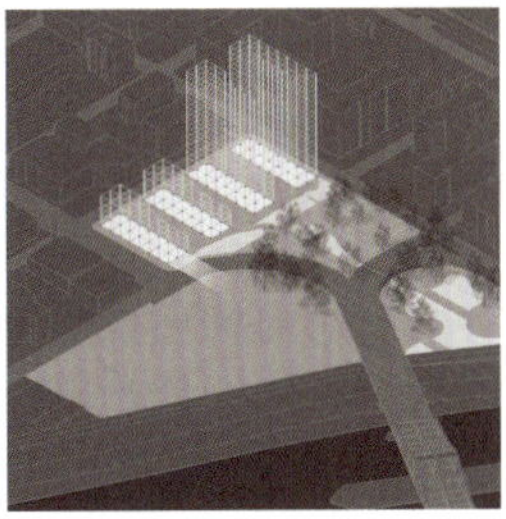
Structural system

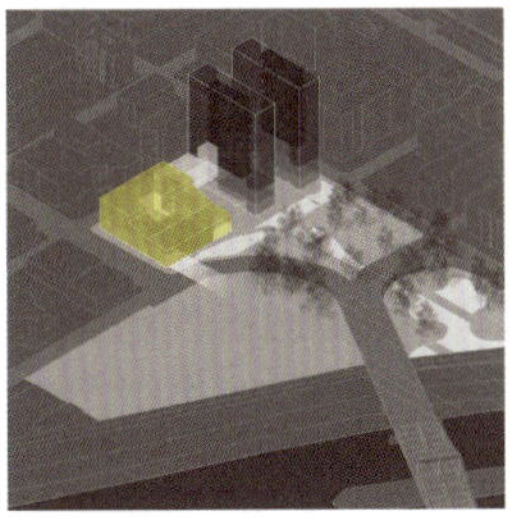
Program

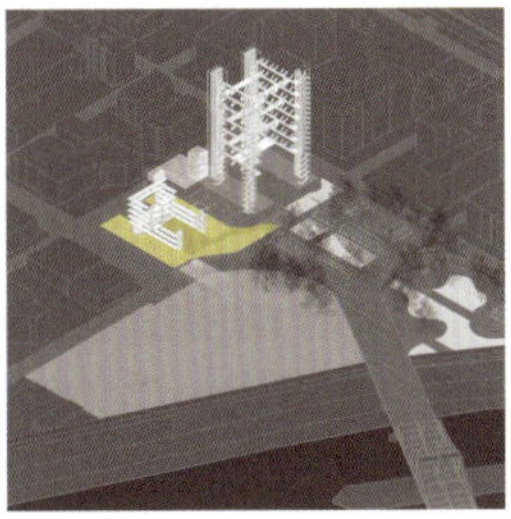
Circulation

Community spaces

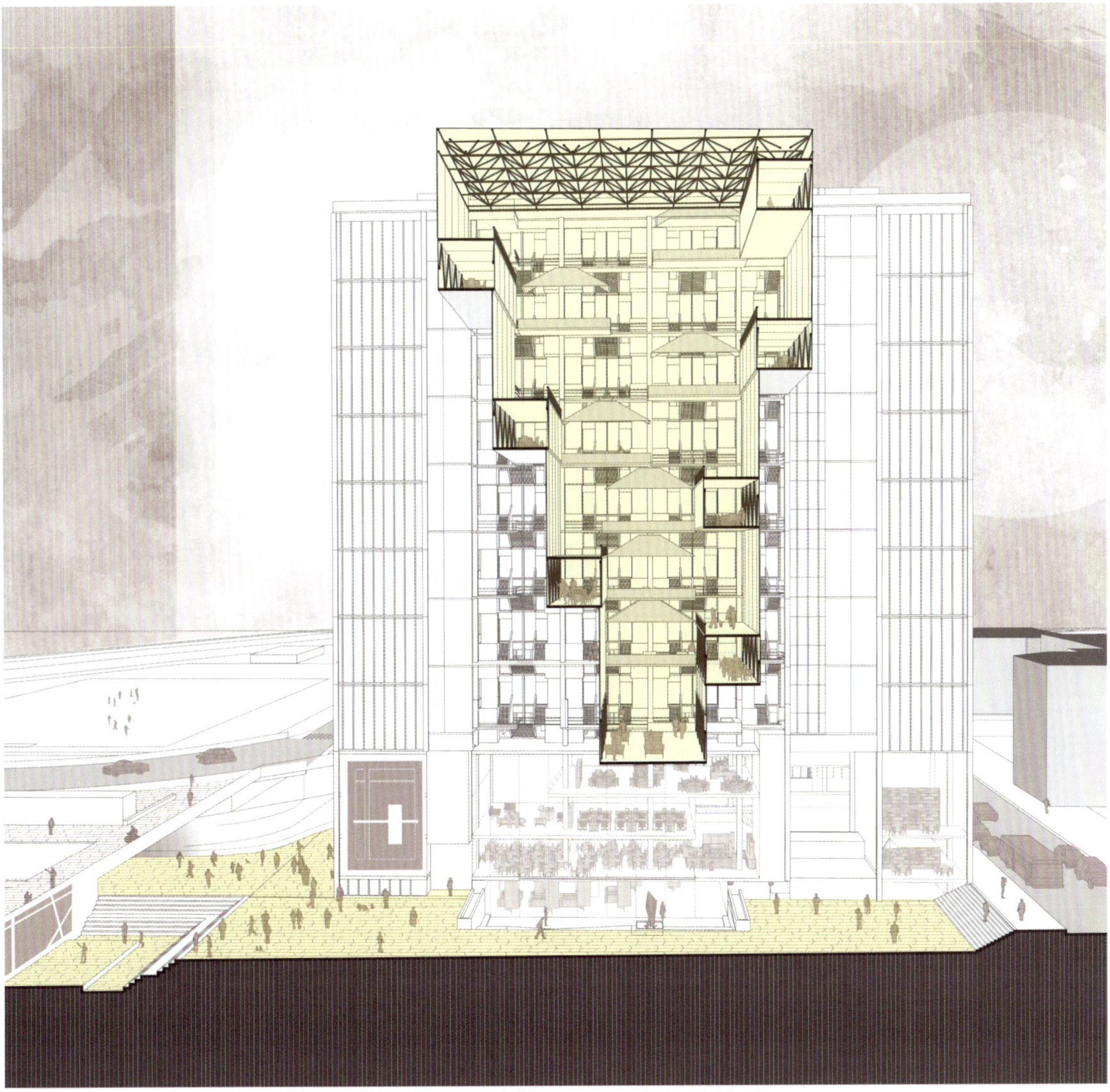
Section perspective showing ground floor public plaza, shared dining areas, and elevated bridges

Circulating Through Scale

Student Team
Alex Kiehl
Jake Gianni

Instructors
Kyriaki Kasabalis

Circulating Through Scale aims to leverage multiple scales of collective space to redefine the site's (site 1) peripheral relationship to the surrounding street grid. A multi-tiered internal courtyard, shared between the site's educational and residential programming, anchors the block and becomes the catalyst for collective interaction and transition among the different site users. Additional community programming is included on both sides of the shared courtyard in two distinct housing typologies: a tower and horizontal bars, both of which generate multiple scales of communal spaces and diverse dwelling unit types. The greatest density of family-scaled residences and collective spaces occurs along the avenues in the bar forms—reflecting the organization of Manhattan's standard block—while the tower features smaller, bi-level apartments and smaller community spaces.

Perspective view of internal public courtyard

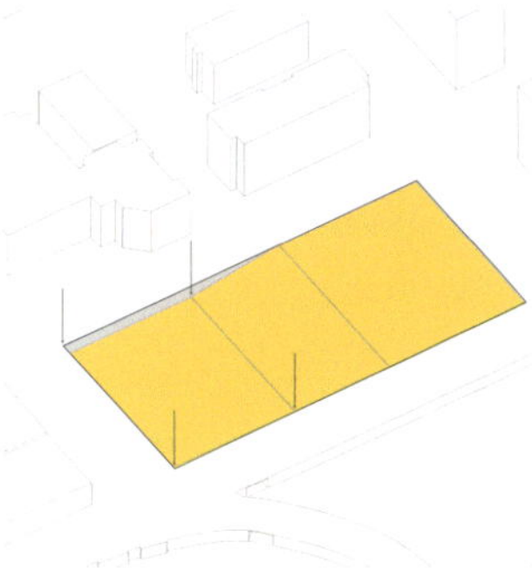
Interior public plaza

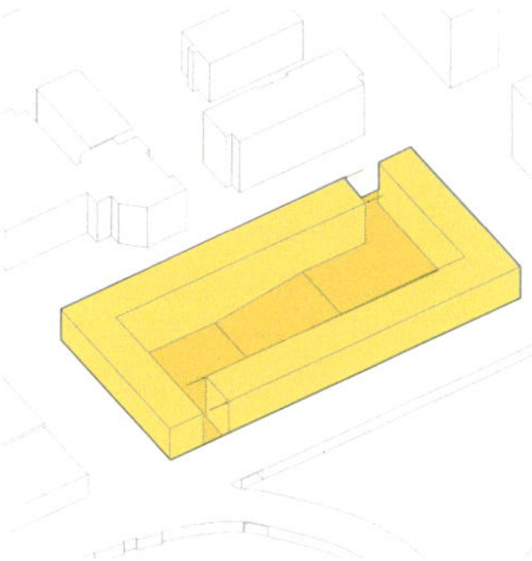
Perimeter blocks

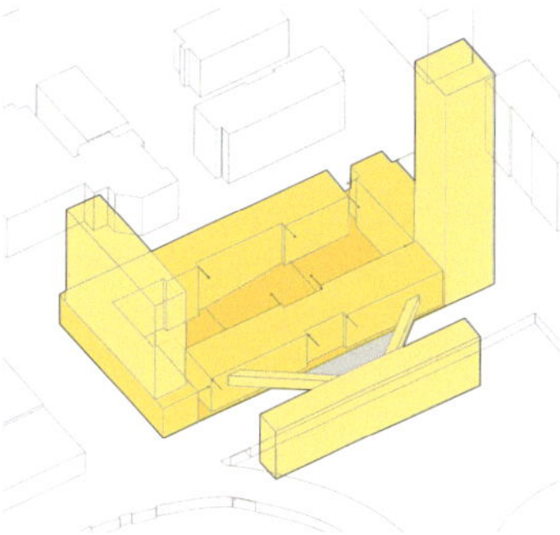
Tower masses

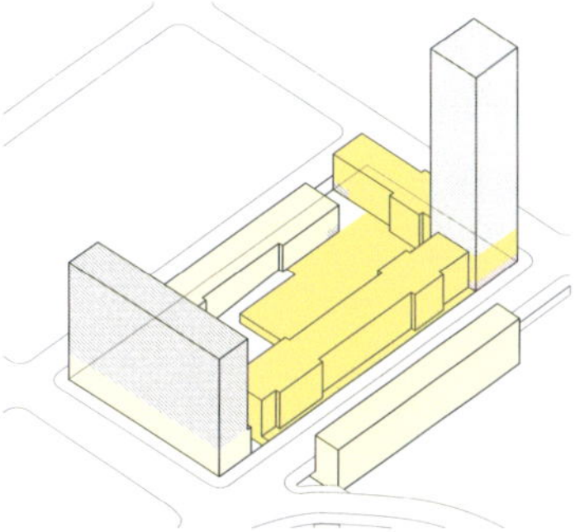
Major program elements

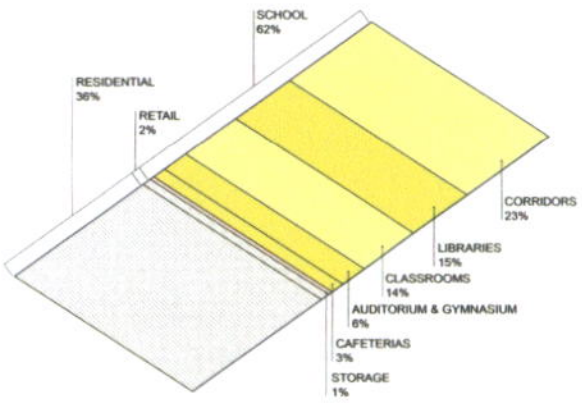

Program distribution

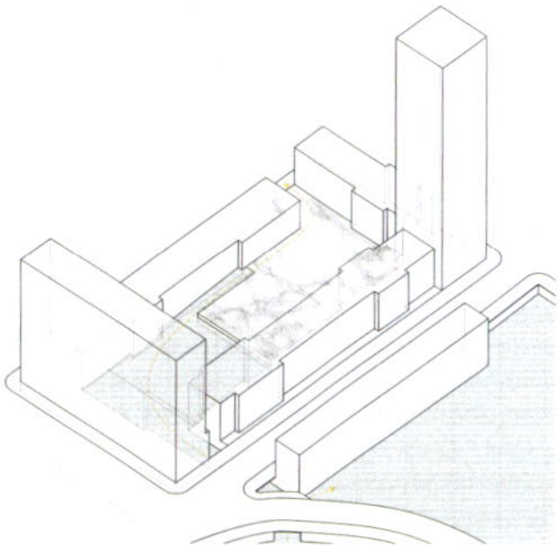
Public interior courtyard

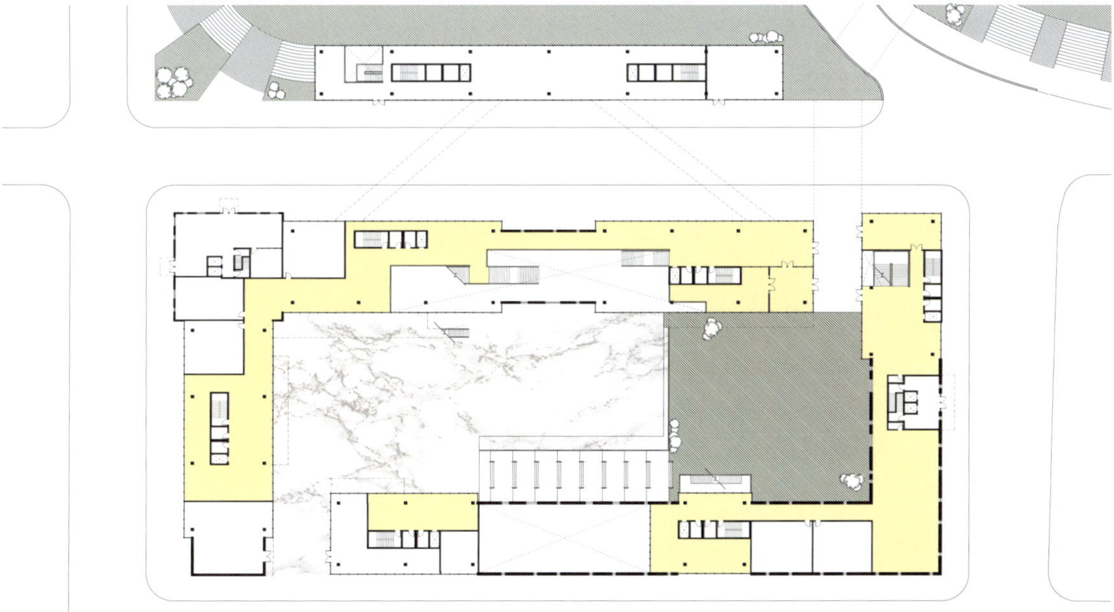
Ground floor plan

Courtyard Unleashed

Student Team
Jing Gu
Yunrui Gao

Instructor
Mona El Khafif

Courtyard Unleashed pays tribute to the historic fabric of the surrounding neighborhood and experiments with the familiar typology of the courtyard through a massing strategy based around three interlocking courtyards. The largest of the three courtyards spans horizontally across the full width of the site, promoting neighborhood pedestrian connections, and offering a large outdoor space which can be shared between the school and the neighborhood. The school's inhabitable rooftop not only generates additional open space, but also provides residential access to two vertically-oriented courtyards containing interior common areas, green spaces, and circulation connections between the other courtyards, sidewalks, and upper-level gardens.

Perspective vignettes

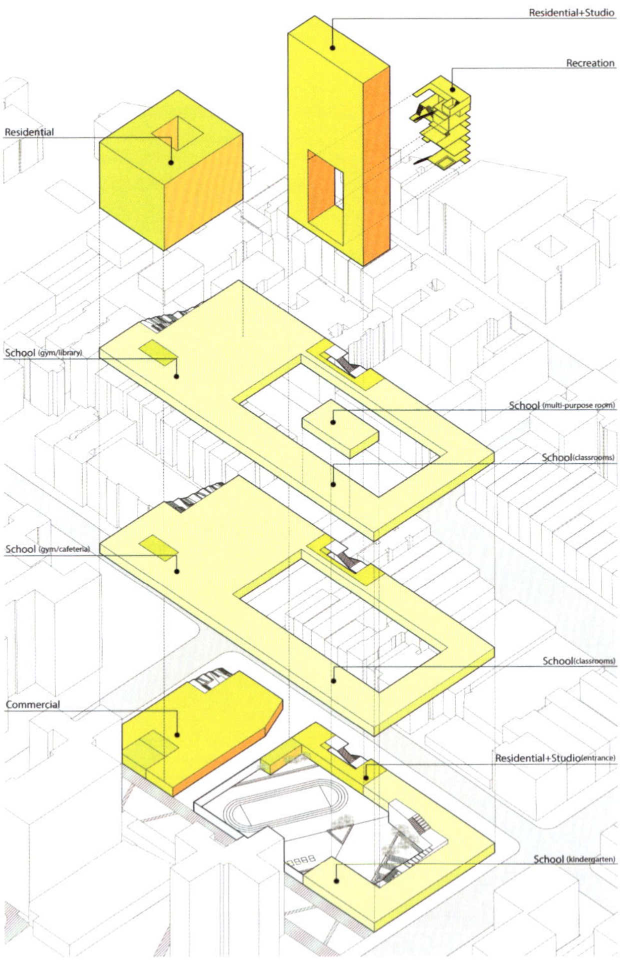

Isometric site strategy and massing diagram, southeast view

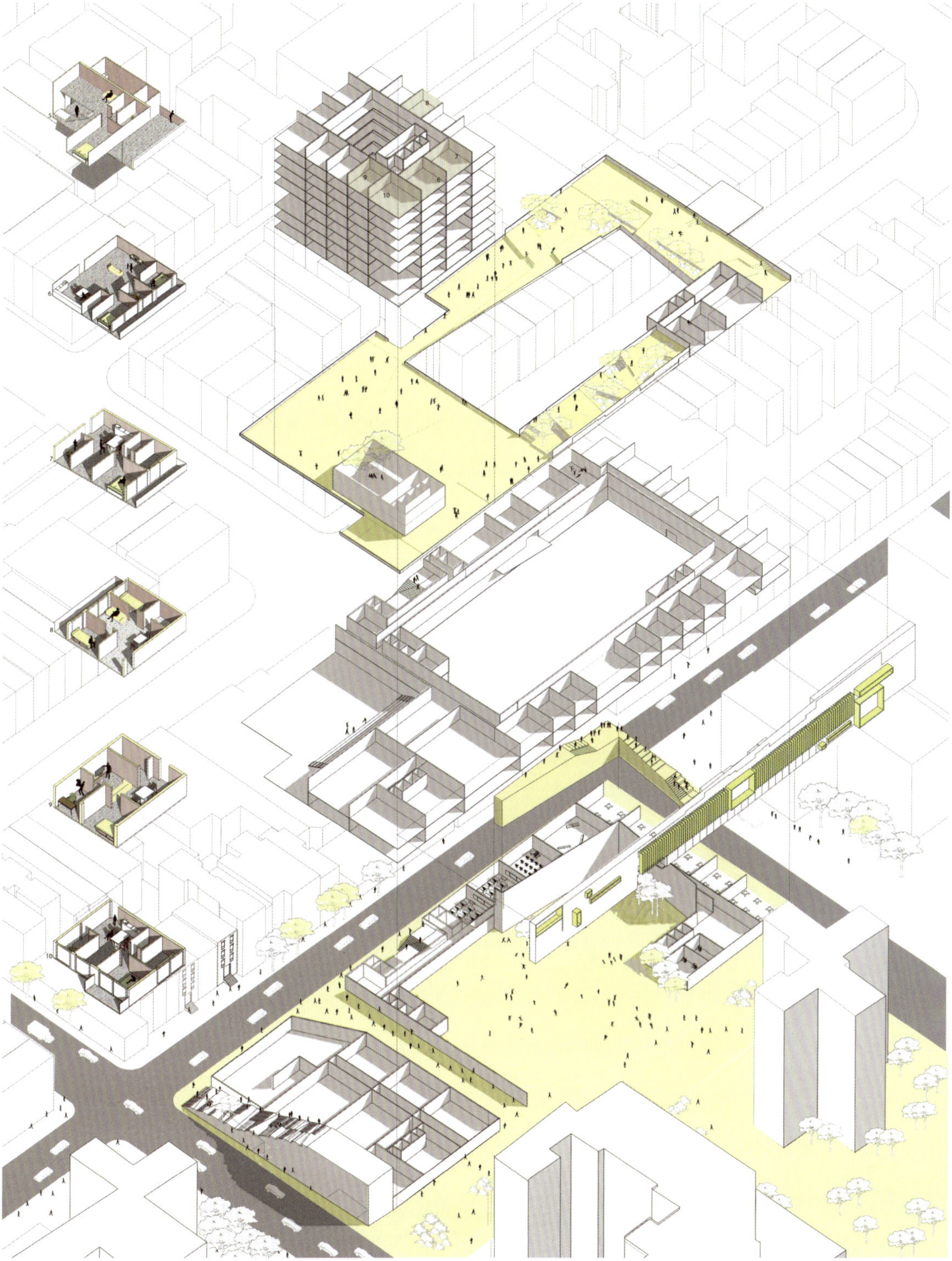

Delayered urban isometric drawing showing shared, public spaces (yellow)

Ground floor plan

Section perspective through tower and interior courtyard

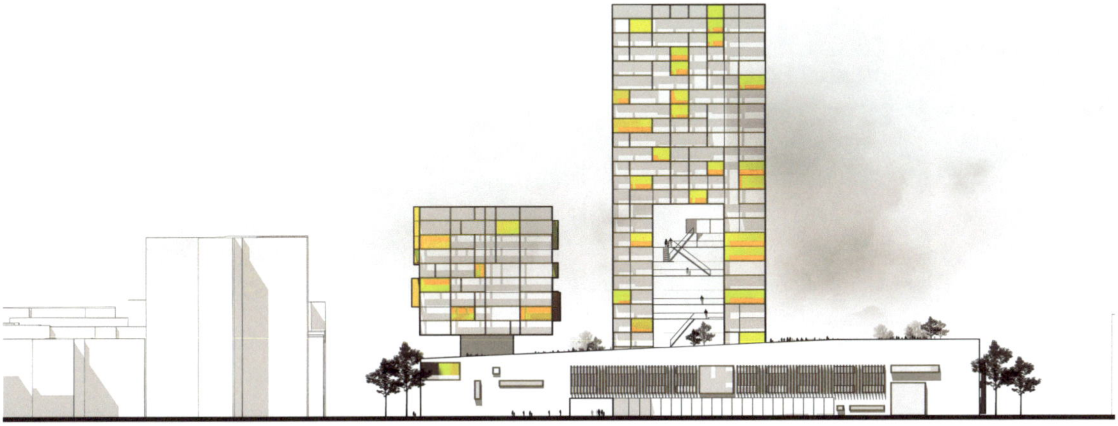

Building elevation, south

Isometric view, southeast

1:200 model, "Courtyard Unleashed"

1:200 model, "Growing Out / Looking In"

Growing Out / Looking In

Student Team
Stephany Stumphauzer
Grace Wills

Instructor
Alexander Yuen

To address the contrast between the large lot (site 2) and the intimacy of the surrounding neighborhood, Growing Out / Looking In aims to establish an active link between the site and the community. Formally, the project adopts a porous perimeter block typology while maintaining a programmatic focus on community infrastructure, multi-generational occupation, and childhood and adolescent development. The proposed combined middle/elementary school and community health center at street level and the ninety-two residential units above encircle a publicly accessible interior courtyard organized through a series of terraced recreational facilities.

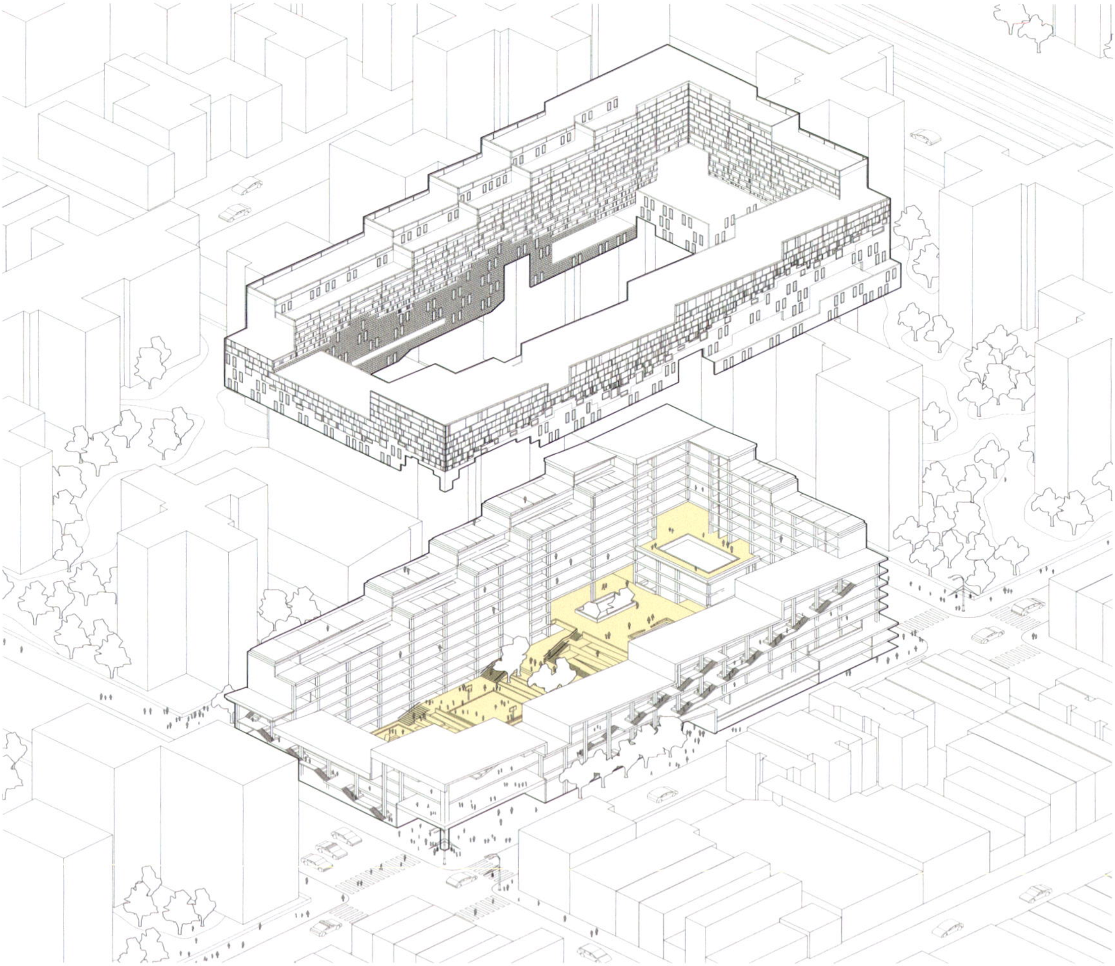

Delayered isometric view, northeast

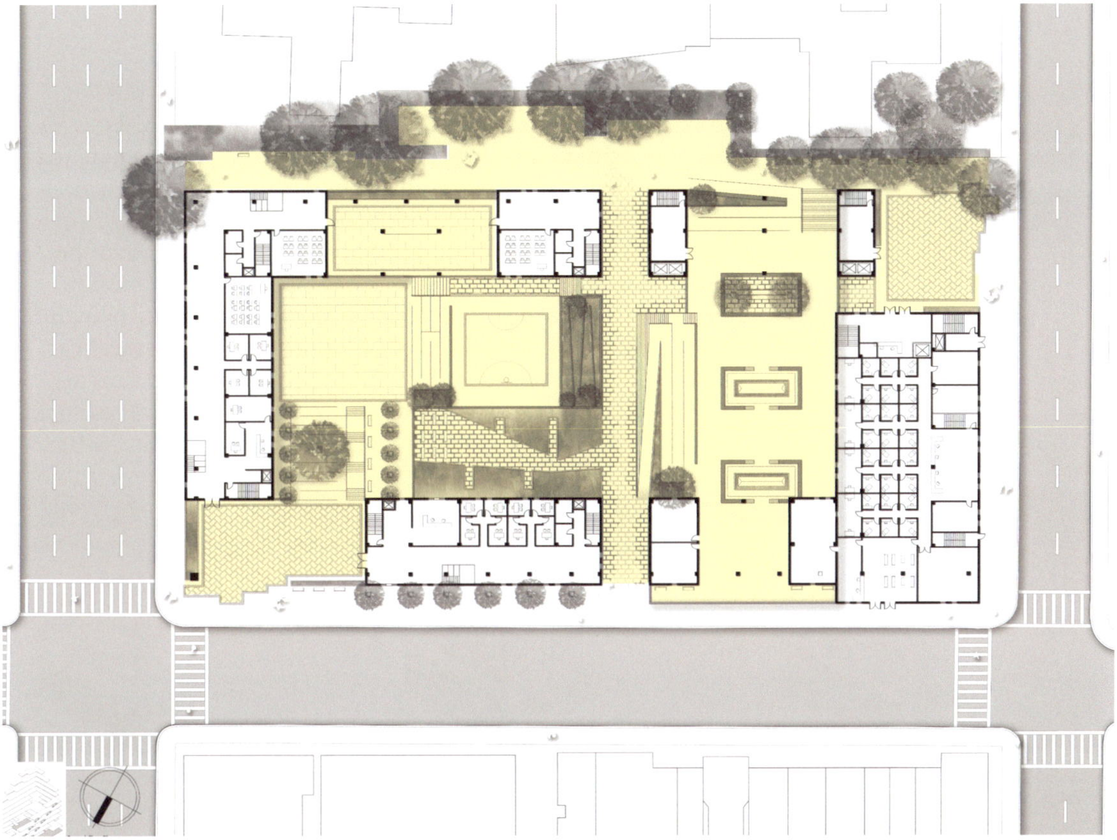

Ground floor plan

Section perspective through multi-level interior courtyard

The Workshop

Student Team
Jacob Blankenship
Kelsey Smith

Instructor
Esther Lorenz

Manhattan is flooded with spaces for viewing art, but it is lacking in those designated for its creation. The WORKSHOP proposes a new home for Fiorello LaGuardia High School (site 2) which would not only act as an extension of nearby institutions such as Lincoln Center and The Juilliard School, but would also help to link the traditionally private realm of performing arts education with the greater urban community through the strategic sharing of internal open spaces. In addition to the school program, the proposal calls for residences and workshop studios. Public outdoor terraces and a circulation bridge not only serve as connective tissue for the block and surrounding neighborhoods, but also as temporally flexible spaces for engaging the public in the collaborative acts of learning and making.

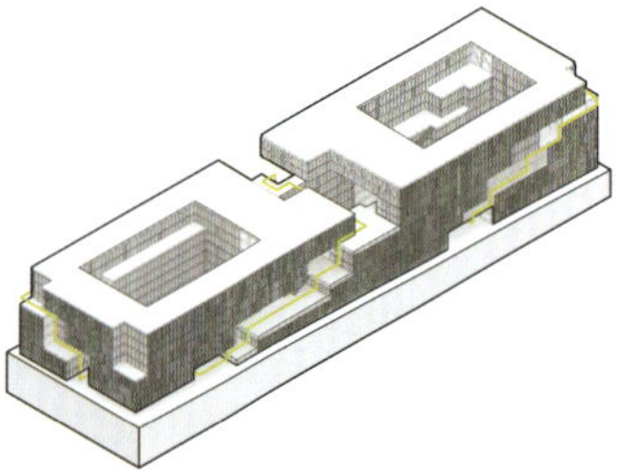

Circulation diagram

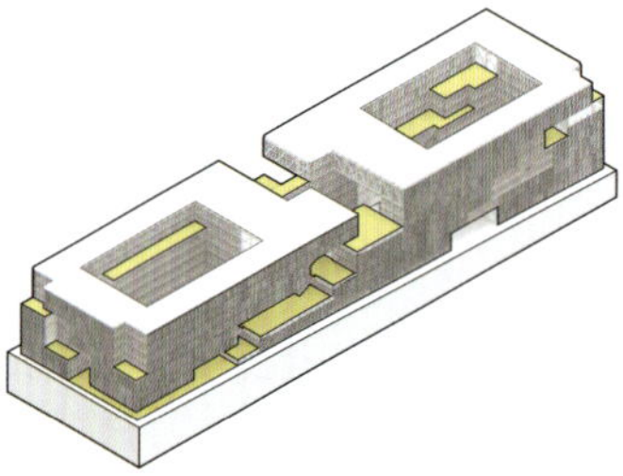

Open space diagram

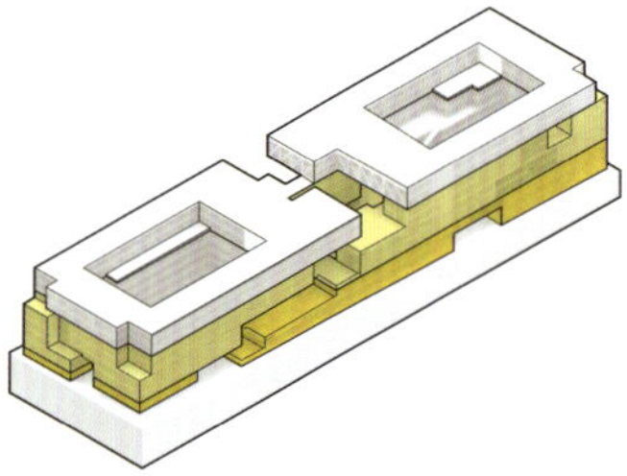

Program diagram

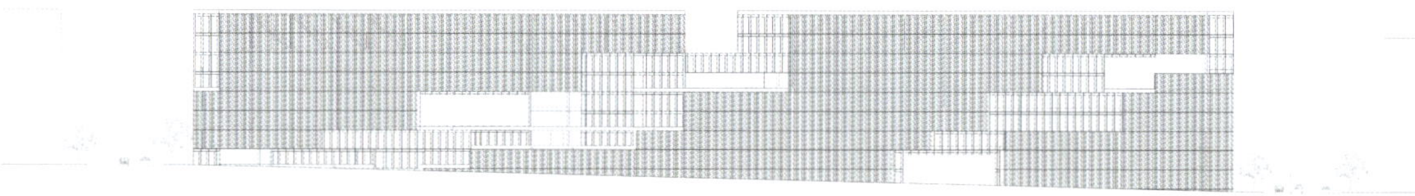

Building elevation, north

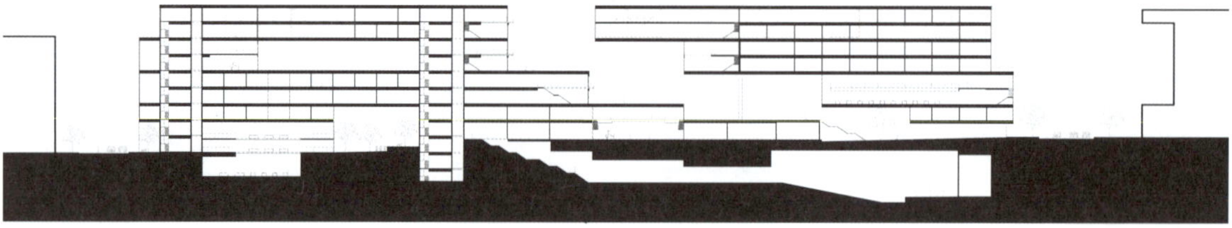

Longitudinal section

Exterior perspective view at street level

Exterior perspective at central courtyard

Courtyard?

Student Team
Irmak Fermen
Iting Chen

Instructor
Matthew Jull

Courtyard? identifies public space as a place for everyday performance in the city. The existing public school on the site, Fiorello H. LaGuardia, is an art and performance high school and located within a neighborhood of "art infrastructures" such as Lincoln Center and the Juilliard School. The project rotates the courtyard block vertically, opening up visual connection and public access to the site. Simultaneously, it provides varying degrees of privacy and connection which merge toward the ground, allowing the distinct programs of education and art to find a shared place in the community through communal workshops and ateliers.

Eighth floor plan

Second floor plan

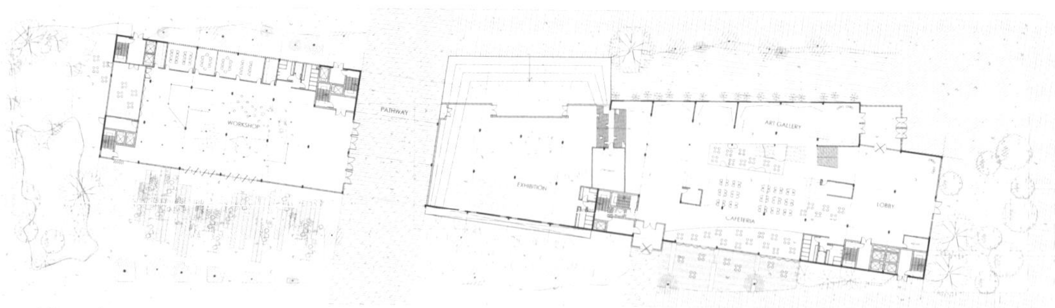

Ground floor plan

Exterior perspective view of sunken courtyard

Exterior perspective view at street level

Interior perspective view at upper level auditorium

Interior perspective view of school library

Cross section through courtyards and shared programming (yellow)

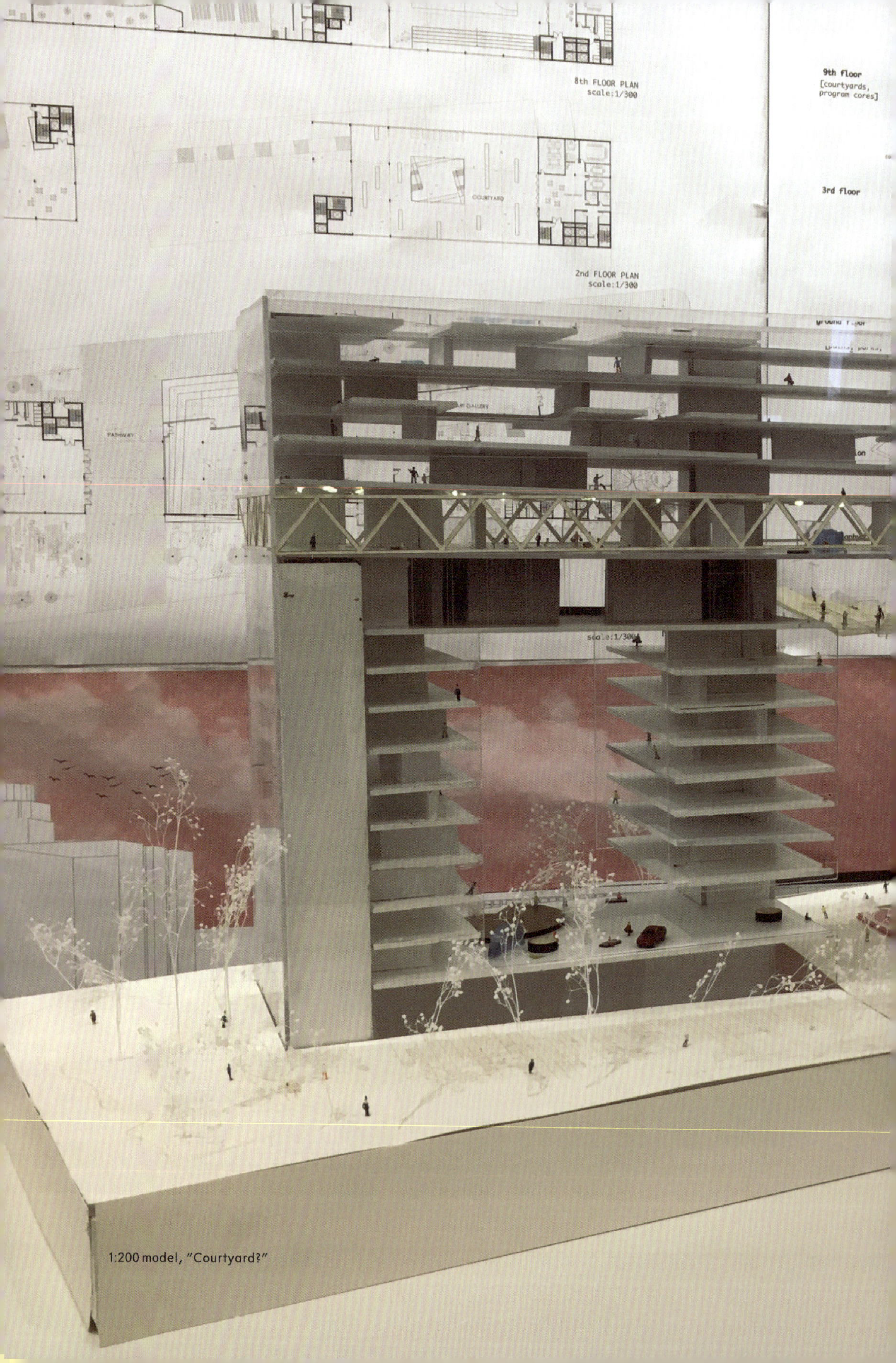

1:200 model, "Courtyard?"

Coutyard
VOLUME DISTRIBUTION
Existing parking
SITE ZONING
[exhibition
hall- square]
Public
Programs
DISTRIBUTION
Visual Permeability
street level

Street Lives In a Block

Student Team
Audrey Liu
Shixun Lyu

Instructor
Mona El Khafif

Street Lives in a Block, conceived as a public-private partnership between a school facility and additional residential units, generates a dense, vibrant, and variegated urban fabric within the confines of a single block through the development and spatial layering of a unique typological "alphabet." This alphabet, rigorously informed by an earlier series of parametrically generated permutations, adapts fluidly to the site's (site 3) edges and adjacencies, and simultaneously maximizes residential FAR while preserving open outdoor spaces and optimizing cross-ventilation, energy efficiency, and daylighting. Through the layering of these alphabet typologies, the project facilitates a flexible, aggregative system of public and semi-public spaces throughout the structure's upper levels.

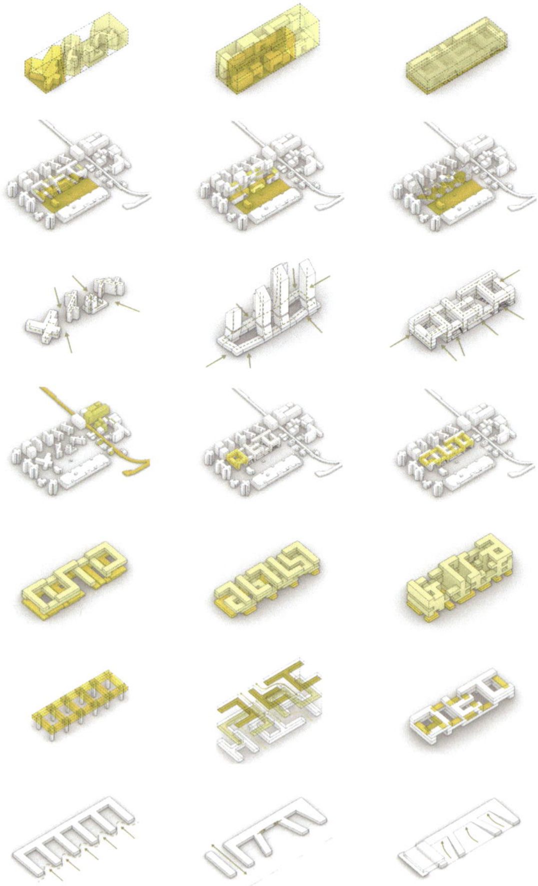

Urban context map and block typologies

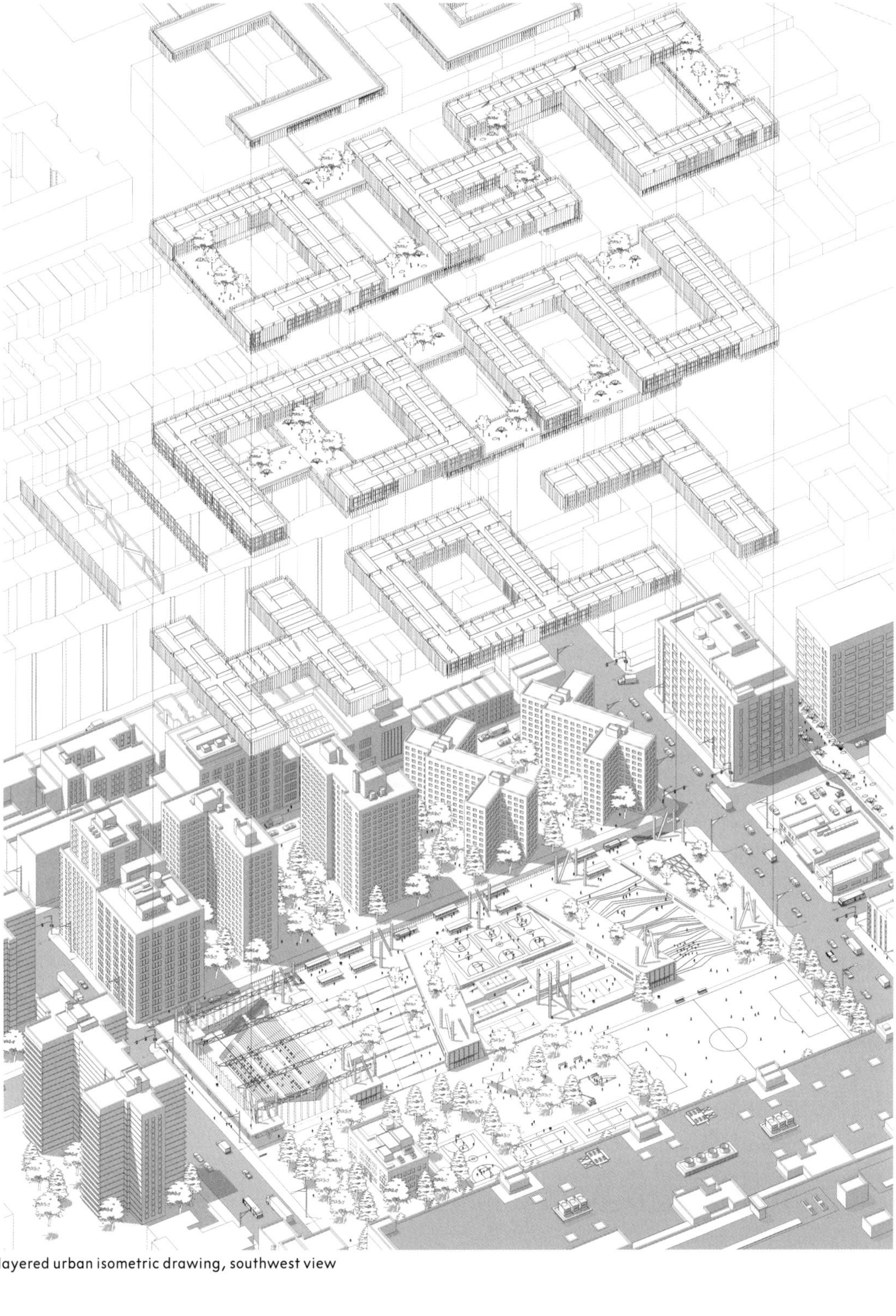

Delayered urban isometric drawing, southwest view

Upper floor plan

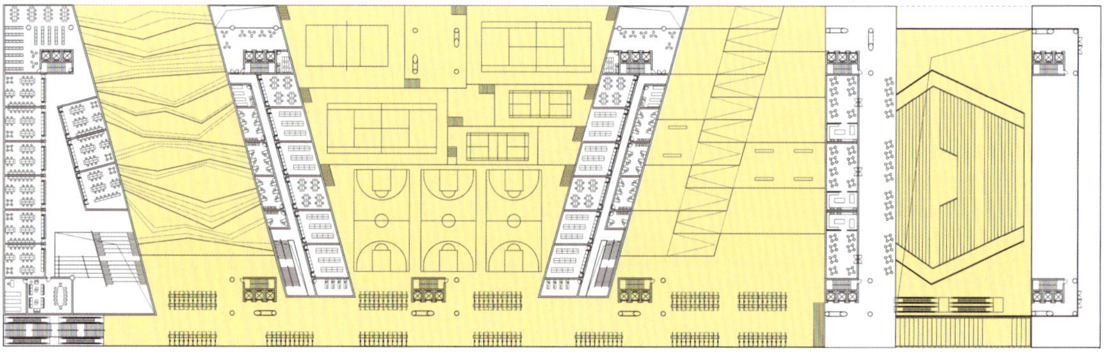

Second floor plan

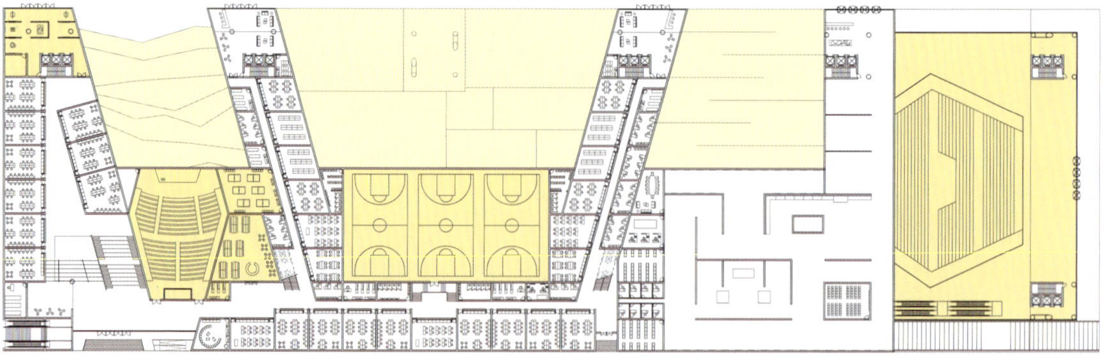

Ground floor plan

Birds-eye perspective view

Street-level perspective view

Building section through public programs (yellow)

1:200 model,
"Street Lives in a Block"

Objection@NYC.edu

Student Team
Jonah Pruitt
Samuel Feldman

Instructor
Matthew Jull

Objection@NYC.edu rejects the privatized excess of recent developments such as the adjacent Hudson Yards, instead prioritizing concerns of affordable housing, accessible public space, and block-scaled street life. The proposal re-articulates the site's (site 4) ground plane as a full-block public zone containing artificially manipulated topographical moments and shared subterranean programming accessible not only to residents and their guests, but to the city as a whole: especially those living in nearby housing projects. To complement the site's current occupant—P.S. 33—the proposal adds a significant volume of residential units within a block-long, diagonally oriented bar, and a multi-sensory exploratorium connecting the residential bar to the public ground plane below through a centrally located, vertical void.

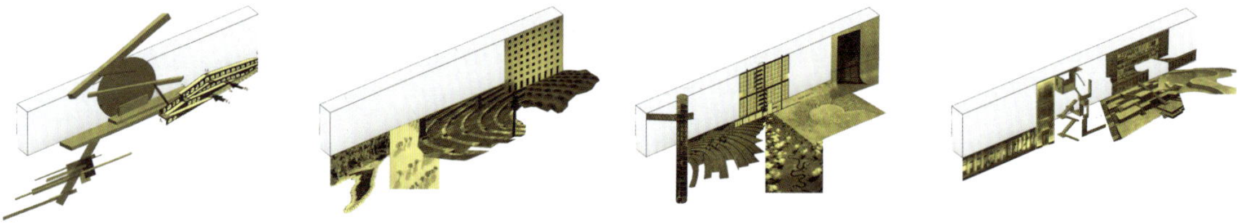

Concept collages

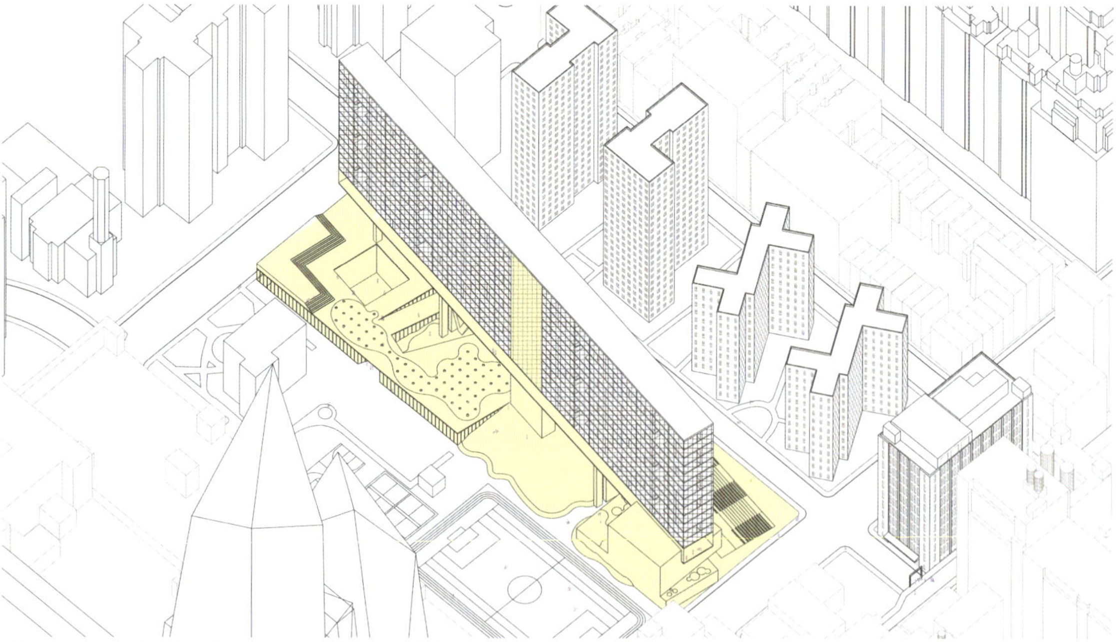

Urban isometric drawing showing ground-level public landscape and vertical exploratorium (yellow)

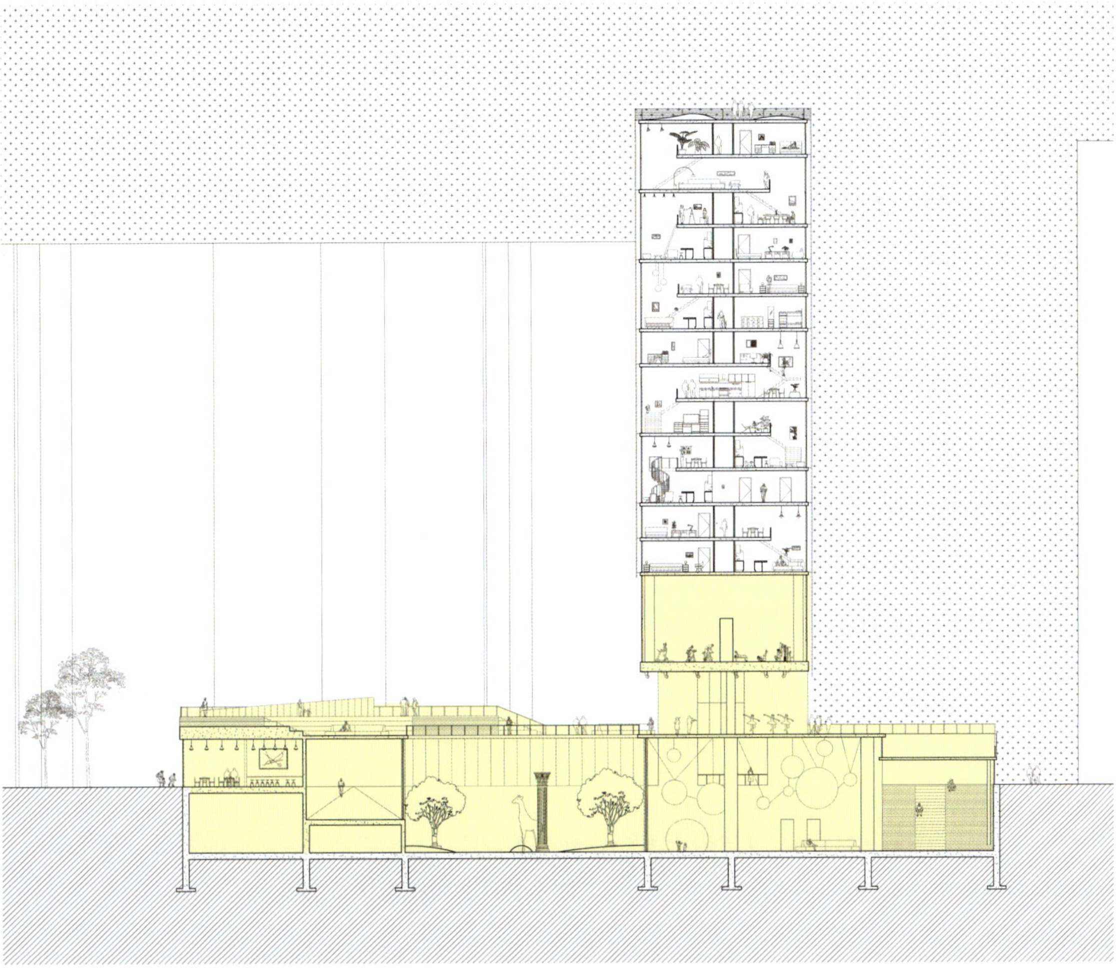

Building section through residential slab and lower level landscape and exploratirum (yellow)

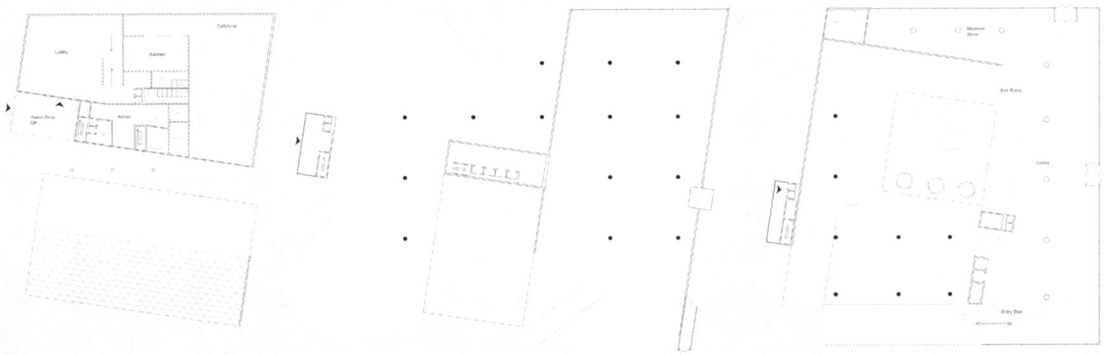

Ground floor plan through public landscape

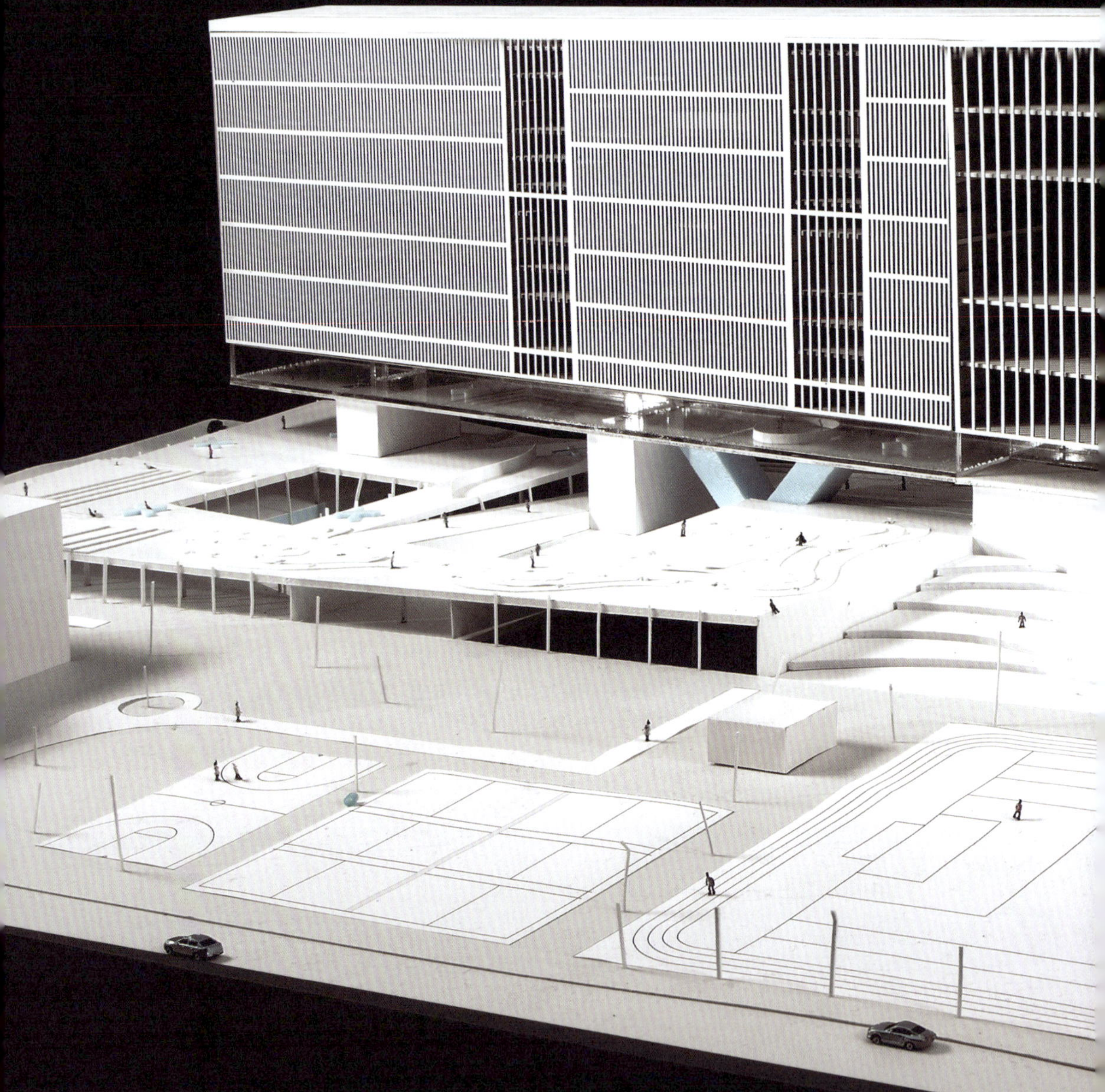

1:200 model,
"Objection@NYC.edu"

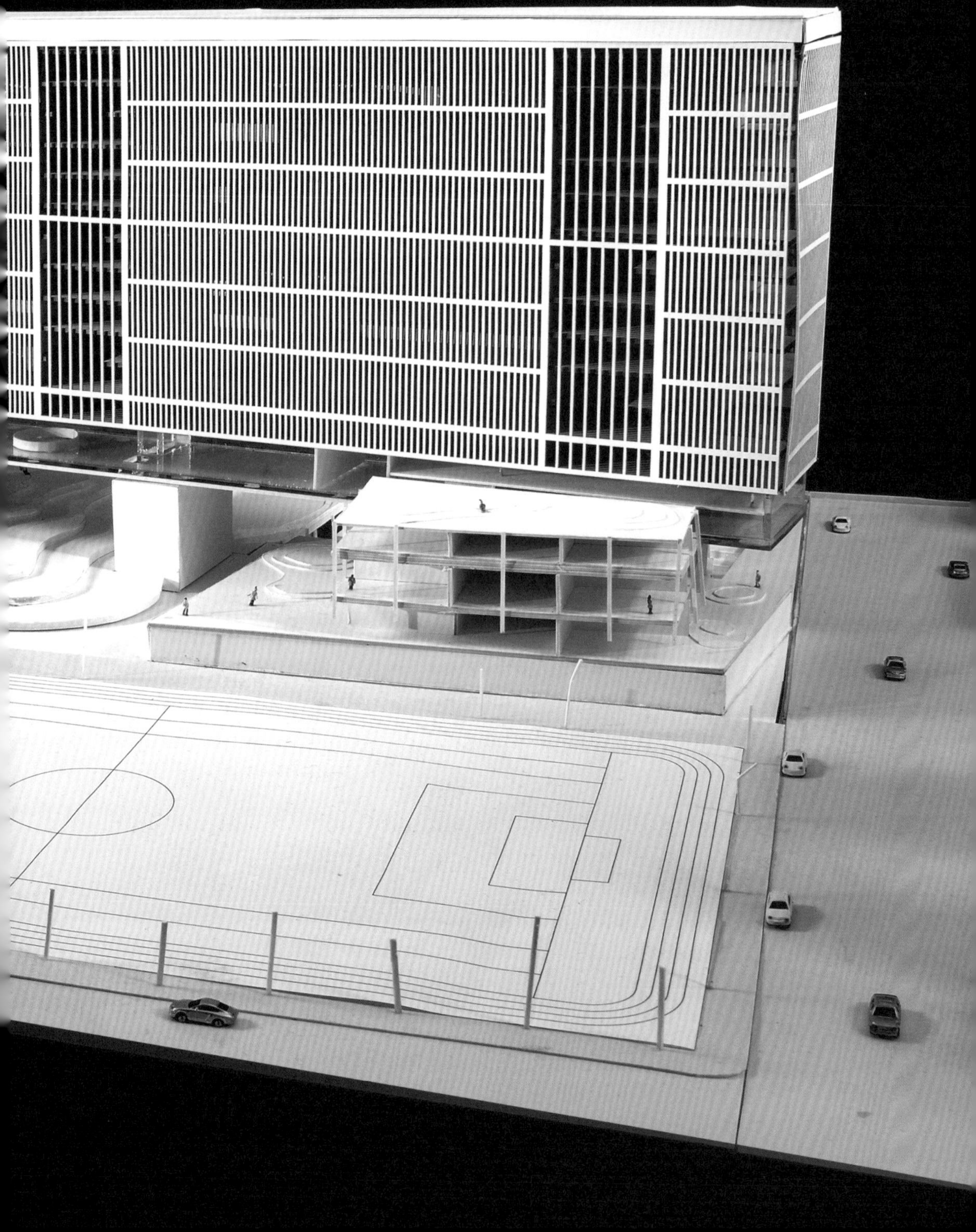

Common Stage

Student Team
Wenyan Yu
Jingyi Shen

Instructor
Mona El Khafif

Common Stage aims to connect P.S. 33 (site 4) to the nearby Hudson riverfront and to three other existing schools nearby. The project proposes a site and massing strategy defined by four residential towers, a low-rise plinth containing the school and public programming, and ground-level courtyards punctuating the plinth and serving as both open spaces and light wells for the surrounding classrooms. The ground floor contains the school's main entrance, offices, and public shared amenities, such as a library, gym, and auditiorium, while the second and third floors contain the majority of the class-rooms and learning spaces. To reinforce the site's connection to its neighbors, the waterfront, and other nearby schools, the plinth roof also features a public recreational area to be shared between residents, the school, and the public.

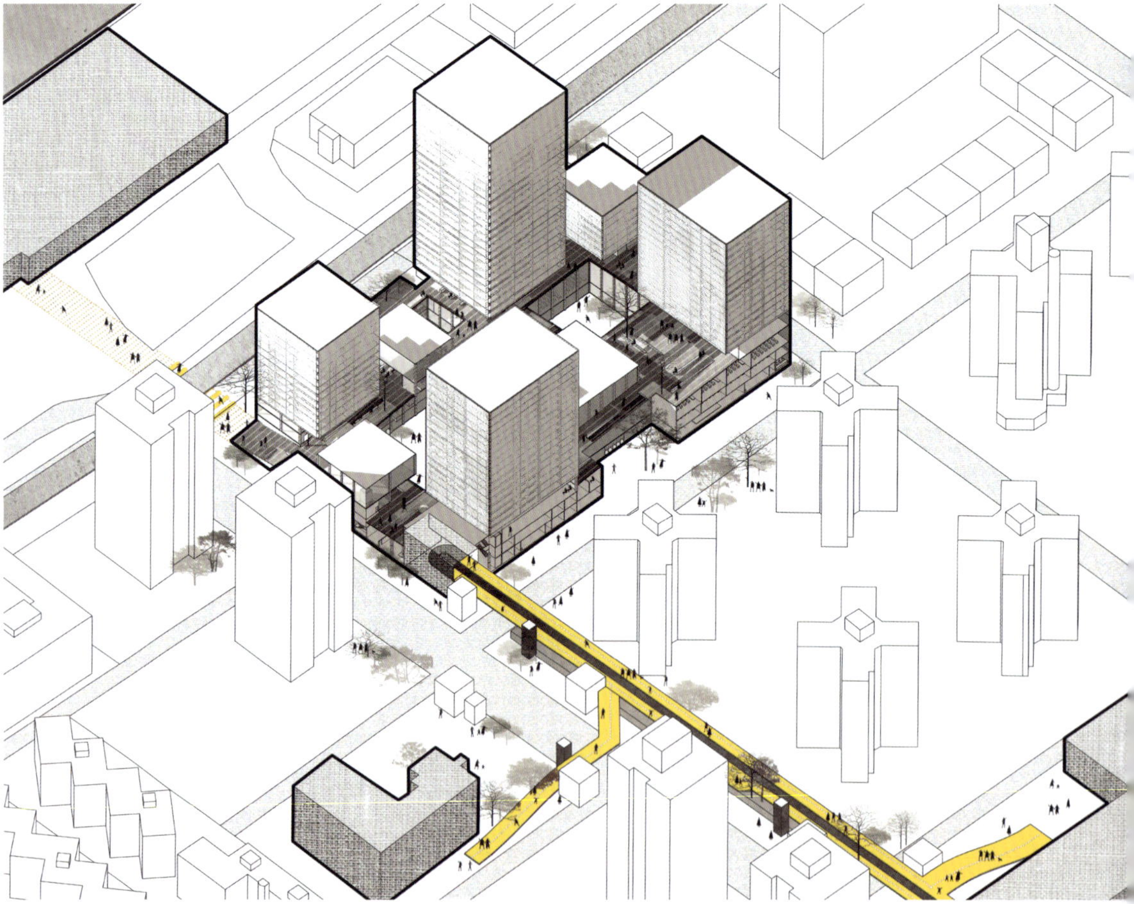

Isometric view, northwest

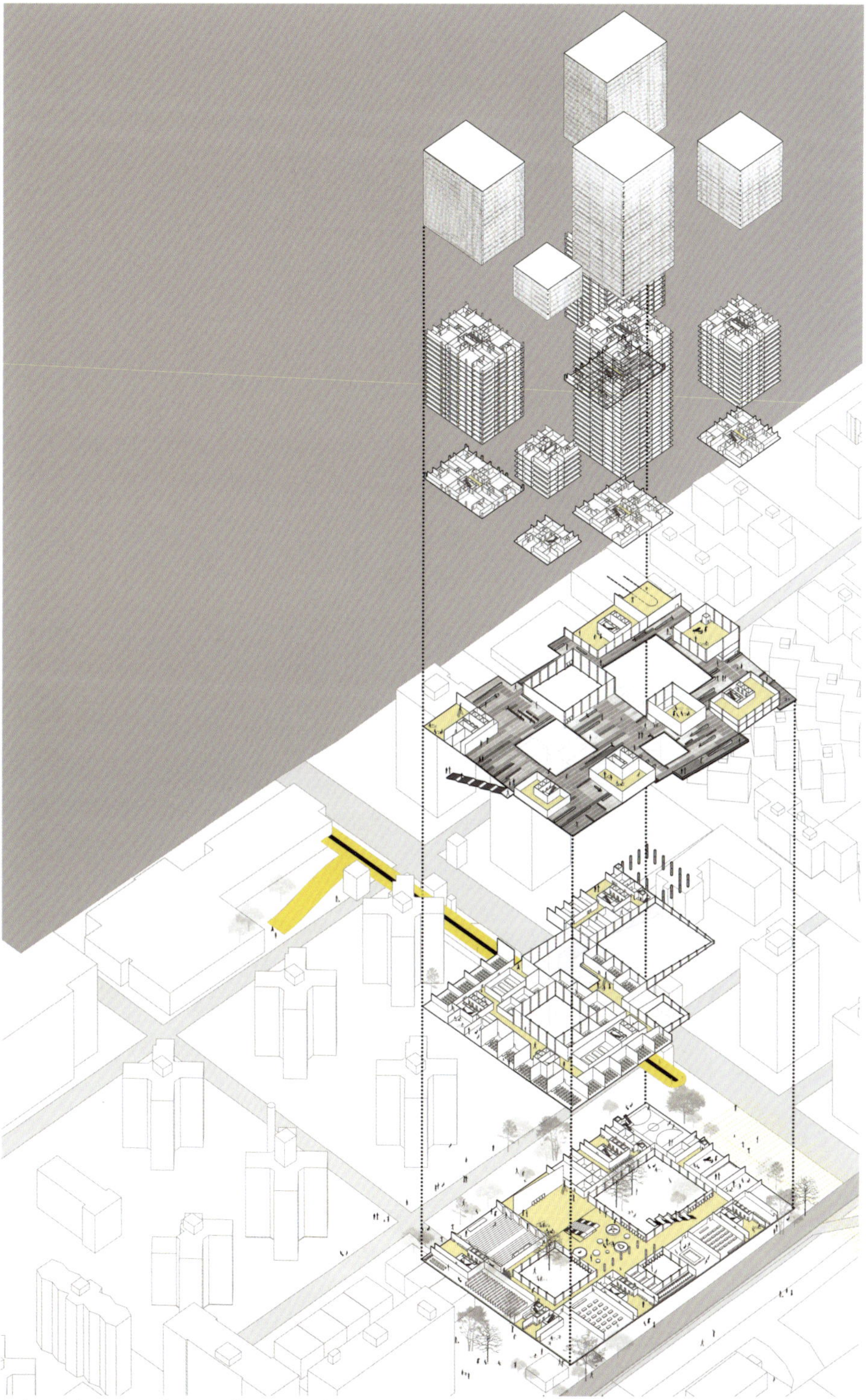

Delayered isometric drawing illustrating the main massing components: towers, plinth, and courtyards

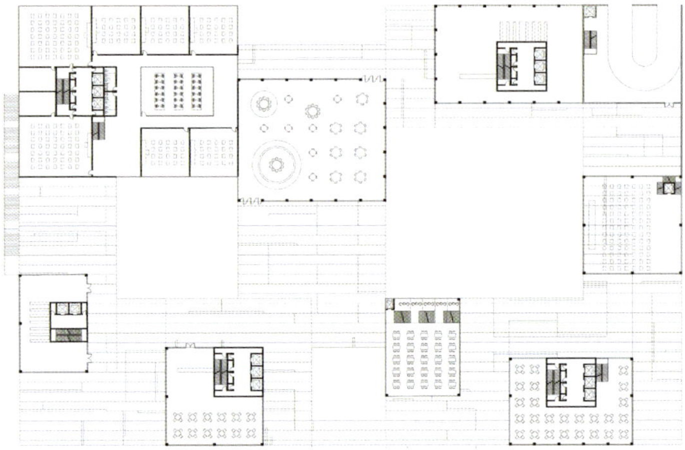

Third floor plan

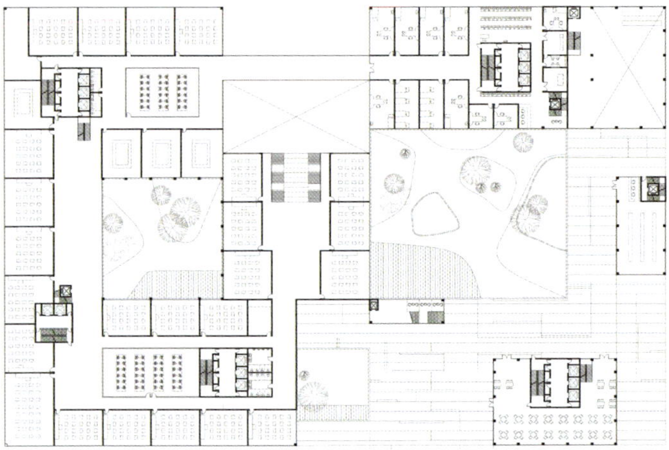

Second floor plan

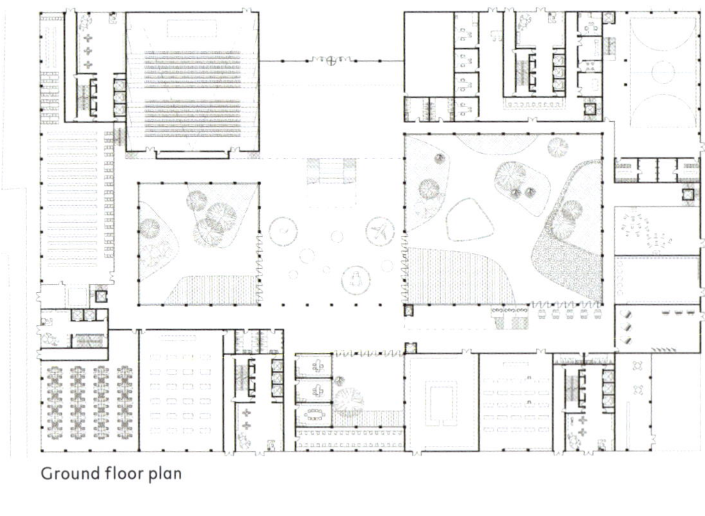

Ground floor plan

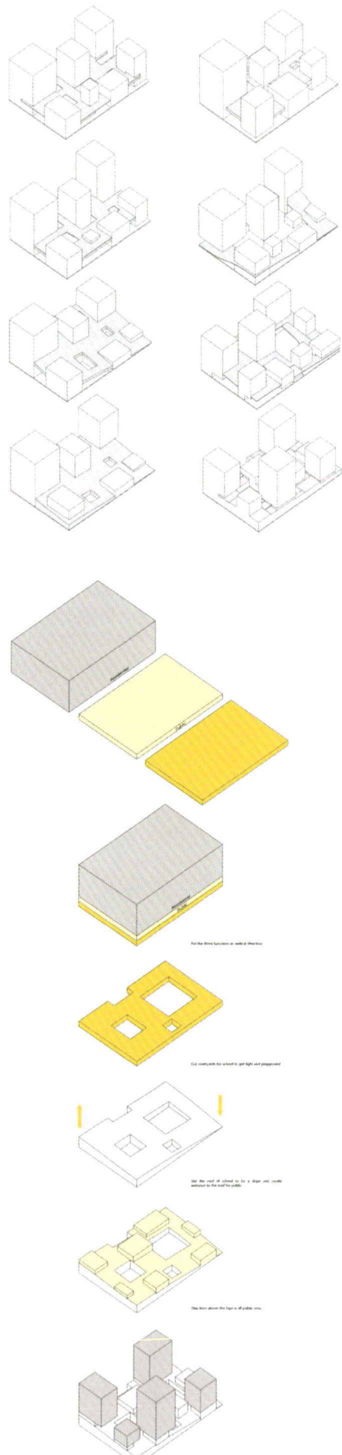

Massing concept diagrams

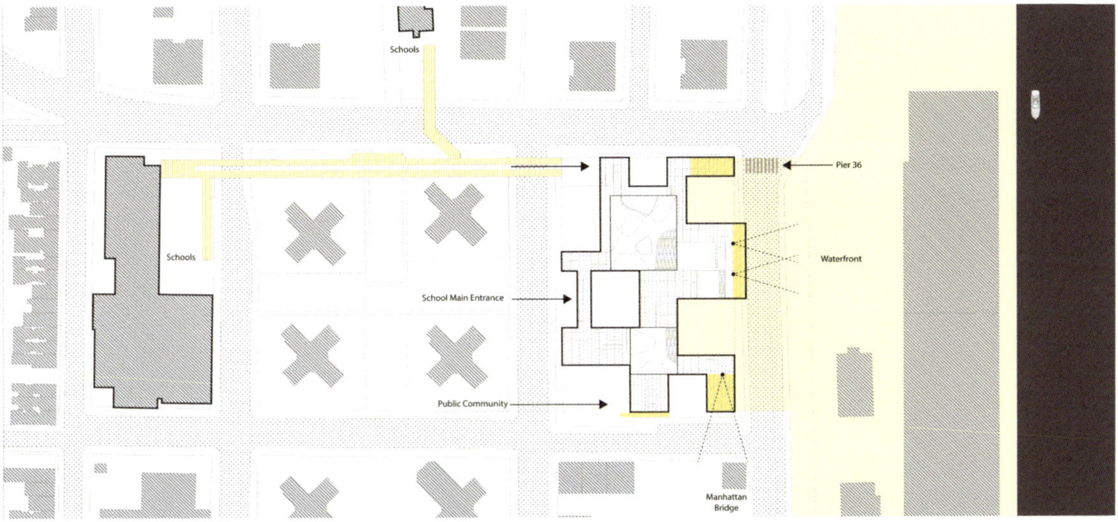

Site context plan showing relationship to East River and nearby schools

Section perspective through towers and shared courtyard

10_Function

Student Team
Xianwen Xu
Xinyi Xia

Instructor
Matthew Jull

Located at the intersection of multiple residential communities, the FDR Drive, and the East River, the Shuang Wen school (Site 5) is physically cut off from its surrounding urban context and nearby waterfront. 10_Function addresses this lack of physical and visual continuity by reconfiguring the school as a multifunctional synthetic landscape connecting two vertical slab towers, each containing a hybridized mix of residential and public programming. At the base of the slabs, the site is divided into three zones: two of which create new public spaces, while the third provides a dedicated outdoor space for the school. Linking these three zones together are ground-level shared spaces and upper-level indoor amenities, which span between the two slabs and establish a new series of vertical neighborhood connections.

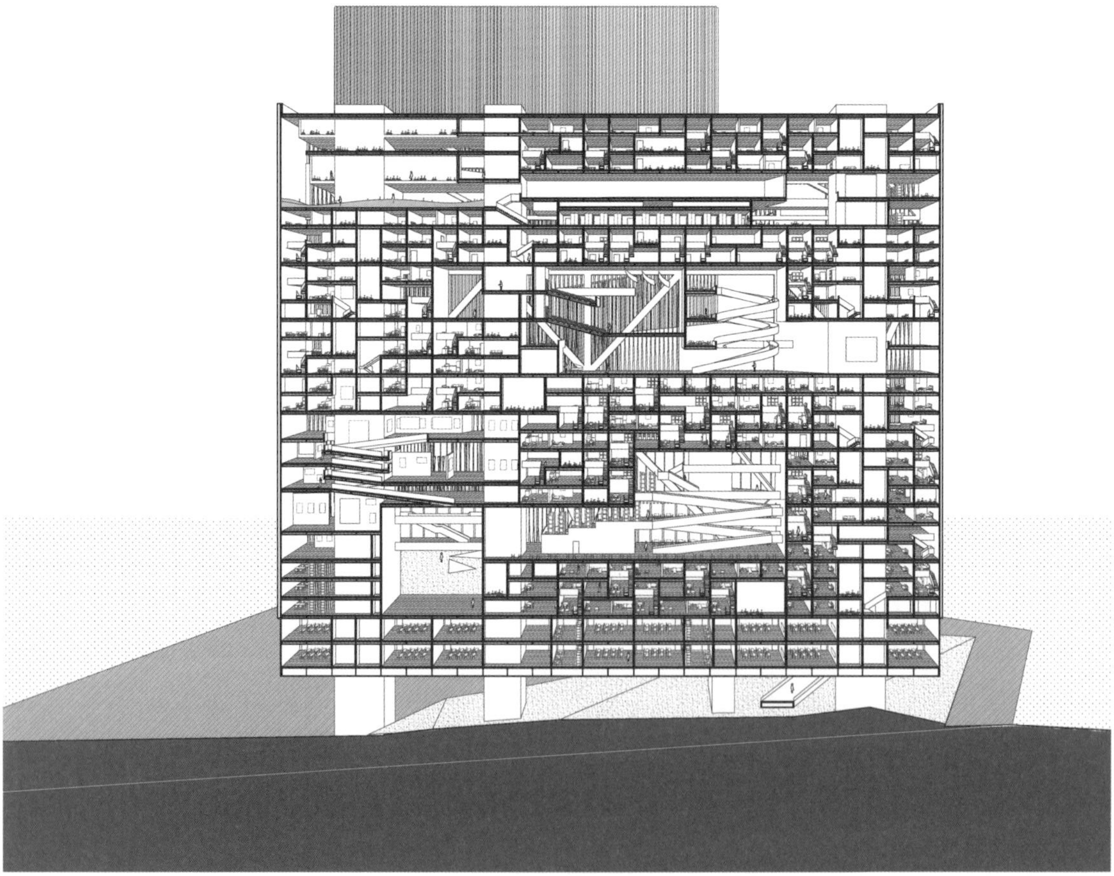

Building section through tower slab

Perspective view from FDR Drive

Perspective view from East River

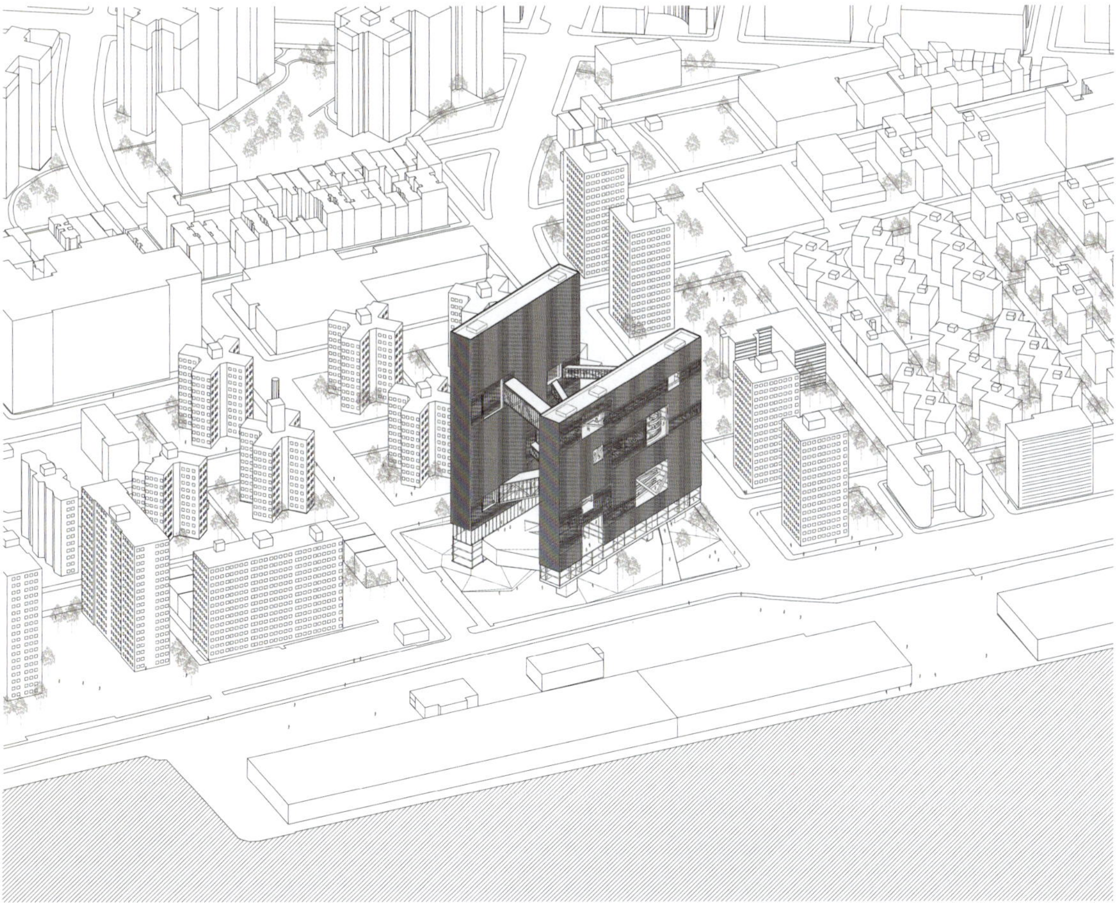

Isometric drawing showing site context, southwest

1:200 model, "10_Function"

Breaking Regularity

Student Team
Tianqi Chu
Jingyao Zhang

Instructors
Kyriaki Kasabalis

Site 5, between the Manhattan and Williamsburg Bridges, is a unique location within the gridiron plan of the city. Not only does the street grid shift its cardinal orientation here, but the neighborhood is also home to a series of hermetic, mid-century, public housing projects. Breaking Regularity—a reference to Camillo Sitte's aversion to symmetry and repetition in the urban fabric—leans into the unique variety of sightlines and axes present at the site by proposing a morphological inversion of this cruciform tower-in-a-park model. Instead of interiorizing the program, however, the project embraces the urban streetscape and organizes its program along the block perimeter. This decision frees up the interior of the site to serve as a collection of irregularly shaped public outdoor plazas. It offers the site a new type of collective space that re-organizes the urban block and redefines its relationship to the rest of the city.

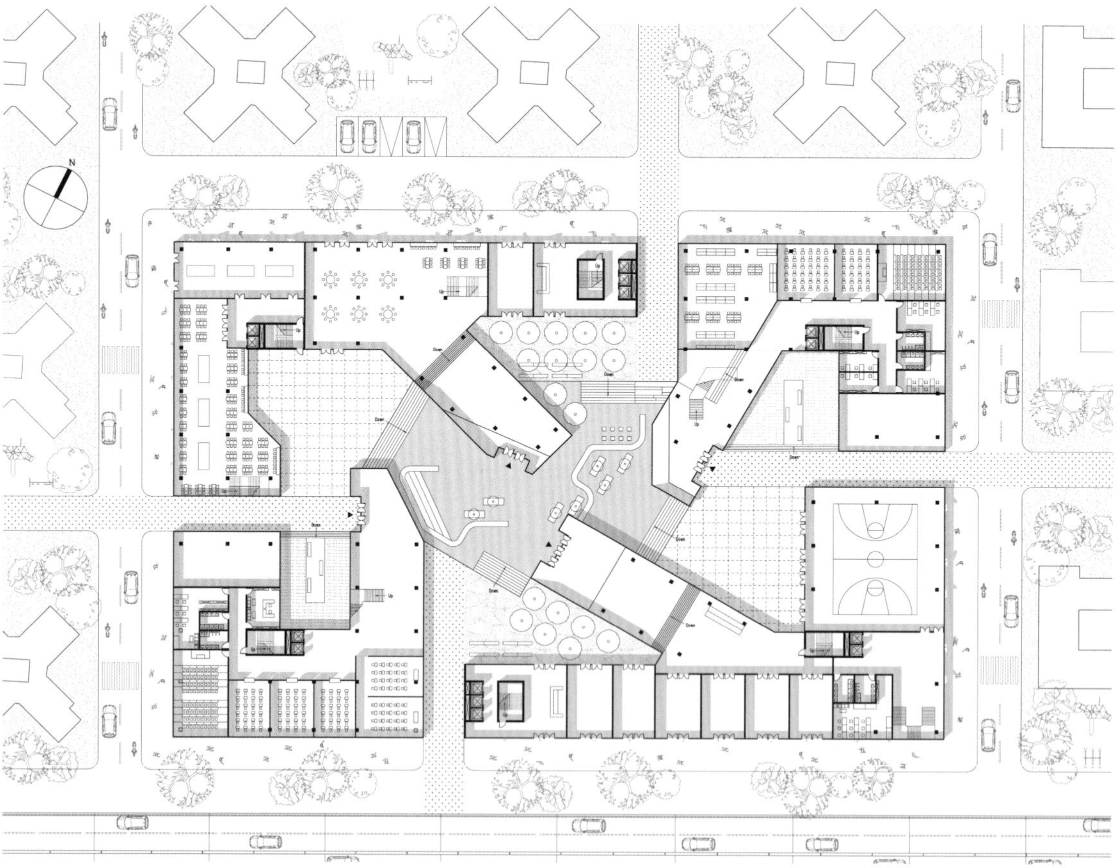

Ground floor plan

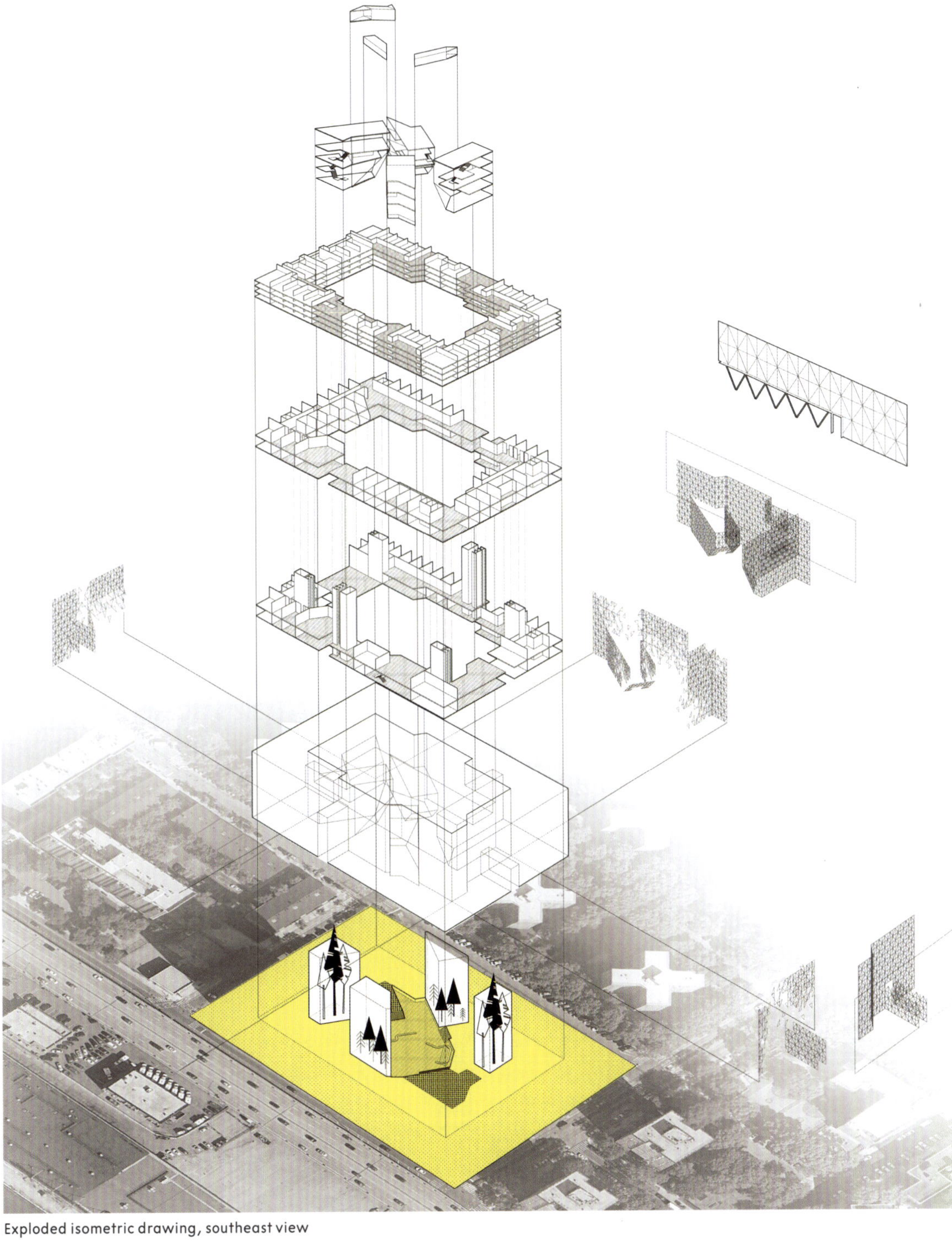

Exploded isometric drawing, southeast view

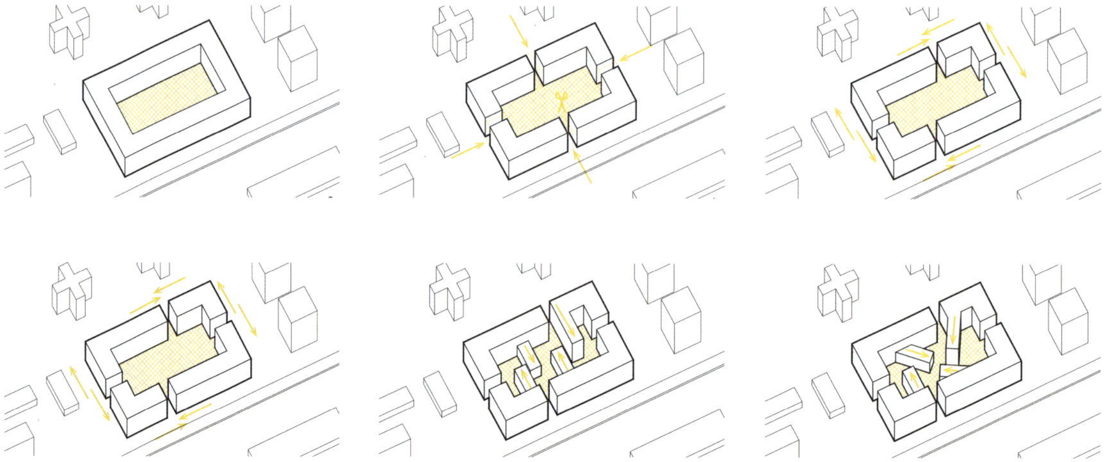

Form generation diagrams showing interior public courtyards (yellow)

Upper level plan

Perspective views at interior public courtyards (yellow)

Section perspective through public courtyards (yellow)

Extended Horizons; Vertical Density

Student Team
Jessica Smith
Evan Sparkman

Instructor
Mona El Khafif

Extended Horizons; Vertical Density establishes a new center of activity at the base of the Brooklyn Bridge (site 6) through a massing strategy that includes a multi-story plinth and three high-rise towers. The plinth's first floor plan expands the site's boundaries by appropriating residual and underutilized spaces around the bridge pier to connect the school with its adjacent neighborhood fabrics. Additionally, the plinth's roof functions as a public space platform, and is organized into four petal-shaped volumes—containing the site's educational program—surrounding a group of interstitial, shared community amenities. Three towers rise above the plinth, and while they all share a basic massing, program, circulation, and facade strategy, each tower is internally unique: not only for its aggregation of housing units, but also for how it weaves pockets of public space into its vertical circulation.

Exterior perspective view illustrating major elements: towers, podium, and elevated plaza

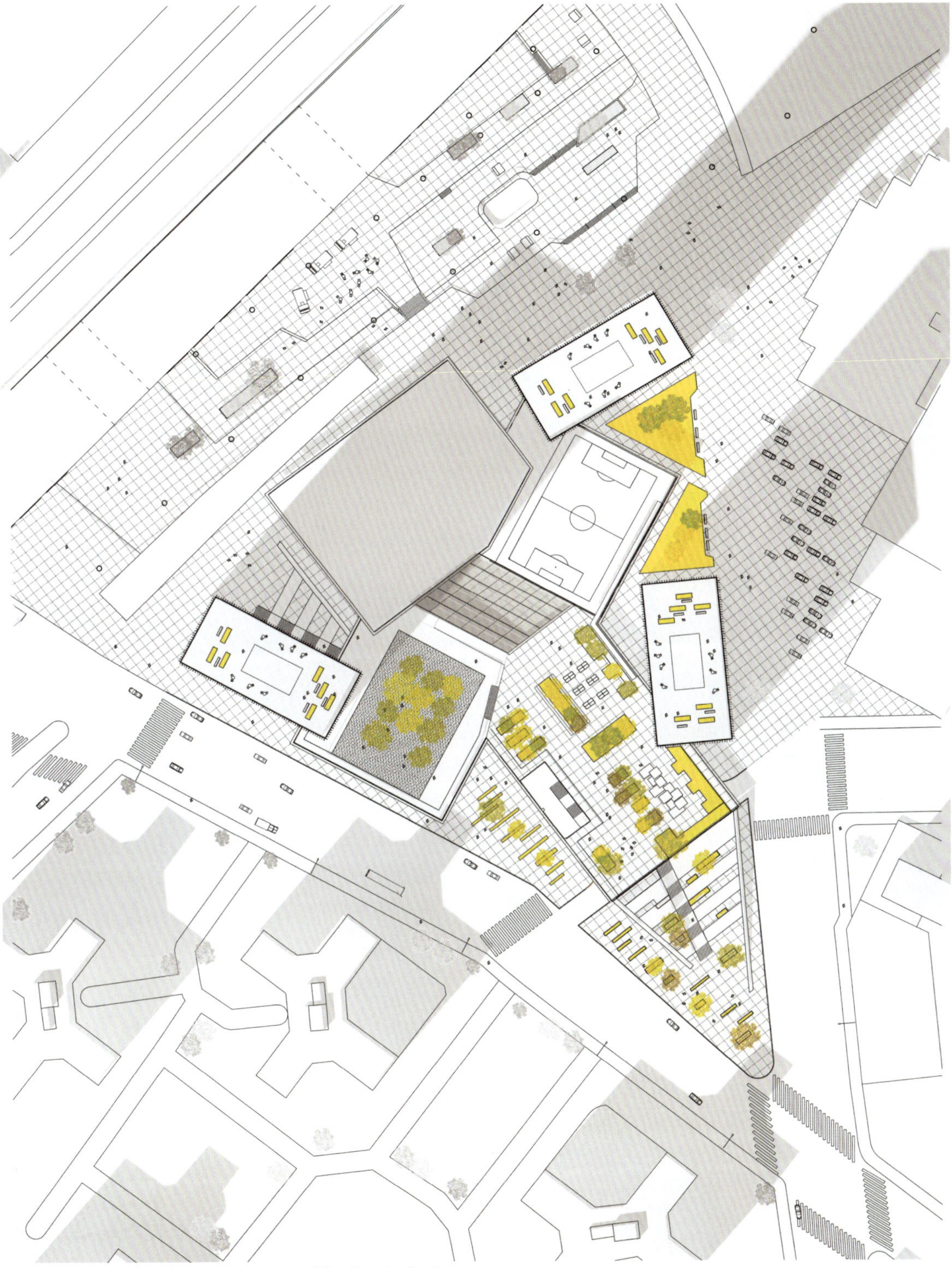

Site plan showing shared amenities within public plaza (yellow)

Section perspective view through multi-story podium and public amenities

Exploded isometric and perspective vignettes, southeast view

1:200 model, "Extended Horizons: Vertical Lines"

1:200 model, "Voxel Grounds"

Voxel Grounds

Student Team
Taha Suhrawardy
Ye Tao

Instructor
Mona El Khafif

Voxel Grounds re-configures the unique, triangular site at the at the base of the Brooklyn Bridge (site 6) into a new urban node of activity, a visibly striking gateway to Manhattan, and an intensified microcosm of the dense and vibrant urban fabrics of nearby neighborhoods. In order to square these intentions with a simultaneous desire to strengthen intimate social interactions and human-scale physical spaces, the proposal suggests an aggregative system of voxelized tower and void modules. These modules, developed as a typological alphabet of program components, not only include massings for the residential areas and the school, but also for outdoor recreational spaces, a library, and a community art gallery. Collectively, these archetypical program blocks establish a new, three-dimensional urban fabric full of shared spaces and elevated grounds.

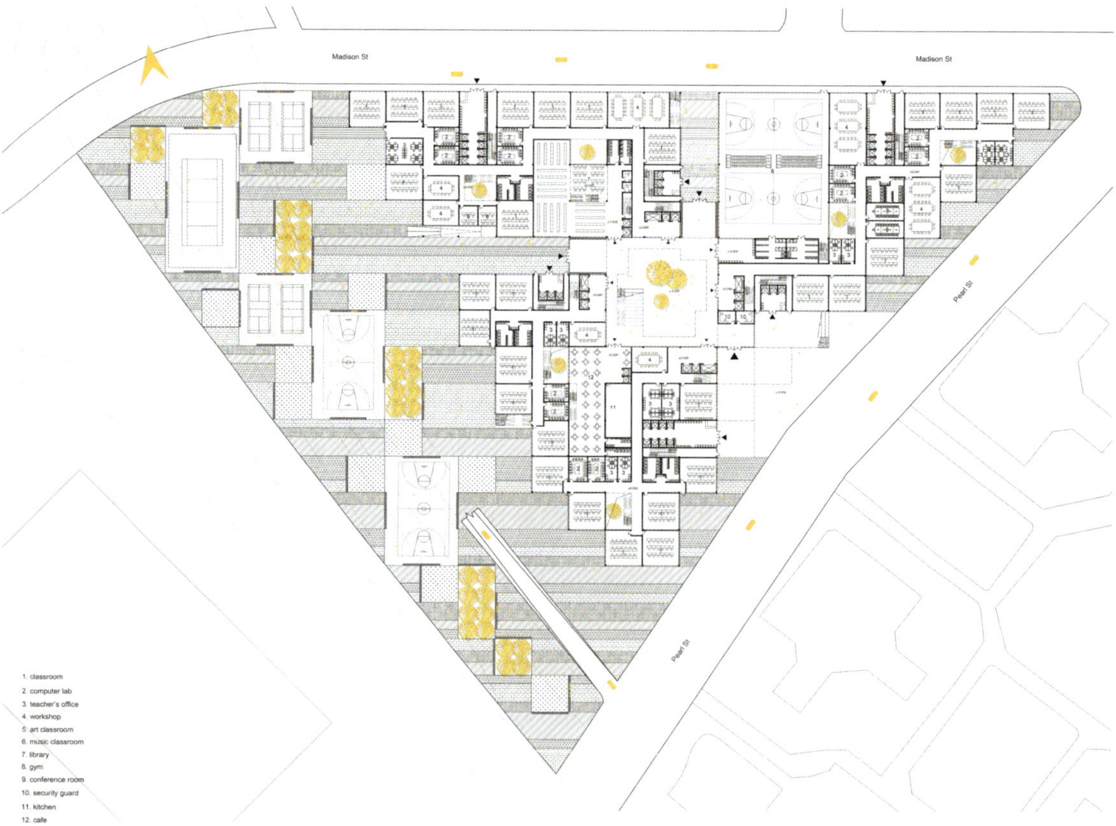

Ground floor plan

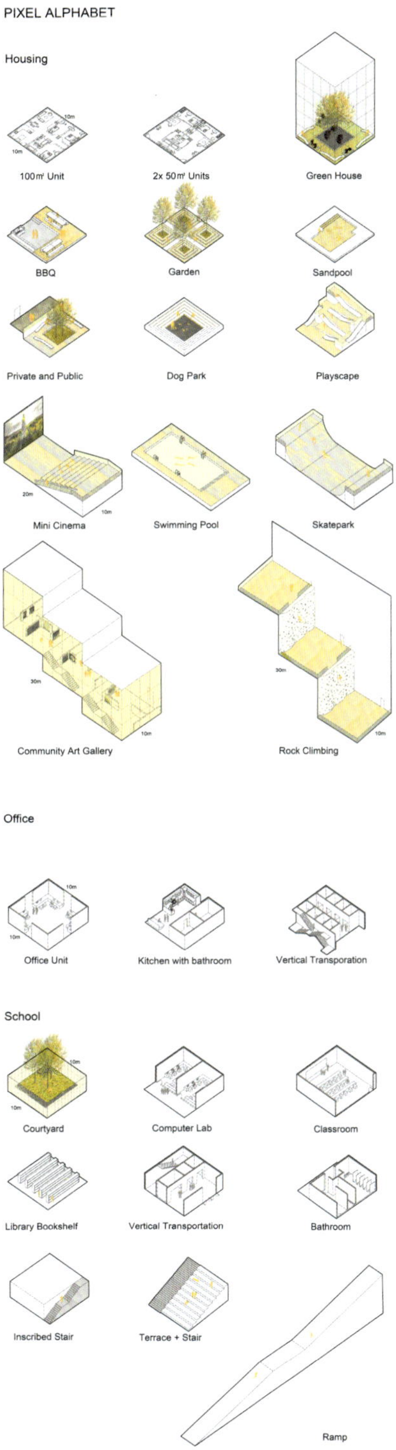

Typology diagrams

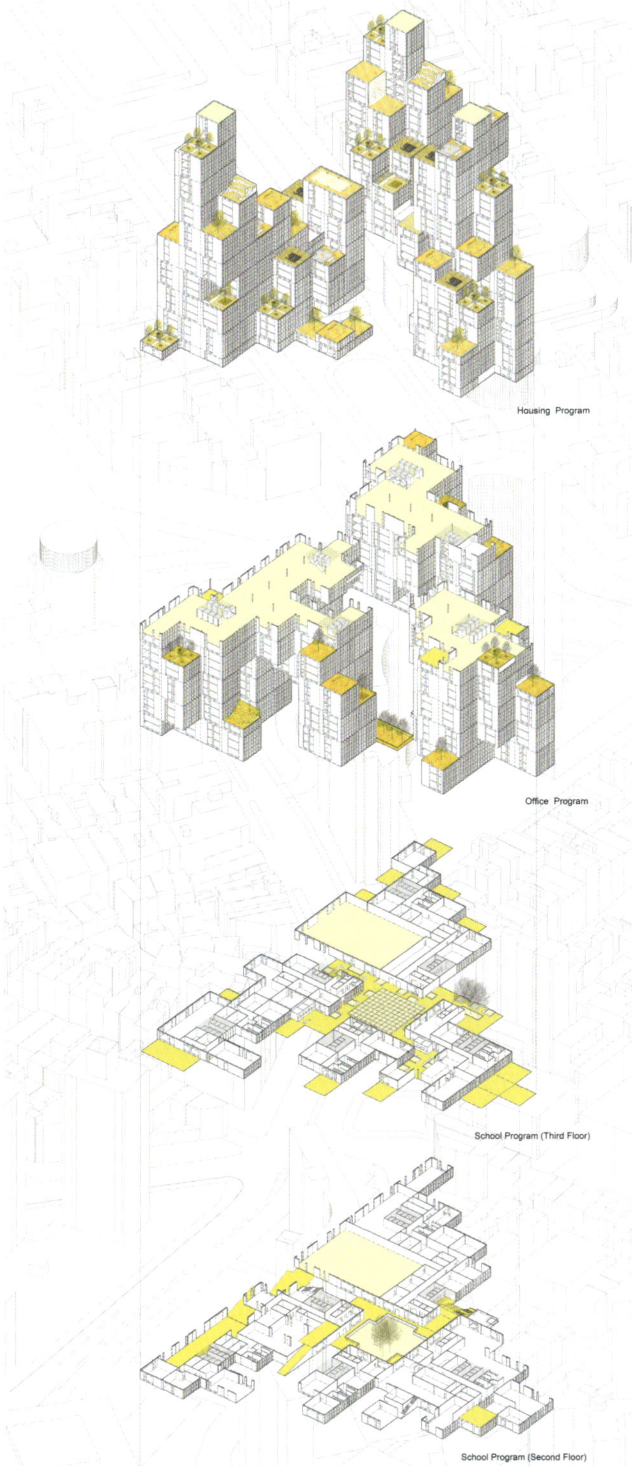

Delayered isometric drawing, southeast view

Billboard Building at the Brooklyn Bridge

Student Team
Harshita Batra
Luis Medina

Instructor
Matthew Jull

This project establishes a center of activity and visibility at the terminus of the Brooklyn bridge, one of the most visited and traveled landmarks in the city (site 6). Conceptualized as a functional wall that exposes the internal life of the building to travelers entering Manhattan from the Brooklyn Bridge, the project is characterized by a diaphanous membrane affixed to the exterior. A space-frame scaffolding system enhances the building's connection to the city, not only by generating unique sight-lines and varying levels of visual porosity specific to each program, but also as an illuminated billboard in constant interaction with passersby on the street. Occupying vertical strata within the space frame are core programs, such as a new school, community greenhouse, offices, and residences: all of which linked together through a vertical circulation network of interior public parks.

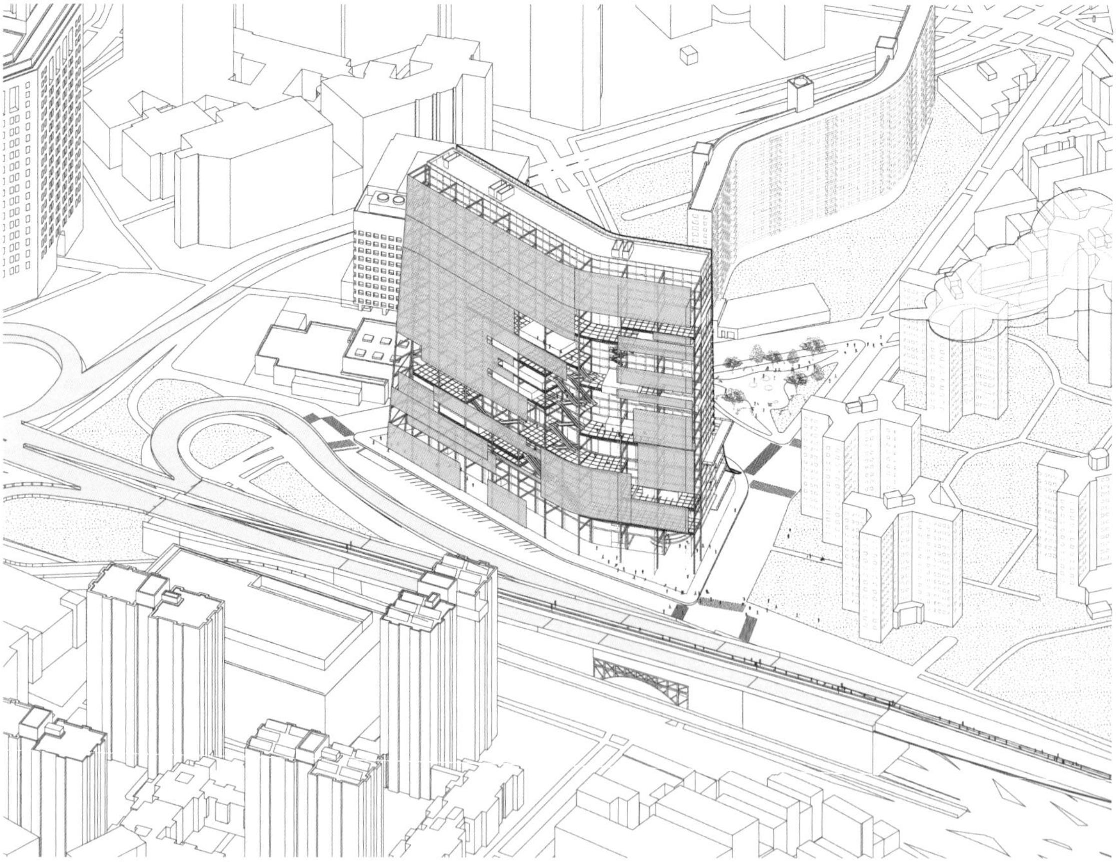

Isometric site drawing, southeast view

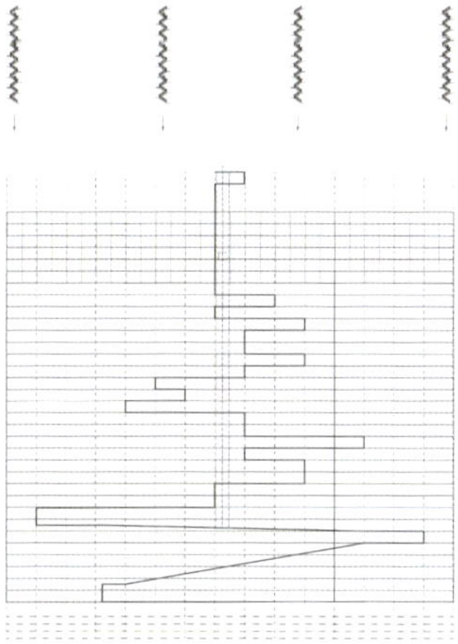

Facade diagram

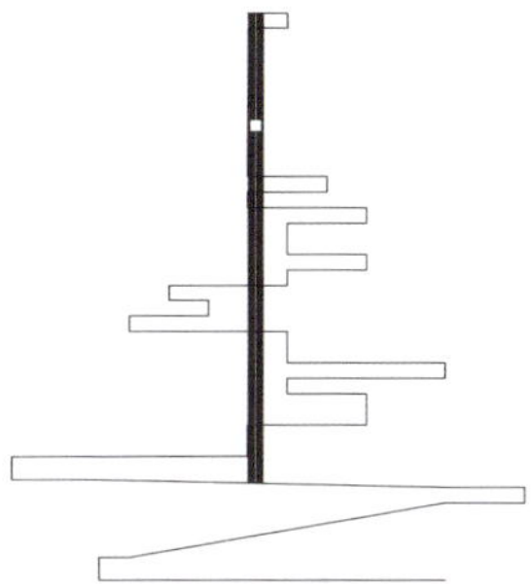

Vertical circulation diagram

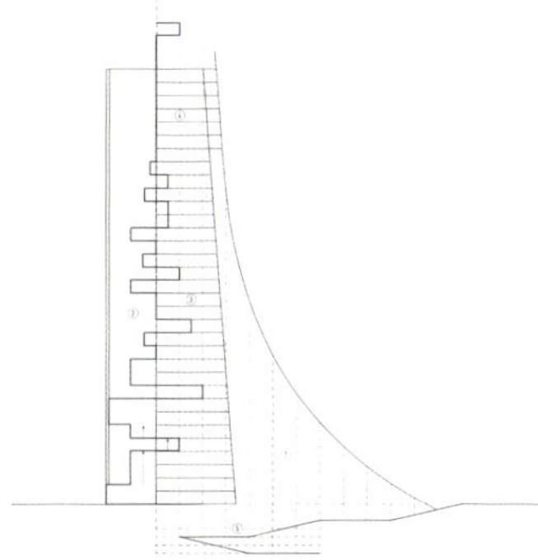

Sectional program diagram

Perspective view, looking west across Brooklyn Bridge promenade

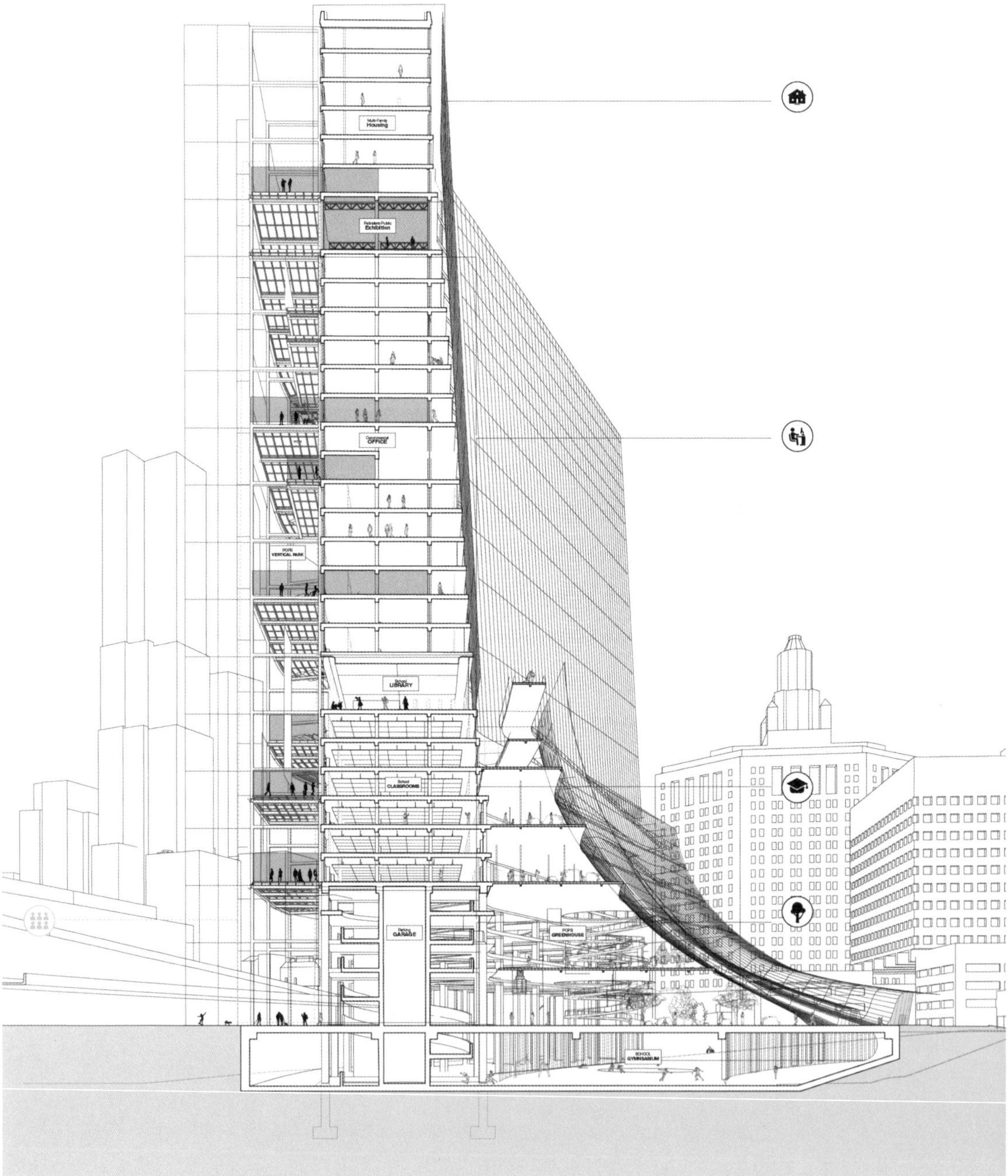

Perspective section through tower

Isometric view of facade screen

375 + 411 Pearl Street

Student Team
Taro Matsuno
Alexander Beranek

Instructor
Alexander Yuen

375 Pearl Street, currently home to Murry Bergtraum High School and the Verizon Building (site 6) was first developed in 1975 through a public-private partnership between the NYC Educational Construction Fund and the NY Telephone Company. This proposal simultaneously reinterprets the site's original financial structure while adaptively reusing the existing tower. In doing so, the project advocates for a new model of high-rise development for downtown Manhattan that accommodates new public and private spaces. The updated massing consists of three components: the existing tower, containing offices and a data center; a series of additions that re-engage the tower's west facade with downtown and house residential units, offices, a conference center, auditoriums, and athletic courts; and a free-standing facade screen, which mediates the change in floor height between the existing and new structures while also creating a central atrium and circulation space.

(Top) Existing Verizon tower
(Above) Project site plan

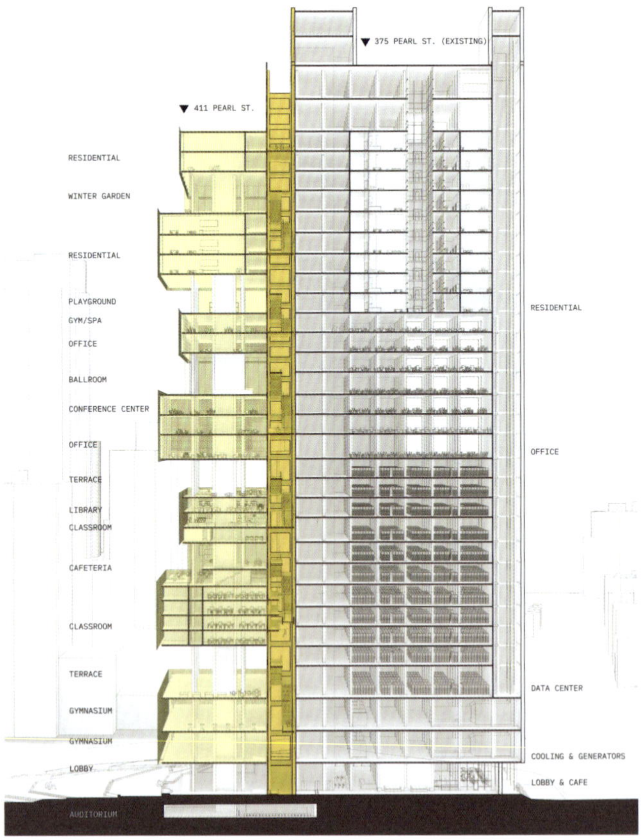

Building cross section through existing structure (gray) and new construction (yellow)

Perspective view at night, looking east

Documenting

Exit
14 St & Union Sq West
4 5 6

Queens

100s of channels for zeros of dollars.
pluto tv
Drop in. It's free.
BRIGH
STORE FOR RENT
212-431-7500
CITY SPEED LIMIT
25
INJURED?
INJURED?
Subway
Canal St Station
N Q R W
CANAL

PEAR

KENDRA SCOT

VAN CLEEF & ARPELS
744
Paris
Geneva
Monte Carlo
London
Tokyo
St. Moritz
Cannes
744
New York
Palm Beach
Beverly Hills
Bal Harbour
Costa Mesa
Chicago

ONE WAY
ONE WAY

Subway
New York City Transit
WIRELESS SERVICE AVAILABLE
Sprint
T··Mobile·
verizon

CITY
CLASS

Music Hall

NO TURNS

FRONT & YORK

CASH
(516)
232
0007

STOP

JUSTICE FOR
BLACK TRANS LIVES

RITY SEATING
ese seats if
nger boards.
Won't y♥u please give
to the elderly or disab
EVERYTHING HURTS ENOUGH
BLACK LIVES MATTER

BLM
STOP
REST IN P
#DEFUND
NYPD
SILENCE
END RACISM
BEFORE WE

DEFUND NYPD
BLACK LIVES MATTER
NOT ONE MORE
BLM
Champion

Saks Fifth Avenue
BLACK LIVES MATTER

No skateboarding
INJUSTICE SYSTEM
SILENCE IS BETRAYAL
BREONNA TAYLOR'S LIFE MATTERS
BLM
I DONT WANT 2
BLACK PANTHER
Yusef, Kevin, Antron, Korey & Raymond

FINDLAY
GALLERIES
TRUMP TOWER

WER

This is exactly the role of the experimental urban project, where a specific project can also become the model. For example, climate change and sea-level rise across the globe raise an important scalar challenge. The scale of the problem and the scale of the different tax bases that would finance urban interventions to mitigate sea-level rise are at odds. Urban projects that operate at a metropolitan or regional scale need to be in alignment with the administrative and tax-base districts that can fund these operations. In the specific case of New York, this work has to happen at a regional scale.
—Felipe Correa

What we're trying to do is move the boundaries of what's possible to discuss, and put ideas out there that can change the way we can think and talk about urban challenges. Our role is not to provide a blueprint to the city of what to do—even if the work of "Rising Currents" somehow impacted the new regional plan—our goal was to communicate these ideas to the public. If somebody wants to pick up on these projects and play ball with the designers and go further, then this was maybe our hidden plan.
—Barry Bergdoll

Discussing

Mona El Khafif and Seth McDowell in Conversation with Barry Bergdoll and Felipe Correa

March 8th, 2020

MK Thank you, Barry and Felipe, for taking time to join us today for a discussion on New York City's past and its future. You are both not only professionals who live and work in New York, but you also both contributed to academic research and curatorial practice dedicated to the city. In alignment with this publication, we would like to discuss today the deceptively simple question of "What is next for New York?"

We structured our discussion into three parts. The first set of questions will engage with New York's past and the most important actions that were taken to secure a successful present. The second part will engage with the actions we should take now, and lastly, we would like to speculate on actions that will address questions of the future. In all cases we would like to link these actions to the discipline of architecture and urban design to investigate the agency of design.

Barry, you are the Meyer Schapiro Professor of Art History in the department of art history at Columbia University, as well as the Philip Johnson Chief Curator of Architecture and Design at the Museum of Modern Art from 2007 to 2013, where you initiated a number of critical exhibitions such as "Home Delivery: Fabricating the Modern Dwelling" (2008), "Rising Currents: Projects for New York's Waterfront" (2010), "Foreclosed: Rehousing the American Dream" (2012), and "Frank Lloyd Wright and the City" (2014). In these exhibitions you engaged designers with urgent social, economic, and environmental issues in New York and elsewhere.

Felipe, you are currently the Vincent and Eleanor Shea Professor and chair of architecture at the University of Virginia. Previously, you served as the director of the Master of Architecture in Urban Design program at the Harvard University Graduate School of Design, where you coordinated a series of Urban Design studios located in New York. You are also a founding principal of Somatic Collaborative, a design research practice based in New York.

To start, could you both discuss what actions allowed New York to become the city that it is today?

BB I think that one of New York's most successful strategies is the enormous number of public parks that have been created, such as Brooklyn Bridge Park, Hunters Point, the transformation of Governors Island, and the High Line. Since the 1990s, there's been incredible investment, not only toward the creation of green spaces, but also their design. Not all of these sites were made fully public, but nonetheless there was an investment in open spaces.

On the other hand, the city hardly invested in its public transit system. I went to Beijing a couple of years ago, and the five-year-old maps I had received from a friend turned out to be completely useless because the city had regenerated its public subway system and added four additional lines since then. Then you look at the New York City subway map and you discover that the city has opened, I think, five or six new subway stations in the last fifty years.

FC I think the incredible investment we've seen in open spaces over the last thirty to forty years is tied to a broader set of political issues. New York politics shifts dramatically between mayoral administration cycles, and in my opinion, two administrations in the last fifty years have put design into the forefront of their agenda. The first is Mayor John Lindsay's administration during the late 1960s. A lot of key architecture and urban planning projects were initiated during this time, although they were implemented much later. For example, the Urban Design Group, which included Jaquelin T. Robertson, former dean of the UVA School of Architecture, was active during this time in the development of district-scale urban design plans utilizing innovative zoning mechanisms to transform areas of Manhattan such as 42nd Street and Battery Park City.

The other very successful era is the Bloomberg administration. Under Bloomberg's leadership, urban and public works projects—from the High Line to the Spring Street Salt Shed—valued what high-quality design brought to the table.

MK Were these developments spread across the city for specific programs like housing, or were these investments made in selected neighborhoods?

FC Some of these projects were initiated by the administration, while others were initiated by the private sector and approved by each administration. For example, the transformation of the Brooklyn Navy Yards, which not only restores post-industrial land and brings new uses to it, but also has become an epicenter of creative industries.

MK Did the city or the administration put specific tools into place to select these projects, like a series of design initiatives, or did the review panel simply pay more attention to design?

FC There were many tools set into place to secure urban development: transfer of development rights, Business Improvement Districts, inclusionary zoning, and FAR bonuses, just to name a few. These are not tools that were original to the Bloomberg administration, but Bloomberg was very effective in using them to generate important capital projects in the city.

MK In their essay contribution to this book, SHoP Architects talks about the transformation of former infrastructures into new public spaces. I think the High Line is a perfect example of how political leadership, retooling, activism, and philanthropy came together in order to make a project happen. A lot of cities tried to have a High Line, but weren't able to realize their projects. We might say that New York produced precedents for other cities.

BB This brings up a very interesting point: New York is currently seen as an alpha city able to implement design projects, but this has not always been the case. Fifteen years ago, New York was not even on the radar screen of a curatorial team sitting on 53rd Street looking internationally at how cities were transforming in regards to open space, landscape, and post-industrial re-utilization. New York was notably absent from that catalog. Most of these changes have actually happened in the last fifteen years, in part because of the keen awareness of the Bloomberg administration that New York's prominence in the global economy was more and more concentrated in Wall Street, and in order to remain competitive with London and Frankfurt, the city needed not only more amenities for those working and investing there, but also for the city to be able to market itself as a tourist destination. Within a matter of months, the High Line, for instance, became one of the prime destinations for foreign tourists.

Going back to your reflection about the Bloomberg administration, many of those projects did segue to other topics. Take Hunters Point. Everything that happened in the Queens and Brooklyn waterfront is also related to the politics of Bloomberg, who developed high-end housing with river views. If you wanted to be the cynic, you could say these are destination parks for people who live in other parts of the borough because the type of adjacent housing that has been created is not affordable for many. These parks are a public amenity, for sure, but they are also an amenity of the co-op or condo package. Those places are destinations that are part of a pattern of condominiumization of the waterfront. But I think that the real test case is going to be the further development of Governors Island because Governors Island, in a certain way, is the leftover piece of the Bloomberg administration.

In the recent history of the city, there's been such a partisan conflict with the handover of the administration from Bloomberg to de Blasio that, to date, they have only done the landscape projects. The public park on Governors Island is finished, but all of the parts that are designated for the developers have yet to begin. I think it's really one of the places we can keep our eyes focused on, not only to see what new relationships can evolve between public and private investment, but also to see if there will be a shift in attitudes toward the waterfront due to sea level rise.

FC I think the shift from Bloomberg to de Blasio is a very important one. In the previous administration, there was a belief that design could actually change the city, and I have not seen this in the current one. De Blasio's housing initiative sounds promising, but there is no clear approach to how this will unfold in form and space.

BB As far as I know from people who are closely involved, it has virtually no design component. It is completely a question of counting the numbers—how many units and where—but there are no aspirations for what all of this will look like. It takes out all of the interesting questions and it just says, "Deliver to me so many units."

MK Could we argue that some of the city's early infrastructures and layouts survived these administrative cycles because of its ability to adapt and absorb all kinds of investments and developments? The street grid of Manhattan, for example—also called the Greatest Grid—survived a lot of administrative cycles as well as economic depressions and booms.

BB I think the so-called Greatest Grid is a strong infrastructure for securing development, but it is a Manhattan-specific thing, and other parts of the city have fewer guiding infrastructures. Interestingly, Manhattan is so often the signifier of New York, but so much of what has really happened in the last fifteen years is the realization of the other boroughs. The development pressures are such that finally the other boroughs

What is fascinating about the Manhattan grid is its ability to constantly reinvent itself. Despite being criticized by some as banal, Manhattan's grid is a brilliant urban project, primarily because of the myriad urban forms its abstract set of relationships can produce.

have entered into that conversation. I just drove in from Long Island; there's a whole new New York that has emerged on the other side of the river, and this New York is exposed to other dynamics.

FC What is fascinating about the Manhattan grid is its ability to constantly reinvent itself. Despite being criticized by some as banal, Manhattan's grid is a brilliant urban project, primarily because of the myriad urban forms its abstract set of relationships can produce. Given the gradual increase in numbers of luxury units, the vacancy rate of many buildings with units used as pied-à-terres, and the construction of affordable housing outside of the borough due to linkage fees, Manhattan today is far less dense than it was throughout the second half of the twentieth century.

BB I think you investigated this trend in your first studio, where you started to show how sharing can be a different way of thinking and designing urban space. The escalation of the number of single-person households in Manhattan is absolutely extraordinary. And that contributes to this perception that there's less density, because how else do you arrive at a less dense grid at the end of a building boom?

This is partly because so many people are living alone in apartments and partly because there are units that had been added to the grid that are actually investments for people who don't need them.

FC I am a firm believer that the grid has the capacity to accommodate a significantly higher FAR in the coming decades. This rezoning, of course, would have to be accompanied by the upgrading of infrastructure and services: mass transit, schools, hospitals, etc.

The Manhattan grid is also the result of all the decisions it has allowed for—for example, the possibility to separate forms of transportation created very efficient systems. There are very few cities in the world that have express versus local subway lines, and this is an incredible invention of New York.

BB Would you say that this a byproduct of the grid or an invention of the subway system?

FC I believe it is both. It is a byproduct of the grid in that it is the urban form that allows for the emergence of a system like this. For instance, the organization generated a hierarchy within the grid between commercial avenues and residential streets, where commerce was supposed to happen on the avenues rather than in alleyways like in Philadelphia or Savannah—other cities with their own great grids. If you were to actually increase the density in those cities to that of Manhattan, however, those alleyways would not work.

MK Could you refer to any notable fictions or design experiments in New York which have had significant impacts on the city and its future? And what do you think is the role of academia and institutions like museums to contribute to these visions?

BB Both academia and museums have an important role in producing fictions, many of which are out there circulating in books like this one. One of the most interesting projects in the 2012 MoMA exhibition "Foreclosed: Rehousing the American Dream" was Studio Gang's contribution, Garden in the Machine, which retroactively edited the building regulations and the codes for Cicero, Illinois, a complex suburb of Chicago. The notion of retrospectively rewriting the codes as a guide is an out-of-the-box way of thinking and designing, yet it is probably only possible in the context of an exhibition. Another example would be The Big U, which was featured in another MoMA exhibition, "Rising Currents: Projects for New York's Waterfront," which we curated in 2010 along with PS1 Contemporary Art Center. The participants in this exhibition developed fabulous visions of how New York could be protected from or constructively live with rising tides in the future.

Superstorm Sandy, it is important to remember, was a superstorm, not a hurricane, and therefore might have actually been a warning for us. Two years after the closing of our exhibition, almost to the day, I received an email asking if I would come to a meeting at the Mayor's Office of Emergency Preparedness. I walked into this room in which there were about twenty people around this big table. And one of the comments they made was that they were very inspired by "Rising Currents," which was enormously gratifying to hear. Then they asked, "What are you going to do next?" And I said, "Excuse me, I am an art historian and a museum curator, but I'm also a citizen and a resident of New York. I actually think on behalf of the eight and a half million others who I'm going to channel now. The better question is, what are you going to do next?"

There is an affinity between the projects you've been doing in the studio and what I tried to do at the museum. What we're trying to do is move the boundaries of what's possible to discuss, and put ideas out there that can change the way we can think and talk about urban challenges. Our role is not to provide a blueprint to the city of what to do—even if the work of "Rising Currents" somehow impacted the new regional plan—our goal was to communicate these ideas to the public. If somebody wants to pick up on these projects and play ball with the designers and go further, then this was maybe our hidden plan. I believe exhibitions, studios, etc., are great vehicles to envision projects. Design studios like yours have perhaps even more freedom to

There is an incredible space for industries and institutions to come together to work on these visions that are not yet tied to political interests or the real estate market.

do so than exhibitions where you have the public walking through the gallery.

We also had a workshop model; city officials, hydraulic engineers, etc., were going through the workshop areas while teams were working on these projects because the actual design process was part of the exhibition, not simply the results. What emerged during the experiment were proposals that were so original that they can't be forgotten, and so realistic that they can't be dismissed. It is important to find that balance between something that is inspiring and encourages other people to think. Simultaneously, these projects move the boundaries but don't enter into the world of Jules Verne or science fiction and therefore cannot be dismissed easily as disconnected from reality.

FC Building on Barry's comment, I think it is important to mention the role of the Regional Plan Association (RPA) in building urban visions for the New York metropolitan area. If you look at the first and second regional plans, they were less about specific planning procedures and more about putting forward an urban agenda with a clear focus on what the form of the city should be. The RPA has been critical in imagining urban projects in relation to larger societal changes in the region. I think initiatives such as "Rising Currents" or the "Four Corridors" are extremely important for New York City, but require significantly more funding than what they have had until now. I think there are very important public-private partnerships to be made in order to continue advancing experimental work regarding the future of the New York metropolitan region. There is an incredible space for industries and institutions to come together to work on these visions that are not yet tied to political interests or the real estate market.

BB When we were working on MoMA's activist exhibitions—"Rising Currents" and "Foreclosed: Rehousing the American Dream"—I said, there's nothing novel about this. This is what goes on in schools of architecture every day of the week. I'm just putting it in the museum and bringing it to the public—which, then, also included guerilla operations and open houses inviting the public to come in and see the work in progress and discuss the projects with the designers. It was important to brief the designers, some of them just out of graduate school, so that the work would be discussed with the public in everyday language and not professional jargon. This would have sunk the whole project, as it was truly important to connect the general public to the design work and the visions developed for the city.

But back to the Regional Plan Association. It brings up an issue which is not unique to New York, but is particularly dramatic in New York, which are the boundaries of New York City that make, from my perspective, zero sense. In the early days, the boundaries had much to do with the logic of transportation and the regional land that was used for those types of infrastructure. But today, we are facing ecological problems and the now century-old work by Patrick Geddes would be more helpful to define boundaries that are based on ecological sheds. Some cities, like San Francisco and Oakland, where bodies of water are connecting and defining the region, operate in a similar way, and you need to think about these ecological sheds rather than administrative boundaries of different municipalities. And that is the only way to do something like the "Rising

Currents" project, as water ignores governmental boundaries.

FC Like the Studio Gang project, we need projects that help rewrite urban codes, not projects that follow urban codes. This is exactly the role of the experimental urban project, where a specific project can also become the model. For example, climate change and sea-level rise across the globe raise an important scalar challenge. The scale of the problem and the scale of the different tax bases that would finance urban interventions to mitigate sea-level rise are at odds. Urban projects that operate at a metropolitan or regional scale need to be in alignment with the administrative and tax-base districts that can fund these operations. In the specific case of New York, this work has to happen at a regional scale.

BB I think he's trying to extend the model that I developed for "Rising Currents," in which two components came together. One was: "let's think in interdisciplinary terms about this issue of sea-level rise and storm surge, etc." The other was that it was conceived in the middle of the last recession. It was meant to support young professionals who might otherwise leave architecture, and challenge them with these urgent questions during a time of recession.

How could this rising current of talent and these rising currents that are threatening be brought together? The generous grant from the Rockefeller Foundation was still minuscule considering the scale of the problem and the twelve weeks of work that was invested into the projects.

MK I would argue that "Rising Currents" also crafted the practice of some of these young professionals, such as Kate Orff, who worked on Oyster-tecture during the exhibition and is now realizing the Living Breakwaters project in Staten Island, NY. Living Breakwaters clearly has its roots in the ideas that were developed during "Rising Currents."

BB Yes, indeed; I think the experience of the workshop and exhibition was transformative for Orff's practice. When she was starting out, Kate proposed to do a lot of groundwork, including surveys and questionnaires and community-based work, and to display the process of fact-finding. There was one moment when I was getting very frightened of the potential visual dryness of her project and I said, "Kate, I'm giving you seventeen feet of wall space at the Museum of Modern Art. We are not exhibiting pamphlets. You have got to come up with something that is a compelling visualization. You've got to seduce us." And she rose to the occasion and developed the panorama section that stole the show and created an iconic image of the whole "Rising Currents" undertaking. It also served as a guide for her future projects.

Her work since then has dealt with these techniques of visualization. She invented it. She very kindly gave me some credit for pushing her to work on graphic visualizations.

MK Living Breakwaters is partly a realization of this project, but on a much larger scale. I find that specifically the work you're doing in the museum is about very critical moments for the city, during which we can strategize about important questions of the future that professional practice is usually not paying attention to until it is too late, after the city has been hit by a storm surge or affected by rising sea level. To me, this should be a much greater part of our common and academic practice, and is a fantastic way to envision our next cities.

BB Yes, I agree, and a lot of it had to do with the unbelievable aura and power of the New York Museum of Modern Art. The exhibition was leveraging the power of MoMA and the shock value of encountering these projects in an art museum where people have come to see Picasso or Jasper Johns. Visitors are coming to see contemporary artists and they're suddenly encountering projects for transforming New York. I overheard people from Brooklyn and Staten Island saying, "Oh, we never saw anything about Staten Island at the Museum of Modern Art before." So that idea that their neighborhood was in the museum was extremely empowering and engaging.

SM While this kind of visualization project enables architecture and design to become accessible to the general public, it also shows that issues of science, ecology, and economics are a provocative territory for designers. I think it tapped into a visual language that spoke to both the public and the profession.

BB It was such a kamikaze operation inside the museum and we had a lot of resistance from the museum's administration because it was a very fast-track project. And we didn't respect any of the conventions of the way projects usually get approved and developed in the museum. One thing I did, which turned out to be a real blessing, was that I invited the exhibition designers who were on the museum exhibition design staff to come to the workshops whenever they could so that the design of the projects and the exhibition were happening at the same time. And the exhibition designers from the museum were in discussion with the five teams of designers. So that was a very interesting two-way street. But it also had the benefit of a ground-up operation because the museum administration was so opposed to this project.

MK What do you both think would be a speculative, but very important action for New York's future that moves beyond what we've discussed so far?

BB We are actually sending out an RFP tomorrow for an exhibition project called "Still Together." It is a deliberate political response to the idea of polarizing us all and "make America great again." The project is about intergenerational living, as originally conceived for two projects that I wanted to do at the MoMA; one was on intergenerational living for an aging population and the other is the anniversary of the passage of the ADA, the Americans with Disabilities Act. How do you create shared environments in which people take care of one another, live together even though they're very different: different ages, different abilities, different backgrounds, etc.?

A part of that is inspired by the Studio Gang project. In these types of exercises, the discussion and the projects are themselves processes of discovery. In particular, we are looking at how residential spaces could be much more flexible, with shared and communal spaces and even different types of ownership. This project is going to pull together historical analysis and show what happens if you edit the history of American architecture to embrace ideas of communal living: being together instead of the heroic history of the individualistic pioneer and high-capitalist mode. As a historian, one thing that I find really fascinating is how history has a progressive prejudice, where if one idea doesn't lead to success, it is considered a failure and relegated to the trash bin. But in reality, when you revisit the trash bin of history, a lot of these discarded things have extraordinary potential. Experiments of the past often gain relevance at unexpected moments in the present or even future.

FC I think New York is an exceptional depository of urban projects. From Grand Central Terminal and the decking over of its rail yards to construct Park Avenue North and Rockefeller Center, the urban project has always played a pivotal role in shaping the city's urban form and metropolitan identity. Today, I believe there are two key urban agendas that the city should consider, and they are highly interrelated. One, how should the city's mobility infrastructure be upgraded to move beyond the monofunctional systems inherited from the post-World War II era? For example, what should be the future of Manhattan's Port Authority? Should it remain in Manhattan or be relocated to New Jersey and linked to the city via rail? Should it still remain as a centralized point, or should it become a more distributed system, with small facilities throughout the metro region that are better integrated to rail transport? The second project for me has to do with a larger study of hydrology in relation to climate change and sea-level rise at a mega-regional scale. I argue that these two are connected, because historically, rights of way for rail infrastructure have followed watersheds; therefore, this opens up an important opportunity to rethink these simultaneously. The Harlem River is the perfect case study for this, as it brings together water ways, rail infrastructure, and the adjacency between two boroughs.

MK Can you explore these a little bit more? Are there other major shifts in addition to sea-level rise?

FC One is the relationship of sea-level rise to the water-edge infrastructure and the capacity of the insurance industry to create change across multiple administrative boundaries. Insurance companies don't act within political boundaries, but within environmental hazard zones, and can therefore impact larger territorial entities.

MK You are referring to the historic precedent of the Sanborn Map Company that published detailed maps of U.S. cities in the nineteenth and twentieth centuries, I assume. These maps were originally created to allow fire insurance companies to assess their liability in urbanized areas of the United States and are today an extremely valuable stock of historic maps. Do you think that what we need today are Sanborn maps that refer to flooding and water hazards?

FC Yes, I think it is important to study how insurance companies can actually be players in this equation. And the other point has to do with the fact that significant amounts of people are unfortunately going to be displaced due to climate change. How do you begin to think about those relocations? How can you actually establish transfer of development rights and transfer of ownership rights in a manner that is equitable and fair to all parties involved? This is a very contested issue in any city. We learned from New Orleans after Hurricane Katrina how difficult it is to do this.

BB This is important. Just look at the way the city is currently approaching its investment into airport infrastructures.

As a historian, one thing that I find really fascinating is how history has a progressive prejudice, where if one idea doesn't lead to success, it is considered a failure and relegated to the trash bin. But in reality, when you revisit the trash bin of history, a lot of these discarded things have extraordinary potential. Experiments of the past often gain relevance at unexpected moments in the present or even future.

LaGuardia is a major infrastructural project, and the city invests enormous expense for an airport that will literally be underwater in twenty years and, in addition, has no fixed rail connection.

FC Right, they will start fixing the project by building polders and seawalls when the water is rising. Nobody does the math though, as retrofitting sites is ten times more expensive than doing it right the first time. The key is to invest in well-thought-out infrastructure now, rather than fixing the mistakes in the aftermath.

SM I would like to go back to one of the things Barry brought up about New York's history: the city's investment in public space or parks. I am curious about what form public space takes in the future. One of the recurring questions that the Next New York studios have engaged in is the role of common, public space in organizing the architecture of the city. One trend that collective housing models have presented in New York is the commodification of interior common space. These are marketed as amenities and become privileged spaces residents must "buy into." This presents serious inequalities and segregation for buildings that are attempting to house a diverse socioeconomic population. We can see this in the Hudson Yards model, where collective space is privatized and condo prices reflect the scale of access to these spaces. Have you seen alternative models for introducing common, collective space within the interior of urban buildings that might be productive within the financial climate of New York City?

BB The problem arises from the fact that we put everything under the umbrella of real estate with the provision of housing in this city and incentivize investment portfolios for people who don't live here. These are two completely different things, but they all get consumed under the notion that somehow this is all housing. What's on 57th Street has absolutely nothing to do with housing, they're just uninhabited investments. It used to be that you had to hide your money in Switzerland; now you put it on display in Midtown. I would just take those off the table, but it does raise the question, what becomes the economic incentive for building different kinds of residential projects?

FC If you leave housing to the market, developers are going to go straight to the bracket that gives them the greatest return on investment. And in a city

How can you actually establish transfer of development rights and transfer of ownership rights in a manner that is equitable and fair to all parties involved? This is a very contested issue in any city.

like New York, this will indefinitely be luxury housing, where investors can park capital. The question is, how do you incentivize the development of housing at a mid-market range? This might have to do with tax breaks, or bonuses, yet developers need incentives that will make it profitable to engage this market range and thereby produce a more diverse and affordable housing market.

BB Let me ask you a question, Felipe, given that you've put together this wonderful book on São Paulo. I wanted to bring Andres Lepik's show "Access for All: São Paulo's Architectural Infrastructures" to AIA New York's Center for Architecture because it presents these incredible hybrid buildings in São Paulo. What did you learn from the São Paulo model?

FC I think the Social Service of Commerce (SESC) model is an incredible invention. As a private federal structure with an autonomous representation in each Brazilian state, the SESC was first created in 1946 in Rio de Janeiro. Since then, it has spread out, with now 572 institutions scattered over more than two thousand Brazilian municipalities. And in São Paulo, there are over forty of them throughout the city. Lina Bo Bardi's SESC Pompeía Cultural Center is the most famous one. A tax on retail stores funds the SESC system. Employees that are affiliated with this retail—all workers and their entire families—have access to the SESC. The centers offer everything from recreational facilities to dental offices to medical facilities and are very well received by the community.

BB If you integrated housing into the SESC, is that an interesting idea?

FC I personally think it's a fascinating idea. I also think it would be a great way to find sites that can accommodate these two programs and be able to increase the critical mass of what the site is occupying. The program of the SESC and housing would make for a great urban adjacency in New York City.

New York has always been in dialogue with other cities, and the exchange of urban ideas and technical expertise has always been productive. The Amsterdam Docklands have a strong relationship to a project like Rockefeller Center, where a plan defines the broader urban morphologies without defining the specificity of its architecture. The idea of transnational dialogues is also a very interesting component from an academic and a pedagogical perspective. The question, however, remains: how do you realize these projects, beyond their formal and spatial nature, to address the economic and political realities of the American city?

MK Thank you, Felipe and Barry, this was a fascinating discussion.

University of Virginia NY Studio Instructors:

Mona El Khafif
Associate Professor

Seth McDowell
Associate Professor

Matthew Jull
Associate Professor

Manuel Bailo Esteve
Associate Professor

Alexander Yuen
Lecturer

Bill Sherman
Lawrence Lewis, Jr.
Eminent Scholar Professor

Esther Lorenz
Associate Professor

Kyriaki Kasabalis
Assistant Professor

Thomas Jefferson Visiting Professors, SHoP Architects:

Gregg Pasquarelli
Founding Principal

Andrew Daley
Senior Associate

John Cerone
Director of Virtual Design & Construction

Contributing Authors:

Ila Berman
Elwood R. Quesada Professor
University of Virginia
School of Architecture

Mona El Khafif
Associate Professor
University of Virginia
School of Architecture

Sharon Haar
Professor
University of Michigan
Taubman College

Matthew Jull
Associate Professor
University of Virginia
School of Architecture

Seth McDowell
Associate Professor
University of Virginia
School of Architecture

Edward Mitchell
Director, Architecture + Interior Design
University of Cincinnati

Carrie Moore
Director
Skidmore, Owings & Merrill

SHoP Architects

Geoffrey Thün
Professor
University of Michigan
Taubman College

Kathy Velikov
Associate Professor
University of Michigan
Taubman College

Thomas Woltz
Principal and Owner
Nelson Byrd Woltz Landscape Architects

Additional Contributors:

Barry Bergdoll
Meyer Schapiro Professor
Columbia University
GSAPP

Felipe Correa
Vincent + Eleanor Shea Professor
University of Virginia
School of Architecture

Photographic Essay (p. 308–329) by:
Tommaso Sacconi

Next New York is the third book in the *Next Cities* publication series by UVA School of Architecture and its Next Cities Institute. The *Next Cities* series disseminates design research by faculty and students at UVA focused on the rapidly changing dynamics of global urban futures. The series expands on how design—in its theory and physical instantiation in the world—probes the questions and controversies of the day, continually writing new expressions of the city.

Authors and Editors:
Mona El Khafif and Seth McDowell

Next Cities Series Editor:
Ila Berman

Series Graphic Design:
Neil Donnelly, Ben Fehrman-Lee, and Siiri Tännler

Volume Graphic Design:
Neil Donnelly and Siiri Tännler

Copy Editor:
Paula Woolley

Managing Editor:
Jake Anderson

Published by Applied Research and Design Publishing, an imprint of ORO Editions.

Publisher: Gordon Goff
www.appliedresearchanddesign.com
info@appliedresearchanddesign.com

10 9 8 7 6 5 4 3 2 1 First Edition
ISBN: 978-1-957183-07-7

Color Separations and Printing:
ORO Group Ltd.
Printed in China

AR+D Publishing makes a continuous effort to minimize the overall carbon footprint of its publications. As part of this goal, AR+D, in association with Global ReLeaf, arranges to plant trees to replace those used in the manufacturing of the paper produced in its books. Global ReLeaf is American Forests' education an action program that helps individuals, organizations, agencies, and corporations improve the local and global environment by planting and caring for trees.

Image Credits:

All images in this book are credited below or in the place where they appear.

Photographs:
p. vi–vii: Mona El Khafif, Seth McDowell
p. 22, Fig. 4: Mona El Khafif
p. 37, Fig. 1: Edward Mitchell
p. 41, Fig. 2: John W. Cahill
p. 48, Fig. 2: Public Domain
p. 53–58, Fig. 4–10: Barrett Doherty
p. 124, Fig 1–2: Courtesy of Brooklyn Daily Eagle photographs, Brooklyn Public Library
p. 125, Fig. 3: Benjamin Norman, The New York Times
p. 132, Fig. 6: Kathy Velikov
p. 142 –145, Fig. 2–9: SHoP Architects
p. 146, Fig. 10: Ty Cole, used with permission
p. 147, Fig. 11: Jeff Goldberg / Esto, used with permission
p. 201, Fig. 1: Mona El Khafif
p. 205, Fig. 6: Mona El Khafif
p. 211, Fig. 1: Dr. T, Flickr
p. 211, Fig. 2: Brian Donovan, Flickr
p. 212, Fig. 3: Iwan Baan and Nic Lehoux, courtesy Diller Scofidio + Renfro
p. 213, Fig. 5: Jim Henderson, Wikimedia
p. 218, Fig. 7: Adriel Hampton, Flickr
p. 222, Fig. 1: Albert Vecerka
p. 228–231, Fig. 4–6: Eduard Hueber
p. 308–329: Tommaso Sacconi

Drawings / Illustrations:
p. 20–21, Fig. 1–3: Austin Edwards, Megan Friedman
p. 46, Fig. 1: Nelson Byrd Woltz Landscape Architects
p. 50–51, Fig. 3: The Related Companies
p. 109, Fig. 1: Yudou Huang, Jiayue Peng, Ziwen Xu
p. 111, Fig. 2: Jing Huang, Sihan Lai, Mengzhe Ye
p. 111, Fig. 3: Yudou Huang, Jiayue Peng, Ziwen Xu
p. 112, Fig. 4: Weiran Jing, Samantha Kokenge
p. 113–114, Fig. 5–6: Darcy Engle, Samuel Johnson, Christoper Weimann
p. 115, Fig. 7: Theodore Bazil, Darcy Engle, Nicholas Grimes, Jing Huang, Samuel Johnson, Sihan Lai, Hutchins Landfair, Mark Meiklejohn, Sherry Ng, Christopher Weimann, Mengzhe Ye, Wan Ziyu
p. 127, Fig. 4: Courtesy of The Miriam and Ira D. Wallach Division of Art, Prints and Photographs, The New York Public Library Digital Collections
p. 128, Fig. 5: Scribner's Magazine v. 52
p. 133–136, Fig. 7–9: Velikov and Thün / RVTR
p. 141, Fig. 1: SHoP Architects
p. 201, Fig. 2: Kristina Fisher, Michael Peterson, Jingyi Shen
p. 202, Fig. 3: Jiaying Deng, Qing Feng, Kate Lipkowitz, Linxi Lu
p. 203, Fig. 4: Ya-Hsin Chiang, Roger Chien, Irmak Fermen, Clare Knecht
p. 204, Fig. 5: Audrey Liu, Shixun Lyu
p. 206, Fig. 7: Lydia Fulton, Yunfan Yang
p. 213, Fig. 4: Courtesy The Architectural League of New York
p. 215, Fig. 6: Brian McGrath
p. 226–227, Fig. 2 - 3: Skidmore, Owings & Merrill